D1478595

PROVERBS

Editorial Consultants

Athalya Brenner-Idan

Elisabeth Schüssler Fiorenza

Editorial Board

Mary Ann Beavis

Carol J. Dempsey

Amy-Jill Levine

Linda M. Maloney

Ahida Pilarski

Sarah Tanzer

Lauress Wilkins Lawrence

Seung Ai Yang

WISDOM COMMENTARY
Volume 23

Proverbs

Alice Ogden Bellis

Sarah Tanzer
Volume Editor

Barbara E. Reid, OP
General Editor

REGIS COLLEGE LIBRARY
100 Wellesley Street West
Toronto, Ontario
Canada M5S 2Z5
WITHDRAWN

BS
1465.53
B45
2018

A Michael Glazier Book

LITURGICAL PRESS
Collegeville, Minnesota

www.litpress.org

A Michael Glazier Book published by Liturgical Press

Cover design by Ann Blattner. *Chapter Letter 'W', Acts of the Apostles, Chapter 4,* Donald Jackson, Copyright 2002, *The Saint John's Bible,* Saint John's University, Collegeville, Minnesota USA. Used by permission. All rights reserved.

Scripture texts in this work are taken from the New Revised Standard Version Bible, © 1989, Division of Christian Education of the National Council of the Churches of Christ in the United States of America. Used by permission. All rights reserved.

The Woman at the Window © The Trustees of the British Museum. Reproduced by permission.

© 2018 by Order of Saint Benedict, Collegeville, Minnesota. All rights reserved. No part of this book may be reproduced in any form, by print, microfilm, microfiche, mechanical recording, photocopying, translation, or by any other means, known or yet unknown, for any purpose except brief quotations in reviews, without the previous written permission of Liturgical Press, Saint John's Abbey, PO Box 7500, Collegeville, Minnesota 56321-7500. Printed in the United States of America.

1	2	3	4	5	6	7	8	9

Library of Congress Cataloging-in-Publication Data

Names: Bellis, Alice Ogden, 1950– author.
Title: Proverbs / Alice Ogden Bellis ; Barbara E. Reid, OP, General Editor.
Description: Collegeville, Minnesota : LITURGICAL PRESS, 2018. | Series: Wisdom commentary ; Volume 23 | Includes bibliographical references and index.
Identifiers: LCCN 2018007466 (print) | LCCN 2018018309 (ebook) | ISBN 9780814681473 (ebook) | ISBN 9780814681220
Subjects: LCSH: Bible. Proverbs—Commentaries. | Bible. Proverbs—Feminist criticism.
Classification: LCC BS1465.53 (ebook) | LCC BS1465.53 .B45 2018 (print) | DDC 223/.707—dc22
LC record available at https://lccn.loc.gov/2018007466

To the Howard University School of Divinity,
faculty, administrators, staff, alumni/ae, and most of all, students,
who together have provided this immigrant from the segregated South
a new home, where I have been gradually transformed by a new
appreciation for gratitude and a glimpse of the wisdom of contemporary
sages. From the day I entered your hallowed halls in 1971 as an MDiv
student, to the day when—to my utter amazement and delight—you
invited me to be on your faculty, to the present day when I continue
to learn from you and thus to thrive in your midst almost fifty years
later, you have welcomed me with a hospitality that, though
completely unmerited, has not gone unnoticed. So, I offer this volume in
your honor, hoping that it may reflect your penetrating insight into
the human condition of which I have been a witness.

Contents

RE   S COLLEGE LIBRARY
100 Wellesley Street West
Toronto, Ontario
Canada M5S 2Z5

Abbreviations

AB	Anchor Bible
ABD	*Anchor Bible Dictionary*. Edited by David Noel Freedman. 6 vols. New York: Doubleday, 1992.
AOTC	Abingdon Old Testament Commentaries
BBR	*Bulletin for Biblical Research*
BDB	Brown, Francis, S. R. Driver, and Charles A. Briggs. *A Hebrew and English Lexicon of the Old Testament*.
BHS	Biblia Hebraica Stuttgartensia
BibInt	Biblical Interpretation Series
BLS	Bible and Literature Series
BZAW	Beihefte zur Zeitschrift für die alttestamentliche Wissenschaft
CBQ	*Catholic Biblical Quarterly*
FCB	Feminist Companion to the Bible
GBS	Guides to Biblical Scholarship
HALOT	*The Hebrew and Aramaic Lexicon of the Old Testament*. Ludwig Koehler, Walter Baumgartner, and Johann J. Stamm. Translated and edited under the supervision of Mervyn E. J. Richardson. 4 vols. Leiden: Brill, 1994-1999.

HSS	Harvard Semitic Studies
HTR	*Harvard Theological Review*
ICC	International Critical Commentary
IFT	Introductions in Feminist Theology
JBL	*Journal of Biblical Literature*
JFSR	*Journal of Feminist Studies in Religion*
JRT	*Journal of Religious Thought*
JSOT	*Journal for the Study of the Old Testament*
JSOTSup	Journal for the Study of the Old Testament Supplement Series
LXX	Septuagint
MT	Masoretic Text
NHC	Nag Hammadi Codices
OBT	Overtures to Biblical Theology
PL	Patrologia Latina
SBL	Society of Biblical Literature
SOTSMS	Society for Old Testament Studies Monograph Series
SymS	Symposium Series
TWOT	*Theological Wordbook of the Old Testament.* Edited by R. Laird Harris, Gleason L. Archer Jr., and Bruce K. Waltke, 2 vols. Chicago: Moody Press, 1980.
USQR	*Union Seminary Quarterly Review*
VT	*Vetus Testamentum*
WCS	Wisdom Commentary

Contributors

(Rev.) Charles Redden Butler, Neto,[1] MDiv, HUSD, 2017, is a writer, scholar, and Pagan minister with Rising Sun Outreach Ministry. He resides in Hyattsville, Maryland, near Washington, DC. He received his baccalaureate from the University of Michigan in Latin American studies in 1975 and studied Hebrew at Wesley Theological Seminary in Washington, DC, in 1981. His scholarly articles include "Psalm 51—A Study in Understanding," for *Early Ethiopian Christianity* (November 2015), comparing Psalm 51 royal theology customs with Egyptian temple custom; "A Great Debate—Or Is It?" (2016) for *Systematic Theology*, giving voice to Eve and Gaia in a theological discussion; "Strangers at the Gate" (2010), a dramatic work of twenty midrash presented at the Women's Expo in Baltimore in 2013; and *According to Us*, an opera created with Rosanna Tufts in 1997. He worked in prison ministry with Wiccan and Santeria women and men at the Federal Correctional Prison at Hazelton, West Virginia.

Sindile Dlamini, a former resident of Johannesburg, South Africa, is an ordained minister currently based in Washington, DC. She is presently an international psychology doctoral student at the Chicago School of Professional Psychology, with research interest in maternal mental health

---

1. Neto is a suffix used in Portuguese-speaking countries to distinguish a grandson from his grandfather when they have the same given name.

in low-income communities, and is a certified Grief to Gratitude Coach. She is also a chaplain at Howard University Hospital and serves as an associate minister at Michigan Park Christian Church. She holds board membership with Life Restoration Ministry, the Caribbean and African Faith-Based Leadership Conference, and Daughters of the African Atlantic Fund. Additionally, she is passionate about service learning and community youth engagement.

Rev. Desiré P. Grogan is a member of the ordained clergy at the historic Shiloh Baptist Church in Washington, DC. In 1992, Rev. Grogan became the first woman to be ordained by the Shiloh congregation, through the American Baptist Churches USA, since the church's inception in 1863. Rev. Grogan holds a bachelor of music degree from the Boston University School of Fine Arts, a master of library science degree from the University of Pittsburgh Graduate School of Library and Information Science, a master of divinity degree from the Howard University School of Divinity, and a master of arts degree in Semitics from The Catholic University of America. In addition to a prolific teaching and preaching ministry, Rev. Grogan has served as the fourth editor of *The WORKER Missionary and Educational Quarterly*, first published by the late Dr. Nannie Helen Burroughs in 1934 and continuously published by the Progressive National Baptist Convention. Rev. Grogan's ministerial and scholarly approach to the biblical text, both in the original languages and in the English translations, involves the discipline of plenary inspiration, that is, comparing Scripture with Scripture (1 Cor 2:13). Rev. Grogan affirms, both personally and experientially, that revelation knowledge is the result of this approach when applied to any biblical text under the anointing of the Holy Spirit.

Glenda F. Hodges, PhD, JD, MDiv, is the founder and CEO of Still I Rise, Inc., a community-based empowerment organization for survivors of domestic violence. She lectures extensively in this area, serves as chairperson of the Domestic Violence Task Force for Prince George's County, and is the county's director for domestic violence services for District 9. She is also the county executive's appointee to the Prince George's County Redevelopment Authority Board. She has done numerous workshops on domestic violence for local and state organizations, and she continues to champion the cause of survivors whose voices have been silenced because of domestic violence. Dr. Hodges is an ordained itinerant elder in the African Methodist Episcopal Church (AMEC), Second Episcopal District, Washington Annual Conference, where she serves as a member of the board of examiners, teaching Christian theology and the legal system to second-year students. She also serves as a member of the judicial council for the AME Church and is an associate minister at Reid Temple African Methodist Episcopal Church, Glen Dale, Maryland, where her pastor is Rev. Dr. Lee P. Washington. Dr. Hodges attended Virginia State University, Howard University, Bowling Green State University, Harvard University, the University of the District of Columbia, and the University of Texas at Austin (School of Law) and holds the following degrees: BA, MA, PhD, JD, and MDiv. Additionally, she has completed several short courses in spirituality and medicine at the Harvard Medical School's Mind Body Medical Institute.

Kristy Hunt is currently an MDiv candidate at Howard University School of Divinity. As a person living with hidden disabilities, managing multiple complex health conditions, Kristy's personal experience as a caregiver and care recipient inform her interest in pastoral care in healthcare settings. Ms. Hunt is a native Philadelphian and longtime, naturalized resident of Washington, DC.

Sehee Kim is a PhD candidate at Boston University School of Theology and earned her MDiv at Harvard Divinity School. Her interests are in the Hebrew Bible and relating it to ancient Near Eastern texts, feminist studies, wisdom literature, archaeology, and classical languages.

NaShieka Knight is an ordained minister from Upper Marlboro, Maryland, who is passionate about women's empowerment and faith-based community outreach. In 2007, she founded Zelophehad's Daughters Inc., a mentoring organization for teen girls in the Washington Metropolitan area. She serves on the board of directors for the Daughters of the African Atlantic Fund and the Prince George's County Human Trafficking Task Force. Ms. Knight is a student member of the Society of Biblical Literature and the American Academy of Religion and is a contributing author to *Unraveling and Reweaving Sacred Canon in Africana Womanhood* (Lexington Books, 2015). She holds an MDiv from Howard University School of Divinity and an MA in Jewish studies with a concentration in biblical and ancient Near Eastern civilizations from Towson University. She is currently a PhD student in Hebrew Bible at Brite Divinity School.

Eunyung Lim is Assistant Professor of New Testament at the Lutheran School of Theology at Chicago. She holds her PhD from Harvard Divinity

School and her doctoral work investigates the cultural valences and rhetorical functions of childlikeness in early Christian literature. Her main areas of research are the New Testament, the Nag Hammadi Library, and ancient Mediterranean cultures, focusing on how the categories of age, gender, and sexuality operate in ancient religious discourse. She served as an editorial assistant for *Harvard Theological Review* and was a visiting lecturer at the College of the Holy Cross.

Sam Perryman is a songwriter, church organist, and music librarian who uses his gifts to inspire others. He studied theology at Howard University, where his interests included comparative religions as well as the intersection of theology with race, gender, and sexuality. Musically, he has served the church for over forty years, and while he continues in that role, he also assists churches in finding creative ways of revitalizing their congregations. Currently, he is studying religion at Lancaster Bible College.

Niciah Petrovic received a master of arts in religious studies from the Howard University School of Divinity. Her focus was on Islamic social ethics and African American religiosity. In 2015, she received a triple major bachelor of arts in political science, Africana studies, and Middle Eastern studies from the University of Notre Dame. Since then, she has worked on local and national political campaigns against mass incarceration, poverty, and institutional racism. Niciah is a community organizer and public speaker, and she most recently sat on a panel for the Juvenile Justice Advocates at Howard University. Niciah has served on the DC Mayor's Commission on Fathers, Men, and Boys, where she applied her knowledge of social ethics to practical community problems stemming from racial disparity.

Beverly A. Reddy holds a BS in business management and an MDiv from the Howard University School of Divinity. Bivocational, she is employed as the director of patient financial services at the Kennedy Krieger Institute, where for twenty-nine years she has dedicated her service to helping children with special needs. She is an ordained Baptist minister. In 2012 she launched the Healing Hurts Domestic Violence Ministry, where she provides support to victims and education to church and community members about the effects of domestic violence. Furthermore, she is a member of the HIV/AIDS ministry and currently serves as director of Christian education at Mount Lebanon Baptist Church in Baltimore,

Maryland. As founder and visionary of Ishshah's Place her goal is to provide a refuge for survivors of intimate partner violence designed to promote holistic lifestyle transformations. Ms. Reddy is mother to Tiffany and Brian and grandmother to eight-year-old Alayna; she enjoys spending quality time with her family.

Alexandrea Rich is a fifth-year doctoral student in sociology at Howard University. With licenses in social work and ministry, she is interested in alternative mental health practices for black women with a focus on the testimony and womanist practices of belonging.

Lawrence W. Rodgers is currently the pastor of the Westside Church of Christ in Baltimore, Maryland. Lawrence graduated with distinction from both Harding University, with a bachelor of Bible and ministry, and Howard University School of Divinity, with a master of divinity. While a student, Lawrence represented the student body in Howard University School of Divinity's envoy to Ethiopia to return manuscript Tweed MS150 to the Ethiopian Orthodox Church. Lawrence is a published author and speaker, focusing on the intersection between theology and prophetic social engagement, particularly concerned with the plight of the marginalized from both a national and global perspective. Furthermore, Lawrence has engaged in religious and cultural studies through teaching in the classroom or participating in field work in Ethiopia, Swaziland, South Africa, and Ghana. Lawrence's work in Africa is occupied with religious imperialism and its remedies on both the continent of Africa, in America, and throughout the diaspora. Lawrence's work in Baltimore includes advocacy and ministry toward homeless individuals, human trafficking victims, and re-entry citizens. In his free time, Lawrence enjoys spending time with his family, cycling, traveling, studying, and enjoying nature.

Teresa L. Smallwood earned a BA from the University of North Carolina at Chapel Hill, where she majored in speech communications and Afro-American studies, a JD from North Carolina Central University School of Law, an MDiv at Howard University School of Divinity, and a PhD from Chicago Theological Seminary in theology, ethics, and human sciences. She is the postdoctoral fellow and associate director of the Public Theology and Racial Justice Collaborative at Vanderbilt Divinity School. Dr. Smallwood was licensed and ordained to public ministry in the Baptist tradition and is presently an active member at New Covenant

Christian Church in Nashville under the pastoral leadership of Rev. Dr. Judy Cummings.

Rev. Anne Troy is a retired United Church of Christ minister who also worked as a government lawyer. Born and raised in New York, she graduated from Case Western Reserve University for her law degree and worked for the US government in Washington, DC, before her retirement. She is also a US Army veteran. Her last ministry before retiring and making Maui her retirement community was at the Shaw Community Center in Washington, DC, a UCC-founded social and racial justice project in the African American community. During her tenure there, she assisted with the acquisition of grant funds in excess of $5 million for that organization. Currently, Anne is writing grants for local churches throughout Hawaii. She continues with Shaw Community Center as their development director.

March M. Wood is a Tibetan Buddhist who focuses on black women's healing and liberation from intersecting oppressions. She is a spiritual activist-organizer with seventeen years of communications and fundraising experience with leading mission-driven organizations. Ms. Wood earned her master of arts in religious studies from the Howard University School of Divinity and her undergraduate degree from Brown University. She has lived in Washington, DC, since 2000 and has been practicing mindfulness meditation for seven years.

Foreword

"Tell It on the Mountain"—or, "And You Shall Tell Your Daughter [as Well]"

Athalya Brenner-Idan

Universiteit van Amsterdam/Tel Aviv University

What can Wisdom Commentary do to help, and for whom? The commentary genre has always been privileged in biblical studies. Traditionally acclaimed commentary series, such as the International Critical Commentary, Old Testament and New Testament Library, Hermeneia, Anchor Bible, Eerdmans, and Word—to name but several—enjoy nearly automatic prestige, and the number of women authors who participate in those is relatively small by comparison to their growing number in the scholarly guild. There certainly are some volumes written by women in them, especially in recent decades. At this time, however, this does not reflect the situation on the ground. Further, size matters. In that sense, the sheer size of the Wisdom Commentary is essential. This also represents a considerable investment and the possibility of reaching a wider audience than those already "converted."

Expecting women scholars to deal especially or only with what are considered strictly "female" matters seems unwarranted. According to Audre Lorde, "The master's tools will never dismantle the master's house."[1] But this maxim is not relevant to our case. The point of this commentary is not to destroy but to attain greater participation in the interpretive dialogue about biblical texts. Women scholars may bring additional questions to the readerly agenda as well as fresh angles to existing issues. To assume that their questions are designed only to topple a certain male hegemony is not convincing.

At first I did ask myself: is this commentary series an addition to calm raw nerves, an embellishment to make upholding the old hierarchy palatable? Or is it indeed about becoming the Master? On second and third thoughts, however, I understood that becoming the Master is not what this is about. Knowledge is power. Since Foucault at the very least, this cannot be in dispute. Writing commentaries for biblical texts by feminist women and men for women and for men, of confessional as well as non-confessional convictions, will sabotage (hopefully) the established hierarchy but will not topple it. This is about an attempt to integrate more fully, to introduce another viewpoint, to become. What excites me about the Wisdom Commentary is that it is not offered as just an alternative supplanting or substituting for the dominant discourse.

These commentaries on biblical books will retain nonauthoritative, pluralistic viewpoints. And yes, once again, the weight of a dedicated series, to distinguish from collections of stand-alone volumes, will prove weightier.

That such an approach is especially important in the case of the Hebrew Bible/Old Testament is beyond doubt. Women of Judaism, Christianity, and also Islam have struggled to make it their own for centuries, even more than they have fought for the New Testament and the Qur'an. Every Hebrew Bible/Old Testament volume in this project is evidence that the day has arrived: it is now possible to read *all* the Jewish canonical books as a collection, for a collection they are, with guidance conceived of with the needs of women readers (not only men) as an integral inspiration and part thereof.

In my Jewish tradition, the main motivation for reciting the Haggadah, the ritual text recited yearly on Passover, the festival of liberation from

---

1. Audre Lorde, "The Master's Tools Will Never Dismantle the Master's House," in *Sister Outsider: Essays and Speeches* (Berkeley, CA: Crossing Press, 1984, 2007), 110–14. First delivered in the Second Sex Conference in New York, 1979.

bondage, is given as "And you shall tell your son" (from Exod 13:8). The knowledge and experience of past generations is thus transferred to the next, for constructing the present and the future. The ancient maxim is, literally, limited to a male audience. This series remolds the maxim into a new inclusive shape, which is of the utmost consequence: "And you shall tell your son" is extended to "And you shall tell your daughter [as well as your son]." Or, if you want, "Tell it on the mountain," for all to hear.

This is what it's all about.

Editor's Introduction to Wisdom Commentary

"She Is a Breath of the Power of God" (Wis 7:25)

Barbara E. Reid, OP

General Editor

Wisdom Commentary is the first series to offer detailed feminist interpretation of every book of the Bible. The fruit of collaborative work by an ecumenical and interreligious team of scholars, the volumes provide serious, scholarly engagement with the whole biblical text, not only those texts that explicitly mention women. The series is intended for clergy, teachers, ministers, and all serious students of the Bible. Designed to be both accessible and informed by the various approaches of biblical scholarship, it pays particular attention to the world in front of the text, that is, how the text is heard and appropriated. At the same time, this series aims to be faithful to the ancient text and its earliest audiences; thus the volumes also explicate the worlds behind the text and within it. While issues of gender are primary in this project, the volumes also address the intersecting issues of power, authority, ethnicity, race, class, and religious belief and practice. The fifty-eight volumes include the books regarded as canonical by Jews (i.e., the Tanakh); Protestants (the "Hebrew Bible" and the New Testament); and Roman Catholic, Anglican, and Eastern Orthodox

Communions (i.e., Tobit, Judith, 1 and 2 Maccabees, Wisdom of Solomon, Sirach/Ecclesiasticus, Baruch, including the Letter of Jeremiah, the additions to Esther, and Susanna and Bel and the Dragon in Daniel).

A Symphony of Diverse Voices

Included in the Wisdom Commentary series are voices from scholars of many different religious traditions, of diverse ages, differing sexual identities, and varying cultural, racial, ethnic, and social contexts. Some have been pioneers in feminist biblical interpretation; others are newer contributors from a younger generation. A further distinctive feature of this series is that each volume incorporates voices other than that of the lead author(s). These voices appear alongside the commentary of the lead author(s), in the grayscale inserts. At times, a contributor may offer an alternative interpretation or a critique of the position taken by the lead author(s). At other times, she or he may offer a complementary interpretation from a different cultural context or subject position. Occasionally, portions of previously published material bring in other views. The diverse voices are not intended to be contestants in a debate or a cacophony of discordant notes. The multiple voices reflect that there is no single definitive feminist interpretation of a text. In addition, they show the importance of subject position in the process of interpretation. In this regard, the Wisdom Commentary series takes inspiration from the Talmud and from *The Torah: A Women's Commentary* (ed. Tamara Cohn Eskenazi and Andrea L. Weiss; New York: Women of Reform Judaism, Federation of Temple Sisterhood, 2008), in which many voices, even conflicting ones, are included and not harmonized.

Contributors include biblical scholars, theologians, and readers of Scripture from outside the scholarly and religious guilds. At times, their comments pertain to a particular text. In some instances they address a theme or topic that arises from the text.

Another feature that highlights the collaborative nature of feminist biblical interpretation is that a number of the volumes have two lead authors who have worked in tandem from the inception of the project and whose voices interweave throughout the commentary.

Woman Wisdom

The title, Wisdom Commentary, reflects both the importance to feminists of the figure of Woman Wisdom in the Scriptures and the distinct wisdom that feminist women and men bring to the interpretive process. In the Scriptures, Woman Wisdom appears as "a breath of the power of God, and a pure emanation of the glory of the Almighty" (Wis 7:25), who was present and active in fashioning all that exists (Prov 8:22-31; Wis 8:6). She is a spirit who pervades and penetrates all things (Wis 7:22-23), and she provides guidance and nourishment at her all-inclusive table (Prov 9:1-5). In both postexilic biblical and nonbiblical Jewish sources, Woman Wisdom is often equated with Torah, e.g., Sirach 24:23-34; Baruch 3:9–4:4; 38:2; 46:4-5; 2 Baruch 48:33, 36; 4 Ezra 5:9-10; 13:55; 14:40; 1 Enoch 42.

The New Testament frequently portrays Jesus as Wisdom incarnate. He invites his followers, "take my yoke upon you and learn from me" (Matt 11:29), just as Ben Sira advises, "put your neck under her [Wisdom's] yoke and let your souls receive instruction" (Sir 51:26). Just as Wisdom experiences rejection (Prov 1:23-25; Sir 15:7-8; Wis 10:3; Bar 3:12), so too does Jesus (Mark 8:31; John 1:10-11). Only some accept his invitation to his all-inclusive banquet (Matt 22:1-14; Luke 14:15-24; compare Prov 1:20-21; 9:3-5). Yet, "wisdom is vindicated by her deeds" (Matt 11:19, speaking of Jesus and John the Baptist; in the Lucan parallel at 7:35 they are called "wisdom's children"). There are numerous parallels between what is said of Wisdom and of the *Logos* in the Prologue of the Fourth Gospel (John 1:1-18). These are only a few of many examples. This female embodiment of divine presence and power is an apt image to guide the work of this series.

Feminism

There are many different understandings of the term "feminism." The various meanings, aims, and methods have developed exponentially in recent decades. Feminism is a perspective and a movement that springs from a recognition of inequities toward women, and it advocates for changes in whatever structures prevent full human flourishing. Three waves of feminism in the United States are commonly recognized. The first, arising in the mid-nineteenth century and lasting into the early twentieth, was sparked by women's efforts to be involved in the public sphere and to win the right to vote. In the 1960s and 1970s, the second wave focused on civil rights and equality for women. With the third wave, from the 1980s forward, came global feminism and the emphasis on the contextual nature of interpretation. Now a fourth wave may be emerging, with a stronger emphasis on the intersectionality of women's concerns with those of other marginalized groups and the increased use of the internet as a platform for discussion and activism.[1] As feminism has matured, it has recognized that inequities based on gender are interwoven with power imbalances based on race, class, ethnicity, religion, sexual identity, physical ability, and a host of other social markers.

Feminist Women and Men

Men who choose to identify with and partner with feminist women in the work of deconstructing systems of domination and building structures of equality are rightly regarded as feminists. Some men readily identify with experiences of women who are discriminated against on the basis of sex/gender, having themselves had comparable experiences; others who may not have faced direct discrimination or stereotyping recognize that inequity and problematic characterization still occur, and they seek correction. This series is pleased to include feminist men both as lead authors and as contributing voices.

Feminist Biblical Interpretation

Women interpreting the Bible from the lenses of their own experience is nothing new. Throughout the ages women have recounted the biblical stories, teaching them to their children and others, all the while interpreting them afresh for their time and circumstances.[2] Following is a very brief sketch of select foremothers who laid the groundwork for contemporary feminist biblical interpretation.

One of the earliest known Christian women who challenged patriarchal interpretations of Scripture was a consecrated virgin named Helie, who lived in the second century CE. When she refused to marry, her

---

1. See Martha Rampton, "Four Waves of Feminism" (October 25, 2015), at http://www.pacificu.edu/about-us/news-events/four-waves-feminism; and Ealasaid Munro, "Feminism: A Fourth Wave?," https://www.psa.ac.uk/insight-plus/feminism-fourth-wave.

2. For fuller treatments of this history, see chap. 7, "One Thousand Years of Feminist Bible Criticism," in Gerda Lerner, *Creation of Feminist Consciousness: From the Middle Ages to Eighteen-Seventy* (New York: Oxford University Press, 1993), 138–66; Susanne Scholz, "From the 'Woman's Bible' to the 'Women's Bible,' The History of Feminist Approaches to the Hebrew Bible," in *Introducing the Women's Hebrew Bible*, IFT 13 (New York: T&T Clark, 2007), 12–32; Marion Ann Taylor and Agnes Choi, eds., *Handbook of Women Biblical Interpreters: A Historical and Biographical Guide* (Grand Rapids: Baker Academic, 2012).

parents brought her before a judge, who quoted to her Paul's admonition, "It is better to marry than to be aflame with passion" (1 Cor 7:9). In response, Helie first acknowledges that this is what Scripture says, but then she retorts, "but not for everyone, that is, not for holy virgins."[3] She is one of the first to question the notion that a text has one meaning that is applicable in all situations.

A Jewish woman who also lived in the second century CE, Beruriah, is said to have had "profound knowledge of biblical exegesis and outstanding intelligence."[4] One story preserved in the Talmud (b. Berakot 10a) tells of how she challenged her husband, Rabbi Meir, when he prayed for the destruction of a sinner. Proffering an alternate interpretation, she argued that Psalm 104:35 advocated praying for the destruction of sin, not the sinner.

In medieval times the first written commentaries on Scripture from a critical feminist point of view emerge. While others may have been produced and passed on orally, they are for the most part lost to us now. Among the earliest preserved feminist writings are those of Hildegard of Bingen (1098–1179), German writer, mystic, and abbess of a Benedictine monastery. She reinterpreted the Genesis narratives in a way that presented women and men as complementary and interdependent. She frequently wrote about feminine aspects of the Divine.[5] Along with other women mystics of the time, such as Julian of Norwich (1342–ca. 1416), she spoke authoritatively from her personal experiences of God's revelation in prayer.

In this era, women were also among the scribes who copied biblical manuscripts. Notable among them is Paula Dei Mansi of Verona, from a distinguished family of Jewish scribes. In 1288, she translated from Hebrew into Italian a collection of Bible commentaries written by her father and added her own explanations.[6]

Another pioneer, Christine de Pizan (1365–ca. 1430), was a French court writer and prolific poet. She used allegory and common sense

3. Madrid, Escorial MS, a II 9, f. 90 v., as cited in Lerner, *Feminist Consciousness*, 140.

4. See Judith R. Baskin, "Women and Post-Biblical Commentary," in *The Torah: A Women's Commentary*, ed. Tamara Cohn Eskenazi and Andrea L. Weiss (New York: Women of Reform Judaism, Federation of Temple Sisterhood, 2008), xlix–lv, at lii.

5. Hildegard of Bingen, *De Operatione Dei*, 1.4.100; PL 197:885bc, as cited in Lerner, *Feminist Consciousness*, 142–43. See also Barbara Newman, *Sister of Wisdom: St. Hildegard's Theology of the Feminine* (Berkeley: University of California Press, 1987).

6. Emily Taitz, Sondra Henry, Cheryl Tallan, eds., *JPS Guide to Jewish Women 600 B.C.E.–1900 C.E.* (Philadelphia: Jewish Publication Society of America, 2003), 110–11.

to subvert misogynist readings of Scripture and celebrated the accomplishments of female biblical figures to argue for women's active roles in building society.[7]

By the seventeenth century, there were women who asserted that the biblical text needs to be understood and interpreted in its historical context. For example, Rachel Speght (1597–ca. 1630), a Calvinist English poet, elaborates on the historical situation in first-century Corinth that prompted Paul to say, "It is well for a man not to touch a woman" (1 Cor 7:1). Her aim was to show that the biblical texts should not be applied in a literal fashion to all times and circumstances. Similarly, Margaret Fell (1614–1702), one of the founders of the Religious Society of Friends (Quakers) in Britain, addressed the Pauline prohibitions against women speaking in church by insisting that they do not have universal validity. Rather, they need to be understood in their historical context, as addressed to a local church in particular time-bound circumstances.[8]

Along with analyzing the historical context of the biblical writings, women in the eighteenth and nineteenth centuries began to attend to misogynistic interpretations based on faulty translations. One of the first to do so was British feminist Mary Astell (1666–1731).[9] In the United States, the Grimké sisters, Sarah (1792–1873) and Angelina (1805–1879), Quaker women from a slaveholding family in South Carolina, learned biblical Greek and Hebrew so that they could interpret the Bible for themselves. They were prompted to do so after men sought to silence them from speaking out against slavery and for women's rights by claiming that the Bible (e.g., 1 Cor 14:34) prevented women from speaking in public.[10] Another prominent abolitionist, Sojourner Truth (ca. 1797–1883), a former slave, quoted the Bible liberally in her speeches[11] and in so doing challenged cultural assumptions and biblical interpretations that undergird gender inequities.

---

7. See further Taylor and Choi, *Handbook of Women Biblical Interpreters*, 127–32.

8. Her major work, *Women's Speaking Justified, Proved and Allowed by the Scriptures*, published in London in 1667, gave a systematic feminist reading of all biblical texts pertaining to women.

9. Mary Astell, *Some Reflections upon Marriage* (New York: Source Book Press, 1970, reprint of the 1730 edition; earliest edition of this work is 1700), 103–4.

10. See further Sarah Grimké, *Letters on the Equality of the Sexes and the Condition of Woman* (Boston: Isaac Knapp, 1838).

11. See, for example, her most famous speech, "Ain't I a Woman?," delivered in 1851 at the Ohio Women's Rights Convention in Akron, OH; http://www.fordham.edu/halsall/mod/sojtruth-woman.asp.

Another monumental work that emerged in nineteenth-century England was that of Jewish theologian Grace Aguilar (1816–1847), *The Women of Israel*,[12] published in 1845. Aguilar's approach was to make connections between the biblical women and contemporary Jewish women's concerns. She aimed to counter the widespread notion that women were degraded in Jewish law and that only in Christianity were women's dignity and value upheld. Her intent was to help Jewish women find strength and encouragement by seeing the evidence of God's compassionate love in the history of every woman in the Bible. While not a full commentary on the Bible, Aguilar's work stands out for its comprehensive treatment of every female biblical character, including even the most obscure references.[13]

The first person to produce a full-blown feminist commentary on the Bible was Elizabeth Cady Stanton (1815–1902). A leading proponent in the United States for women's right to vote, she found that whenever women tried to make inroads into politics, education, or the work world, the Bible was quoted against them. Along with a team of like-minded women, she produced her own commentary on every text of the Bible that concerned women. Her pioneering two-volume project, *The Woman's Bible*, published in 1895 and 1898, urges women to recognize that texts that degrade women come from the men who wrote the texts, not from God, and to use their common sense to rethink what has been presented to them as sacred.

Nearly a century later, *The Women's Bible Commentary*, edited by Carol Newsom and Sharon Ringe (Louisville: Westminster John Knox, 1992), appeared. This one-volume commentary features North American feminist scholarship on each book of the Protestant canon. Like Cady Stanton's commentary, it does not contain comments on every section of the biblical text but only on those passages deemed relevant to women. It was revised and expanded in 1998 to include the Apocrypha/Deuterocanonical books, and the contributors to this new volume reflect the global face of contemporary feminist scholarship. The revisions made in the third edition, which appeared in 2012, represent the profound advances in feminist biblical scholarship and include newer voices. In both the second and third editions, *The* has been dropped from the title.

12. The full title is *The Women of Israel or Characters and Sketches from the Holy Scriptures and Jewish History Illustrative of the Past History, Present Duty, and Future Destiny of the Hebrew Females, as Based on the Word of God.*
13. See further Eskenazi and Weiss, *The Torah: A Women's Commentary*, xxxviii; Taylor and Choi, *Handbook of Women Biblical Interpreters*, 31–37.

Also appearing at the centennial of Cady Stanton's *The Woman's Bible* were two volumes edited by Elisabeth Schüssler Fiorenza with the assistance of Shelly Matthews. The first, *Searching the Scriptures: A Feminist Introduction* (New York: Crossroad, 1993), charts a comprehensive approach to feminist interpretation from ecumenical, interreligious, and multicultural perspectives. The second volume, published in 1994, provides critical feminist commentary on each book of the New Testament as well as on three books of Jewish Pseudepigrapha and eleven other early Christian writings.

In Europe, similar endeavors have been undertaken, such as the one-volume *Kompendium Feministische Bibelauslegung*, edited by Luise Schottroff and Marie-Theres Wacker (Gütersloh: Gütersloher Verlagshaus, 2007), featuring German feminist biblical interpretation of each book of the Bible, along with apocryphal books, and several extrabiblical writings. This work, now in its third edition, has recently been translated into English.[14] A multivolume project, *The Bible and Women: An Encylopaedia of Exegesis and Cultural History*, edited by Irmtraud Fischer, Adriana Valerio, Mercedes Navarro Puerto, and Christiana de Groot, is currently in production. This project presents a history of the reception of the Bible as embedded in Western cultural history and focuses particularly on gender-relevant biblical themes, biblical female characters, and women recipients of the Bible. The volumes are published in English, Spanish, Italian, and German.[15]

Another groundbreaking work is the collection The Feminist Companion to the Bible Series, edited by Athalya Brenner (Sheffield: Sheffield Academic, 1993–2015), which comprises twenty volumes of commen-

---

14. *Feminist Biblical Interpretation: A Compendium of Critical Commentary on the Books of the Bible and Related Literature*, trans. Lisa E. Dahill, Everett R. Kalin, Nancy Lukens, Linda M. Maloney, Barbara Rumscheidt, Martin Rumscheidt, and Tina Steiner (Grand Rapids: Eerdmans, 2012). Another notable collection is the three volumes edited by Susanne Scholz, *Feminist Interpretation of the Hebrew Bible in Retrospect*, Recent Research in Biblical Studies 7, 8, 9 (Sheffield: Sheffield Phoenix, 2013, 2014, 2016).

15. The first volume, on the Torah, appeared in Spanish in 2009, in German and Italian in 2010, and in English in 2011 (Atlanta: SBL Press). Five more volumes are now available: *Feminist Biblical Studies in the Twentieth Century*, ed. Elisabeth Schüssler Fiorenza (2014); *The Writings and Later Wisdom Books*, ed. Christl M. Maier and Nuria Calduch-Benages (2014); *Gospels: Narrative and History*, ed. Mercedes Navarro Puerto and Marinella Perroni; English translation ed. Amy-Jill Levine (2015); and *The High Middle Ages*, ed. Kari Elisabeth Børresen and Adriana Valerio (2015); and *Early Jewish Writings*, ed. Eileen Schuller and Marie-Theres Wacker (2017). For further information, see http://www.bibleandwomen.org.

taries on the Old Testament. The parallel series, Feminist Companion to the New Testament and Early Christian Writings, edited by Amy-Jill Levine with Marianne Blickenstaff and Maria Mayo Robbins (Sheffield: Sheffield Academic, 2001–2009), contains thirteen volumes with one more planned. These two series are not full commentaries on the biblical books but comprise collected essays on discrete biblical texts.

Works by individual feminist biblical scholars in all parts of the world abound, and they are now too numerous to list in this introduction. Feminist biblical interpretation has reached a level of maturity that now makes possible a commentary series on every book of the Bible. In recent decades, women have had greater access to formal theological education, have been able to learn critical analytical tools, have put their own interpretations into writing, and have developed new methods of biblical interpretation. Until recent decades the work of feminist biblical interpreters was largely unknown, both to other women and to their brothers in the synagogue, church, and academy. Feminists now have taken their place in the professional world of biblical scholars, where they build on the work of their foremothers and connect with one another across the globe in ways not previously possible. In a few short decades, feminist biblical criticism has become an integral part of the academy.

Methodologies

Feminist biblical scholars use a variety of methods and often employ a number of them together.[16] In the Wisdom Commentary series, the authors will explain their understanding of feminism and the feminist reading strategies used in their commentary. Each volume treats the biblical text in blocks of material, not an analysis verse by verse. The entire text is considered, not only those passages that feature female characters or that speak specifically about women. When women are not apparent in the narrative, feminist lenses are used to analyze the dynamics in the text between male characters, the models of power, binary ways of thinking, and the dynamics of imperialism. Attention is given to how the whole text functions and how it was and is heard, both in its original context and today. Issues of particular concern to women—e.g., poverty, food, health, the environment, water—come to the fore.

16. See the seventeen essays in Caroline Vander Stichele and Todd Penner, eds., *Her Master's Tools? Feminist and Postcolonial Engagements of Historical-Critical Discourse* (Atlanta: SBL Press, 2005), which show the complementarity of various approaches.

One of the approaches used by early feminists and still popular today is to lift up the overlooked and forgotten stories of women in the Bible. Studies of women in each of the Testaments have been done, and there are also studies on women in particular biblical books.[17] Feminists recognize that the examples of biblical characters can be both empowering and problematic. The point of the feminist enterprise is not to serve as an apologetic for women; it is rather, in part, to recover women's history and literary roles in all their complexity and to learn from that recovery.

Retrieving the submerged history of biblical women is a crucial step for constructing the story of the past so as to lead to liberative possibilities for the present and future. There are, however, some pitfalls to this approach. Sometimes depictions of biblical women have been naïve and romantic. Some commentators exalt the virtues of both biblical and contemporary women and paint women as superior to men. Such reverse discrimination inhibits movement toward equality for all. In addition, some feminists challenge the idea that one can "pluck positive images out of an admittedly androcentric text, separating literary characterizations from the androcentric interests they were created to serve."[18] Still other feminists find these images to have enormous value.

One other danger with seeking the submerged history of women is the tendency for Christian feminists to paint Jesus and even Paul as liberators of women in a way that demonizes Judaism.[19] Wisdom Commentary aims to enhance understanding of Jesus as well as Paul as Jews of their day and to forge solidarity among Jewish and Christian feminists.

---

17. See, e.g., Alice Bach, ed., *Women in the Hebrew Bible: A Reader* (New York: Routledge, 1998); Tikva Frymer-Kensky, *Reading the Women of the Bible* (New York: Schocken Books, 2002); Carol Meyers, Toni Craven, and Ross S. Kraemer, *Women in Scripture* (Grand Rapids: Eerdmans, 2000); Irene Nowell, *Women in the Old Testament* (Collegeville, MN: Liturgical Press, 1997); Katharine Doob Sakenfeld, *Just Wives? Stories of Power and Survival in the Old Testament and Today* (Louisville: Westminster John Knox, 2003); Mary Ann Getty-Sullivan, *Women in the New Testament* (Collegeville, MN: Liturgical Press, 2001); Bonnie Thurston, *Women in the New Testament: Questions and Commentary*, Companions to the New Testament (New York: Crossroad, 1998).

18. Cheryl Exum, "Second Thoughts about Secondary Characters: Women in Exodus 1.8–2.10," in *A Feminist Companion to Exodus to Deuteronomy*, FCB 6, ed. Athalya Brenner (Sheffield: Sheffield Academic, 1994), 75–97, at 76.

19. See Judith Plaskow, "Anti-Judaism in Feminist Christian Interpretation," in *Searching the Scriptures: A Feminist Introduction*, ed. Elisabeth Schüssler Fiorenza (New York: Crossroad, 1993), 1:117–29; Amy-Jill Levine, "The New Testament and Anti-Judaism," in *The Misunderstood Jew: The Church and the Scandal of the Jewish Jesus* (San Francisco: HarperSanFrancisco, 2006), 87–117.

Feminist scholars who use historical-critical methods analyze the world behind the text; they seek to understand the historical context from which the text emerged and the circumstances of the communities to whom it was addressed. In bringing feminist lenses to this approach, the aim is not to impose modern expectations on ancient cultures but to unmask the ways that ideologically problematic mind-sets that produced the ancient texts are still promulgated through the text. Feminist biblical scholars aim not only to deconstruct but also to reclaim and reconstruct biblical history as women's history, in which women were central and active agents in creating religious heritage.[20] A further step is to construct meaning for contemporary women and men in a liberative movement toward transformation of social, political, economic, and religious structures.[21] In recent years, some feminists have embraced new historicism, which accents the creative role of the interpreter in any construction of history and exposes the power struggles to which the text witnesses.[22]

Literary critics analyze the world of the text: its form, language patterns, and rhetorical function.[23] They do not attempt to separate layers of tradition and redaction but focus on the text holistically, as it is in

20. See, for example, Phyllis A. Bird, *Missing Persons and Mistaken Identities: Women and Gender in Ancient Israel* (Minneapolis: Fortress, 1997); Elisabeth Schüssler Fiorenza, *In Memory of Her: A Feminist Theological Reconstruction of Christian Origins* (New York: Crossroad, 1984); Ross Shepard Kraemer and Mary Rose D'Angelo, eds., *Women and Christian Origins* (New York: Oxford University Press, 1999).

21. See, e.g., Sandra M. Schneiders, *The Revelatory Text: Interpreting the New Testament as Sacred Scripture*, rev. ed. (Collegeville, MN: Liturgical Press, 1999), whose aim is to engage in biblical interpretation not only for intellectual enlightenment but, even more important, for personal and communal transformation. Elisabeth Schüssler Fiorenza (*Wisdom Ways: Introducing Feminist Biblical Interpretation* [Maryknoll, NY: Orbis Books, 2001]) envisions the work of feminist biblical interpretation as a dance of Wisdom that consists of seven steps that interweave in spiral movements toward liberation, the final one being transformative action for change.

22. See Gina Hens-Piazza, *The New Historicism*, GBS, Old Testament Series (Minneapolis: Fortress, 2002).

23. Phyllis Trible was among the first to employ this method with texts from Genesis and Ruth in her groundbreaking book *God and the Rhetoric of Sexuality*, OBT (Philadelphia: Fortress, 1978). Another pioneer in feminist literary criticism is Mieke Bal (*Lethal Love: Feminist Literary Readings of Biblical Love Stories* [Bloomington: Indiana University Press, 1987]). For surveys of recent developments in literary methods, see Terry Eagleton, *Literary Theory: An Introduction*, 3rd ed. (Minneapolis: University of Minnesota Press, 2008); Janice Capel Anderson and Stephen D. Moore, eds., *Mark and Method: New Approaches in Biblical Studies*, 2nd ed. (Minneapolis: Fortress, 2008).

its present form. They examine how meaning is created in the interaction between the text and its reader in multiple contexts. Within the arena of literary approaches are reader-oriented approaches, narrative, rhetorical, structuralist, post-structuralist, deconstructive, ideological, autobiographical, and performance criticism.[24] Narrative critics study the interrelation among author, text, and audience through investigation of settings, both spatial and temporal; characters; plot; and narrative techniques (e.g., irony, parody, intertextual allusions). Reader-response critics attend to the impact that the text has on the reader or hearer. They recognize that when a text is detrimental toward women there is the choice either to affirm the text or to read against the grain toward a liberative end. Rhetorical criticism analyzes the style of argumentation and attends to how the author is attempting to shape the thinking or actions of the hearer. Structuralist critics analyze the complex patterns of binary oppositions in the text to derive its meaning.[25] Post-structuralist approaches challenge the notion that there are fixed meanings to any biblical text or that there is one universal truth. They engage in close readings of the text and often engage in intertextual analysis.[26] Within this approach is deconstructionist criticism, which views the text as a site of conflict, with competing narratives. The interpreter aims to expose the fault lines and overturn and reconfigure binaries by elevating the underling of a pair and foregrounding it.[27] Feminists also use other postmodern approaches, such as ideological and autobiographical criticism. The former analyzes the system of ideas that underlies the power and

24. See, e.g., J. Cheryl Exum and David J. A. Clines, eds., *The New Literary Criticism and the Hebrew Bible* (Valley Forge, PA: Trinity Press International, 1993); Edgar V. McKnight and Elizabeth Struthers Malbon, eds., *The New Literary Criticism and the New Testament* (Valley Forge, PA: Trinity Press International, 1994).

25. See, e.g., David Jobling, *The Sense of Biblical Narrative: Three Structural Analyses in the Old Testament*, JSOTSup 7 (Sheffield: University of Sheffield Press, 1978).

26. See, e.g., Stephen D. Moore, *Poststructuralism and the New Testament: Derrida and Foucault at the Foot of the Cross* (Minneapolis: Fortress, 1994); *The Bible in Theory: Critical and Postcritical Essays* (Atlanta: SBL Press, 2010); Yvonne Sherwood, *A Biblical Text and Its Afterlives: The Survival of Jonah in Western Culture* (Cambridge: Cambridge University Press, 2000).

27. David Penchansky, "Deconstruction," in *The Oxford Encyclopedia of Biblical Interpretation*, ed. Steven McKenzie (New York: Oxford University Press, 2013), 196–205. See, for example, Danna Nolan Fewell and David M. Gunn, *Gender, Power, and Promise: The Subject of the Bible's First Story* (Nashville: Abingdon, 1993); David Rutledge, *Reading Marginally: Feminism, Deconstruction and the Bible*, BibInt 21 (Leiden: Brill, 1996).

values concealed in the text as well as that of the interpreter.[28] The latter involves deliberate self-disclosure while reading the text as a critical exegete.[29] Performance criticism attends to how the text was passed on orally, usually in communal settings, and to the verbal and nonverbal interactions between the performer and the audience.[30]

From the beginning, feminists have understood that interpreting the Bible is an act of power. In recent decades, feminist biblical scholars have developed hermeneutical theories of the ethics and politics of biblical interpretation to challenge the claims to value neutrality of most academic biblical scholarship. Feminist biblical scholars have also turned their attention to how some biblical writings were shaped by the power of empire and how this still shapes readers' self-understandings today. They have developed hermeneutical approaches that reveal, critique, and evaluate the interactions depicted in the text against the context of empire, and they consider implications for contemporary contexts.[31] Feminists also analyze the dynamics of colonization and the mentalities of colonized peoples in the exercise of biblical interpretation. As Kwok Pui-lan explains, "A postcolonial feminist interpretation of the Bible needs to investigate the deployment of gender in the narration of identity, the negotiation of power differentials between the colonizers and the colonized, and the reinforcement of patriarchal control over spheres where these elites could exercise control."[32] Methods and models from sociology and cultural anthropology are used by feminists to investigate

---

28. See Tina Pippin, ed., *Ideological Criticism of Biblical Texts: Semeia* 59 (1992); Terry Eagleton, *Ideology: An Introduction* (London: Verso, 2007).

29. See, e.g., Ingrid Rosa Kitzberger, ed., *Autobiographical Biblical Interpretation: Between Text and Self* (Leiden: Deo, 2002); P. J. W. Schutte, "When *They, We,* and the Passive Become *I*—Introducing Autobiographical Biblical Criticism," *HTS Teologiese Studies / Theological Studies* 61 (2005): 401–16.

30. See, e.g., Holly Hearon and Philip Ruge-Jones, eds., *The Bible in Ancient and Modern Media: Story and Performance* (Eugene, OR: Cascade, 2009).

31. E.g., Gale Yee, ed., *Judges and Method: New Approaches in Biblical Studies* (Minneapolis: Fortress, 1995); Warren Carter, *The Gospel of Matthew in Its Roman Imperial Context* (London: T&T Clark, 2005); *The Roman Empire and the New Testament: An Essential Guide* (Nashville: Abingdon, 2006); Elisabeth Schüssler Fiorenza, *The Power of the Word: Scripture and the Rhetoric of Empire* (Minneapolis: Fortress, 2007); Judith E. McKinlay, *Reframing Her: Biblical Women in Postcolonial Focus* (Sheffield: Sheffield Phoenix, 2004).

32. Kwok Pui-lan, *Postcolonial Imagination and Feminist Theology* (Louisville: Westminster John Knox, 2005), 9. See also, Musa W. Dube, ed., *Postcolonial Feminist Interpretation of the Bible* (St. Louis: Chalice, 2000); Cristl M. Maier and Carolyn J. Sharp,

women's everyday lives, their experiences of marriage, childrearing, labor, money, illness, etc.[33]

As feminists have examined the construction of gender from varying cultural perspectives, they have become ever more cognizant that the way gender roles are defined within differing cultures varies radically. As Mary Ann Tolbert observes, "Attempts to isolate some universal role that cross-culturally defines 'woman' have run into contradictory evidence at every turn."[34] Some women have coined new terms to highlight the particularities of their socio-cultural context. Many African American feminists, for example, call themselves *womanists* to draw attention to the double oppression of racism and sexism they experience.[35] Similarly, many US Hispanic feminists speak of themselves as *mujeristas* (*mujer* is Spanish for "woman").[36] Others prefer to be called "Latina feminists."[37] Both groups emphasize that the context for their theologizing is *mestizaje* and *mulatez* (racial and cultural mixture), done *en conjunto* (in community), with *lo cotidiano* (everyday lived experience) of Hispanic women as starting points for theological reflection and the encounter with the divine. Intercultural analysis has become an indispensable tool for working toward justice for women at the global level.[38]

Prophecy and Power: Jeremiah in Feminist and Postcolonial Perspective (London: Bloomsbury, 2013).

33. See, for example, Carol Meyers, *Discovering Eve: Ancient Israelite Women in Context* (New York: Oxford University Press, 1991); Luise Schottroff, *Lydia's Impatient Sisters: A Feminist Social History of Early Christianity*, trans. Barbara and Martin Rumscheidt (Louisville: Westminster John Knox, 1995); Susan Niditch, *"My Brother Esau Is a Hairy Man": Hair and Identity in Ancient Israel* (Oxford: Oxford University Press, 2008).

34. Mary Ann Tolbert, "Social, Sociological, and Anthropological Methods," in *Searching the Scriptures*, 1:255–71, at 265.

35. Alice Walker coined the term (*In Search of Our Mothers' Gardens: Womanist Prose* [New York: Harcourt Brace Jovanovich, 1967, 1983]). See also Katie G. Cannon, "The Emergence of Black Feminist Consciousness," in *Feminist Interpretation of the Bible*, ed. Letty M. Russell (Philadelphia: Westminster, 1985), 30–40; Renita Weems, *Just a Sister Away: A Womanist Vision of Women's Relationships in the Bible* (San Diego: Lura Media, 1988); Nyasha Junior, *An Introduction to Womanist Biblical Interpretation* (Louisville: Westminster John Knox, 2015).

36. Ada María Isasi-Díaz (*Mujerista Theology: A Theology for the Twenty-First Century* [Maryknoll, NY: Orbis Books, 1996]) is credited with coining the term.

37. E.g., María Pilar Aquino, Daisy L. Machado, and Jeanette Rodríguez, eds., *A Reader in Latina Feminist Theology* (Austin: University of Texas Press, 2002).

38. See, e.g., María Pilar Aquino and María José Rosado-Nunes, eds., *Feminist Intercultural Theology: Latina Explorations for a Just World*, Studies in Latino/a Catholicism (Maryknoll, NY: Orbis Books, 2007).

Some feminists are among those who have developed lesbian, gay, bisexual, and transgender (LGBT) interpretation. This approach focuses on issues of sexual identity and uses various reading strategies. Some point out the ways in which categories that emerged in recent centuries are applied anachronistically to biblical texts to make modern-day judgments. Others show how the Bible is silent on contemporary issues about sexual identity. Still others examine same-sex relationships in the Bible by figures such as Ruth and Naomi or David and Jonathan. In recent years, queer theory has emerged; it emphasizes the blurriness of boundaries not just of sexual identity but also of gender roles. Queer critics often focus on texts in which figures transgress what is traditionally considered proper gender behavior.[39]

Feminists also recognize that the struggle for women's equality and dignity is intimately connected with the struggle for respect for Earth and for the whole of the cosmos. Ecofeminists interpret Scripture in ways that highlight the link between human domination of nature and male subjugation of women. They show how anthropocentric ways of interpreting the Bible have overlooked or dismissed Earth and Earth community. They invite readers to identify not only with human characters in the biblical narrative but also with other Earth creatures and domains of nature, especially those that are the object of injustice. Some use creative imagination to retrieve the interests of Earth implicit in the narrative and enable Earth to speak.[40]

Biblical Authority

By the late nineteenth century, some feminists, such as Elizabeth Cady Stanton, began to question openly whether the Bible could continue to be regarded as authoritative for women. They viewed the Bible itself as

39. See, e.g., Bernadette J. Brooten, *Love between Women: Early Christian Responses to Female Homoeroticism* (Chicago and London: University of Chicago Press, 1996); Mary Rose D'Angelo, "Women Partners in the New Testament," *JFSR* 6 (1990): 65–86; Deirdre J. Good, "Reading Strategies for Biblical Passages on Same-Sex Relations," *Theology and Sexuality* 7 (1997): 70–82; Deryn Guest, *When Deborah Met Jael: Lesbian Feminist Hermeneutics* (London: SCM, 2011); Teresa Hornsby and Ken Stone, eds., *Bible Trouble: Queer Readings at the Boundaries of Biblical Scholarship* (Atlanta: SBL Press, 2011).

40. E.g., Norman C. Habel and Peter Trudinger, *Exploring Ecological Hermeneutics*, SymS 46 (Atlanta: SBL Press, 2008); Mary Judith Ress, *Ecofeminism in Latin America*, Women from the Margins (Maryknoll, NY: Orbis Books, 2006).

the source of women's oppression, and some rejected its sacred origin and saving claims. Some decided that the Bible and the religious traditions that enshrine it are too thoroughly saturated with androcentrism and patriarchy to be redeemable.[41]

In the Wisdom Commentary series, questions such as these may be raised, but the aim of this series is not to lead readers to reject the authority of the biblical text. Rather, the aim is to promote better understanding of the contexts from which the text arose and of the rhetorical effects it has on women and men in contemporary contexts. Such understanding can lead to a deepening of faith, with the Bible serving as an aid to bring flourishing of life.

Language for God

Because of the ways in which the term "God" has been used to symbolize the divine in predominantly male, patriarchal, and monarchical modes, feminists have designed new ways of speaking of the divine. Some have called attention to the inadequacy of the term *God* by trying to visually destabilize our ways of thinking and speaking of the divine. Rosemary Radford Ruether proposed *God/ess*, as an unpronounceable term pointing to the unnameable understanding of the divine that transcends patriarchal limitations.[42] Some have followed traditional Jewish practice, writing *G-d*. Elisabeth Schüssler Fiorenza has adopted *G*d*.[43] Others draw on the biblical tradition to mine female and non-gender-specific metaphors and symbols.[44] In Wisdom Commentary, there is not one standard way of expressing the divine; each author will use her or his preferred ways. The one exception is that when the tetragrammaton, YHWH, the name revealed to Moses in Exodus 3:14, is used, it will be without vowels, respecting the Jewish custom of avoiding pronouncing the divine name out of reverence.

---

41. E.g., Mary Daly, *Beyond God the Father: A Philosophy of Women's Liberation* (Boston: Beacon, 1973).

42. Rosemary Radford Ruether, *Sexism and God-Talk: Toward a Feminist Theology* (Boston: Beacon, 1983).

43. Elisabeth Schüssler Fiorenza, *Jesus: Miriam's Child, Sophia's Prophet; Critical Issues in Feminist Christology* (New York: Continuum, 1994), 191 n. 3.

44. E.g., Sallie McFague, *Models of God: Theology for an Ecological, Nuclear Age* (Philadelphia: Fortress, 1987); Catherine LaCugna, *God for Us: The Trinity and Christian Life* (San Francisco: Harper Collins, 1991); Elizabeth A. Johnson, *She Who Is: The Mystery of God in Feminist Theological Discourse* (New York: Crossroad, 1992). See further Elizabeth A. Johnson, "God," in *Dictionary of Feminist Theologies*, 128–30.

Nomenclature for the Two Testaments

In recent decades, some biblical scholars have begun to call the two Testaments of the Bible by names other than the traditional nomenclature: Old and New Testament. Some regard "Old" as derogatory, implying that it is no longer relevant or that it has been superseded. Consequently, terms like Hebrew Bible, First Testament, and Jewish Scriptures and, correspondingly, Christian Scriptures or Second Testament have come into use. There are a number of difficulties with these designations. The term "Hebrew Bible" does not take into account that parts of the Old Testament are written not in Hebrew but in Aramaic.[45] Moreover, for Roman Catholics and Eastern Orthodox believers, the Old Testament includes books written in Greek—the Deuterocanonical books, considered Apocrypha by Protestants.[46] The term "Jewish Scriptures" is inadequate because these books are also sacred to Christians. Conversely, "Christian Scriptures" is not an accurate designation for the New Testament, since the Old Testament is also part of the Christian Scriptures. Using "First and Second Testament" also has difficulties, in that it can imply a hierarchy and a value judgment.[47] Jews generally use the term Tanakh, an acronym for Torah (Pentateuch), Nevi'im (Prophets), and Ketuvim (Writings).

In Wisdom Commentary, if authors choose to use a designation other than Tanakh, Old Testament, and New Testament, they will explain how they mean the term.

Translation

Modern feminist scholars recognize the complexities connected with biblical translation, as they have delved into questions about philosophy of language, how meanings are produced, and how they are culturally situated. Today it is evident that simply translating into gender-neutral formulations cannot address all the challenges presented by androcentric texts. Efforts at feminist translation must also deal with issues around authority and canonicity.[48]

45. Gen 31:47; Jer 10:11; Ezra 4:7–6:18; 7:12-26; Dan 2:4–7:28.
46. Representing the *via media* between Catholic and reformed, Anglicans generally consider the Apocrypha to be profitable, if not canonical, and utilize select Wisdom texts liturgically.
47. See Levine, *The Misunderstood Jew*, 193–99.
48. Elizabeth Castelli, "*Les Belles Infidèles*/Fidelity or Feminism? The Meanings of Feminist Biblical Translation," in *Searching the Scriptures*, 1:189–204, here 190.

Because of these complexities, the editors of the Wisdom Commentary series have chosen to use an existing translation, the New Revised Standard Version (NRSV), which is provided for easy reference at the top of each page of commentary. The NRSV was produced by a team of ecumenical and interreligious scholars, is a fairly literal translation, and uses inclusive language for human beings. Brief discussions about problematic translations appear in the inserts labeled "Translation Matters." When more detailed discussions are available, these will be indicated in footnotes. In the commentary, wherever Hebrew or Greek words are used, English translation is provided. In cases where a wordplay is involved, transliteration is provided to enable understanding.

Art and Poetry

Artistic expression in poetry, music, sculpture, painting, and various other modes is very important to feminist interpretation. Where possible, art and poetry are included in the print volumes of the series. In a number of instances, these are original works created for this project. Regrettably, copyright and production costs prohibit the inclusion of color photographs and other artistic work. It is our hope that the web version will allow a greater collection of such resources.

Glossary

Because there are a number of excellent readily available resources that provide definitions and concise explanations of terms used in feminist theological and biblical studies, this series will not include a glossary. We refer you to works such as *Dictionary of Feminist Theologies*, edited by Letty M. Russell with J. Shannon Clarkson (Louisville: Westminster John Knox, 1996), and volume 1 of *Searching the Scriptures*, edited by Elisabeth Schüssler Fiorenza with the assistance of Shelly Matthews (New York: Crossroad, 1992). Individual authors in the Wisdom Commentary series will define the way they are using terms that may be unfamiliar.

Bibliography

Because bibliographies are quickly outdated and because the space is limited, only a list of Works Cited is included in the print volumes. A comprehensive bibliography for each volume is posted on a dedicated website and is updated regularly. The link for this volume can be found at wisdomcommentary.org.

A Concluding Word

In just a few short decades, feminist biblical studies has grown exponentially, both in the methods that have been developed and in the number of scholars who have embraced it. We realize that this series is limited and will soon need to be revised and updated. It is our hope that Wisdom Commentary, by making the best of current feminist biblical scholarship available in an accessible format to ministers, preachers, teachers, scholars, and students, will aid all readers in their advancement toward God's vision of dignity, equality, and justice for all.

───────◆───────

Acknowledgments

There are a great many people who have made this series possible: first, Peter Dwyer, director of Liturgical Press, and Hans Christoffersen, publisher of the academic market at Liturgical Press, who have believed in this project and have shepherded it since it was conceived in 2008. Editorial consultants Athalya Brenner-Idan and Elisabeth Schüssler Fiorenza have not only been an inspiration with their pioneering work but have encouraged us all along the way with their personal involvement. Volume editors Mary Ann Beavis, Carol J. Dempsey, Amy-Jill Levine, Linda M. Maloney, Ahida Pilarski, Sarah Tanzer, Lauress Wilkins Lawrence, and Seung Ai Yang have lent their extraordinary wisdom to the shaping of the series, have used their extensive networks of relationships to secure authors and contributors, and have worked tirelessly to guide their work to completion. Two others who contributed greatly to the shaping of the project at the outset were Linda M. Day and Mignon Jacobs, as well as Barbara E. Bowe of blessed memory (d. 2010). Editorial and research assistant Susan M. Hickman has provided invaluable support with administrative details and arrangements. I am grateful to Brian Eisenschenk and Christine Henderson who have assisted Susan Hickman with the Wiki. There are countless others at Liturgical Press whose daily work makes the production possible, including Colleen Stiller, production manager; Stephanie Nix, production assistant; and Tara Durheim, associate publisher for accademic and monastic markets. I am especially thankful to Lauren L. Murphy and Justin Howell for their work in copyediting.

Author's Introduction

As I begin this commentary on Proverbs in the Wisdom Commentary, a series devoted to a feminist approach to interpretation of Scripture, it is useful to define my approach to the task at hand. For reasons that I will explain below, the term "feminist" has become freighted. Thus, I would prefer to say that this commentary represents a gender-sensitive reading of Proverbs. What that means is that I try to be alert to the codes that affected women (but also men) in the text, as in life. Some of these are explicit, as in the fact that the Proverbs are addressed to young men, even though the NRSV translates the singular בֵּן as "[my] child" when its literal translation is "[my] son."[1] In some biblical texts, this may be a correct translation, but in Proverbs, the literary environment makes it clear that the addressees are usually, if not exclusively, young men, as will be discussed in the commentary. Some of the gender codes are less obvious and must be teased out of the text. For example, wisdom is depicted and personified as a woman, especially in chapters 8–9, but often the human teachers who are depicted in literary texts are male, though not always. Proverbs 31:1-9 is devoted to the teaching of Lemuel's mother to her son! In this volume I am primarily focusing on aspects of the text that affected ancient Israelite women and the implications of this for today.

---

1. See Translation Matters on Son (Child), בֵּן, at 1:8.

The word "feminism" is obviously related to "feminine," but one can be feminine, i.e., a female gendered person in body and/or mind, without considering oneself a feminist. In general, feminists read texts, as I do, with a lens focused on the experiences of women, the codes—both written and unwritten—that govern their conduct, their roles, and for what they are valued or devalued in the society in which they live. Ideally, if we are reading texts (or life) in this fashion, we should not limit our field of vision to women of one ethnicity, class, or religion, or, if we do, we should have a good reason for so doing. In practice, those who are part of a dominant culture have tended to focus on women in that dominant culture and their issues, thus creating a situation where feminism and feminists were correctly perceived as mostly limited in the United States to white middle-class women.

As a result, women of color developed womanism and called themselves womanists in response to the limitations of the feminist movement. The term "womanism" was coined by Alice Walker in her 1983 collection, *In Search of Our Mothers' Gardens*.[2] It is a term that comes from African American folk tradition, in which to act "womanish" means for a girl to act older than her age, to the dismay of her elders.[3]

The emergence of womanism has created a bit of a semantic conundrum, and for me a personal dilemma, because although a few African Americans describe themselves as black feminists, the term "feminist" is tinged with whiteness (why else would those who call themselves black feminists need to preface the term "feminist" with "black"?), so that I am somewhat uncomfortable with the term "feminist." After all, it would seem odd to call myself a white feminist.[4] It is akin to the problem of the word "man" used generically to refer to all humanity and the masculine

2. Alice Walker, *In Search of Our Mothers' Gardens: Womanist Prose* (New York: Harvest/Harcourt Brace Jovanovich, 1983).

3. "Womanish" in Urban Dictionary, http://www.urbandictionary.com/define.php?term=womanish.

4. I became especially aware of this in the early 1990s when I wrote an article on the Queen of Sheba, which I had originally planned to call a feminist reading. When I decided to publish it in our journal at Howard University School of Divinity, the *Journal of Religious Thought*, I realized that I was not comfortable calling myself a feminist in the context of my professional setting in a historically black school. So instead of calling my reading of the Queen of Sheba a feminist reading, I called it a gender-sensitive reading: "(The Queen of) Sheba: A Gender-Sensitive Reading," in *JRT* 51 (1994–1995): 17–28. Although I have not been consistent in my use of language on this issue, at this relatively late stage in my career I would prefer not to use a label, as none quite fits my social context.

pronoun "he" used generically to refer to either a male or a female. Thus, my preference is for the term "gender-sensitive reading" and no label at all for myself other than biblical scholar or the like.

Hebrew Poetry

By training, I am a Semitic philologist, which means that my area of expertise is in ancient Semitic languages, primarily northwest Semitic languages, of which the most well-known one is biblical Hebrew, though I learned other sister languages for comparative purposes. Through many years of study, I became aware of the prose and poetic styles of the ancient Hebrew authors, their typical rhetorical devices, as well as the culture that informed the literature they wrote. All of this is important for the book of Proverbs, which is ancient Hebrew poetry.

Hebrew poetry is very different from most Western poetry. It does not rhyme or have regular rhythm. The primary distinction from prose is parallelism. A typical line of poetry has two cola (half-lines); the first colon (a single half-line) briefly states an idea and the second colon usually restates it using different language. For example, we find in Proverbs 1:2:

> For learning about wisdom and instruction   A
> For understanding words of insight . . .   B

I have labeled the first half-line, or colon, A and the second one B. In the first colon, "for learning about" translates a Hebrew infinitive לדעת, "to learn," and "wisdom and instruction," חכמה ומוסר, are the two objects of the preposition "about" but only in English; the nouns are a compound direct object in Hebrew where there is no preposition needed. In the second colon, "for understanding" again translates a Hebrew infinitive להבין, and the phrase "words of insight" renders the object of the infinitive אמרי בינה, which is in turn a prepositional phrase (in Hebrew an equivalent structure). So, the first colon may be diagrammed grammatically as follows:

> I (infinitive) O (object) + O (object) or I OO, or, more conventionally, ABB.
> The second one may be diagrammed as I O, or, again more conventionally, A'B'.

In terms of what the two cola say, the semantic parallelism, we can also see that the two cola are parallel, because the verbs "learning" and "understanding" are synonyms, and the objects "wisdom," "instruction," and "words of insight" are all in the same semantic domain. Thus, although the first colon has two objects and the second one has only one, a prepositional phrase, this is typical of the kinds of variation that we find in Hebrew poetry.

In addition to parallelism, Hebrew poetry also exhibits rhythm and euphonic sound patterns. In terms of rhythm, most cola present either a two-stress or three-stress pattern, with most Hebrew words being short enough that they have only one stress. This is subjective, but those familiar with the language can feel the rhythmic patterns. This rhythm is somewhat similar to what is called free verse in modern English poetry, which, it can be argued, is partly derived from the King James Version of the Psalms, which goes back to John Wycliffe's fourteenth-century translation.[5] In Proverbs 1:2, the first colon has three beats and most people would probably hear the second one as having two. It is possible to sense this even in the English translation.

Hebrew poetry also exhibits euphony (alliteration and assonance). An example of both in an English poem can be found in Edgar Allen Poe's "The Raven," of which the first three lines are presented below (consonants occurring at least three times are in boldface; repeated vowels are italicized; note that *v* and *f* are considered one sound):

> *O*nce up*o*n a m*i*dnight dr*ea*ry, while I p*o*ndered, **w**eak and **w**e*a*ry,
> *O*ver **m**any a quaint and curious v*o*lume of f*o*rgotten lore—
> While I **n**odded, **n**early **n**app*i*ng, suddenl*y* there came a tapp*i*ng . . .

To give a sense of the euphonic sound pattern of Proverbs 1:2, it will be helpful to provide an informal transliteration of each colon (the letters in bold are consonants that are repeated; the italicized vowels are the ones that are repeated, so that the reader can easily see which sounds are emphasized):

לדעת חכמה ומוסר
leda'at chochm*a*h *ou*m*ou*sar
להבין אמרי בינה
leh*a*veen 'eemray veen*a*h

The consonants *m* (3x), *l* (2x), *n* (2x), *r* (2x), and *v* (2x) are each repeated at least once in the two cola. The *ch* sound (as in Bach, not church) is created by two different consonants (כ and ח), but it is the same sound, so it counts. The vowels *a* (6x), *ee* (3x), and *ou* (2x) are repeated multiple times. The alliteration (repetition of consonants) and assonance (repeti-

---

5. Charles Allen, "Cadenced Free Verse," *College English* 9 (January 1948), 195–99.

tion of vowels), added to the rhythm (3-2 stresses) and the parallelism (ABB/A'B'), give the line its poetic character.

Hebrew poets love to play with the language, as poets are wont to do, sometimes creating complex wordplays that are usually not easily translatable into another language. There will not be time to go into much of this in a commentary of this length and focus, but the poetic structure of Proverbs needs to be kept in mind as we consider the nature of the material before us. As Marshal McLuhan famously said in in the 1960s, "The medium is the message."

Wisdom Literature

The book of Proverbs is Wisdom literature, a genre that also includes the books of Qohelet (Ecclesiastes), Job, and three deutero-canonical works: Baruch, Wisdom of Ben Sira (aka Sirach or Ecclesiasticus), and Wisdom of Solomon.[6] Proverbs, Qohelet, and Job are part of the third division of the Jewish canon, the *Ketubim* or Writings, which were canonized after the Torah and Prophets. Wisdom literature includes both oral folk sayings and the literature of the elite, reflecting on the nature of life and offering didactic advice. The word "proverb" (משל) may refer to a pithy saying written in terse poetic parallelism (like "You can have it all; you just can't have it all at once" [Oprah Winfrey]) or to an extended poem. Both types of משל are found in Proverbs. They are almost impossible to translate well into English, because of the interplay in the Hebrew between the sounds, rhythm, and meaning of the few words in each line. Additionally, double meanings and complex wordplays add to the translation problems. For example, the double meaning of the name of the pet supply store PetSmart would be impossible to render into another language.

Author and Date

The book of Proverbs is traditionally attributed to Solomon (Prov 1:1; 10:1; 25:1), but other authors are also named (22:17; 24:23; 30:1; 31:1). The authors of the sayings in chapters 10–29 are diverse in social location: urban and rural, elite and ordinary. Others are apparently foreign (Agur [30:1]; Lemuel's mother [31:1]). It is for this reason that scholars

---

6. "Apocryphal" in Protestant parlance.

do not believe that Solomon is responsible for all, or even most, of the proverbs. Although the individual proverbs cannot be dated, the date of the collection can be narrowed to within a few centuries. The earliest possible date would be the time of Hezekiah (late eighth to early seventh century BCE), since he is mentioned in 25:1. The collection is likely to have been complete before the time of Ben Sira (author of Sirach), who was writing in the early second century BCE, since he shows the influence of Proverbs in his book. Most commentators, however, date the latest segments of the book, chapters 1–9 and 31, which seem to form a kind of envelope around the middle section, to either the Persian Period or the Hellenistic Period (see the next section), i.e., between the last half of the sixth century and the first half of the fourth century BCE.

Social Setting

One question that has been discussed at length is the social setting of the teaching of wisdom. Were boys or young men (the original intended audience) taught in a school or at home? There is no definitive evidence for schools in ancient Israel until quite late, and the fact that mothers as well as fathers are depicted as authoritative teachers suggests that the home was the more likely setting.

Most scholars believe that the father was the one who did the vast majority of the teaching, but there are thirteen references to the word "mother" and seventeen to the word "father" in Proverbs, suggesting that the teaching roles were somewhat balanced. Focusing on the six texts that deal specifically with instruction, three verses mention both mother and father (1:8; 6:20; 30:17); two, only the father (3:12; 4:1); and one, solely the mother (31:1; Lemuel's mother's teaching her son, which goes on for the next eight verses!). Based on the information available, it is impossible to determine the degree to which mothers may have been involved in ancient Israelite instruction, but the possibility that mothers were deeply involved should not be dismissed. Gerlinde Baumann notes that Egyptian wisdom texts do not include mothers as teachers. She suggests that the depiction of mothers as teachers in Proverbs is not just for reasons of parallelism. Unless mothers actually functioned as teachers, they would not have been included in this literature.[7]

---

7. Gerlinde Baumann, "A Figure with Many Facets: The Literary and Theological Functions of Personified Wisdom in Proverbs 1–9," in *Wisdom and Psalms*, ed. Athalya Brenner and Carole R. Fontaine, FCB 2, 2nd ser. (Sheffield: Sheffield Academic, 1998), 49–52.

Wisdom as the Feminine Principle

The Buddhist concept of wisdom, or *prajna*, is related to the supreme thought of achieving buddhahood to liberate all beings from suffering. When we manifest *prajna* we directly see the nature of reality and are free from the delusion that we are separate, unchanging, independent selves. With this understanding of the independent self as an illusion, we clearly see the nature of the relationship between self and other. This clarity leaves no need for an enemy. *Prajna* is the awareness that all phenomena are connected, which naturally brings about vast compassion.

Though Buddhism is not a theistic tradition, the Hebrew concept of wisdom, *hokmah*, aligns with *prajna* because both point toward correct relationships. *Prajna* enables us to see ourselves in all beings, and *hokmah* demands that we live in right relation to God and God's people. Neither forms of wisdom are conceptual but are, rather, active states of engagement that can be cultivated only through direct experience. *Prajna* and *hokmah* reflect the truth that actions have consequences, and when we choose wisely we can expect to lessen our suffering and the suffering of those around us.

Interestingly, wisdom is characterized as female in the Hebrew and Buddhist traditions. Tibetan Buddhists venerate *Yeshe Tsogyal* as a female Buddha, or "Awakened One." *Yeshe Tsogyal* was a real woman who lived in Tibet during the eighth century and is considered to be the human manifestation of the feminine principle of "experiential nondual wisdom."[8] In Proverbs, *Hokmah* is repeatedly portrayed as a woman whose wrath and compassion offer warnings and blessings.

In both spiritual traditions, wisdom is the ground of right action. Without her counsel we are incapable of acting skillfully and more likely to cause harm. Listening to wisdom means dropping our grasping egos and returning to proper relations with ourselves and others.[9]

March M. Wood

---

8. Judith Simmer-Brown, "Yeshe Tsogyal: Woman and Feminine Principle," *Shambhala Times* (August 19, 2009); http://shambhalatimes.org/2009/08/19/yeshe-tsogyal-woman-and-feminine-principle/.

9. See Katherine Murphey Hayes, *Proverbs*, ed. Daniel Durken, New Collegeville Bible Commentary 18 (Collegeville, MN: Liturgical Press, 2013); Trinley Dradül Jampal, the Kongma Sakyong II, *The Supreme Thought: Bodhichitta and the Enlightened Society Vow* (Halifax and Cologne: Dragon, 2013), esp. 32.

Contemporary biblical scholarship tends to view Proverbs as the work of conservative elite scribes whose comfortable position in society facilitated their view that God recompenses humans according to their deeds. Those who see Proverbs as reflecting easy, simple, complacent, or naive optimism often prefer the books of Qohelet (Ecclesiastes) and Job, which are thought to question this traditional view.[10] Feminist scholars often join in the negative judgment of Proverbs, adding concerns about the implied reader being a son, which requires women to read as if they were men.[11] This concern will be addressed below.

Intended Audience

Since the original intended audience comprised boys/young men (especially evident in chaps. 1–9 and 31:10-31 with their sexual imagery), it is sometimes considered difficult for readers who are not male to identify with the intended audience. Not only women but gay men and heterosexual men who are not looking for love may not find the sexual imagery relevant. Most contemporary readers must edit the material or adapt ourselves to make this aspect of it meaningful for our experience.

There are two responses to this concern. First, every time we read a novel or watch a movie in which the protagonist is a man, we read from the point of view of a male. In addition, we identify temporarily with the main character each time the protagonist is of a different ethnicity than we are or a different age or from a different social or economic class. There is nothing inherently evil in this unless there is something inherently evil about men or groups who are different from ourselves and we should thus never put ourselves in their shoes.

Most of us, men and women alike, have been socialized into certain attitudes toward women (and men) that are not ideal. That does not make men evil or make it a violation of one's womanhood to temporarily step into male shoes any more than it violates one's selfhood to step into the fictional shoes of a person of a different ethnicity, class, religion, or whatever. It is one way we learn about others. If we are threatened by

10. Peter T. H. Hatton, *Contradiction in the Book of Proverbs: The Deep Waters of Counsel*, SOTSMS (Burlington, VT: Ashgate, 2008), 18–38.

11. Judith E. McKinlay, *Gendering Wisdom the Host: Biblical Invitations to Eat and Drink*, Gender, Culture, Theory 4, JSOTSup 216 (Sheffield: Sheffield Academic, 1996), 99.

temporarily identifying with a young male student, then one's identity as a woman is weak indeed.

We may well lament that there is not a version of Proverbs in the Bible directed toward young women. The reality is that a small elite group of male royal and priestly figures held much of the limited power that there was in a rural agrarian society beyond the power that everyone had within the group-oriented household.[12] Women occasionally wielded power, as various biblical stories make evident, but often their power was covert rather than overt, and/or limited to the domestic sphere.[13] In any event, we must deal with the literature that we have and the society that it reflects, trying to understand it and critique it, as well as to understand and critique our own culture, in part by looking at our reflection in ancient texts such as Proverbs.

There is a second response to the concern about the implied audience. If we are women, gay men, or beyond the age of seeking mates, it is not necessary to identify with teenage males to usefully read the book of Proverbs; rather, we can acknowledge the antiquated imagery in Proverbs and recast it in more congenial terms. Today the strange woman (to be

12. Carol Meyers in *Discovering Eve: Ancient Israelite Women in Context* (Oxford: Oxford University Press, 1991), 122–97, makes it clear that in the period before the monarchy there was greater equality and complementarity between the sexes than afterward. In the typical household everyone had to work hard in order for the extended family to survive. The rigid gender roles that developed later were much more fluid in the earlier periods. During the monarchic period, women lost power, but in the pioneer time after the exile, they regained it and then some.

13. Eve had agency but in Christian tradition is depicted negatively (Gen 3); Sarah had agency with regard to her handmaid Hagar, a domestic matter (Gen 16, 21); Rebekah had agency, using it for her favorite son, in a domestic setting (Gen 27:5-13); Rachel too had agency, stealing her father's gods, again in a largely family quarrel (Gen 31:34); she and Leah are depicted as not getting along but do cooperate, again in the domestic sphere (Gen 29:1–30:34); they also have agency with regard to their handmaids (30:3-13); Miriam had agency, but her song of the sea is mostly attributed to Moses (Exod 15:1-18, 20-21), and she is depicted as a complaining, jealous sibling to Moses (Num 12:1). Deborah acted overtly as a judge, but Jael, acting covertly, sealed the victory (Judg 4–5); the wise woman of Abel (2 Sam 20) is largely a puppet for the prophet Nathan; Bathsheba acted behind the scenes to ensure that her son Solomon would be king (1 Kgs 11–17); Jezebel acted through her husband but did not last for long (1 Kgs 16:31; 18:4-19; 19:1, 2; 21:5-25; 2 Kgs 9). Athaliah was monarch in her own right but also did not endure long (2 Kgs 11:1, 14-16; 2 Chr 23:12-15). Huldah had her own agency, but we know little of her (2 Kgs 22 and 2 Chr 34). Ruth, Naomi, Esther, and Judith all have agency, but they are probably fictional characters whose stories make various important moral points about Judah.

discussed below) may be seen as a sexual predator or pedophile, and these come in more than one gender, though they tend to be male. The ultimate point of Proverbs is not about finding the right mate, though for some demographics this is a significant quest, but about bonding with wisdom, which is a gender-neutral activity, even if in Hebrew the word for wisdom is grammatically and culturally feminine. Finding the right partner is an important element of happiness if we are inclined to mate, but it is only one element of life. Marriage with wisdom is universally necessary.

In spite of some very negative feminine imagery, discussed below, Proverbs includes perhaps the most positive female imagery of the divine in the entire Jewish and Christian canons, reflecting high social status for at least some women at the time it was being brought into final form, also discussed below.[14]

The book of Proverbs does reflect the world in which it was produced. How could it do otherwise? The question is whether it is a reactionary, conservative, or subversive text. In the last case, it would be challenging readers to reconsider their perspective on the world. If it is a product of the postexilic period, a time when the trauma of exile had called into question much traditional thinking, it is possible that Proverbs is reactionary, or just conservative. There is enough contradictory material in the book, however, to suggest that the authors intended it to cause its readers to ponder and question, not simply to learn old saws by heart. If this is the case, Proverbs is a profoundly more subversive and interesting book than is generally believed.[15] That is the position argued in this commentary.

The editors of the book of Proverbs engage their audience, enticing them to think deeply about important questions such as wealth and poverty, diligence and laziness, reward and punishment, and their relationship. Is poverty always a result of laziness? What is the responsibility of the person of integrity toward the poor? Where does God fit in? The perspective of the sages is more subtle than they are sometimes given credit for. Wealth is good, but seeking after it too vigorously is not, and it is not as important as integrity. Poverty is often caused by laziness and diligence certainly tends to lead to wealth, but other factors also lead to poverty. In the last analysis, a poor integrity is better and more

---

14. Claudia Camp, "The Female Sage in Ancient Israel and in the Biblical Wisdom Literature," in *The Sage in Ancient Israel and the Near East*, ed. John G. Gammie and Leo G. Perdue (Winona Lake, IN: Eisenbrauns, 1990), 127.

15. Hatton, *Contradiction*.

satisfying than a rich corruption. There are tensions within the book of Proverbs, which the compilers who brought it into final form present to the audience/reader to ponder, but they have structured the material in such a way that they provide guidance as to what answers they hope we will find. These are lessons we need to hear today in our culture, as much as the ancient Hebrews needed to hear them in their day, for our society is far more consumerist, materialistic, and coarse than the ancient Israelite one was.

Gender Roles

One of the major issues at play in Proverbs is gender roles. At the time the book came into final form (most likely the postexilic period), women's roles seem to have changed. By the evidence in Proverbs itself (31:16) as well as other sources, women could own property and engage in business activities. One imagines that some parts of ancient Israelite culture were not pleased with these advances for women. Indeed, one can see some of the negative attitudes toward women in Proverbs, such as the strange woman passages in 2:16-19; 5:1-11, 15-23; and 7:14-20, as well as proverbs such as 19:13; 21:9, 19; 25:24; 27:15, which complain about unpleasant wives. Proverbs 19:13 is a good example:

> A stupid child is ruin to a father,
> and a wife's quarreling is a continual dripping of rain.

The sages include these negative sentiments, perhaps because they were so much a part of traditional wisdom that they could not be omitted, but they are undercut by the strong and positive image of the strong woman (אשת־חיל ["capable wife" in NRSV]) in 31:10-31 (see also 12:4), as well as the personified feminine figure of Wisdom in 8:4–9:6. Christl Maier suggests that the old traditions were not erased but passed on in creative new ways.[16] In addition, they are balanced by many more statements about quarrelsome men. (See discussion and note at 21:9, 19.) Using old traditions, Proverbs makes bold, new statements within the well-known format of a collection of bromides and stereotyped complaints. Think of it as a way of providing a kind of corrective lens through which the reader can see the old proverbs anew.

---

16. Christl Maier, "Proverbs," in *Feminist Biblical Interpretation: A Compendium of Critical Commentary on the Books of the Bible and Related Literature*, ed. Luise Schottroff and Marie-Theres Wacker (Grand Rapids, MI: Eerdmans, 2012), 255–72.

An example of a negative version of this process is the way American slave owners embedded the story of the so-called curse of Ham in their interpretive traditions. The biblical story clearly says that it was not Ham but Canaan who was cursed (Gen 9:18-27), yet without changing a word of the text, the slave owners were able to interpret the story in such a way as to make it say that it was Ham who was cursed, and therefore slavery of Africans was justified.[17] In a similar but constructive, progressive manner, the sages who brought the book of Proverbs into its final form were providing corrective lenses for some of the out-of-date proverbs, which could not be discarded, because they were too much a part of the community tradition, but needed to be understood fresh in a new era.

Structure

One other matter is worth considering at the outset. Most scholars hold that the sayings in chapters 10–29 are mostly a hodge-podge, thrown together without any ordering principle. Although the ordering principles are not always easy to discern, at times the proverbs do seem to have been gathered in a fashion intended to help the wisdom seeker contemplate the issues created by the juxtaposition of various proverbs, as mentioned above. I will make an attempt at grouping the proverbs to show their interrelatedness and subversive potential, following Knut Heim's divisions of 10:1–22:16, though not rigidly.[18]

The book of Proverbs divides into the following sections (Hebrew titles in parentheses):

Section	Chapters	Heading(s)
1	1–9	Advice to Young Men about Women and Wisdom, Concluding with Wisdom's and Folly's Banquets (The Proverbs of Solomon, Son of David, King of Israel)
2a	10:1–15:33	A Collection Marked by Antithetic Parallelism (The Proverbs of Solomon)
2b	16:1–22:16	A Courtly/Royal Collection

17. See Gene Rice, "The Curse That Never Was (Genesis 9:18-27)," *JRT* 29 (1972): 5–27.

18. Knut M. Heim, *Like Grapes of Gold Set in Silver: An Interpretation of Proverbial Clusters in Proverbs 10:1–22:16* (Berlin: de Gruyter, 2001).

3a	22:17–24:22	A Free Adaptation of the Egyptian Wisdom Text, *The Instruction of Amenemope* (The Words of the Wise)
3b	24:23-34	A Small Collection of Miscellaneous Proverbs (These Also Are the Sayings of the Wise)
3c	25:1–29:27	A Collection with Courtly/Royal Focus (These Are Other Proverbs of Solomon That the Officials of King Hezekiah of Judah Copied)
4a	30:1-14	Sayings of an Unknown Individual, Possibly a Non-Judahite (The Words of Agur Son of Jakeh. An Oracle)
4b	30:15-33	Numerical and Other Sayings
4c	31:1-9	The Words of King Lemuel. An Oracle That His Mother Taught Him
5	31:10-31	Poem on the אשת־חיל, Strong Woman/Wife (Capable Wife) (A Strong Woman/Wife Who Can Find?)

The Significance of the Structure of Proverbs

The structure of Proverbs suggests that the editors were making a point about women and wisdom, especially since the first nine chapters and the last chapter were probably added late (see below). Part 1 is advice mainly of fathers to sons about women but concludes with the banquets of Wisdom and Folly, where the feminine divine Wisdom clearly has the upper hand (A). This is balanced by part 5, which is the Ode to the Strong Woman/Wife ("Capable Wife" in NRSV), divine Wisdom's human counterpart (A'). Parts 2, 3, 4a, and 4b are again advice mainly of *fathers* to sons (B), which is balanced by part 4c, which is advice of a *mother* to her son. This may be represented diagrammatically as follows:

1 Fathers to sons about women/**Wisdom** over Folly	A
2–4b **Fathers to sons** about everything including women	B
4c Lemuel's **mother's advice to Lemuel** about women among other things	B'
5 Ode to the Strong Woman/Wife, who on a human level represents **Wisdom**	A'

TRANSLATION MATTERS

A few words are in order about the NRSV translation. To make Proverbs relevant to a contemporary audience, the NRSV translates some words generically that originally were undoubtedly understood in their masculine sense, for example, Hebrew בֵּן, "son," is translated as "child," as discussed above, though NRSV does not follow this principle consistently. The NRSV also translates some words in a way that constitutes an interpretation rather than a translation, for example, אשה זרה, literally, the "strange woman," is translated as "loose woman" (5:3; 7:5; 22:14), interpreting her strangeness as sexual rather than ethnic or a combination of these aspects of her character.

Although I am an advocate of inclusive language in contemporary speech and writing, I do not think it is helpful to impose it on ancient texts where it is clearly not the intention of the authors; nor do I think it is helpful to translate terms such as אשה זרה, which are multivalent in meaning, with a single meaning other than a literal one. It is better to translate them literally, in this case "strange woman," so that the ambiguity of the original can be heard in the translation. If the ancient text was sexist by our standards, we cannot change that through translation sleight of hand, and it is better not to be dishonest with the public.

In addition, some common words, like צדק, translated as "righteous," are perhaps better translated differently, as noted in Translation Matters below.[19] Finally, some Hebrew words used regularly in Proverbs need explanation. Where I disagree with NRSV, which is fairly frequently, since some of the words are key ones in Proverbs, I use my preferred translation in the commentary, putting NRSV's translation in parentheses the first time I use the word in that section. The NRSV is no worse than other translations done by committees; it is better than many, but most such translations cater to an ecclesiastical market that wants to hear what it is used to hearing rather than a newer, more accurate understanding and/or to hear religiously unoffensive renderings. Translations sold to the public are inherently the result of religio-political and economic factors that sadly do not result in more excellent products. In other words, translation by compromise muddies the waters instead of sifting the wheat from the tares, to mix metaphors horribly.

---

19. See Translation Matters on Just/Integrity/Honesty (Righteous[ness]), צדיק/צדק/צדקה, at 1:2.

Part 1
Proverbs 1:1–9:18

Advice to Young Men about Women and Wisdom, Concluding with Wisdom's and Folly's Banquets

Introduction

Chapters 1–9 differ from 10–29 in that they mainly consist of long poems rather than short, pithy sayings. This does not require a single author, but it makes it more likely than for parts 2–4b (chaps. 10–29) and part 5 (chap. 31). These introductory chapters use the imagery of Wisdom[1] and its antithesis, Folly, personified poetically as female figures.[2] Wisdom is a personification rather than a divine hypostasis in that divine Wisdom is depicted as if it were a person, like giving fictional consciousness and personality to an aspect of a person like one's eyes or mind (as if one's eyes and one's mind had separate existence

---

1. For recent overviews of the biblical wisdom figure, see Gerlinde Baumann, "Personified Wisdom: Contexts, Meanings, Theology," in *The Writings and Later Wisdom Books*, ed. Christl M. Maier and Nuria Calduch-Benages, The Bible and Women: An Encyclopedia of Exegesis and Cultural History; Hebrew Bible/Old Testament, vol. 1.3 (Atlanta: SBL Press, 2014), 57 n. 1.

2. Ibid., 58; Silvia Schroer, *Wisdom Has Built Her House: Studies in the Figure of Sophia in the Bible*, trans. Linda Maloney (Collegeville, MN: Liturgical Press, 2000).

and each had individual agency; "Mine eyes have seen the glory of the coming of the Lord"). In hypostasis, the entity is viewed as an actual being separate from its source, as in Pinocchio becoming a real boy. (For a detailed discussion of personified Wisdom, see the commentary on 8:22.) The personified figure of Wisdom in 1–9 was probably drawn in part from images of the God of Israel and in part from goddess mythology.[3] It is also likely that personified Wisdom emerged in the theological and political crisis brought about by the loss of kingship and temple during the postexilic period. In that destabilized environment, this figure took over functions that the king and perhaps even the priests had formerly performed. Even after a new temple was built, its functionaries may not have had the same status as previously.[4] In transitional periods, women often gain authority, both practically and in the abstract realm.

The personified figures of Wisdom and Folly are also tied to their human counterparts: the respectable wife a young man should marry and stay with exclusively, and her opposite, אשה זרה, the "strange" woman, also known as נכריה, the "foreign" woman (2:16; 5:20; 7:5). In this context these terms do not necessarily denote ethnic foreignness but might only indicate otherness or deviation from the norm.[5] It is possible, however,

3. Bernhard Lang, "Lady Wisdom: A Polytheistic and Psychological Interpretation of a Biblical Goddess," in *Reading the Bible: Approaches, Methods and Strategies*, ed. Athalya Brenner and Carole Fontaine (Sheffield: Sheffield Academic, 1997), 400–423; Judith M. Hadley, "Wisdom and the Goddess," in *Wisdom in Ancient Israel: Essays in Honour of J.A. Emerton*, ed. John Day et al. (Cambridge: Cambridge University Press, 1995), 234–43; Michael D. Coogan, "The Goddess Wisdom—Where Can She Be Found? In Literary Reflexes of Popular Religion," in *Ki Baruch Hu: Ancient Near Eastern, Biblical, and Judaic Studies in Honor of Baruch A. Levine*, ed. Robert Chazan, William W. Hallo, and Lawrence H. Schiffman (Winona Lake, IN: Eisenbrauns, 1999), 203–9; Gerlinde Baumann, "A Figure with Many Facets: The Literary and Theological Functions of Personified Wisdom in Proverbs 1–9," in *Wisdom and Psalms*, ed. Athalya Brenner and Carole A. Fontaine, FCB 2, 2nd ser. (Sheffield: Sheffield Academic, 1998), 62–66; and Baumann, "Personified Wisdom," 57–63.

4. Alice M. Sinnott, *The Personification of Wisdom*, SOTSMS (Aldershot: Ashgate, 2005), 9.

5. Athalya Brenner, "Proverbs 1–9: An F Voice?," in *On Gendering Texts: Female and Male Voices in the Hebrew Bible*, ed. Athalya Brenner and Fokkelien van Dijk-Hemmes, BibInt 1 (Leiden: Brill, 1993), 113–30; Christl Maier, "Conflicting Attractions: Parental Wisdom and the 'Strange Woman' in Proverbs 1–9," in Brenner and Fontaine, *Wisdom and Psalms*, 92–108; Carol A. Newsom, "Women and the Discourse of Patriarchal Wisdom: A Study of Proverbs 1–9," in *Gender and Difference in Ancient Israel*, ed. Peggy Day (Minneapolis: Fortress Press, 1989), 142–60; Harold C. Washington, "The Strange Woman אשה זרה/נכריה of Proverbs 1–9," in *Temple and Community in the Persian Period* 2, ed. Tamara Eskenazi and Kent H. Richards, JSOTSup 175 (Sheffield: JSOT Press,

that, in the context of a xenophobic Persian Period, ethnic otherness was part of the intended meaning.[6] Other phrases used to describe this woman are רע אשת, "evil woman" (6:24), and כסילו אשת, "a woman of foolishness." Her speech is described as smooth, deceptive, and false (2:16; 5:3; 6:24; 7:5), and her ways lead to Sheol and death (2:18; 5:5; 6:26; 7:26-27). It is possible to read the references to the Strong Woman/Wife (31:10-31)[7] as applying on one level to Wisdom and the contrasting verses on the foreign or evil woman as being tied to Folly.

It is likely that for the most part the same strange woman is being depicted in all of these chapters, because personified Wisdom is the same character throughout and the strange woman is her human antithesis.[8] The structure of chapters 1–9 also suggests that even if the individual pieces were originally written separately, they have been brought together into an editorial whole in which the strange woman units are identified with each other. The structure is a double chiasm, a chiasm being a symmetrical pattern, e.g., ABBA.

| Prov 1:11-14 | Speech of the gang | A |
| Prov 1:22-33 | Speech of Wisdom | B |

Warning against the strange woman—2:16-19

| Prov 4:4-9 | Speech of the father's father | B' |

Warning against the strange woman—5:1-11, 15-23

| Prov 5:12-14 | Speech of the son | A' |

Warning against the evil woman—6:23-35

Prov 7:14-20	Speech of the strange woman	A
Prov 8:4-36	Speech of Wisdom	B
Prov 9:5-6	Speech of Wisdom	B'
Prov 9:16-17	Speech of the foolish woman/Folly[9]	A'

1994), 217–42; Jane S. Webster, "Sophia: Engendering Wisdom in Proverbs, Ben Sira and the Wisdom of Solomon," *JSOT* 78 (1998): 63–79.

6. Christl M. Maier, "Good and Evil Women in Proverbs and Job," in Maier and Calduch-Benages, *The Writings and Late Wisdom Books*, 86.

7. See Translation Matters on Strong Woman/Wife (Capable Wife), אשת־חיל, at 12:4.

8. Gale A. Yee, "'I Have Perfumed My Bed with Myrrh': The Foreign Woman (*'iššâ zārâ*) in Proverbs 1–9," in *A Feminist Companion to Wisdom Literature*, ed. Athalya Brenner, FCB 9 (Sheffield: Sheffield Academic, 1995), 53–68.

9. Ibid., 113.

Because the theme of advice to sons to avoid women appears at the beginning of chapter 31, mirroring chapters 1–7, and 31:10-31 is a poem in praise of the ideal wife, the human counterpart to divine Wisdom (mirroring 8:1–9:6), chapters 1–9 and 31 form a literary frame around the book of Proverbs.[10] These two sections were written down after the rest of the book as a kind of envelope for the older material, recontextualizing it and giving it a new focus. It is not just a compendium of proverbs; it is a book about Wisdom and Folly. The date of chapters 1–9 is generally believed to be postexilic, during either the Persian Period (538–333 BCE)[11] or the first half of the fourth century BCE.[12] Whatever the date of chapters 1–9, the social setting is urban and the audience is upper-class boys/young men.

It is possible that the creator(s) of Proverbs 1–9 and 31 developed the personified figures of Wisdom and Folly from the reference to them in Proverbs 14:1:

> Wisdom builds her house,
>> but Folly tears it down with her own hands.[13]

In a similar fashion, each of the two words in the strange/foreign woman pair is present once in chapters 10–29:

> The mouth of a loose [Hebrew זרות, strange, (plural)] woman is a deep pit; he with whom the LORD is angry falls into it. (22:14)

> For a prostitute is a deep pit;
>> an adulteress [Hebrew נכריה, foreign woman] is a narrow well. (23:27)

Again, these occurrences provide the material from which the author(s) of chapters 1–9 may have developed the strange/foreign woman figure. (See the commentary for a detailed discussion.)

---

10. Claudia V. Camp, *Wisdom and the Feminine in the Book of Proverbs*, BLS 11 (Sheffield: Almond Press, 1985), 207–8.

11. Christine Roy Yoder, *Wisdom as a Woman of Substance: A Socioeconomic Reading of Proverbs 1–9 and 31:10-31*, BZAW 304 (Berlin: de Gruyter, 2001); Gale A. Yee, *Poor Banished Children of Eve: Woman as Evil in the Hebrew Bible* (Minneapolis: Fortress Press, 2003), 136; Washington, "The Strange Woman."

12. Maier, "Conflicting Attractions," 100–104.

13. Author's translation. The NRSV renders it: "The wise woman builds her house, but the foolish tears it down with her own hands." See Translation Matters at 14:1. See also the contrast between wisdom and prostitutes in 29:3.

Many interpretations of the strange woman in chapters 1–9 have been offered: a foreigner,[14] a figure combining ethnic otherness and foreign worship,[15] a social outsider, a prostitute (foreign or not), and someone else's wife. Gale Yee interprets the prohibitions against sex with the strange woman on two levels, literal and figurative. On the figurative level, sex—usually adultery—with the strange woman represents marriage with a woman outside the *golah* community, those who had returned to Judah from Babylonian exile. These marriages are the ones prohibited by Ezra and Nehemiah (Ezra 9–10; Neh 13:23-30).[16]

My view is like that of Gale Yee. The strange woman may have represented the lower-class women who did not go into Babylonian captivity but remained in the land. When the exiles returned, the men may have married the local women to get access to the land they had once owned but had lost when they went to Babylon. These non-elite women may have been viewed as strange, even ethnically other, given that the Judahites were endogamous (married within their own tribes). Perhaps their worship customs had become somewhat different as well, which would have added to their being viewed as social outsiders from the perspective of the upper-crust group who had been in Babylonian exile.

Feminist evaluations of the feminine imagery in these chapters range from somewhat positive to mostly negative. On the positive side, divine Wisdom is personified as a female figure. On the negative side, she has two antitheses: on an abstract level, Folly; and on a human level, the strange woman. Moreover, the critics assert that Wisdom is at best God's diminutive sidekick, almost a plaything. Although it is true that Wisdom has a playful side in chapter 8, for the most part she is a powerful, serious figure who essentially speaks for God. One may even go so far as to speculate that she represents the absent prophetic voice. Wisdom calls from the streets and rebukes those who do not answer her call. Even prescinding from the later Christian interpretations of Wisdom as the Logos, she is no mere sidekick. Some feminist scholars, such as Silvia Schroer and Christl Maier, view her as the basis of a new feminist spirituality.[17]

---

14. Nancy Nam Hoon Tan, *The "Foreignness" of the Foreign Woman in Proverbs 1–9: A Study of the Origin and the Development of a Biblical Motif*, BZAW 381 (Berlin: de Gruyter, 2008).

15. Claudia V. Camp, *Wise, Strange, and Holy: The Making of the Bible*, JSOTSup 320 (Sheffield: Sheffield Academic, 2000).

16. Yee, *Poor Banished Children of Eve*, 135–58, 220–31.

17. Schroer, *Wisdom Has Built Her House*, 39–41; and Maier, "Proverbs," 264.

Perhaps most troubling is the polarization of the human counterparts of Wisdom and Folly, the strong woman/wife and the strange woman. At least the poles are wife and strange woman rather than the virgin-and-whore dichotomy of Christian polemics. Nevertheless, in real life, individuals (male and female) are usually mixtures of good and bad. Two of the most highly thought of "saints" in contemporary America are Martin Luther King Jr. and John F. Kennedy. Yet, it is well known that both of these men were far from pure in matters of sexuality. That does not seem to matter. It is understood that men have weaknesses.

Yet, women are not allowed the same freedom. When Rosa Parks refused to give up her seat on the bus in Montgomery, Alabama, in 1955, her action was used by the NAACP rather than a similar action by a fifteen-year-old who was pregnant as a result of statutory rape, because they understood that Rosa Parks would "sell" better than the fifteen-year-old pregnant woman; she would be seen as a woman of virtue; no sexual scandal could be attached to her. And for years she was seen by the public as a tired old woman rather than the trained civil rights worker that she was.[18]

Even in the twenty-first century, though mores have changed, a sexual double standard persists. On the one hand, in 2017 the president of the United States could boast of certain sexually aggressive actions toward women;[19] on the other hand, men in high places were beginning to be called on their sexually predatory practices, and men of goodwill were beginning to join in the chorus to say "no more."[20]

Women are freer than ever before but often are still expected to uphold traditional sexual values more than men, especially in ecclesiastical circles. How much of this can be attributed to the influence of an ancient text like Proverbs and its twin figures of Wisdom and Folly and human

18. Josh Moon, "Bus Boycott Took Planning, Smarts," *USA Today*, November 29, 2015, https://www.usatoday.com/story/news/local/blogs/moonblog/2015/11/29/bus -boycott-took-planning-smarts/76456904/.

19. "Transcript: Donald Trump's Taped Comments about Women," *New York Times*, October 8, 2016, https://www.nytimes.com/2016/10/08/us/donald-trump-tape -transcript.html.

20. It is not just women who are calling men to task; it is also men, who in the past were bystanders but now, emboldened by the change in climate, are beginning to see the power in numbers. See Robert Lypsyte, "Sexual Harassment: How We Men Can— and Must—Help Bring Down Sexual Predators," *The Guardian*, November 19, 2017, https://www.theguardian.com/world/2017/nov/19/sexual-harassment-assault -men-jock-culture.

counterparts of the strange woman and the strong woman/wife is hard to say, especially given how biblically illiterate the American population is.[21] Nevertheless, influences of ancient texts do tend to linger, even after the active consciousness of such texts has all but disappeared. Whether the contemporary double standard can be blamed in part on Proverbs, it must be acknowledged that at least in this regard the book is, unfortunately, not out of date.

Prologue (1:1-7)

Proverbs 1:1-7 forms a prologue to the whole book, emphasizing that the proverbs are intended for learning wisdom, knowledge, justice, and related virtues. Proverbs 1:2 begins a series of Hebrew infinitives (translated as "learning," "understanding," etc.) with direct objects ("wisdom," "instruction," etc.) in 1:2-4 and 1:6 that describe the purpose of the book. This series begins in 1:2 with the expression "to know" or "learn to know" wisdom and instruction.

TRANSLATION MATTERS

The Hebrew root ידע and the derived infinitive דעת in Proverbs 1:2 can be translated as both "learning" and "knowledge" and means (1) know and learn but also (2) to know a person—both socially and carnally (sexually)—and (3) to know how to do things on a practical level.

The second colon of 1:2 uses the verb להבין, meaning "understand" but also "perceive" and "discern." The object of this verb, בינה, "words of insight," includes the same root. In 1:3, the idea is that one is to take the discipline (the word is מוסר) in wise dealing (השכל) to heart. The verb השכל, "understand, make wise," is sometimes used as a synonym for דעת, knowledge, and other nouns from the root ידי. The second colon adds three more objects: righteousness, justice, and equity.

The verb in 1:3, translated as "gaining," literally "taking," is parallel to the infinitive "learning" in 1:2. The meanings of the objects of the infinitive are discussed in Translation Matters.

---

21. Albert Mohler, "The Scandal of Biblical Illiteracy: It's Our Problem," January 20, 2016, https://albertmohler.com/2016/01/20/the-scandal-of-biblical-illiteracy-its-our-problem-4/m.

Prov 1:1-7

¹The proverbs of Solomon son of David, king of Israel:
²For learning about wisdom and instruction,
for understanding words of insight,
³for gaining instruction in wise dealing, righteousness, justice, and equity;
⁴to teach shrewdness to the simple, knowledge and prudence to the young—

⁵let the wise also hear and gain in learning,
and the discerning acquire skill,
⁶to understand a proverb and a figure, the words of the wise and their riddles.

⁷The fear of the LORD is the beginning of knowledge;
fools despise wisdom and instruction.

TRANSLATION MATTERS

Just/Integrity/Honesty (Righteous[ness]), צדק, צדקה, and צדיק; the root behind these words means conformity to an ethical standard, what is just, lawful, or right.[22] The NRSV translation, "righteous[ness]" is too narrow and misleading, suggesting superficial piety, especially given the fact that the word is most often used today in the combination self-righteous. The terms צדקה and צדק (righteousness) are roughly synonymous.[23] Although no single translation will always work, "integrity" (or "honesty") is a better translation than "righteousness" for these terms. Similarly, (the) "just" (or in some contexts innocent) is a better rendering for צדיק than "righteous."

Justice/Right/Rectitude, משפט, are among the range of meanings.

Uprightness/Equity, מישרים, means what is upright, equitable. So, all three—צדק, משפט, and מישרים—are nuances of wisdom.

Proverbs 1:4 indicates that the audience includes the simple, naive individuals (פתאים) and the young (נער), but 1:5 broadens the audience to the mature persons, designated as wise (חכם), who already have a measure of understanding. The objects of the verb לתת, "to teach," in 1:4 are prudence (ערמה, "shrewdness"), knowledge (דעת), and discretion (מזמה, "prudence"). In Wisdom literature, דעת means discernment, understanding, and wisdom.

---

22. Harold G. Stigers, "1879 צָדֵק," in *TWOT*, 752–55.
23. Jutta Leonhardt-Balzer, "צדק," in *New Interpreter's Dictionary of the Bible*, vol. 4, ed. Katherine Doob Sakenfeld (Nashville: Abingdon, 2009), 808.

TRANSLATION MATTERS

Prudence/Prudent (Shrewdness/Clever), ערום/ערמה; the related words ערמה and ערום have a consistently positive meaning in Proverbs.[24] The rendering of the noun ערמה as "shrewdness" and the adjective ערום as "clever" by NRSV is ambiguous, as these words can have pejorative connotations, as in "too clever for her own good." It would be better to translate as "prudence/prudent."

Foresight/Discretion/Purposes/Plans, מזמה; the noun מזמה connotes hidden plans or purposes, which because of their hiddenness require discretion and suggest a person of foresight.

Proverbs 1:6 promises that the addressees will be able to understand proverbs and figures of speech, the words of the wise and their enigmatic sayings. The verb להבין, "to understand," is the same one used in 1:2b. The term משל, translated as "proverb" in 1:6, is used of brief, popular, wise sayings, prophetic figurative discourse, parables, poems, and the sayings collected in the book of Proverbs. The word מליצה, translated as "figure" in 1:6, is used only here and in Habakkuk 2:6, where it refers to a mocking poem. Here, in parallelism with משל, it must refer to some poetic figure. The wise (חכמים) in Proverbs refers to those who are learned in ethical and religious matters. The final word in the verse, חידתם, means "riddles" in the sense of allegorical and figurative sayings that need interpretation.

TRANSLATION MATTERS

Know, the verb ידע, from which the infinitive דעת, translated as both "learning" in 1:2 and "knowledge" in 1:7, has a broad range of meanings, including to know a person—both socially and carnally (sexually). Since one of the objects of the verb is wisdom, which is later personified as a female figure who invites young men to a banquet, the sexual meaning of the verb is relevant and serves to emphasize the intimate relationship required with wisdom. Here wisdom is paralleled with מוסר, discipline, chastening, or correction (instruction).

Wisdom, חכמה, which can also be rendered as "skill" or "prudence," is primarily a religious and ethical concept, though it includes practical aspects as well. It is, first of all, an attribute of God (2:6; 3:19); its fundamental principle is fear of YHWH[25] (9:10; 15:33). In 8:22-31 it is personified as a female figure.

---

24. A. Luc, "ערם," in *New International Dictionary of Old Testament Exegesis and Theology*, vol. 1, ed. Willem A. Van Gemeren (Grand Rapids, MI: Zondervan, 1997), 539–40.
25. See discussion of this phrase at 1:7.

Discipline/Chastening/Correction, מוּסָר; the NRSV rendering as "instruction" in 1:2 and 1:7 is a mild translation of the word. The concept of מוּסָר involves the student undergoing a difficult, life-changing process and includes notions of discipline, chastening, and correction. Today we hear a lot about transformative leadership and the training required for it, but most of it is shallow. We are drawn to the stories of the Olympic athletes because we can tell the years of dedication it took for them to mold their bodies into the perfection required to win at the Olympic level. But there is another kind of transformation that the book of Proverbs is talking about and that liberal education was originally intended to convey, one that deeply impacts the student's moral core. Heroes of this sort include people like Mary McLeod Bethune,[26] Nannie Helen Burroughs,[27] Mary Lyon,[28] Pauli Murray,[29] Mary Church Terrell,[30] and Ida B. Wells-Barnett[31]—each in her own way fought for women's rights and the rights of the underprivileged and marginalized. These were women of deep character and determination.

26. Mary McLeod Bethune, born in the late nineteenth century, an educator and activist, served as president of the National Association of Colored Women, founded the National Council of Negro Women, and founded the Daytona Normal and Industrial Institute in 1904, which later became Bethune-Cookman College. (See https://www.biography.com/people/mary-mcleod-bethune-9211266.) A statue of her erected in the 1970s is in Lincoln Park in Washington, DC.

27. Nannie Helen Burroughs, born in the late nineteenth century, opened the National Trade and Professional School for Women and Girls in Washington, DC, in 1909, when she was twenty-six. Her motto for the school was "We specialize in the wholly impossible." She trained her faculty to teach students through a curriculum that emphasized both vocational and professional skills. Her students were to become self-sufficient wage earners and "expert homemakers." Nannie Helen Burroughs never married. She devoted her life to the National Trade and Professional School for Women and Girls and remained its principal until her death in 1961. Three years later the institution she founded was renamed the Nannie Burroughs School.

28. Mary Lyon, women's rights activist and educator, was born in the late eighteenth century. She founded the first women's college in the United States, now known as Mount Holyoke College, in South Hadley, Massachusetts. See https://www.biography.com/people/mary-lyon-9389865.

29. Pauli Murray was a twentieth-century civil rights activist, an original member of the Congress of Racial Equality (CORE), the first African American woman ordained by the Episcopal Church, a lawyer, and a gay rights activist. Her autobiography was rereleased in 1987 as *Pauli Murray: The Autobiography of a Black Activist, Feminist, Lawyer, Priest and Poet*. See https://paulimurrayproject.org/pauli-murray/biography/.

30. Mary Church Terrell's life spanned the second half of the nineteenth century and the first half of the twentieth. She was a suffragette, a civil rights advocate, a charter member of the NAACP, and its first president.

31. Ida B. Wells, born in Mississippi, in the last third of the nineteenth century, was a journalist and became an antilynching advocate as a result of a triple lynching that

Proverbs 1:7 declares the central tenet of the book of Proverbs. Since knowledge and wisdom are virtually synonymous, the saying that the fear of YHWH is the beginning of knowledge means likewise that it is the beginning of wisdom. Fear of YHWH is not much in fashion today. The pendulum swung from fear to praise to apathy some time ago for many people. Fear, in the proper sense of the word, however, is magisterial. C. S. Lewis describes it in an especially affecting way:

> Those who have not met this term may be introduced to it by the following device. Suppose you were told there was a tiger in the next room: you would know that you were in danger and would probably feel fear. But if you were told "There is a ghost in the next room," and believed it, you would feel, indeed, what is often called fear, but of a different kind. It would not be based on the knowledge of danger, for no one is primarily afraid of what a ghost may do to him, but of the mere fact that it is a ghost. It is "uncanny" rather than dangerous, and the special kind of fear it excites may be called Dread. With the Uncanny one has reached the fringes of the Numinous. Now suppose that you were told simply "There is a mighty spirit in the room" and believed it. Your feelings would then be even less like the mere fear of danger: but the disturbance would be profound. You would feel wonder and a certain shrinking—a sense of inadequacy to cope with such a visitant and of prostration before it—an emotion which might be expressed in Shakespeare's words "Under it my genius is rebuked." This feeling may be described as awe, and the object which excites it as the Numinous.
>
> A modern example may be found (if we are not too proud to seek it there) in *The Wind in the Willows* where Rat and Mole approach Pan on the island:
>
> "Rat," he found breath to whisper, shaking, "Are you afraid?" "Afraid?" murmured the Rat, his eyes shining with unutterable love. "Afraid? of Him? O, never, never. And yet—and yet—O Mole, I am afraid."[32]

Here for the first time the opposite of the wise are mentioned: אֱוִילִים, fools.

---

occurred in her hometown while she was out of town, in which a friend was one of the victims. See https://www.biography.com/people/ida-b-wells-9527635.

32. C. S. Lewis, introduction to *The Problem of Pain*, in *The Complete C. S. Lewis Signature Classics*, rev ed. (New York: HarperOne, 2007; original, 1940), 554.

TRANSLATION MATTERS

Jerk/Schmuck/Folly (Fool/Folly), אולת/אויל, is the worst sort of fool and folly that is encountered in Proverbs. The word for the person occurs seventeen times in Proverbs. The אוילים despise wisdom and instruction (see also 17:28). They are not just dumb, mindless idiots. From the point of view of the sages, they are morally corrupt creatures. They talk too much (10:14; 14:3; 17:28) and are arrogant (12:15) and contentious (e.g., 12:16; 20:3; 28:3). We might in our less charitable moments call them jerks or even schmucks. Today we may suspect that they are covering up insecurity, but whatever the reason for their behavior we view it as obnoxious. This root occurs forty times in Proverbs.

This type of fool should be distinguished from the כסיל, a word that is also translated as "fool" by NRSV but is a different sort of person. He is inept, bumbling, and stupid, but not evil. When the sages speak of Folly, they are talking about moral corruption, אולת, not just bumbling stupidity. Because there is no good substitute for the English translation of Folly, and since it is still used in contemporary speech, I have retained the traditional translation. It only translates אולת and thus if we were looking for a synonym in English it would be recklessness or irresponsibility rather than mere madness or idiocy, and certainly not silliness, though "recklessness" does not feel like a strong enough word. Strangely, it is usually associated with the ignorant types of fools or the naive rather than the type being described here. The two exceptions are 16:22 and 27:22. We do not seem to have a perfect synonym for the Hebrew concept of Folly in English with its connotations of serious moral corruption.

There is one other type of fool mentioned in Proverbs called a נבל, a nickname given to the character in the story of Abigail's first husband, Nabal, who acts foolishly in his dealings with David (1 Sam 25). This sort of fool is presumptuous, ignoble, and churlish. Variations on this word occur three times in Proverbs, in 17:7, 17:21, and 30:22.

Proverbs 1:7, with its repetition of the key words from 1:2, forms an *inclusio* around the prologue.

> ²For **learning** [דעת] about *wisdom* [חכמה] and instruction [מוסר],
>   for understanding words of insight,
> ⁷The fear of the Lord is the beginning of **knowledge** [דעת];
>   fools despise *wisdom* [חכמה] and instruction [מוסר].

In addition, words from the same root as wisdom occur in 1:5-6, strongly binding the prologue together:

> ⁵let the *wise* [חכם] also hear and gain in learning,
>   and the discerning acquire skill,
> ⁶to understand a proverb and a figure,
>   the words of the *wise* [חכמים] and their riddles.

Exordium to Pay Attention to Parents' Instruction (1:8-19)

Proverbs 1:8-9 is an exordium or exhortation, in which the addressee is urged to pay attention to the parents' instruction. The fact that the child is called בני, *my* son (*my* child), is significant. The pronoun makes it clear that the place of instruction was probably originally within the home rather than in a more institutional setting such as in a school; "my son" is a term of endearment as well as of authority. It could be used in a school setting, but it seems more natural at home. The verb שמע, "hear," means much more than to casually listen. To really hear the father's correction (instruction, מוסר), the same word that was used in the prologue[33] is to get it, to understand it at a deep level. Ancient Israel's creed, the *Shema*, begins: "Hear [שמע], O Israel, YHWH is our God, YHWH alone" (Deut 6:4). In the second colon (half line), the child is told not to reject the mother's teaching either. The word used for teaching, תורה, *torah*, is the same one used of God's law, but here that is clearly not what the word means. It is *torah* with a small *t*. This is not to say that the word is insignificant; it parallels מוסר, the instruction the father gives. The image is of the two parents standing before the son, teaching him.

Proverbs 1:9 provides a metaphorical motivation for why the child should heed the parents' instruction. The word translated as "garland" (לויה) occurs only here and in 4:9. Here it is parallel to ענקים, necklaces, neck-pendants; there it is parallel to עטרה, crown, wreath. Thus, it seems to mean something like wreath or garland granted as an honor, perhaps like our athletic medals worn around the neck.

Proverbs 1:10-16 presents the instructions to avoid what we might call street gangs. Verse 10 begins with a general warning against being enticed by sinners. As in 1:8, the parents address the son (child)[34] as "my son," adding to the intimacy and the urgency of the appeal. The verb used is denominated from the noun for a naive, simple individual, פתי. So, the parents are pressing the son not to let anyone pull the wool over his eyes; rather, he should be wise to the ways of such people and just say no. Then, in 1:11-14, to help him avoid falling in with the wrong crowd, the parents give him a sample of the words of the gang. The parents say, "If they say," then for three verses quote what they might say. Noteworthy are all the first common plural verb forms ("let us lie in wait," "let us

---

33. See Translation Matters on Discipline/Chastening/Correction (Instruction), מוסר, at 1:2.

34. See Translation Matters on Son (Child), בן, at 1:8.

Prov 1:8-19

⁸Hear, my child, your father's
instruction,
and do not reject your mother's
teaching;
⁹for they are a fair garland for your
head,
and pendants for your neck.
¹⁰My child, if sinners entice you,
do not consent.
¹¹If they say, "Come with us, let us lie
in wait for blood;
let us wantonly ambush the
innocent;
¹²like Sheol let us swallow them alive
and whole, like those who go
down to the Pit.
¹³We shall find all kinds of costly
things;

we shall fill our houses with
booty.
¹⁴Throw in your lot among us;
we will all have one purse"—
¹⁵my child, do not walk in their way,
keep your foot from their paths;
¹⁶for their feet run to evil,
and they hurry to shed blood.
¹⁷For in vain is the net baited
while the bird is looking on;
¹⁸yet they lie in wait—to kill
themselves!
and set an ambush—for their own
lives!
¹⁹Such is the end of all who are
greedy for gain;
it takes away the life of its
possessors.

wantonly ambush" [1:11], "let us swallow them alive" [1:12], "we shall find, we shall fill" [1:13], "we will all have" [1:14]), which give the son a false sense of intimacy in the gang. The parents are painting a picture of the gang as quite brazen about what they plan to do, lying in wait for blood, wantonly ambushing the innocent, even swallowing them alive and whole like Sheol. They claim that they will divide the spoils evenly, but who can trust this sort?

The "then" part after the "if" clause begun in 1:11 finally begins in 1:15 with another vocative, "my son." The advice is not to walk the walk with the bad guys (1:15), for their feet run to evil and they rush to spill blood (1:16). The words of the father are again heard in the remaining verses, exhorting the son to avoid their path (1:15), explaining that the gang's way runs to blood and violence (1:16), but what they are really doing is setting a trap for themselves (1:17-18). Finally, 1:19 generalizes the stupidity of the gang and the terrible end that comes to all who try to get rich quick through violent and selfish schemes.

TRANSLATION MATTERS

Son (Child). Hebrew בֵּן, "son," is translated by NRSV as "child"; the plural בנים could designate the people of a place, as in the sons of Israel = Israelites. The plural could also be used for male and female children (Gen 3:16; 21:7; Exod 21:5; 22:23). Even so, the original addressees of the final form of the book of Proverbs were boys and young men, given the focus on avoiding the wrong kind of women and finding the right kind of wife, especially in chapters 1–9 and 31. Nevertheless, the term could have been understood more inclusively in some individual proverbs. In a new and radically different social context, the text can be updated to allow it to continue to speak to new generations, though it is important that readers understand that this is what is being done.

Father/Parent/Ancestor. Hebrew אָב meant father, grandfather, ancestor, patriarch, and the like. Unless אָב could be used generically, there is no word for "parent" in biblical Hebrew. It may be that אָב could have been used for "parent," just as בֵּן, especially in the plural, could be used generically for "children." NRSV translates it as "parent" in 17:21.

Wisdom Calls, Mostly to Deaf Ears (1:20-33)

In 1:20-33, we meet personified divine Wisdom for the first time. In 1:20-21, Wisdom speaks out in the open, unlike the street gangs whose invitations are secret. She cries out outside in the street, in the plaza near the city gate, in the busy tumultuous areas, and at the city gates themselves, where commercial and legal business was conducted. Wisdom was not limited to a privileged few but was available to everyone, at least in theory; the invitation was freely extended to anyone who was out and about. At the time the concluding poem in 31:10-31 was written, in praise of the strong woman/wife (capable wife),[35] women were apparently moving freely, doing business in the city, so in theory the invitation was available for women as well as men, even though it was not originally intended for their ears.

In 1:22, Wisdom addresses three groups: the simple (פתים), the scoffers (לצים), and the dolts ("fools," כסילים), asking with frustration, how long? Proverbs 1:4 says that one of the purposes of the book is to teach prudence (shrewdness[36]) to the simple, so it is not surprising that Wisdom calls to the simple. They may be naive, but they are open to learning.

---

35. See Translation Matters on Strong Woman/Wife (Capable Wife), אשת־חיל, at 12:4.

36. See Translation Matters on Prudent/Prudence (Clever[ness]), ערמה and ערום, at 1:4.

Prov 1:20-33

²⁰Wisdom cries out in the street;
in the squares she raises her
voice.
²¹At the busiest corner she cries out;
at the entrance of the city gates
she speaks:
²²"How long, O simple ones, will you
love being simple?
How long will scoffers delight in their
scoffing
and fools hate knowledge?
²³Give heed to my reproof;
I will pour out my thoughts to you;

I will make my words known to
you.
²⁴Because I have called and you
refused,
have stretched out my hand and
no one heeded,
²⁵and because you have ignored all
my counsel
and would have none of my
reproof,
²⁶I also will laugh at your calamity;
I will mock when panic strikes
you,

The scoffers are a much harder group to reach. They are the egotistical detractors. Wisdom herself says in 9:7-8 that people who try to correct scoffers get only abuse and hatred for their efforts. Proverbs 15:12 expresses a similar sentiment. Proverbs 14:6 goes so far as to assert that this kind of individual seeks knowledge in vain. Yet Wisdom reaches out even to them.

TRANSLATION MATTERS

In 1:20, the word translated as "Wisdom," חכמות, is plural rather than the more usual singular form: חכמה.[37] The word is considered to be an abstract form and should be understood as singular grammatically because of the singular verbs used with it. The plural form is also used in 9:1, where it is personified, and 24:7, where it is not.

TRANSLATION MATTERS

Dolt/Chump/Oaf/Inept (Fool), כסיל; the fools addressed in 1:22 are different from those mentioned at the end of the prologue in 1:7 (אוילים). The כסילים are not morally corrupt, just stupid and inept. But they are almost as bad. They take no pleasure in understanding (18:2), even beating (rebuking) does not work on them (17:10), and they have no mind to learn (17:16), not that beating is recommended today.

37. See Translation Matters on Wisdom, חכמה, at 1:1.

²⁷when panic strikes you like a
   storm,
and your calamity comes like a
   whirlwind,
when distress and anguish come
   upon you.
²⁸Then they will call upon me, but I
   will not answer;
they will seek me diligently, but
   will not find me.
²⁹Because they hated knowledge
and did not choose the fear of the
   LORD,

³⁰would have none of my counsel,
   and despised all my reproof,
³¹therefore they shall eat the fruit of
   their way
and be sated with their own
   devices.
³²For waywardness kills the simple,
   and the complacency of fools
   destroys them;
³³but those who listen to me will be
   secure
and will live at ease, without dread
   of disaster."

Despite their ineptitude, Wisdom calls them. She asks how long they will continue loving and desiring their current condition and hating knowledge. The verbs used all express strong emotion. It may seem odd to think of a simple, naive person loving being that way, but according to the sages such an individual loves their condition more than the work required to become wise. Similarly, it may seem an overstatement to suggest that such a person hates knowledge, but from the sages' perspective anyone who does not make knowledge a top priority hates it. The strong emotionally evocative language is intended to motivate the addressee to become activated in the process of becoming wise, not necessarily just to condemn them. Such a psychological approach can sometimes be effective.

In 1:23, Wisdom asks those to whom she calls to return to her correction (reproof), as though they have just wandered away and need to get back on the path. The verb used, שוב, which literally means "turn around," is sometimes associated with repentance. This is the first instance of the important word תוכחת, which can mean, in a milder sense, reproof or, in its stronger meaning, rebuke, as in 29:15 where it is parallel to the rod. Coupled with this negative concept, however, are two positive phrases. Wisdom will cause her breath or spirit to flow out, נבע, like water, but in parallelism with words in the next colon, NRSV is not incorrect in translating the Hebrew usually rendered as "my breath/spirit," רוחי, as "my thoughts." The idea, though, is that Wisdom will share not simply thoughts and words but the essence of her being, which will come out in her speech. The picture is of a teacher who is firm but wise and caring.

The parallel verb in 1:23b is "to know," ידע. As in 1:2 and 1:7 in the prologue, this knowing is of a profound sort. It is not rote knowledge but learning that goes deep within the student's being. In 1:24-25, Wisdom gives the reasons for what she will say in the remainder of her speech in 1:26-31. Because the simple, scoffers, and dolts would not respond to her, when they get into trouble, she will not answer them. The verb used in 1:25 to describe their lack of consent to her reproof (אבה) is the same one used in 1:10, where the parents tell the child not to consent if a gang tries to persuade the son[38] to join up.

Proverbs 1:26 begins the litany of the ways in which Wisdom will disregard the simple, scoffers, and inept fools. When some calamity hits that causes these people panic, Wisdom will laugh and mock them.

TRANSLATION MATTERS

In 1:27 the NRSV is reading the *Qeré*,שואה, "storm," rather than the *Ketib*, שאוה, "emptiness." The *Ketib* is the written consonantal text the Masoretic scribes found and the *Qeré* is what they intended to be read based on the vowels they added, which forced a reading different from what the consonantal text would normally dictate.

Proverbs 1:27 continues but adds weather imagery, comparing their panic to a storm (שואה, *šôʾâ*) and a whirlwind (סופה, *sûpâ*). This adds to the calamity and the panic that it causes distress (צרה, *ṣārâ*) and anguish (צוקה, *ṣûqâ*). The storm words and these last two words all begin with sibilants (s sounds), so the effect is a piling up of s's that makes the line quite alliterative.

Proverbs 1:28 describes how those who have been hit by calamities change their tune from ignoring Wisdom to calling and seeking her diligently. Only she will not answer and will not be able to be found. Part of the motivational strategy is to explain that if they do not answer her in a timely fashion, she will not be available to them later. But why not? The reason is that wisdom takes time to cultivate. It cannot be called upon on short notice any more than one can learn a language or learn to play a sport overnight.

Proverbs 1:29-30 form the first half of the next sentence. These two lines again explain why Wisdom will not be available to those who do not an-

38. See Translation Matters on Son (Child), בן, at 1:8.

swer her call early in life. As in 1:22, the phrase שנאו דעת, "hate knowledge," is used. They hated knowledge and did not choose the fear of YHWH,[39] which 1:7 says is the beginning of knowledge. The sages believed that knowledge and wisdom, for the two are used virtually synonymously in Proverbs, are a matter of choice. Proverbs 1:30 repeats the ideas expressed in 1:25, wording them slightly differently. The same words for "counsel," עצה, and "correction," תוכחה, are used, and the verb "[not] to consent to," לא אבה, translated by NRSV as "to have none of," is switched from referring to counsel to reproof. Otherwise, 1:25 and 1:30 are very similar.

Proverbs 1:31 is a "therefore" clause that concludes the sentence begun in 1:29-30. Two mixed metaphors are involved. First, "they shall eat the fruit of their way." The word דרך, "road, path, way, manner," is used frequently in Proverbs as a metaphor for an individual's life journey. One eats the fruit of one's labors, which can be compared to one's way, but the metaphor seems strained. The second metaphor is equally so. One is satisfied by food, so here an individual will be sated by the results of his (or her) devices, plans, or principles.

In 1:32-33, Wisdom completes her speech with two antithetical general statements that the bad attributes of the simple (פתים) and dolts kill them and that those who listen to Wisdom will be secure. In 1:32, the waywardness, משובת, of the simple kills them. The noun משובת usually means "apostasy," "backsliding," but here that does not fit the context. The idea is rather that the simple turn away from Wisdom, and that is a death-dealing choice. Similarly, the ושלות כסילים, the complacency of dolts—their self-satisfied false sense of security—will cause them to perish. On the other hand, in 1:33 Wisdom states that those who listen, meaning really listen to her, will truly be secure and will rest at ease without any concern of disaster. The word NRSV translates as "dread," פחד, is the one translated as "panic" in 1:26-27. So those who ignore Wisdom will experience panic, with no one to help them, but those who answer her call have no fear of experiencing such panic. Wisdom is not promising wealth here, nor ease, but what today might be called the peace of mind that comes from deep self-knowledge. Maya Angelou comes to mind, whose poems exude this quality.[40]

---

39. See discussion of this phrase at 1:7.

40. Maya Angelou (1928–2014), an American poet, memoirist, and civil rights activist, published autobiographies, essays, and poetry and was credited with plays, movies, and television shows spanning over fifty years. See https://www.poets.org/poetsorg/poet/maya-angelou. For some of her most famous poems, see "Maya Angelou" on poemhunter.com, for example, https://www.poemhunter.com/poem/still-i-rise/.

This first appearance of Wisdom belies those who would argue that she is merely a sidekick. Her voice has the same tone and content as the words of God as represented in prophetic literature (see, e.g., Jer 4:1-2).

Advice to Value Wisdom (2:1-9)

Proverbs 2:1-9 begins with an exordium in the parent's speech to the son (child).[41] In 2:2b, "the heart," לב, means what we think of as mind, so the son should incline his heart/mind to the advice.

Proverbs 2:3 continues by encouraging the young man to call out for insight and understanding, just as Wisdom called out in her speech in 1:20, and to search out insight and understanding like silver or hidden booty (treasures; 2:4). For the son will then succeed in finding the fear, יראה, of YHWH (meaning reverence) and knowledge, דעת, of God (2:5),[42] closely related concepts. The piling up of multiple verbs and various body parts involved in the process of acquiring wisdom, as well as the variety of synonyms for wisdom, gives the impression that the acquisition of wisdom is an arduous, complex, all-consuming affair. It involves the senses, the intelligence, and the depths of one's being. Proverbs 2:6-8 identifies YHWH as the source of wisdom, חכמה;[43] knowledge, דעת; and understanding, תבונה; 2:7 makes it clear that this is not simply an intellectual pursuit but a moral one, since God stores up sound wisdom, or in this context perhaps enduring (abiding) success (תושיה), for the upstanding (upright; ישרים) and is a shield, as was used in war, for those who walk with integrity (blamelessly; תם).

A Father Living Vicariously through His Son

After wrestling with the text of Proverbs, I felt saddened because it reminded me of a father who lives vicariously through his son. I concluded that the father tried to live his life through his son based on how the father asserted his intolerance (Prov 2:1), how he marginalized men and women (Prov 2:12-19), and how he established a binary relationship between good and evil (Prov 2:20-22). In addition, the father reinforced his power and control over the son through the son's silence.

Recently, a devotee of Hare Krishna shared a thought on

---

41. See Translation Matters on Son (Child), בן, at 1:8.
42. See discussion of the root ידע at 1:7.
43. See Translation Matters on Wisdom, חכמה, at 1:1.

¹My child, if you accept my words
 and treasure up my
   commandments within you,
²making your ear attentive to wisdom
 and inclining your heart to
   understanding;
³if you indeed cry out for insight,
 and raise your voice for
   understanding;
⁴if you seek it like silver,
 and search for it as for hidden
   treasures—
⁵then you will understand the fear of
 the LORD

and find the knowledge of God.
⁶For the LORD gives wisdom;
 from his mouth come knowledge
  and understanding;
⁷he stores up sound wisdom for the
 upright;
 he is a shield to those who walk
  blamelessly,
⁸guarding the paths of justice
 and preserving the way of his
  faithful ones.
⁹Then you will understand
 righteousness and justice
 and equity, every good path;

Proverbs 1:7, the passage that reads, "the fear of the LORD is the beginning of wisdom." My friend said that children won't learn from people whom they don't respect. His interpretation caused me to reflect on what it must have meant to a son to have an overbearing father who may have thought that his son wasn't very intelligent (Prov 2:1). How would the son feel toward the father? I then concluded that, perhaps, the son might not respect his father, although he loved him enough to marry the woman the father chose for him. This is likely because it's rather normal for a person to want to please someone they love, even if they don't love everything about that person.

Many Christians believe it possible to love a sinner while hating the sin in him. In that context, it's possible for the son to love his father deeply (enough to remain silent while his father speaks) and also to fear him. This kind of relationship is rooted in power and control and, I would imagine, is not very healthy. It is possible that the son could marry the wrong woman for himself and wind up resenting himself as well as his father; he might beat up on himself for not standing up to his father's evil tendencies.

As a middle-aged, educated, African American church musician who has never been married and has no biological children, I can identify with the son who (clearly) succumbed to external pressures. As a church musician and choir director, I am used to folk, including pastors, making assumptions about who I am based on stereotypes about artists. Some of their ideas are probably right. The good news is, however, that over time I've learned to live with whispers and silent elephants in the room. One advantage is that I feel very capable of teaching young people how to be tolerant and accepting of difference. As a matter of fact, that's been one of my life passions.

In the case of the heteronormative paradigm well established in Proverbs, it seems to me that the son would have at least two choices in dealing with an overbearing father. Either, he could ignore the father's overbearing tendencies and marry whomever he pleases (see 2:16-19) or he can confront his father. I would probably do both.

Sam Perryman

TRANSLATION MATTERS

The heart, לב, was the seat of intelligence and higher emotions, the equivalent of the mind in modern Western thought.

TRANSLATION MATTERS

Upstanding/Straight/Straightforward (Upright), ישר/ישרים; the words mean, in addition, what is pleasing to God, what is just. Of individuals, I am using "upstanding" rather than NRSV's "upright" simply because no one uses the word "upright" of people any more. We occasionally may speak of persons as upstanding, as in upstanding citizens.

Integrity/Whole/Complete (Blameless), תם; those who walk in this quality have a quality of wholeness in their lives; they are undivided, not living/talking one way at home/church and another at the office or the gym.

Proverbs 2:8 goes on to promise that God guards the paths of justice on which God's faithful walk. The word used for "paths" in the first colon, ארחות, is a synonym for דרך in the second colon. The word translated by NRSV as "faithful ones" (חסידיו, *Qerê*)[44] is related to the noun חסד, meaning kindness, and is the root from which the Orthodox Jewish Chasidim's name is taken.

---

44. See above on 1:20 for an explanation of *Qerê/Ketib*.

TRANSLATION MATTERS

The noun חסד is best understood as "kindness," "mercy," rather than "loyalty," as the NRSV often renders it. In Proverbs 2:8, NRSV renders the plural חסידיו as "his faithful ones," whereas older translations, such as KJV, translate it as "his saints."[45]

Proverbs 2:9 grammatically is another "then" clause like the one in 2:5. In that instance, the son is expected to understand fear of YHWH[46] and knowledge of God; this time it is integrity (righteousness)[47] and justice, equity, and every good path—in other words, the moral life. The word used here for "path," מעגל, is different from the two words encountered thus far (דרך and ארח), but it has a similar meaning. The מעגל was an entrenchment or track.

Wisdom Will Protect the Son (2:10-22)

Proverbs 2:10-22 continues the parent's speech, now focusing on the ways in which wisdom will save the young man from evil men and women (2:10-19). Verses 10-15 focus on evil men, while verses 16-19 focus on the נכריה/אשה זרה, "strange" and "foreign woman" (rendered "loose woman," "adulteress" in NRSV). The vocabulary shared by the two segments and the structuring of the two units make it clear that the latter is being identified with the former as is shown below; both are considered evil.[48]

TRANSLATION MATTERS

Soul/Neck/Person/Desire, נפש; the original meaning of this word was "neck" or "gullet" (esophagus), from which was derived the meanings breath, life, and soul, but also desire, appetite, and passion.

45. Katherine Doob Sakenfeld, *The Meaning of Ḥesed in the Hebrew Bible*, HSS 17 (Missoula, MT: Scholars Press, 1978).

46. See discussion of this phrase at 1:7.

47. See Translation Matters on Just/Integrity/Honesty (Righteous[ness]), צדקה/צדיק/צדק, at 1:2.

48. Yee, "I Have Perfumed My Bed with Myrrh," 56–57.

Prov 2:10-22

¹⁰for wisdom will **come** into your heart,
and knowledge will be pleasant to your soul;

¹¹prudence will watch over you;
and understanding will guard you.

¹²It will **save** you from the way of evil,   A
from those who **speak** perversely,   B

¹³who **forsake** the **paths** of uprightness   C
to walk in the ways of darkness,

¹⁴who rejoice in doing evil
and delight in the perverseness of evil;

¹⁵those whose **paths** are crooked,   D
and who are devious in their ways.   E

¹⁶You will be **saved** from the loose woman,   A'
from the adulteress with her smooth **words**,   B'

¹⁷who **forsakes** the partner of her youth   C'

Proverbs 2:10-11 speaks of how wisdom will come into the son's heart (mind),[49] knowledge will even be delightful (pleasant) in the soul, and prudence and understanding will guard the child. The phrase לנפשך ינעם, "be pleasant in the soul" (2:10), has a double meaning. Because נפש, "soul," originally meant "neck" or "gullet" (esophagus), and because the verb נעם, "be pleasant," can have the connotation of "being tasty" (see 9:17), the meaning was heard by the original addressees in two ways.

The two virtues in 2:11 are practical. Foresight (מזמה)[50] involved the inner thoughts of an individual, those plans that could be used for good or ill. תבונה involved understanding in the practical arena. Wisdom was not just esoteric philosophical knowledge, though it included this; it had very practical, down-to-earth aspects. As in 2:8, 2:12 begins with a Hebrew infinitive, להציל, "save," so this material is connected structurally with the infinitives in 2:2, 3, and 8. The subject is not stated; it could be YHWH or wisdom or any of the preceding nouns. The phrase at the end of the first colon can be rendered as "way of evil" or "way of an evil one," or both meanings may have been intended and understood by the original audience. Because the second colon focuses on a person who speaks duplicitously (perversely), it is likely that the phrase was intended to include the notion of the way of an evil individual, to parallel the double-talker, תהפכות, in the second half of the line.

49. See Translation Matters on the Heart, לב, at 2:2.
50. See Translation Matters on Foresight/Discretion/Purposes/Plans, מזמה, at 1:4.

and forgets her sacred covenant;
[18]**for** her **way** leads down to death,
and her paths to the shades;
[19]those who **go** to her never come back,
nor do they regain the **paths** of life.

E'

D'

[20]Therefore walk in the way of the good,
and keep to the **paths** of the just.
[21]For the **upright** will abide in the land
and the innocent will remain in it;
[22]but the wicked will be cut off from the land,
and the treacherous will be rooted out of it.

TRANSLATION MATTERS

Duplicitously (Perversely), תהפכות; this word occurs eight times in Proverbs and only once elsewhere (in Deut 32:20). It usually refers to speech and often to slanderous speech or to evil plans and devices. Because the term "perverse" often has a sexual connotation, I prefer to use a different translation. NRSV translates three other words as "perverse," which also will be noted and rendered differently for the same reason.

Proverbs 2:13-15 gives a fuller description of the people who speak duplicitously. Verse 13 indicates that they abandon the straight paths (of uprightness; ישר),[51] the same root as ישרים, and walk instead in dark paths (paths of darkness; דרכי-חשך). (See Isa 9:2 for the prophetic parallel.) The darkness is, of course, metaphorical. In a time before electricity and when oil for lamps was expensive, the darkness of night became a metaphor for moral blindness. It should be noted that the Bible includes no texts in which Africans are denigrated for their skin color.[52] In this period the darkness of night was not associated with complexion.

51. See Translation Matters on Upstanding/Straight/Straightforward (Upright), ישר/ישרים, at 2:7.
52. Randall C. Bailey, "Beyond Identification: The Use of Africans in Old Testament Narrative and Poetry," in *Stony the Road We Trod: African American Biblical Interpretation*, ed. Cain Hope Felder (Minneapolis: Fortress Press, 1991), 165–69. See also Rodney Sadler, *Can a Cushite Change His Skin? An Examination of Race, Ethnicity, and Othering in the Hebrew Bible* (New York: Bloomsbury, 2005); Marta Høyland Lavik, "Are the Kushites Disparaged in Isaiah 18? Kush Applied as a Literary Motif in the Hebrew Bible," in *How Plausible Is a Kushite Role in Sennacherib's Retreat? A Conversation with Henry Aubin's* The Rescue of Jerusalem, ed. Alice Ogden Bellis (Piscataway Township, NJ: Gorgias Press, forthcoming).

Verse 14 indicates that those who speak duplicitously (perversely)[53] enjoy doing evil and delight in its deceitfulness (the same word as in 2:12). Proverbs 2:15 rounds out the portrait with the observation that their paths are crooked, twisted (perverted), עקשים, and they are devious, נלוזים, in their ways.

TRANSLATION MATTERS

Strange/Foreign/Alien Woman (Loose Woman, Adulteress), אשה זרה/נכריה; the NRSV translations of אשה זרה as "loose woman" in 2:16 and נכריה as "adulteress" in 2:16; 5:20; 6:24; 7:5; and 23:27 is a paraphrase, based on the context of some of the occurrences, but the context does not always require this interpretation. It is better to translate more neutrally as "strange" or "foreign woman" and let the context speak for itself.

In 2:16-19, the parent turns the attention from duplicitous men to strange women. The same infinitive is used in 2:16 as at the beginning of 2:12 (נצל, "save"). The NRSV translation overemphasizes the sexual implication. The Hebrew זרה does not mean "loose woman" but rather "strange, foreign woman." Similarly, the woman in the second colon, נכריה, is "foreign/alien," or simply different, not an adulteress. Furthermore, the partner of her youth in 2:17 is not necessarily her husband but could be YHWH,[54] opening the possibility that we are talking, at least on one level, of the young man being seduced from his faith. The reference to the woman making her words smooth in 2:16 suggests that she is enticing the youth with her smooth talk. Exactly what she is enticing the young man to do is not specified.

Proverbs 2:18 indicates that her way was headed down to death and her paths to the shades, i.e., the dead who resided in Sheol. Verse 19 concludes the section on the strange woman by saying that those who come (English "go") to her won't ever return, nor will they regain the path of life. The verb "come," בוא, can have a sexual connotation of penetration and may stress that if you dally with foreign influences, they may bind you like a disruptive sexual relationship.

---

53. See Translation Matters on Duplicitously (Perversely), תהפכות, at 2:12.
54. Christine Roy Yoder, *Proverbs*, AOTC (Nashville: Abingdon, 2009), 31.

Verses 20-22 bring chapter 2 to a close with advice for the youth to stay on the path(s) of the good and the just (righteous; 2:20),[55] meaning tested ways of living that have been found to benefit the community. Those who do so will be rewarded. The upstanding will dwell in the land and those with integrity (the innocent; תמימים) will remain in it (2:21). (For a similar sentiment, see 3:9-10.) The chapter ends on a negative note, with punishments for failure to walk in the right paths described. Unlike the upstanding and persons of integrity who will abide in the land, the corrupt, unscrupulous, reprehensible people (wicked; רשעים) will be cut off from the land; similarly, those who act or deal treacherously, the duplicitous, deceitful, and deceptive, בוגדים, will be pulled out of it (2:22). For the opposite perspective, however, see 11:16.

TRANSLATION MATTERS

Corrupt/Unscrupulous/Reprehensible (Wicked), רשעים; the word that is usually translated "wicked" has the connotation in Hebrew of someone convicted of a serious crime and thus deserving of serious punishment. Its opposite is צדיק (*tsaddik*), usually translated as "righteous," but I prefer "just."[56] In a time when there were no prisons or complicated judicial structures, justice was for the most part handled by the elders in each community. Typical punishments for crimes such as theft or misappropriation of property were restitution and, for serious crimes such as murder, execution, which was carried out by a relative of the victim.[57] Today with the problem of mass incarceration created by overzealous prosecution of minor drug offenses, we may hear words with criminal nuances differently than the original audience did. We also simply do not use the word "wicked" in everyday speech, except in slang where it means wonderful, like "wicked good punch," so I will translate this root as corrupt, unscrupulous, or reprehensible.

Trust the Father's Advice and Honor YHWH (3:1-12)

Proverbs 3 begins with an exordium in 3:1-4, in which the parent counsels the child to let the heart/mind (לב)[58] guard what is being taught for the sake of quantity (length of days and years) and quality of life

---

55. See Translation Matters on Just/Integrity/Honesty (Righteous[ness]), צדקה/צדיק/צדק, at 1:2.

56. See Translation Matters on Just/Integrity/Honesty (Righteous[ness]), צדקה/צדיק/צדק, at 1:2.

57. Gordon Wenham, "Law and the Legal System in Ancient Israel: Part 2," https://www.the-highway.com/law2b_Wenham.html.

58. See Translation Matters on the Heart, לב, at 2:2.

Prov 3:1-12

¹My child, do not forget my teaching,
   but let your heart keep my
      commandments;
²for length of days and years of life
   and abundant welfare they will
      give you.
³Do not let loyalty and faithfulness
      forsake you;
   bind them around your neck,
   write them on the tablet of your
      heart.

⁴So you will find favor and good
      repute
   in the sight of God and of people.

⁵Trust in the LORD with all your
      heart,
   and do not rely on your own
      insight.
⁶In all your ways acknowledge him,
   and he will make straight your
      paths.
⁷Do not be wise in your own eyes;

(שלום). *Shalom* means much more than peace; it means wholeness, completeness, and welfare. Verse 3a is difficult, interrupting the flow. It is better to interpret the kindness (חסד, loyalty)[59] and faithfulness as God's, because חסד is frequently a divine attribute.[60] What we expect to be tied around the child's neck and written on the heart/mind,[61] however, are the teachings from 3:1, not divine or human kindness and faithfulness. This was the case in 1:9, where the parents' instruction was said to be a garland on the child's head and pendants hung around the neck. Thus, in the context 3:3a should be read as going with 3:2, being a reminder to the youth that the quantity and quality of life experienced on one level as a result of receiving a parent's teaching comes at a deeper level from the kindness and faithfulness of God.

In 3:3b, the result of placing the teachings around the neck is that they are an external reminder; the result of writing them, figuratively speaking, on the tablet of one's heart/mind is that one is also internalizing them. The tablet is a reference to the tablets on which the Ten Commandments were written as well as to the new covenant in Jeremiah that was to be written on human hearts/minds rather than on stone (Jer 31:31-34). By both externalizing and internalizing parental teaching, the student

59. See Translation Matters on Kindness/Mercy (Loyalty), חסד, at 2:8. The Hebrew חסד is best understood as mercy or kindness rather than loyalty (NRSV).

60. "[I]t is obvious that God was in covenant relation with Israel, also that he expressed this relation in *ḥesed*, that God's *ḥesed* was eternal (Note the refrain of Ps 136)—though the *ḥesed* of Ephraim and others was not (Hos 6:4)." *TWOT*, 698. See also II under †I. חֶסֶד in BDB, 339.

61. See Translation Matters on the Heart, לב, at 2:2.

fear the LORD, and turn away from
evil.
⁸It will be a healing for your flesh
and a refreshment for your body.

⁹Honor the LORD with your substance
and with the first fruits of all your
produce;
¹⁰then your barns will be filled with
plenty,

and your vats will be bursting with
wine.

¹¹My child, do not despise the LORD's
discipline
or be weary of his reproof,
¹²for the LORD reproves the one he
loves,
as a father the son in whom he
delights.

will, according to 3:4, gain favor, which is to say a good reputation, with
both God and the human community. The term used for people, אדם, is a
generic term for humanity, including men and women. The word is best
known from the story of the Garden of Eden where the first human character is named Adam, but the character is given that name because Adam
represents all humanity. The fact that Adam turns out to be male—it is
not clear what sex he is at the beginning of the story[62]—has colored the
Hebrew word אדם in an unfortunate way.

Trusting in the Lord and Relying on One's Own Insight (Prov 3:5)

The turbulence of life is often overwhelming. Though I have not struggled with addiction, other factors such as anxiety, illness, unhealthy behaviors and relationships, and the chaos of the universe have led me to find comfort and guidance from the Serenity Prayer. I imagine that Reinhold Niebuhr found himself grappling with many of the same harsh, complicated, multilayered challenges of the human condition that we all experience when he wrote this prayer. A simple set of instructions to meditate on, the Serenity Prayer, implores us to know the difference between what we must accept and learn to live with, and what we must reject to make ourselves—and the world—better. In asking the Creator for the ability to wisely discern for ourselves the best course of action to take in any given moment we acknowledge our agency and freedom of will.

As a child I would often keep information from my mother

62. Phyllis Trible, *God and the Rhetoric of Sexuality*, OBT (Philadelphia: Fortress Press, 1978), 80.

I thought she would find displeasing. When the truth of whatever unpleasantness I was too afraid to admit or confront was revealed, my mother would always encourage me to be honest by gently reminding me, "With information comes understanding." The lesson my mother patiently instilled with this oft-repeated maxim was the need to have as much relevant information (no matter how bad or good) as possible to have the most correct grasp of a situation and figure out the most beneficial action or inaction needed to resolve the matter. In other words, the more complete the available knowledge, the more insight there is to decide how to react and respond in a manner to yield the most favorable outcome. Because we have the freedom to choose what to think, how to behave, and with whom we interact, human beings rely on their ability to gain an accurate and deeply intuitive understanding of the people, places, and things around them. Therefore, the instruction of this proverb to not rely on my own insight is antithetical to my trusting in the Lord with all my heart. I trust the creator has instilled in me the grace, mercy, and wisdom to carefully consider my knowledge of the world to live with integrity and to speak and act with loving kindness. To live is to make choices every moment we are not asleep. We choose which thoughts to cultivate and which to discard, what we will do and not do, with whom and where we will do these things, etc. Every choice we make is done using our own insight.

We turn to prayer in times of great difficulty, seeking divine counsel to inform the tough decisions made in the face of adversity. Though we look for and often receive the wisdom of the Spirit, it is people who act. Divine intervention is most often in the form of human actions. My trust in the Universe requires me to rely on my own insight. Through prayer and contemplative meditation, I can gain the clarity of mind and spirit needed to see the difference between the blessings and burdens about myself and my environment that I must assume and those that must be rejected to make space for positive change. My faith in the power of prayer and quiet reflection to open the human spirit to the sage knowing, loving kindness, and compassionate blessings of the ancestors and the Creator needs me to have faith in the integrity of my critical thinking, listening, and other skills of observation.

Formal education, emotional intelligence, and lived experiences deepen the understanding a person has of themselves, as well as the people, places, and things they meet, enabling them to interact in more kind, loving, and nurturing ways. Greater insight into the self is often the catalyst for spiritual, intellectual, and emotional growth, resulting in a deepening and widening of personal faith. In this way spiritual growth is an intellectual and emotional activity reliant on the insight a person has gained throughout their lives. Greater understanding of the consequences of our thoughts and actions on ourselves and the lives of others helps us to better understand the stranger, making them neighbors and kindred spirits. For this reason, to trust in the Lord with all your heart, one must rely on and cultivate one's own insight.

Kristy Hunt

Proverbs 3:5-8 focuses on the need to trust in God rather than one-self. The point is not passivity but rather humility. Verse 5 begins with the imperative to trust in YHWH with all of one's heart/mind and not depend exclusively on one's reasoning. The sages did not believe that the human brain was worthless. They did believe that arrogance was a grave sin because human reasoning is limited. One must use one's mental capacities, develop them, but never overrate them and always trust in YHWH from whom they come in the first place. Wisdom is not simply an intellectual pursuit, devoid of religious and moral concerns (3:6). Rather, one must know and acknowledge God as one journeys through life. If one does this, God will make the paths straight. That is, God will make the road easier, because a straight path is easier to walk on than one that bends and turns. It might seem that doing it God's way would take all the fun out of life. From the sages' perspective, however, it makes life easier and more pleasurable, though one does have to learn how to go about it, which takes effort.

Proverbs 3:7 carries on in the same line of thought. It is very easy to think ourselves quite smart. Indeed, this is a particular weakness of the young. The second half of the verse urges the young person to fear YHWH, in the sense of awe and respect,[63] and turn away from evil. When we think we are smart, we tend to get into trouble, because we don't see our weaknesses. When we acknowledge our shortcomings, we know enough to fear the divine. In that mind-set we are paradoxically a little less likely to fall into serious error than when we think ourselves hyper bright.

Verse 8 concludes this section, saying that if you do the things in 3:5-7, it will result in "healing for your flesh and refreshment for your bones (body)." This is an ancient version of the mind/spirit/body connection.

63. See discussion of this phrase at 1:7.

Excursus on Women's Sins 1: Arrogance

The academic discipline of feminist theology may have begun with Valerie Saiving's 1960 essay, "The Human Situation: A Feminine View,"[64] in which she argued that male theologians, in particular Reinhold Niebuhr, wrote theology from a male perspective that excluded women's experience. Her work made an initial splash but was quiescent until it was reprinted in *Womanspirit Rising* in 1979, where it was the lead essay.[65] She argued that sins such as pride (in the negative sense of the word, i.e., overweening pride) and arrogance are typical for men but not for women, whose usual sins are rather subservience, acquiescence, failure to develop one's gifts, triviality, distractibility, etc.

Saiving has herself been criticized for her exclusivism, as her view of women tended to be that of the white middle class. She has acknowledged this and matured in her thinking.[66] The question remains to what degree it is true in the twenty-first century that pride and arrogance are sins more typical of men than women. The world is changing. And within some cultures in North America women have very strong personalities where subservience, acquiescence, and the like are not typical.

In *The Confidence Code: The Science and Art of Self-Assurance— What Women Should Know*, Katty Kay and Claire Shipman argue that the gap between men's and women's pay is a result of women's lack of confidence but that with the right training women can overcome their confidence issues.[67] There is also significant evidence, however, that women are often penalized for acting in ways that are counter-stereotypical, i.e., that are perceived as aggressive and therefore inappropriate, and thus women do not do what they understand will be ineffective. The good news is that this backlash effect begins to taper off when even as little as 15 percent of the upper management is composed of women.[68]

64. Valerie Saiving, *The Journal of Religion* 40/2 (1960): 100–12.

65. Valerie Saiving, "The Human Situation: A Feminine View," in *Womanspirit Rising: A Feminist Reader in Religion*, ed. Carol P. Christ and Judith Plaskow (San Francisco: Harper and Row, 1979), 25–42.

66. Rebekah Miles, "Valerie Saiving Reconsidered," *JFSR* 28 (2012): 79. See Valerie Saiving, "A Conversation with Valerie Saiving," *JFSR* 4 (1988): 99–115.

67. Katty Kay and Claire Shipman, *The Confidence Code: The Science and Art of Self-Assurance—What Women Should Know* (New York: HarperBusiness, 2014).

68. Rebecca Mitchell, "Gap or Trap? Confidence Backlash Is the Real Problem for Women," *The Conversation*, June 12, 2014, https://theconversation.com/gap-or-trap-confidence-backlash-is-the-real-problem-for-women-27718.

It may be true that men in general are more prone to arrogance due to having a greater amount of testosterone than women, but culture also plays a huge role in the way we express attitudes such as arrogance, confidence, and the like, and with more women currently going to college and graduate school than men, the upper echelons of business, government, and the professional world could become primarily a woman's world in the near future, hard as that is to believe today.[69] The evidence suggests that such a situation will free women to express their confidence without fear of negative repercussions. It could lead to a situation in which women may actually need to worry about the sin of arrogance on a more regular basis.

Proverbs 3:9-12 presents two commands, which seem oriented toward men with their own estates, living independently, rather than youths living under their parents' roofs. Verses 9-10 advise the young adult student to honor YHWH with the first fruits of the crops; as a result the storehouses and wine vats will be full to overflowing. These verses also suggest that a wise person shows compassion for the poor. Although a number of proverbs indicate that some poverty is a result of laziness, proverbs such as this one are an implicit acknowledgment that the sages understood that life was more complicated than a model of simple retribution would suggest.

We do not know a great deal about the poverty of women *per se* in biblical times. We do know that the economy was fundamentally a farm-based one with minimal technology and that everyone in the household had to work on the farm in order for the extended family to survive. Most people were poor by modern standards. There was no running water, no electricity, no indoor plumbing, etc. Carol Meyers estimates that in the premonarchic period, women were doing about 40 percent of the farm labor in addition to being pregnant, nursing, and caring for small children most of the time, since they had to produce as many workers for the farm as they could. Mortality was high due to poor nutrition and

69. Even now I chair an academic committee composed of three women, reporting to a female academic dean serving under the first female dean of my divinity school!

lack of advanced medical care.[70] If a woman's husband died, she had to rely either on her parents if they still lived or on one of her sons, as she would have no land of her own since there is no evidence of women owning land until after the exile. So, if a woman's husband died and she had neither parents nor grown sons, she was in a bad way. This is the reason there are so many exhortations in Deuteronomy to take care of the widows (as well as the orphans and sojourners). Consider the widow of Zarephath in 1 Kings 17:8-24, an unnamed widow in 2 Kings 4:1-7, and the story of Naomi and Ruth, both widows, in the book of Ruth. These biblical women were not poor because they were lazy or evil. They were just unlucky. It was hard for anyone to make a living and, sad to say, the deck was stacked against single women.

Today women and children comprise much of the world's poor, many living much as the biblical characters did, certainly not because of their own evil ways, but mostly through the economic and political structures that keep the world's affluent rich. That includes the author of this book and many of its readers, even if we do not feel wealthy. (See the discussion in the Excursus on Disproportion of Wealth and Poverty in the Contemporary World at 13:22.)

Verses 11-12 return explicitly to education, with a brief exordium, counseling the young person concerning divine discipline, comparing it to fatherly reproof. Although the NRSV consistently translates בֵּן generically, in the original context it referred to a son rather than a daughter.[71] We really do not know much about women's education. We do know that there were a few educated women, for example, the prophet Huldah to whom the book of the law that was found under Josiah's administration was taken for authentication (2 Kgs 22). Since we do not even know whether there were formal schools for boys, much less girls, until late in the biblical period, she was likely privately educated at home, as were probably many boys.

A Tribute to Wisdom (3:13-20)

Proverbs 3:13-20 is a tribute to wisdom. Verse 13 is one of the "blissful" proverbs. The others are 3:18; 8:32, 24; 14:21; 16:20; 20:7; 28:14; 29:18; and 31:28. The word תְּבוּנָה, "understanding," can mean the act of understanding, the faculty of understanding, or, as is the case here, the object

---

70. Carol Meyers, *Discovering Eve: Ancient Israelite Women in Context* (New York: Oxford University Press, 1988), 169–70.

71. See Translation Matters on Son (Child), בֵּן, at 1:8.

¹³Happy are those who find wisdom,
and those who get understanding,
¹⁴for her income is better than silver,
and her revenue better than gold.
¹⁵She is more precious than jewels,
and nothing you desire can
compare with her.
¹⁶Long life is in her right hand;
in her left hand are riches and
honor.
¹⁷Her ways are ways of pleasantness,
and all her paths are peace.

¹⁸She is a tree of life to those who lay
hold of her;
those who hold her fast are called
happy.

¹⁹The LORD by wisdom founded the
earth;
by understanding he established
the heavens;
²⁰by his knowledge the deeps broke
open,
and the clouds drop down the dew.

of understanding. It is also paired with חכמה, wisdom,[72] in 3:19, where it refers to divine wisdom and understanding, and also in 5:1, where it is the parent's wisdom and understanding that is involved. Proverbs 3:14 is the first of the "better than/more than" proverbs, in which one thing is compared with another. The other "better than/more than" proverbs are 3:15; 8:11, 19; 12:9; 15:16, 17; 16:8, 16, 19, 32; 17:1, 12; 19:1, 22; 21:3; 22:1; 25:7, 24; 26:12; 27:5, 10; 28:6, 23; 29:20; and 31:10. All of the "better than" proverbs are stated in the form of an apparent paradox, many of them articulating the subversive notion that being poor or weak, but just, is to be preferred over being rich or powerful. It is not simply that virtue is praised but that virtue even in a disadvantaged or oppressed person is more to be desired than wealth and power. Although this is addressed to a son in its original context, it is applicable to anyone, like Jesus' beatitudes, which are similar in their paradoxical quality.

In the second colon of 3:14 where gold is mentioned, it is clear that we are talking about elite households. The silver and gold might have been in the form of coins or jewelry. The second colon of these proverbs generally has an object that is of a higher degree than in the first colon. So in 3:14 wisdom is better than silver, but since fine gold is more valuable than silver, gold is placed in the second colon. The point was not only to compare spiritual gain with material, although there was undoubtedly an element of this. Wisdom was not just a philosophical concept; its religious and moral qualities were not divorced from business and

72. See Translation Matters on Wisdom, חכמה, at 1:1.

commerce, which at least elite women could engage in, as is evidenced in 31:10-31. As such, its revenue was quite concrete. From the perspective of the sages, those who incorporated wisdom into their manner of life would prosper economically as well as spiritually; indeed, these two spheres were not separate or separable. Yet the point of this proverb is that the most important product of wisdom is in another realm entirely.

TRANSLATION MATTERS

Blissful (Happy), אשרי; this is a very difficult word to translate, like the similar Greek word μακάριος in the beatitudes. It means much more than happy, because in Western culture happiness is a shallow emotion often acquired through consumption rather than more profound experiences. Blessed (now pronounced as one syllable, rather than two) expresses part of the meaning, but in some ways, it is too confining to the religious sphere and this word goes beyond religion as it is often narrowly construed. To be blissful, deeply blessed, truly happy is to have come to the point where we can be grateful in almost all circumstances, even as we fight the terrible injustices and pain that is all around us. David Bentley Hart uses this translation of μακάριοζ in the beatitudes in Matthew and Luke in his translation of the New Testament.[73]

Proverbs 3:15 is another "more than" proverb, adding additional degrees of intensity to what was said in 3:14. Jewels were considered yet more valuable than silver and fine gold, but the most valuable thing is left to last and that is anything you can desire. Even that does not compare to wisdom. Purchasable things can be stolen and used up, but once you have wisdom, as long as you have your mental faculties and life itself, no one can take it away from you and with it you can live an abundant life. No physical thing can do that for you. Proverbs 8:11 is worded almost identically.

Verses 16-18 then proceed to describe what wisdom can do for you. The right hand was considered the more important hand, the left being unclean. This, along with the fact that length of days is listed first, tells us that a long life was regarded as more valuable than wealth and honor. Nevertheless, the ancient Hebrews did not esteem riches lightly, and they certainly did not consider honor to be insignificant. These attributes are

---

73. David Bentley Hart, *The New Testament: A Translation* (New Haven: Yale University Press, 2017), 7, 118.

held in wisdom's left hand, balancing out the more desirable gifts that she offers in her right hand. Verse 17 continues the thought begun in verse 16 with imagery of the road.

Women as well as men would have used the roads. Women were apparently not sequestered. Consider Jacob's first meeting Rachel when she brought the sheep to the well; she would have followed a well-worn path. The same Hebrew word is used in the story of Hannah going on a path after she meets with Eli as is used here, דרך (1 Sam 1:18). Wisdom's roads are pleasant or delightful and her paths are *shalom*—peaceful, safe, secure, healthy, and prosperous.

Proverbs 3:18 invokes the tree of life from the Garden of Eden (Gen 2:9) to describe wisdom's benefits. The tree of life is a symbol across cultures worldwide.[74] In the garden Adam and Eve were permitted to eat of the tree of life; it was only the tree of the knowledge of good and evil that was forbidden (Gen 2:16-17). After they ate, however, they were expelled from the garden, so that they would not eat of the tree of life and live forever (Gen 3:22-23). Thus, the tree of life would seem to represent, if not eternal life, either a very long life or a high-quality life. In those days, a long life was much shorter than today due to the more limited diet, lack of advanced medicine (resulting especially in infant mortality and death in childbirth), and, for most people, physical labor. For the average person, man or woman, forty years was probably typical if they did not die due to the direct or indirect effects of war.

The tree of life appears in three other proverbs. In 11:30 the fruit of the just (righteous)[75] is compared with the tree of life; in 13:12 fulfilled desire is the compared quality; and in 15:4 the comparison is with a gentle tongue.

Proverbs 3:19-20 changes the focus from wisdom to YHWH, who through wisdom, understanding, and knowledge created the cosmos. As in 3:13, חכמה and תבונה, wisdom and understanding, are paired in 3:19, where the heavens and the earth are said to have been established. Verse 20 continues the thought, adding that through divine דעת, knowledge, the primordial seas were broken open and the clouds drip dew. So, not only

---

74. These include ancient Iran, Egypt, and Mesopotamia and Urart, Hinduism, Buddhism, Christianity, Judaism including the Kabbalah, Islam, the Baha'i faith, Latter Day Saints, Germanic paganism and Norse mythology, China, Europe, Georgia, Mesoamerica, North America.

75. See Translation Matters on Just/Integrity/Honesty (Righteous[ness]), צדקה/צדק/צדיק, at 1:2.

was divine wisdom/understanding/knowledge (for these are essentially synonymous) involved in creating the world, but these attributes continue to sustain it, as the dew arrives each morning.

> ### Excursus on Contemporary Longevity
>
> As of 2017, women's average life span in the United States was slightly longer than for men; for women the number was 81.2; for men it was 76.4. A person who was sixty-five in 2012, however, could expect to live on average another 19.3 years (20.5 for women; 17.9 for men), or to 85.5 for women and 82.9 for men. The death rates for African American men are higher than for men in general, and for African American women are higher than for other women.[76] The differences are probably due to improper diet and lack of exercise and access to good medical care, in part resulting from higher levels of poverty as well as to greater stress. Longer life has its benefits but with it come challenges in terms of saving enough money for retirement, especially for those who are not able to find good work and benefits.

Seek Wisdom; Find Security (3:21-26)

Proverbs 3:21-26 begins with another exordium in 3:21-22. Proverbs 3:23-26 provides the motivations for the student to follow the advice. Verse 21 exhorts the addressee not to let some initially undisclosed object(s) out of his sight. Since 3:21 follows 3:19-20, we assume that the objects are wisdom/understanding/knowledge from 3:19-20, and this is not entirely wrong, but the second colon presents two specific objects of the verb in this verse: תושיה, sound wisdom, and מזמה, foresight (prudence). The former word is used in 2:7, where YHWH stores it up for the upstanding (upright),[77] and in 8:14, where it is one in a list of attributes that personified Wisdom claims. מזמה, foresight,[78] is used in 1:4, where it is one of the

76. Larry Copeland, "Life Expectancy in the USA Hits a Record High," *USA Today*, October 9, 2014, https://www.usatoday.com/story/news/nation/2014/10/08/us-life-expectancy-hits-record-high/16874039/.

77. See Translation Matters on Upstanding/Straight/Straightforward (Upright), ישר/ישרים, at 2:7.

78. See Translation Matters on Foresight/Discretion/Purposes/Plans, מזמה, at 1:4.

Prov 3:21-26

²¹My child, do not let these escape
    from your sight:
    keep sound wisdom and prudence,
²²and they will be life for your soul
    and adornment for your neck.
²³Then you will walk on your way
    securely
    and your foot will not stumble.
²⁴If you sit down, you will not be
    afraid;

when you lie down, your sleep will
    be sweet.
²⁵Do not be afraid of sudden
    panic,
    or of the storm that strikes the
    wicked;
²⁶for the LORD will be your
    confidence
    and will keep your foot from being
    caught.

attributes that the book of Proverbs is intended to teach. These qualities will be life for the soul/neck (נפש)[79] and favor, grace, or elegance for the גרגרות, another word for neck (3:22). Just as the parents' teaching is said to be a garland on the child's head and pendants around the neck in 1:9, and as the parents' teaching is to be bound around the neck in 3:3, so here the abstract qualities are to be worn figuratively in a similar way. Whether the student is walking or sitting or lying down, there need be no fear of the kind of panic that strikes the corrupt (wicked),[80] for YHWH is one's confidence. The student will move without stumbling on the road (3:23) if sound wisdom and foresight are retained. The student of wisdom can sleep without fear (3:24), unlike those who plotted evil schemes, who are likely to experience bad things. The addressee should fear neither a sudden dread nor the devastation of the corrupt that comes upon them (3:25). See 11:16 for the opposite perspective. Proverbs 3:26 concludes this section by saying that YHWH will be your confidence and will keep your foot from being caught, confirming the high status given to wisdom.

Treat Your Neighbor Kindly and Inherit Honor (3:27-35)

Proverbs 3:27-35 begins in verses 27-31 with a series of behaviors to avoid, ending in verse 32 with the first of a series of reasons behind these. The reasons continue in verses 33-35 with a list of antitheses. Verse 27

79. See Translation Matters on Soul/Neck/Person/Desire, נפש, at 2:10.
80. See Translation Matters on Corrupt/Unscrupulous/Reprehensible (Wicked), רשע/רשעים, at 2:22.

²⁷Do not withhold good from those to
whom it is due,
when it is in your power to do it.
²⁸Do not say to your neighbor, "Go,
and come again,
tomorrow I will give it"—when you
have it with you.
²⁹Do not plan harm against your
neighbor
who lives trustingly beside you.
³⁰Do not quarrel with anyone without
cause,
when no harm has been done to
you.
³¹Do not envy the violent
and do not choose any of their
ways;
³²for the perverse are an abomination
to the LORD,
but the upright are in his
confidence.
³³The LORD's curse is on the house of
the wicked,
but he blesses the abode of the
righteous.
³⁴Toward the scorners he is scornful,
but to the humble he shows
favor.
³⁵The wise will inherit honor,
but stubborn fools, disgrace.

opens the list of proscribed behaviors with the command not to withhold a service that is owed, which the addressee has a responsibility to perform. This saying is advising the young man not to shirk duty, not to put off fulfilling an obligation, not to make excuses, but to do it at once if able to do so. Verse 28 continues the same line of thinking, but now the issue concerns an item that is presumably owed to the neighbor. The young person is again advised not to put off giving to the neighbor what is owed. Verse 29 turns to an even worse offense: it is one thing not to give the neighbor what is owed as soon as it is asked for (3:28), but actively plotting against the neighbor is a much more serious crime. Verse 30 forbids baseless quarrels; it does not suggest that one should avoid a lawsuit if one has been legitimately wronged. One should not, however, pick a fight. Since this saying follows 3:29, it may be that quarreling with someone for no reason is related to devising evil against a neighbor, for one way of devising evil would be through trumped-up charges. Verse 31 goes on to urge the youth not to envy the violent (whose gains from violence may be the cause for envy), nor should the addressee choose any of the paths of the violent. This saying may have 16:29 in mind, which says that the violent try to entice their neighbors into walking on paths that are not good, or it may be a recapitulation of 1:15-19.

Proverbs 3:32 begins the reasons that are given for the prohibitions in 3:27-31. It is a YHWH saying and the first one in Proverbs that uses the term תועבה, "abomination," which in Proverbs is used in an ethical sense, unlike its earlier purely ritual usage, and means a person or practice that is loathed or repugnant either to God or to people. The other instances are 6:6; 8:7; 11:1, 20; 12:22; 13:19; 15:8, 9, 26; 16:5, 12; 17:15; 20:10, 23; 21:27; 24:9; 26:25; 28:9; and 29:7. This proverb states that the devious (perverse; נלוז)[81] are an abomination to YHWH;[82] the antithesis is stated in the second colon, that the upright are in God's confidence. Verse 33 continues the thought of verse 32, saying that YHWH's curse is on the house, in the sense of the family, of the corrupt (wicked),[83] but God blesses the habitation, again in the extended sense of the family, of the just (righteous).[84] This does not necessarily mean that God actively manipulates events so that the just are blessed and the corrupt are cursed. It may simply mean that, the way God has set the world up, for the most part, it pays to be honest. Verse 34 deals, at least tangentially, with the issue of poverty. The first colon says that God scorns the לצים, the scornful, but in the second colon we read that God shows favor to the עניים, the humble, poor, weak, and oppressed. In its present context opposite of scornful, the primary meaning must be humble, but the other meanings—poor, weak, and oppressed—are suggested as well.

Here for the first time in Proverbs, we get an explicit statement indicating God's positive attitude toward the poor. The kinds of specific behavior described in 3:27-30 (withholding what is owed, planning harm against someone, quarreling without cause) as well as the types of people described in 3:31-34 (the violent, the devious [perverse], the corrupt, and the scorners) are what can drive individuals into poverty. Given the large number of proverbs commenting negatively on laziness and evil behavior leading to poverty, in this section not only are the types of behavior that can lead to poverty described but we find a positive statement about the poor in 3:34, where we read, "to the humble he shows favor." Here it is not bad behavior or lack of diligence that leads to destitution.

81. Like the other instances of the NRSV translations of perverse used for other Hebrew words, I prefer to avoid this word because of its sexual connotations. The term means devious or crooked.

82. See discussion of the term "abomination" at 3:32.

83. See Translation Matters on Corrupt/Unscrupulous/Reprehensible (Wicked), רשעים/רשע, at 2:22.

84. See Translation Matters on Just/Integrity/Honesty (Righteous[ness]), צדקה/צדק/צדיק, at 1:2.

Excursus on Women's Pay Gap in the United States

We are reminded of the contemporary world. Even in the United States, where much progress has been made in women's rights, women are still paid on average 80 percent of what their male colleagues make, and the gap is not expected to close until at least 2059, if not later. The gap is worse for women of color.[85] And this is only one of the problems women face. Women are more likely to be single parents. Out of about twelve million single-parent families with children under the age of eighteen, more than 80 percent were headed by single mothers in 2016.[86] In addition, 75 percent of women who reported sexual harassment at work experienced retaliation when they brought it to the attention of the authorities.[87] It is not surprising that it is estimated that 70 to 90 percent of victims (most of whom are women) do not report their complaints.[88] And the list of concerns could go on.

Due to all of this, women in the United States were 35 percent more likely to be poor than men in 2015. More than 16.9 million, better than one in eight women, were poor. Of these women, 45.7 percent (=16 percent of US population) lived in extreme poverty (defined as income at or below 50 percent of the federal poverty level). Thus, one in sixteen women were in extreme poverty.[89]

Finally, verse 35 concludes the reasons that a young man should follow the advice in 3:27-31, saying that the wise will inherit honor while the rebellious, incompetent dolts (fools; כסילים)[90] will inherit disgrace (understood). The word כבוד, honor, abundance, was an extremely im-

85. AAUW, "The Simple Truth about the Gender Pay Gap," https://www.aauw.org/research/the-simple-truth-about-the-gender-pay-gap/.
86. US Census Bureau, "Table FG10: Family Groups: 2016," https://singlemotherguide.com/single-mother-statistics/accessed.
87. Tara Golshan, "Study Finds 75 Percent of Workplace Harassment Victims Experienced Retaliation When They Spoke Up: What We Know about Sexual Harassment in America," *Vox*, October 17, 2017, https://www.vox.com/identities/2017/10/15/16438750/weinstein-sexual-harassment-facts.
88. National Women's Law Center Fact Sheet, November 2016, "Workplace Justice: Sexual Harassment in the Workplace," https://nwlc.org/wp-content/uploads/2016/11/Sexual-Harassment-Fact-Sheet.pdf.
89. National Women's Law Center, "National Snapshot: Poverty Among Women and Families, 2015," September 14, 2016, https://nwlc.org/resources/national-snapshot-poverty-among-women-families-2015/.
90. See Translation Matters on Dolt/Chump/Oaf/Inept (Fool), כסילים, at 1:22.

portant concept in ancient Mediterranean cultures, including ancient Israel. Honor involved a man's reputation and was considered his most important asset. קָלוֹן, ignominy, dishonor, was the opposite of honor and was to be avoided at almost all cost.

Excursus on Honor and Shame in the Ancient Mediterranean World

The ancient Mediterranean world, of which Israel and Judah were a part, entailed what is called an honor-shame culture. It must be stated at the outset that shame is not the same as guilt. Guilt is the fact of having done something considered wrong, whether by the one who did the action or others. On the other hand, shame is a feeling that we can have, whether we are guilty or not. For example, persons may feel shame(d) for having been raped, but they should not be considered guilty of the crime perpetrated against them.

In the ancient Mediterranean world for men, many of the values that are taught in Proverbs are what gave them honor. Today honor comes mostly from money and reputation. The biblical masculine values included protecting the women from bodily harm and ensuring that they remained sexually pure.[91] When men failed to live up to these ideals, shame and dishonor fell upon them. Women also were expected to live up to ideals, including being sexually chaste and taking care of their households. When women lived up to these ideals they had the positive quality of shame. When they did not, they were said to be shameless. A good example is when Tamar is raped by her half-brother Amnon (2 Sam 13). She asks him, "Where can I carry my shame?" meaning that she will no longer have shame.

This lack of symmetry in the honor-shame system to some degree persists today in the unwritten sexual codes that still operate in the contemporary Western world, though they have less force today than even fifty years ago and less power in urban areas than in rural ones. The fact that we still understand the word "shameless" to mean someone who has done something reprehensible, however, shows how deeply rooted the ancient codes are. The spate of outings of sexual predators and sexual harassers in 2017 brought with it a new form of sexual shame, experienced not by the victims, as has often been the most common form of shame in modern times, but by the perpetrators.[92]

---

91. The story of Dinah in Genesis 34 is a good example of this culture at work.

92. Joseph Burgo, "Why We Should Humiliate Harassers," *The Washington Post*, November 19, 2017.

A Father's Advice to a Son to Get Wisdom and Live (4:1-9)

Proverbs 4:1-9 begins with another exordium in 4:1-2. The opening command, "listen," שמעו, really means to listen carefully, to listen up, we might say in the vernacular. This is one of three instances (including 7:24 and 8:32) where sons[93] (בנים, plural) are addressed, rather than the more common singular familiar addressee, my son. This usage is consistent with either a home or a more formal school setting. Even though the teacher calls himself a father, he could do that in a school as well as at home. The second colon in 4:1 begins with a second verb, "be attentive," קשב, parallel to "listen," שמע, which also makes it clear that the students are supposed to be listening carefully to what the teacher is saying.

The purpose is then introduced, that the students may know, דעת, or, really, come to know or gain insight, בינה. Verse 2 continues the purpose statement, explaining that the teacher will be providing good precepts, לקח. The word is from a root meaning "take," so we might say that the teacher is giving the students good take-away. In the second colon he urges them not to forget his (literally "my") teaching, תורתי. Proverbs 4:3-4a describes the father's experience with his own parents and then prepares to quote the son's paternal grandfather in 4:4b-9, showing that what he is teaching goes back to what he was taught and to generations before that. In 4:3, the teacher tells the students about his own experience as a student, mentioning both his father and his mother (see 1:8). The words "tender," רך, and "only," יחד, suggest that he was young and an only child. Although the mother is mentioned, her role in teaching is not clearly identified. Proverbs 4:4 indicates that the teacher's father taught him and says nothing about the mother. It goes on to begin the quotation of his father's words, which continues through the end of 4:9. The teacher's father admonishes him to hold on to the teaching to live. Both quantity and quality of life are envisioned.

The youths are told (4:6) to acquire (4:5a) wisdom, חכמה,[94] and insight, בינה, and not forget (cease to care about) them or neglect the teacher's words (4:5b). They are told not to leave/abandon/forsake her, i.e., wisdom/insight, and she will keep them; the second colon states the antithesis: love her and she will guard you. The verb love, אהב, in Hebrew has a wide range of meanings from appetites, like food and drink, to friendship, to sexual love. It is evident that it is the last meaning that is involved here since in 4:8 the sons are told to embrace (חבק) wisdom.

---

93. See Translation Matters on Son (Child), בן, at 1:8.
94. See Translation Matters on Wisdom, חכמה, at 1:1.

Prov 4:1-9

¹Listen, children, to a father's instruction,
and be attentive, that you may gain insight;
²for I give you good precepts: do not forsake my teaching.
³When I was a son with my father, tender, and my mother's favorite,
⁴he taught me, and said to me,
"Let your heart hold fast my words; keep my commandments, and live.
⁵Get wisdom; get insight: do not forget, nor turn away from the words of my mouth.

⁶Do not forsake her, and she will keep you;
love her, and she will guard you.
⁷The beginning of wisdom is this: Get wisdom,
and whatever else you get, get insight.
⁸Prize her highly, and she will exalt you;
she will honor you if you embrace her.
⁹She will place on your head a fair garland;
she will bestow on you a beautiful crown."

Proverbs 4:7 continues with what at first glance seems an odd statement: the first thing to do regarding wisdom is get wisdom. There is no shortcut. You just have to begin the process. The second colon then says that of all the things you may want to acquire, get insight. Wisdom, חכמה, and insight, בינה, are also paired in 4:5. They are virtual synonyms. In 4:8-9 the students are told that there is a sort of *quid pro quo* with wisdom. If you esteem her, then she will exalt you. If you embrace her, she will honor you. She will also put a graceful garland on your head, and you'll get a glorious crown. This is wedding imagery,[95] which picks up from the language of love in 4:6. Proverbs 4:9b involves wordplay, for the root of the verb that is translated as bestow, מגן, calls to mind the noun מגן, (shield), suggesting that wisdom will both bestow a beautiful crown and shield you.

Stay on the Right Path and Avoid the Path of Evildoers (4:10-19)

Proverbs 4:10-19 again begins with an exordium. The son (child)[96] is encouraged to listen carefully, שמע, and accept the teacher's words. The result will be long life because wisdom provides the means for successful living. This does not guarantee a long life, but the sages believed that a

95. Camp, *Wisdom and the Feminine*, 93–94, 100.
96. See Translation Matters on Son (Child), בן, at 1:8.

Prov 4:10-19

[10]Hear, my child, and accept my words,
    that the years of your life may be many.
[11]I have taught you the way of wisdom;
    I have led you in the paths of uprightness.
[12]When you walk, your step will not be hampered;
    and if you run, you will not stumble.
[13]Keep hold of instruction; do not let go;
    guard her, for she is your life.
[14]Do not enter the path of the wicked,
    and do not walk in the way of evildoers.

[15]Avoid it; do not go on it;
    turn away from it and pass on.
[16]For they cannot sleep unless they have done wrong;
    they are robbed of sleep unless they have made someone stumble.
[17]For they eat the bread of wickedness
    and drink the wine of violence.
[18]But the path of the righteous is like the light of dawn,
    which shines brighter and brighter until full day.
[19]The way of the wicked is like deep darkness;
    they do not know what they stumble over.

wise person had a better chance at a successful life than one lacking in wisdom. Verse 11 is still in the first person. The teacher emphasizes that he has taught the student the path of wisdom. In the second colon he even says that he has caused the student to walk on the paths of uprightness, using a verb from the same root as the most common word for path, דרך. One almost pictures a father taking a son by the hand and the two of them walking down a path together. Verse 12 continues the theme of the road or path, which is found also in 4:14-15 and 18-19. Because of the parent's discipline (instruction),[97] the student's pace will not be impeded and, when running, there will be no stumbling (see 3:23). If one has gained wisdom and is walking on the way of wisdom, one will have the tools needed to handle the obstacles along the way, not that there will be no obstacles. Verse 13 moves away from road imagery briefly. Discipline (מוסר) is normally masculine in Hebrew, but here it is grammatically treated as feminine, as it seems to be identified with wisdom. The youth is advised to take hold of discipline and not to relax the hold. "Hold on for dear life" is a reasonable paraphrase of the second colon.

---

97. See Translation Matters on Discipline/Chastening/Correction (Instruction), מוסר, at 1:2.

The point here seems to be a reminder that the attainment of wisdom is a slow process in which one must be constantly vigilant. The slightest slacking off could be deadly.

Proverbs 4:14-15 returns to the road image, telling the students not to enter the path of the corrupt (wicked)[98] in the first place, nor to walk in the way of unethical people (evildoers, רעים; 4:14).

TRANSLATION MATTERS

The word רע, when used of people, has a range of meanings, from unpleasant to ill-tempered to evil, but in this context it must principally refer to the latter meaning. The problem is that we do not use this language much in contemporary English. We call people immoral, unethical, unscrupulous, etc., but rarely do we label someone evil. Therefore, I prefer "unethical" for this term.

They are to avoid it completely and pass on. The same verb is used at the end of both cola in 4:15 with different meanings (עבר; turn away, pass on). Verses 16-17 then give the reason for all of this careful avoidance of the road of the wicked who cannot even sleep until they have committed a crime. They are addicted to it and without their fix they are jumpy. The two paths are contrasted in 4:18-19. The path of the just (righteous)[99] is compared with the light of dawn, which gradually gets brighter until the full light appears. Youths, as they grow in wisdom, shine brighter and brighter metaphorically. The antithesis is in 4:19, where the way of the corrupt is said to be so dark that they don't even know what they have stumbled over. This relates back to 4:12, where there won't be any stumbling for those who get wisdom.

Advice to Walk, Look, and Talk Straight (4:20-27)

Proverbs 4:20-27 yet again begins with an exordium. The son (child)[100] should attend with ears, eyes, and heart/mind[101]—with the whole person.

---

98. See Translation Matters on Corrupt[ion]/Unscrupulous/Reprehensible (Wicked[ness]), רשע/רשעים, at 2:22.

99. See Translation Matters on Just/Integrity/Honesty (Righteous[ness]), צדקה, צדיק, and צדק, at 1:2.

100. See Translation Matters on Son (Child), בן, at 1:8.

101. See Translation Matters on the Heart, לב, at 2:2.

Prov 4:20-27

²⁰My child, be attentive to my words;
   incline your ear to my sayings.
²¹Do not let them escape from your
   sight;
   keep them within your heart.
²²For they are life to those who find
   them,
   and healing to all their flesh.
²³Keep your heart with all vigilance,
   for from it flow the springs of life.

²⁴Put away from you crooked speech,
   and put devious talk far from you.
²⁵Let your eyes look directly forward,
   and your gaze be straight before
   you.
²⁶Keep straight the path of your feet,
   and all your ways will be sure.
²⁷Do not swerve to the right or to the
   left;
   turn your foot away from evil.

The reasons are given in 4:22: The parent's words are life-giving for those who find them, meaning, those who can truly lay hold of them. The second colon seconds this thought by stating that they are healing to all flesh. As in 3:8, the sages understood the mind-body connection. Verses 23-27 present a series of behaviors to do or avoid.

Proverbs 4:23 begins with the counsel to be especially vigilant in guarding your heart/mind, because this is the source of the springs of life. The heart/mind is the center of the human psyche. We have to guard it lest what springs forth from it into audible speech does not represent the person we want to be. This becomes clear in 4:24, where the teacher tells the youth to put crooked speech and devious talk far away, but since speech springs from within, this is not possible unless one has learned how to guard one's heart/mind. Proverbs 4:25-27 moves from speech to sight. The advice here is to look straight ahead and not to either side. The point is not to get distracted but to move down the path directly, not allowing the various evils to the left or right to distract our attention. If you look straight ahead, it is easier to keep walking straight down the path (4:26). When one turns the head to the right, one tends to walk to the right. The feet naturally follow the eyes. When we stay on the morally correct path, then, the sages believed, all our ways would be established. Verse 27 makes explicit that turning to the right or left represents various forms of evil.

Excursus on the Nature of Contemporary Evil

Of course, life often seems more ambiguous than the picture painted in Proverbs, but frequently in retrospect it is easy to see what was murky while living through it. There is much we do not see because we do not want to see it or are too busy and really do not want our lives disrupted. Many of the German Christians did not see, or refused to see, what was happening around them during and leading up to World War II, even though the signs were all around them. Many of the slave owners in the United States could not see the evil of their ways or found biblical "excuses,"[102] even though in retrospect the evil is obvious. Similarly, we do not seem to see what we are doing to the planet today or how we are perpetuating the slavery of the past in mass incarceration.[103] These matters are no more ambiguous than the evils of the past. How to fix them is always hard, but the evils are not difficult to see nor is our involvement in them if we care to look.

First Warning against the Strange Woman (5:1-6)

Proverbs 5 begins with an exordium in 5:1-2 where the speaker asks the son (child)[104] to listen to *my* wisdom, חכמתי, *my* understanding, תבונתי. This is the first time that these terms have been personalized in this way, yet the speaker is not undercutting the claim to universality by calling the wisdom and teaching "mine." Rather, the speaker is identifying with the teaching. Wisdom and understanding are not only out there. The teacher has incorporated them internally and now embodies them. Wisdom and understanding are also paired in 3:13; 10:23; and 21:30. As is true in many of the exordia, the student is urged to listen carefully to the parent's teaching. Proverbs 5:2 provides the motivation. The first colon says, "so that you may hold on to discretion" (prudence; מזמות),[105] a word that means one's purposes or plans. In parallelism with the second

---

102. Gene Rice, "The Curse That Never Was (Genesis 9:18-27)," *JRT* 29 (1972): 5–27.

103. See *Thirteenth*, the award-winning Netflix film on the loophole provided by the Thirteenth Amendment, which allows prisons to function as the new plantation: https://www.netflix.com/title/80091741. See also Michelle Alexander, *The New Jim Crow: Mass Incarceration in the Age of Colorblindness* (New York: New Press, 2012).

104. See Translation Matters on Son (Child), בן, at 1:8.

105. See Translation Matters on Foresight/Discretion/Purposes/Plans, מזמה, at 1:4.

Prov 5:1-6

¹My child, be attentive to my wisdom;
   incline your ear to my
     understanding,
²so that you may hold on to prudence,
   and your lips may guard
     knowledge.
³For the lips of a loose woman drip
   honey,
   and her speech is smoother than
     oil;

⁴but in the end she is bitter as
   wormwood,
   sharp as a two-edged sword.
⁵Her feet go down to death;
   her steps follow the path to
     Sheol.
⁶She does not keep straight to the
   path of life;
   her ways wander, and she does
     not know it.

colon, which says, "so that your lips may guard or watch knowledge," it is evident that the first colon must mean that you need to keep your plans to yourself and not go blurting them out. So, we might translate loosely, "so that you may have discretion and watch your mouth."

Proverbs 5:3-6 describes the strange woman,[106] first encountered in 2:16-19. Who is she? The LXX translates as if the word were זונה, "prostitute," rather than the Hebrew MT's זרה, "strange" or "foreign woman." Is she a prostitute, adulterer, foreigner? Based on 5:7-14, it is hard to tell, other than that she is one who entices young men into doing something they should not. When these lines are combined with the explicit sexual images of 5:15-20, however, it appears evident that her strangeness is in her illicit sexuality, though the exact nature of the sexuality is not clear based on the material in this chapter. We cannot tell whether she is a prostitute or a married woman who is luring young married men into sex. Sex between a married man and a prostitute was not illegal, but it was frowned upon by the sages. Sex between any man and a married woman was a serious crime.[107] It is possible that the sexual imagery is partly a metaphor for the abandonment of Wisdom for Folly, though the word "Folly" is not explicitly used.

Whatever the exact nature of the sexuality, this sexually dangerous woman implicitly represents Folly. She is the antithesis of Wisdom. Both the depiction of this woman as a real woman and as a symbol is offensive

106. See Translation Matters on Strange/Foreign/Alien Woman (Loose Woman/Adulteress), אשה זרה, at 2:16.
107. Elaine Adler Goodfriend, "Adultery," in *ABD*, 1:82–86.

to some. A similar picture may be drawn, however, of the sexually dangerous man who is cute, cool, and charming, or fat, ugly, and powerful, and who smoothly or gracelessly tries to seduce every woman who comes near him, just because he is under the narcissistic illusion that his sexually predatory practices of various sorts are desired by his victims. Just as the strange woman is an apt symbol of Folly for men, the sexual harasser may be the equivalent for women.

In 5:3 the strange woman's lips are described as dripping honey (נפת תטפנה). The same phrase is found in Song of Songs 4:11: "Your lips drip honey, my bride." Thus, the parent is acknowledging that the strange woman is very enticing. She appears to be offering the same goods as the kind of woman the speaker would want for her son, but the parent claims there is a significant difference despite superficial similarities. Folly can masquerade as Wisdom.

In 5:4 the strange woman is said to be bitter as wormwood, also known as *Artemisia absinthium*, a plant used in making various modern concoctions including absinthe, vermouth, and some bitters. The apparent sweetness of Folly turns to bitterness when the consequences come home to roost. In 5:5 the phrase "her feet," רגליה, is a double entendre, meaning both legs and genitals. Her paths don't stay on the path of life but wander, but she is unaware of the fact (5:6). This could be taken to mean that she is naive and inept or rather that she is intentionally ignoring the obvious. This applies equally well to those who pursue Folly as to those who follow a dangerous woman or man.

More Advice to Avoid the Strange Woman to Avoid Disaster (5:7-14)

Proverbs 5:7 is another exordium addressed to בנים, children (presumably male youth),[108] as in 4:1; 7:24; 8:24; and 8:32, but in the LXX to my son, υἱέ. The MT's plural address suggests the possibility of a school setting, although a home situation is not ruled out. Even if we knew where education took place, the place of education does not tell us anything in and of itself about whether girls and young women were included in formal instruction in reading, writing, etc.

As in many of the exordia, this one begins with the command to listen (carefully) to the speaker. The second colon follows up with the charge

---

108. See Translation Matters on Son (Child), בן, at 1:8.

Prov 5:7-14

⁷And now, my child, listen to me,
  and do not depart from the words
    of my mouth.
⁸Keep your way far from her,
  and do not go near the door of her
    house;
⁹or you will give your honor to others,
  and your years to the merciless,
¹⁰and strangers will take their fill of
    your wealth,
  and your labors will go to the
    house of an alien;
¹¹and at the end of your life you will
    groan,
  when your flesh and body are
    consumed,
¹²and you say, "Oh, how I hated
    discipline,
  and my heart despised reproof!
¹³I did not listen to the voice of my
    teachers
  or incline my ear to my instructors.
¹⁴Now I am at the point of utter ruin
  in the public assembly."

not to turn away from the teacher's words. The concern was not so much idle distraction as the lures of the world. The teacher is especially concerned about the strange woman of 5:3. The teacher says simply to keep your distance (5:8). If you don't let your path get near her and if you don't get close to her door, then you should be fine. There is a margin of error.

Proverbs 5:9-14 presents the consequences if the young man succumbs to the enticing woman's wiles. In 5:9, vigor (honor, הוד) in the context probably includes the connotation of sexual virility. In terms of the whole line the idea seems to be that the young man would be wasting sexual vigor in the prime years of life. The people with whom he is consorting are cruel because they are taking away from him something that they should not be taking, that should be reserved for the man's wife. Verse 10 continues the thought by saying that strangers (זרים, the masculine plural form of זרה, the word used of the woman in 5:3; 7:5; 22:14) and aliens (נכרי, masculine form of foreign/alien woman used in 2:16; 5:20; etc.) will possess your wealth. It is not clear how this is connected. Either the young man will have had to pay handsomely for prostitutes or, if adultery has been involved, he will have had to pay a large penalty.[109] The strangers and aliens are not necessarily foreigners but people who are outsiders to one's family. Identifying the strange woman with Folly means that the young man in pursuing her/Folly will neglect Wisdom and place his fortune (both literally and metaphorically) in the hands of outsiders.

109. Goodfriend, "Adultery."

Proverbs 5:11-14 imagines the youth deeply regretting having not paid attention to teachers and discipline as public ruin now looms. Verse 11 depicts the student in old age, his flesh and body כלות, spent, exhausted, consumed. It is always difficult for young people to imagine themselves old, but the teacher is trying to get the student to picture this, putting it in vividly unpleasant terms. It is not old age *per se* that is unpleasant but senior years without wisdom. Proverbs 5:12-14 describes the former pupil's self-reproach. The verbs used are highly emotional: hate, שנא, and despise or spurn, נאץ. The teacher understands how difficult discipline (מוסר, "instruction")[110] and correction (תוכחת, "reproof") are and thus hopes by showing empathy to win the student over. The quotation continues in 5:13 with the student saying that he did not do what was commanded in the exordia in 5:7a (שמע, "listen") and in 5:13b (נטה, "incline [your ear]"). There is a difference, however. The verb "listen" when followed by the phrase בקול, to the voice of, means obey or heed. It is stronger than the verb used alone. Two words are used here for "teacher," which are used only here in Proverbs: מורה, which is from the same root as Torah, and מלמד. These words are suggestive of a formal school setting. Verse 14 completes the student's quotation. The total evil (כל־רע, "utter ruin") that is the focus here is some sort of public shaming. Whether it is a formal censure or simply the bad reputation that the person gets from the vulgar sort of life that he has led is not clear, but it is certainly one or the other, since one's honor counted for so much in ancient Israel.[111]

Advice to Stick with the Wife of One's Youth (5:15-23)

Proverbs 5:15-20 presents advice to stick with one's wife, the only passage in chapters 1–9 with such a focus. In 5:15, the young man is urged to drink from his own well, בארך. In Song of Songs 4:15, the male lover compares his beloved with a cistern, באר, and with flowing water, נזלים. In both cases, the well/cistern and the flowing water, the center of life in a desert culture, are identified as a woman. Water is traditionally, along with earth, associated with the female in many ancient religious and mythological systems, because of its ability to bring forth life. In Latin

---

110. See Translation Matters on Discipline/Chastening/Correction (Instruction), מוסר, at 1:2.

111. Lyn M. Bechtel, "Shame as a Sanction of Social Control in Biblical Israel: Judicial, Political, and Social Shaming," *JSOT* 49 (1991): 47–76.

Prov 5:15-23

[15]Drink water from your own cistern,
   flowing water from your own well.
[16]Should your springs be scattered abroad,
   streams of water in the streets?
[17]Let them be for yourself alone,
   and not for sharing with strangers.
[18]Let your fountain be blessed,
   and rejoice in the wife of your youth,
[19]a lovely deer, a graceful doe.
May her breasts satisfy you at all times;
   may you be intoxicated always by her love.

[20]Why should you be intoxicated, my son, by another woman
   and embrace the bosom of an adulteress?
[21]For human ways are under the eyes of the LORD,
   and he examines all their paths.
[22]The iniquities of the wicked ensnare them,
   and they are caught in the toils of their sin.
[23]They die for lack of discipline,
   and because of their great folly they are lost.

tradition, the vulva and vagina could be represented by a fountain.[112] There is also a tradition of lactating breast sculpture in Italy.[113] In Jungian psychology the anima is also associated with water.[114]

Proverbs 5:16 is difficult. Both this verse and Song of Songs 4:15 use the word "spring," מעין. In Song of Songs the male lover is again comparing his lover to the fountain. If the fountain represents the wife's sexuality in Proverbs 5:16, however, the meaning has shifted, for the point would be that the woman is now active sexually outside her marriage! This is possible, because if the man has been too busy satisfying his needs outside the marriage, then the woman may need to find her satisfaction outside as well, and this verse could be a warning to the young man about that possibility. He has not kept her in the center of his life. Alternatively, the spring here may not be referring to the woman's sexuality; rather,

112. Havelock Ellis, *Studies in the Psychology of Sex*, vol. 5 (1927), in *Art and Popular Culture* (website), http://www.artandpopularculture.com/Sexual_symbolism.

113. *Slow Italy* (website), Lactating Breast Italy, http://slowitaly.yourguidetoitaly.com/2012/11/lactating-fountains-of-italy/.

114. Joan Relke, "The Archetypal Female in Mythology and Religion: The Anima and the Mother," *Europe's Journal of Psychology* 3 (2007), https://ejop.psychopen.eu/article/view/389/html.

a different kind of shift in meaning has occurred and now its referent is the man. The question, then, would be whether his sexual vitality should be dispersed outside. He has wandered from the center. A third possibility is to read "springs" as referring to his offspring. The following verse (5:18) complicates matters, for there the young man is told to let the fountains be for himself alone and not for strangers who are with him. This suggests the merits of the third reading, for the sages were unlikely to have been counseling the young man to share his wife with strangers who were with him, in a sort of ancient version of group sex, making the first reading implausible. And they hardly would have been telling the young man to reserve his sexual vitality for himself, striking out the second reading. Verse 18 continues the water imagery, adding a new word, מקור, another word for "fountain," one that clearly refers to the young man's wife because of the parallelism of the verse. The reference to the "wife of your youth" is a reminder that ancient Israelite youth were often betrothed and married quite young. They frequently did not have any choice in the matter of their spouse, so learning to love someone with whom they had never felt an initial romantic attraction was a very different process than the marital journey known to many readers of this commentary.

Proverbs 5:19 continues the focus on the wife, calling her animal names. It counsels the young man in sensual terms to drink his fill from (his wife's) breasts and to go astray, שגה, in her love. We might paraphrase "to get lost in the love of his wife," not that of another.[115] The chapter concludes in 5:21-23 with statements about (a) God's watching human ways, (b) the entrapment of the corrupt (wicked)[116] by their own iniquities, and (c) that they die by their lack of discipline and their folly.[117] A pun is probably involved in 5:22. As young people walk along the way, they become ensnared in cords of their own making, the results of the toil or birth pains of their iniquity, and they trip and fall, destruction being their lot. Due to their lack of discipline, they die.

115. See Translation Matters on Strange/Foreign/Alien Woman (Loose Woman, Adulteress), אשה זרה, at 2:8.
116. See Translation Matters on Corrupt[ion]/Unscrupulous/Reprehensible (Wicked[ness]), רשע/רשעים, at 2:22.
117. See Translation Matters on Jerk/Schmuck/Folly (Fool/Folly), אויל/אולת, at 1:7.

TRANSLATION MATTERS

In 5:22, there is probably a double or triple entendre involving חֶבֶל (*ḥebel*), meaning "cords, bands," and a homonym חֶבֶל (*ḥebel*),[118] meaning "destruction." Another similar sounding word, חֵבֶל (*ḥēbel*), means "labor pains, toil," but cords or bands is the primary meaning.

Various Groups of Sayings with Advice to Stay Out of Trouble (6:1-19)

Proverbs 6:1-19 contains four groups of sayings: dealing with loan guarantees (6:1-5), dealing with sloth and industriousness (6:6-11), about a scoundrel and villain (6:12-15), and concerned with what is loathsome to YHWH (6:16-19). In the first group of sayings, 6:1 presumes a situation in which the addressee has given a pledge, i.e., guaranteeing a loan to a neighbor, the lender in the scenario, to an outsider, the recipient of the loan. If the recipient defaults, then the loan guarantor can only beg mercy from the lender if short of funds to cover the loan (6:3). But the real point is not to encourage such groveling but rather to discourage guaranteeing loans in the first place. Why would someone guarantee a loan? Presumably there was a large fee involved.

Proverbs 6:6-11 deals with indolence and advises the loafer to observe the ways of the ant. This section concludes with the statement that it doesn't take a whole lot of sloth to result in poverty. The ancient Israelites were poor agrarian people. They had to work hard to make ends meet, even before the days when the various governments to which they were subjected added a heavy tax burden on top of the simple problem of getting the soil to produce enough food to feed one's family. It is easy to imagine that it did not take much getting off of the schedule of planting, weeding, harvesting, etc., before one faced starvation, especially given the vagaries of the weather. As in developing nations today, women shouldered much responsibility for the work of the farm as well as the nurture of the family, including the production of clothing and food. There was no sick leave, maternity leave, or vacation time.

Proverbs 6:12-15 describes a worthless individual, the kinds of behavior typical of such a person, and his sudden expected demise. Although

---

118. See Mic 2:10; Job 21:17.

Prov 6:1-19

¹My child, if you have given your
  pledge to your neighbor,
  if you have bound yourself to
  another,
²you are snared by the utterance of
  your lips,
  caught by the words of your mouth.
³So do this, my child, and save
  yourself,
  for you have come into your
  neighbor's power:
  go, hurry, and plead with your
  neighbor.
⁴Give your eyes no sleep
  and your eyelids no slumber;

⁵save yourself like a gazelle from the
  hunter,
  like a bird from the hand of the
  fowler.
⁶Go to the ant, you lazybones;
  consider its ways, and be wise.
⁷Without having any chief
  or officer or ruler,
⁸it prepares its food in summer,
  and gathers its sustenance in
  harvest.
⁹How long will you lie there, O
  lazybones?
  When will you rise from your sleep?
¹⁰A little sleep, a little slumber,

---

some of the description is vague, crooked speech suggests a liar, shuffling the feet represents unwillingness to work hard, and finger pointing indicates someone who blames others for his own wrongdoing. The fact that the person is actively devising evil and creating discord suggests not a passive person but one who is trying to get rewards dishonestly. The sages believed such a person would eventually experience a dramatic calamity.

Proverbs 6:16-19 lists the seven things that YHWH loathes. These may be boiled down to arrogance, dishonesty, violence, and a love of discord; they are among the worst character flaws described in Proverbs. (See the Excursus on Women's Sins 1: Arrogance, at 3:8, and the Excursus on Women's Sins 4: Anger, at 14:16.)

TRANSLATION MATTERS

In 6:1, זר means "stranger" (rendered "another" in the NRSV), though it does not have to mean a foreigner; it can mean someone outside one's group.[119]

---

119. See Translation Matters on Strange/Foreign/Alien Woman (Loose Woman, Adulteress), אשה זרה, at 2:8.

Prov 6:1-19 (cont.)

a little folding of the hands to rest,
[11]and poverty will come upon you like
a robber,
and want, like an armed warrior.

[12]A scoundrel and a villain
goes around with crooked speech,
[13]winking the eyes, shuffling the feet,
pointing the fingers,
[14]with perverted mind devising evil,
continually sowing discord;
[15]on such a one calamity will descend
suddenly;
in a moment, damage beyond
repair.

[16]There are six things that the LORD
hates,
seven that are an abomination to
him:
[17]haughty eyes, a lying tongue,
and hands that shed innocent
blood,
[18]a heart that devises wicked
plans,
feet that hurry to run to evil,
[19]a lying witness who testifies
falsely,
and one who sows discord in a
family.

Practical Admonitions for Living an Upright Life— Proverbs 6:1-22

As a retired pastor on Maui, Hawaii,[120] I have always felt that there was a strong nexus between the Hebrews and the Hawai'ians in spiritual thought. Both cultures value the wisdom of elders and appreciate how troubled relationships can hurt oneself and others with whom we interact. This concept is reflected in the Hawaiian words, *pono* and *ho'oponopono*.

Pono is a Hawaiian word that has many meanings but is commonly rendered as "righteousness." Depending on the context, it can mean "goodness, uprightness, morality, moral qualities, correct or proper procedure, excellence, well-being, prosperity, in perfect order, or accurate."[121] It shares similarities to the Hebrew word *shalom*, and, like *shalom*, the word has strong cultural and spiritual connotations of "a state of harmony or balance" and is the aim of the *ho'oponopono* practice. *Ho'oponopono* is a combination of *ho'o* (to make) and *pono*. It also has several meanings, but generally it means to make right, to do justice, to make amends in a fractured relationship, and to seek forgiveness.

120. The writer is not Hawai'ian, however, she has studied both the Hebrew and Hawai'ian languages and takes a keen interest in linguistic and cultural similarities.
121. Mary Kawena Pukui and Samuel H. Elbert, *Hawaiian Dictionary* (Honolulu: University of Hawai'i, 1986), 340–41.

Hawai'ian scholar Nana Veary, in her book *Change We Must: My Spiritual Journey*,[122] writes that *ho'oponopono* was a practice in ancient Hawaii. She describes it as a practice of extended family members meeting to "make right" broken family relations. Some families met daily or weekly, to prevent problems from erupting. Others met when a person became ill, believing that illness was caused by the stress of anger, guilt, recriminations, and lack of forgiveness.[123]

Ho'oponopono corrects, restores, and maintains good relationships among family members and with their gods or God by getting to the causes and sources of trouble. Usually the most senior member gathers the family together and conducts the process. If the family is unable to work through a problem, they turn to a respected outsider.

In the modern times, courts in Hawai'i began to order juvenile and adult offenders to work with an elder who would conduct *ho'oponopono* for their families, as a form of alternative dispute resolution. You will find *ho'oponopono* in *lomilomi* (Hawai'ian healing massage), *'ohana* (family) conferencing, judicial and court systems, drug addiction recovery, restorative justice in the prison system, and in mental health counseling. There are many expressions of *ho'oponopono* in the world today.

Ho'oponopono played an integral part in the United Church of Christ's Apology to the Hawai'ian People. [124] On January 17, 1993, which marked the hundredth anniversary of the overthrow of Queen Liliuokalani, the United Church of Christ, through its president, Dr. Paul Sherry, issued a formal Apology to *Na Kanaka Ma'oli* (the Native Hawai'ian people) at Iolani Palace, and later at Kaumakapili Church. The address acknowledged the complicity of the Sons of the Mission (the descendants of the original American Board of Commissioners for Foreign Missions [ABCFM] missionaries, one of the predecessor entities of the United Church of Christ) in the overthrow of the monarchy.

During a recent phone interview with Rev. Kekapa Lee, who led the vote on the resolution to adopt the Apology, he felt that the Apology itself constituted *ho'oponopono*. Once the resolution was adopted, the Hawai'ians showed their appreciation by singing

---

122. Nana Veary, *Change We Must: My Spiritual Journey* (International Zen Dojo, 2000), 34.

123. Mary Kawena Pukui, E. W. Haertig, and Catherine A. Lee, *Nānā I Ke Kumu: Look to the Source* (Queen Lili'uokalani Children's Center, 1971), 60–70.

124. See Pacific Justice and Reconciliation Center website: http://pjrcpeace.org, "UCC Apology."

Hawai'ian songs, surely a gracious act of forgiveness.[125]

According to the Pacific Justice and Reconciliation Center, Sherry's remarks "focused on the courage and nonviolence of the Queen Liliuokalani, in her efforts to right the wrongs, and that her life is an example to all today, to study, train, and practice peace and nonviolence in our personal lives, to be hopeful in our vision and work together for social transformation." Later, the United States also issued an Apology to the Hawaiian people.[126]

Likewise, the book of Proverbs constitutes "practical admonitions" for living an upright life that appears to resonate deeply in the Hawai'ian culture. In chapter 6, the wisdom to be gleaned is to live in right relationship with one's neighbor. How does one do this? A righteous person is not snared by the utterance of his or her mouth, not caught in lies or gossip that tend to place stress on or fracture relationships (Prov 6:2-3). A righteous person places himself or herself in a covenantal relationship with family members and outsiders, reflecting the covenantal relationship one has with God. Verse 3 underscores the dynamic of the power shift when the relationship is broken, that is, when forgiveness is not freely given for intentional or unintentional acts. The righteous person must save himself or herself by seeking the neighbor's forgiveness lest they fall under the neighbor's power. Implicit is this understanding of human nature: when we allow ourselves to burn in anger, wallow in self-pity, or ruminate bitterly, we are giving over our peace of mind, our power of the Spirit, to another. Healing and reconciliation cannot occur, and we remain mired in an unprofitable and impoverished state of mind.

Proverbs 6:3-11 advises the reader "to go, hurry, and plead with our neighbor quickly, not to sleep," emphasizing swiftness like an ant scurrying, or a gazelle running from a hunter, or a bird escaping from a fowler, recognizing that human nature is to dwell on the hurts rather than address them.

I can imagine that the Hebrews, if they knew what the elements of *ho'oponopono* were, would have practiced something similar. The elements of *ho'oponopono*:

---

125. Many thanks to Rev. Kekapa Lee, pastor at First Chinese Church in Honolulu, Hawai'i, for sharing his *mana'o* (thoughts) about the Apology during a phone interview on December 6, 2017.

126. See Pacific Justice and Reconciliation Center website: http://pjrcpeace.org, "U.S. Apology."

- Opening *pule* (prayer) and prayers any time they seem necessary.

- A statement of the obvious problem to be solved or prevented from growing worse. This is sometimes called *kukulu kamahana* in its secondary meaning.

- The "setting to rights" of each successive problem that becomes apparent during the course of *ho'oponopono*, even though this might make a series of *ho'oponopono* necessary (*mahiki*).

- Self-scrutiny and discussion of individual conduct, attitudes, and emotions.

- A quality of absolute truthfulness and sincerity. Hawaii called this *'oia'i'o*, the "very spirit of truth."

- Control of disruptive emotions by channeling discussion through the leader.

- Questioning of involved participants by the leader.

- Honest confession to the gods (or God) and to each

other of wrongdoing, grievances, grudges, and resentments.

- Immediate restitution or arrangements to make restitution as soon as possible.

It is hoped that mutual forgiveness and releasing from the guilts, grudges, and tensions occasioned by the wrongdoing (*hala*) will result. Nearly always a closing prayer is made. The leader calls for the periods of silence called *ho'omalu*. *Ho'omalu* was invoked to calm tempers; to encourage self-inquiry into actions, motives, and feelings; or simply for rest during an all-day *ho'oponopono*. And once a dispute was settled, the leader decreed *ho'omalu* for the whole subject, both immediately and long after *ho'oponopono* ended.[127]

Hawaiians believe that *ho'oponopono* is not just a concept, method, or technique; it is a way of life for all people.[128] I believe that the Hebrews would have understood this based on my reading of Proverbs and other books of the Hebrew Bible.

Anne Troy

127. Pukui et al., *Nānā I Ke Kumu*, 60–70.
128. See Pacific Justice and Reconciliation Center website: http://pjrcpeace.org.

Excursus on Women's Sins 2: Violence

We tend to think of women as being less violent than men and thus women's sins being passivity rather than violence. It is certainly true that the most violent crimes are committed primarily by men, but at least concerning intimate partner violence (IPV), there is apparently more symmetry at lower levels of violence than one might expect, though this is a contentious area. Based on the findings of the US National Family Violence Survey in 1975,[129] Suzanne K. Steinmetz wrote an article in 1977 in which she coined the term "battered husband," to parallel "battered wife."

In 1997, Martin S. Fiebert, of the University of California at Long Beach, began compiling an annotated bibliography of research relating to spousal abuse by women. As of June 2012, this bibliography included 286 scholarly investigations demonstrating gender symmetry between the sexes relating to physical aggression. The overall sample size was over 371,600.[130] In 2000, John Archer of the University of Central Lancashire and president of the International Society for Research on Aggression did a meta-analysis of eighty-two IPV studies. His analysis showed that women were slightly more likely to use an act of physical aggression and to use it more frequently than men, but men were more likely to inflict injury.[131] By contrast, in 2017 the US Department of Justice found that women comprise 84 percent of reported spouse abuse victims and 86 percent of victims of abuse by a boyfriend or girlfriend.[132] The only way that the above statistics could be true and at the same time there could be the kind of symmetry reported in IPV would be for there to be a much greater level of nonreporting by men than by women. This is theoretically

129. Richard J. Gelles and Murray A. Straus, *Intimate Violence: The Causes and Consequences of Abuse in the American Family* (New York: Simon & Schuster, 1988).

130. Martin S. Fiebert, "References Examining Assaults by Women on Their Spouses or Male Partners: An Annotated Bibliography," *Sexuality and Culture* 18 (2014): 405–67, https://link.springer.com/article/10.1007%2Fs12119-013-9194-1.

131. John Archer, "Sex Differences in Aggression between Heterosexual Partners: A Meta-Analytic Review," *Psychological Bulletin* (2000), http://psycnet.apa.org /doiLanding?doi=10.1037%2F0033-2909.126.5.651.

132. Bureau of Justice Statistics, US Department of Justice, "Family Violence Statistics: Including Statistics on Strangers and Acquaintances," June 2005, https://www.bjs .gov/content/pub/pdf/fvs03.pdf.

possible due to two factors: shame and fear that reporting might lead to being viewed as the perpetrator rather than the victim. Whether it is true is hard to know based on the current data.

What we do know is that women are perceived as less violent. Only recently have they been approved for combat roles in the military in the United States. There is also the phenomenon known as passive aggression, which may be typical of women who were taught that aggression was not proper feminine behavior. All humans have aggressive instincts that will emerge in either healthy or unhealthy fashions. Perhaps the sin is not in aggression *per se* but in how it is expressed. And those criteria may be applied in a gender-neutral fashion.

None of this addresses the reasons for women's violence, but a great deal of anger among women is created by sexual harassment at work, with over 50 percent of adult working-age women having experienced it during their careers,[133] and in traditional family arrangements when the woman is expected to shoulder a disproportionate amount of the domestic responsibilities, even if she is working as many hours as the man.[134] Among ethnic minority women, there are additional causes for anger.

The types of behavior described in 6:16-19 are destructive of community in any day and place. It is interesting that only sowing discord in a family could possibly be taken as referring to a sexual offense. It is possible that the discussion of adultery in 6:20-35 should be evaluated in the context of these social offenses.

133. Patrick Worrall, "Fact Check: How Many Women Face Sexual Harassment in the Workplace?," *4 News*, October 12, 2017, https://www.channel4.com/news/factcheck/factcheck-how-many-women-face-sexual-harassment-in-the-workplace.

134. Amanda Marcotte, "Think Today's Couples Split Household Chores? Think Again," *LA Times* (May 11, 2015), http://beta.latimes.com/opinion/op-ed/la-oe-0512-marcotte-housework-men-20150512-story.html.

> *Excursus on Women's Sins 3: Dishonesty*
>
> According to a 2016 survey, women are more dishonest than men at work, concerning their health, and in relationships. The motivations, however, are sometimes to avoid hurting someone's feelings.[135] On the other hand, women (and other marginalized people) may also be dishonest due to power differentials. Dishonesty sometimes serves to protect the individual telling the lie or someone close to that person. People with full access to power often do not understand this behavior and find it irritating.
>
> Here we think of the biblical tricksters like Rebekah deceiving Isaac to ensure that Jacob would receive his blessing in Genesis 27 and Tamar deceiving her father-in-law Judah into having sex with her because he would not give her his third son Shelah in levirate marriage, which he was legally required to do (Gen 34).
>
> On the other hand, another study by Jessica Kennedy of Vanderbilt University has found that both men and women try to deceive women more than men in business dealings, because they are viewed as easier targets.[136] So, women apparently both use deception and are vulnerable to it.

Advice Not to Commit Adultery (6:20-35)

Proverbs 6:20-35 deals explicitly with adultery. It begins with an exordium in 6:20-21 (with echoes of 1:9; 4:9; and others), which includes both the mother and the father. Verses 22-23 allude to the Shema, Deuteronomy 6:4-9 (and its twin text, Deut 11:18-20[137]):

> Hear, O Israel: The LORD is our God, the LORD alone. You shall love the LORD your God with all your heart, and with all your soul, and with all your might. Keep these words that I am commanding you today in your heart. Recite them to your children and talk about them when you are at home and when you are away, when you lie down and when you rise. Bind them as a sign on your hand, fix them as an emblem on your forehead, and write them on the doorposts of your house and on your gates.

135. Sarah O'Grady, "Women Are MORE Dishonest Than Men: Females More Likely to Tell Every Day Fibs," *Express*, October 11, 2016, http://www.express.co.uk/life-style/life/719589/Women-more-dishonest-men-females-more-likely-tell-every-day-fibs.

136. Jim Patterson, "Women Face Dishonesty More Often Than Men during Negotiations," *Research News at Vanderbilt*, October 2, 2014, https://news.vanderbilt.edu/2014/10/02/women-face-dishonesty/.

137. Baumann, "A Figure with Many Facets," 95.

Prov 6:20-35

²⁰My child, keep your father's commandment,
and do not forsake your mother's teaching.
²¹Bind them upon your heart always;
tie them around your neck.
²²When you walk, they will lead you;
when you lie down, they will watch over you;
and when you awake, they will talk with you.
²³For the commandment is a lamp
and the teaching a light,
and the reproofs of discipline are the way of life,
²⁴to preserve you from the wife of another,
from the smooth tongue of the adulteress.
²⁵Do not desire her beauty in your heart,
and do not let her capture you with her eyelashes;
²⁶for a prostitute's fee is only a loaf of bread,

Because these texts were central to ancient Israelite religion, the author suggests that the teaching of the parents is of great consequence. The main subject is introduced in 6:24.

TRANSLATION MATTERS

The Hebrew עָר, *rā ʿ*, in 6:24 does not mean "another" but rather "unethical" (evil).[138] There is no need to revocalize (change the vowels) based on the Septuagint's ὑπάνδρου, "wife of a man," to רֵעַ (*rēʿā*), "friend, companion/another." In the context, unethical woman/wife has much the same sense. (On adulteress, see Translation Matters on Foreign/Alien Woman at 2:16.)

The MT of 6:24a says: "to guard you from a woman/wife of evil," מאשת רע. By revocalizing the last word, NRSV reads "wife of another" (see 6:29). This makes the first colon parallel semantically to the second, with "adulteress," but the Hebrew נכריה does not mean adulteress; it means foreign or alien woman.[139] Nevertheless, given the explicit mention in 6:26 of the wife of a man, adultery is what the author has in mind. In ancient Israel, marriages were arranged by parents so that the young people did not have much say in the matter of who their spouses would be. In addition, they were often engaged from a young age. Sex with a

---

138. See Translation Matters on Unethical (Evil/Bad/Wicked), רע/רעים, at 4:14.
139. See Translation Matters on Foreign/Alien Woman, נכריה, at 2:16.

Prov 6:20-35 (cont.)

but the wife of another stalks a
man's very life.
[27]Can fire be carried in the bosom
without burning one's clothes?
[28]Or can one walk on hot coals
without scorching the feet?
[29]So is he who sleeps with his
neighbor's wife;
no one who touches her will go
unpunished.
[30]Thieves are not despised who steal
only
to satisfy their appetite when they
are hungry.
[31]Yet if they are caught, they will pay
sevenfold;

they will forfeit all the goods of
their house.
[32]But he who commits adultery has
no sense;
he who does it destroys
himself.
[33]He will get wounds and dishonor,
and his disgrace will not be wiped
away.
[34]For jealousy arouses a husband's
fury,
and he shows no restraint when
he takes revenge.
[35]He will accept no compensation,
and refuses a bribe no matter how
great.

betrothed woman was considered adultery, so even if a young woman was years away from her wedding, she may have been considered as good as married in the eyes of the law and the community.

It is not clear to what degree girls were just betrothed at an early age and to what degree they were considered married in biblical culture. We do not know how old Rebekah or Rachel and Leah were when they married Isaac and Jacob, for example. What we do know is that we have several stories of "barren" women. Wilma Bailey suggests that this indicates that prepubescent marriage was practiced when various factors warranted it. The kind of factors that warranted it were the need of families with daughters to reduce the number of mouths to feed (though marrying a daughter usually required a dowry to compensate the husband for the cost of maintaining the bride, in spite of the fact that it was supposed to be for the benefit of the wife) and the need of husbands to secure the most capable baby producer along with the best dowry as soon as possible.[140]

Today the practice of marrying girls to men continues, especially in developing countries, resulting from the same sort of forces that made it happen in the ancient world. In 2013, Stephanie Sinclair wrote that more than 10 percent of girls in developing countries were married by the age

---

140. Wilma Bailey, "Baby Becky, Menarche and Prepubescent Marriage in Ancient Israel," *The Journal of the Interdenominational Theological Center*, 37 / 1–2 (2011): 113–37.

of fifteen, according to the United Nations. Worse yet, an estimated 14.2 million girls a year would become child brides by 2020 if nothing changes.[141] Several organizations are now advocating an end to this practice.[142]

Proverbs 6:26 compares sex (with prostitutes) to adultery, showing that the former was accepted, if not condoned, but the latter had serious consequences (see Lev 20:10; Deut 22:22).[143]

Proverbs 6:27-28 presents rhetorical questions, the answers to which are: Of course not. Committing adultery in ancient Israel was like playing with fire. You would get burned. Similarly, 6:29 says that a man who committed adultery would be punished. Verses 30-31 talk about thieves who steal only to satisfy their hunger and thus are not scorned (since they are not greedy), yet they still must pay dearly for their crime. In 6:32-33 the adulterer is shown to be worse than the hungry thieves, because he does not need sex, but if he is stupid enough to commit adultery, he will self-destruct. Such a man has no sense, according to the sages; he is lacking heart/mind, חסר־לב.[144] This is the same phrase used to describe the strange woman's prey in 7:7 and the invitees to the banquets of both Wisdom and Folly in 9:4 and 16. Proverbs 6:34-35 concludes, focusing on the cuckolded husband's jealousy, which is part of the reason that the adulterer will self-destruct; the husband is so outraged that he will not accept any amount of money to calm his wounded ego and hush the matter up.

The Messianic Thief: The Redeemer of His Bride
Proverbs 6:30-31

Proverbs 6:30-31 introduces a "situational" *hapax legomenon*, the only stated occurrence of an unusual scenario: a thief who is not despised if carrying out the vice of stealing to satisfy a basic need, like hunger, but who is required to restore sevenfold if caught. Though the NRSV presents this perpetrator in the plural, i.e., "thieves," the original Hebrew casts this character in the singular גנב, "thief," who

---

141. Rena Silverman, "Millions of Young Girls Forced into Marriage," *National Geographic* (March 15, 2013), https://news.nationalgeographic.com/news/2013/13/130313-child-brides-marriage-women-sinclair-photography/.

142. See "The Pixel Project's '16 For 16' Campaign: 16 Organisations Working to Stop Child Marriage," December 12, 2013, http://16days.thepixelproject.net/16-organisations-working-to-stop-child-marriage/; https://www.girlsnotbrides.org/child-marriage-advocacy-successes-2014/; http://www.care.org/work/womens-empowerment/child-marriage.

143. Goodfriend, "Adultery," 82–86.

144. See Translation Matters on the Heart, לב, at 2:2.

is further identified by the masculine singular pronouns "he" and "his" and by the masculine singular conjugation of verbs associated with his activities.

The significance in retaining the original language designation of this thief is that it points directly to the Messianic Thief who came to do what no ordinary thief could do: for the Messianic Thief came to take back what had been stolen from him by the one who "comes only to steal and kill and destroy" (John 10:10). As this latter thief is the cohort of the proverbial whore (see Prov 5:5; 7:27; Rev 17:1-6), the Messianic Thief is the Redeemer of His Bride—the Church.[145]

The Messianic Thief's "hunger" was to fulfill his Father's will (John 4:32, 34) by redeeming his Bride from the Satanic thief's control. While doing so, the Messianic Thief was "caught" by those who were threatened by his power to upset their status quo hold on the people and who condemned him to death by crucifixion. It was, however, in his "caught" state that the Messianic Thief redeemed his bride through the shedding of his blood for the forgiveness of her sins.

If the fate of the Messianic Thief had ended in the tomb, then the activities of restoration in verse 31 would not have been achievable. The resurrection of the Messianic Thief, however, guaranteed his ability to pay sevenfold,[146] thus enfranchising his redeemed bride as joint heir to seven new things that constitute all the goods of his house: the new heaven, the new earth (Rev 21:1), new bodies (Rom 8:23; Phil 3:20-21), the new Jerusalem (Rev 21:2, 9-21), the new temple (Rev 21:22), the new light (Rev 21:23-25; 22:5), and the new paradise (Rev 22:1-4). Instead of "forfeiting," as the NRSV states, the Messianic Thief will "give" all the goods of his house, as the Hebrew verb יִתֵּן ("he will give") clearly denotes. Even the repentant thief recognized the Messianic Thief as the more excellent thief in whose kingdom he desired to reside (Luke 23:39-43)!

Though the Messianic Thief was despised by those who rejected him (Isa 53:3), he was dearly beloved and highly exalted by the God who sent him (Matt 3:17; Phil 2:9-11). And this

---

145. For a feminist critique of the metaphor of the church as the bride of Christ, see Elisabeth Schüssler Fiorenza, *Ephesians*, WCS 50 (Collegeville, MN: Liturgical Press, 2017), 89–104.

146. Though an ordinary thief was commended for making some measure of restoration (Luke 19:8), only the Messianic Thief is recorded as making a complete restoration, symbolized by the term "sevenfold."

same Messianic Thief has alerted his redeemed bride of the sure character of his return: "See, I am coming like a thief" (Rev 16:15). The Messianic Thief who has come and will come, is Jesus, the Wisdom of God (1 Cor 1:30), and the redeemer of his bride—the church!

Rev. Desiré P. Grogan

There are very few biblical stories of women who commit adultery intentionally. Potiphar's wife tries unsuccessfully to seduce Joseph, but her husband is called a eunuch. The term סריס may, however, also mean a high government official. If Potiphar was a sexual eunuch, it is easy to understand Potiphar's wife's motives (both to get pregnant and sexual satisfaction) and easy also to understand why Potiphar did not have Joseph executed but instead merely threw him in jail. If he was not a eunuch, but only a government official, the story is harder to understand.

The other story that comes to mind is that of Bathsheba and David (2 Sam 11). Scholars debate whether Bathsheba was trying to seduce David, with most, though not all, feminist scholars on the negative side of this debate.[147] In any case, the fact that Uriah, when offered a chance to go home to his wife while on furlough so that he could sleep with her, refuses to do so, suggests that he knew what had happened and was not willing to play David's game. His honor would not allow it. He was not in a position to retaliate against David, but he would not pretend to be the father of David's child by sleeping with Bathsheba one night.

Finally, the story of Hosea and Gomer involves Hosea's belief that he was cuckolded when his wife committed adultery (at least so he imagined) and that at least two of his children were apparently children of adultery (Hos 2:2). Because in this story Hosea's experience with Gomer represents God's experience with unfaithful Israel, Hosea's focus is on Gomer and not on the other man/men. He loves her, wants her back, and goes to lengths that today create problems for modern readers, because they involve threats of abuse (Hos 2:3, 6, 10),[148] but to the original readers

147. See discussion in Alice Ogden Bellis, "Bathsheba," and the literature cited there, in *Helpmates, Harlots, and Heroes: Women's Stories in the Hebrew Bible*, 2nd ed. (Louisville: Westminster John Knox, 2007), 130–33.

148. For discussion of the threats of abuse, see Renita J. Weems, "Victim of Violence or Victim of Metaphor," in *Interpretation for Liberation*, ed. Katie Geneva Canon and Elisabeth Schüssler Fiorenza, *Semeia* 47 (1989): 87–104.

living in an entirely different world were intended to send the message that God loves us so much that no matter how much we "screw up," God will never forsake us.

A Play with the Message: Avoid the Strange Woman (7:1-27)

Proverbs 7:1-27 is the longest of the sections dealing with the strange woman and displays a narrative sensibility lacking in other parts of Proverbs. It begins with an exordium in 7:1-5. In 7:4 the youth is to call wisdom "sister" and intimate friend. Sister can mean lover. The word is parallel to bride, כלה, in Song of Songs 4:9, 10, 12; 5:1, 2. (For other bridal imagery, see 4:8-9.) In 7:5, the main theme is introduced. As indicated in previous chapters, the Hebrew does not say "loose woman" or "adulteress" but rather "strange" or "foreign woman," אשה זרה,[149] and "foreign" or "alien woman," נכריה,[150] respectively. The exact nature of the woman's strangeness in this chapter is not entirely clear. It cannot be assumed that we are dealing with the same type of strangeness in this chapter as in the previous chapter. It is possible, however, that the character is intended to be read on two levels, a flesh-and-blood woman to be avoided and Folly personified as such a woman.

> ### The Maneaters
>
> Proverbs 7, in its entirety, calls to mind the lyrics of a popular 1980s song by Hall & Oates, "Maneater." Both the writer and the performers claim the motivation for the song was not, in fact, women but rather New York City.[151] Women were used in the iconography for the video as a metaphor for the fast-paced New York City life because it is a widely held consensus that "the big apple" can "chew you up." In this way, the apple is synonymous with the Genesis creation story in which the socially constructed "Eve," cast as the evil woman, led the socially constructed, male-dominated-by-the-female "Adam" to sin. Contextually, the father in Proverbs 7 wants his *son* to be "the apple of his

---

149. See Translation Matters on Strange/Foreign/Alien Woman (Loose Woman, Aduleress), אשה זרה, at 2:8.

150. See Translation Matters on Foreign/Alien Woman, נכריה, at 2:16.

151. Leslie Richin, "Watch Out Boy! Today in 1982 Hall & Oates Took on a 'Maneater,'" *Billboard.com*, December 17, 2014, https://www.billboard.com/articles/news/6406621/hall-and-oates-maneater-anniversary.

Prov 7:1-27

[Exordium]

¹ My child, keep my words
    and store up my commandments
        with you;
²keep my commandments and live,
    keep my teachings as the apple of
        your eye;
³bind them on your fingers,
    write them on the tablet of your
        heart.
⁴Say to wisdom, "You are my sister,"
    and call insight your intimate friend,
⁵that they may keep you from the
        loose woman,
    from the adulteress with her
        smooth words.

[Setting the Scene]

⁶For at the window of my house
    I looked out through my lattice,
⁷and I saw among the simple ones,
    I observed among the youths,
    a young man without sense,
⁸passing along the street near her
        corner,
    taking the road to her house
⁹in the twilight, in the evening,
    at the time of night and darkness.

[Description of the Woman]

¹⁰Then a woman comes toward him,
    decked out like a prostitute, wily
        of heart.
¹¹She is loud and wayward;
    her feet do not stay at home;
¹²now in the street, now in the squares,
    and at every corner she lies in wait.

[What the Woman Says and Does]

¹³She seizes him and kisses him,
    and with impudent face she says
        to him:
¹⁴"I had to offer sacrifices,
    and today I have paid my vows;
¹⁵so now I have come out to meet you,
    to seek you eagerly, and I have
        found you!
¹⁶I have decked my couch with
        coverings,
    colored spreads of Egyptian linen;
¹⁷I have perfumed my bed with
        myrrh,
    aloes, and cinnamon.
¹⁸Come, let us take our fill of love
        until morning;
    let us delight ourselves with love.
¹⁹For my husband is not at home;
    he has gone on a long journey.
²⁰He took a bag of money with him;
    he will not come home until full
        moon."

[The Young Man Is Captivated]

²¹With much seductive speech she
        persuades him;
    with her smooth talk she compels
        him.
²²Right away he follows her,
    and goes like an ox to the
        slaughter,
    or bounds like a stag toward the
        trap
²³until an arrow pierces its entrails.
He is like a bird rushing into a snare,
    not knowing that it will cost him
        his life.

[Final Exordium]

²⁴And now, my children, listen to me,
    and be attentive to the words of
        my mouth.
²⁵Do not let your hearts turn aside to
        her ways;
    do not stray into her paths.
²⁶for many are those she has laid low,
    and numerous are her victims.
²⁷Her house is the way to Sheol,
    going down to the chambers of
        death.

eye" (v. 2), thereby admonishing him to strictly comply with the father's instructions to avoid temptations of a sexual nature with a specified woman, the one who is a "maneater" (vv. 21-23). The theme of domination and seduction takes center stage (vv. 26-27). There is a crippling naiveté undergirding this line of reasoning. As a philosophical thinker, I call it *post hoc ergo propter hoc*—a hasty generalization, fallacious in its conclusion. Eroticism suffers at the hands of this reasoning as something unholy. Consequently, Eros, one of four Greco-Christian terms for love, is instantly reduced to something sinister and vile. This, then, translates into broad-scale condemnation of sexual diversity. Lesbians, gays, bisexuals, transgender persons, intersexed individuals, their allies, and those who are questioning and discerning their identities are consequentially easily lumped into harrowed tales that mirror this faulty thought.

The proverb evinces disgust for eroticism. The feminine is the scapegoat for intolerance and fear of the "other." The characterization speaks to the grossly exaggerated posturing of patriarchal hegemony as trope for the incessant deluge of hate-talk disguised as God-talk. Heterosexism has obscured the ground for sexuality toward a compendium of acceptable norms that hinder eroticism in general and squelch homoeroticism particularly. Here, eroticism is feminized as a "strange woman" (v. 5). Consequentially, sexuality's conformability as a mandate in Western constructs of sociality and governance serves a prominent role in the suppression of sexual desire. The question is: how does the suppression of sexual expression equate to wisdom? The answer is: it does not. It is not wise to suppress one's sexual desire or to imprison desire within a cultural enclave of constrictions having little meaning or gravitas. What is helpful are the parameters placed on their mutual sexual expression between consenting adults in covenanted relationships, in whatever prisms they are configured. But not here. Here, a woman, a feminized subject, serves as catalyst for the demise of an innocent, unassuming male who is forced to come into her bedroom and perform sexual exploits—a seduction of epic proportion, the work of a maneater.

The root cause of the vitriolic rhetoric against sexual diversity pervasive in theological communions derives from the thought patterns in this proverb resulting in a huge swath of theological thinking that borders on the absurd. The ridiculous conclusions drawn because of an inability to appreciate the complexity of sexual attraction bespeaks the nature of a contrived sexual (im)morality and a misplaced condemnation.

Teresa L. Smallwood, JD, PhD

Proverbs 7:6-24 is a narrative account of a fictitious event, depicted to scare the young man (son)[152] away from "bad" women. It can be broken down into the following segments: setting the scene (7:6-9), description of the woman (7:10-12), what she does and says (mostly, 7:13-20), and the result of her persuasive speech, which is that he is persuaded/captured (7:21-23).

In 7:7 someone looks out of a latticed window. This is usually assumed to be a man, even among feminist commentators,[153] but in most cases where such an individual is identified, she is a woman. This is the case with Michal (2 Sam 6:16), Jezebel (2 Kgs 9:30), and Sisera's mother (Judg 5:28). The one exception is Genesis 26:8, where Abimelech looks out the window and sees Abraham fondling Rebekah. The Samaria ivories, which include an image of a woman looking through a latticed window (see below),[154] also provide archaeological evidence supporting this feminine image. These images, dating from 900 to 700 BCE, are associated with the reign of King Ahab of Israel.

152. See Translation Matters on Son (Child), בֵּן, at 1:8.

153. Claudia V. Camp, "What's So Strange about the Strange Woman?," in *The Bible and the Politics of Exegesis: Essays in Honor of Norman K. Gottwald on His Sixty-Fifth Birthday*, ed. D. Jobling et al. (Cleveland: Pilgrim Press, 1991), 17–31; Carol A. Newsom, "Woman and the Discourse of Patriarchal Wisdom," 142–60; Kathleen M. O'Connor, *The Wisdom Literature* (Wilmington, DE: Glazier, 1988), 61–63; Yee, "I Have Perfumed My Bed with Myrrh," 53–68.

154. *The Woman at the Window*, British Museum, http://www.britishmuseum.org /research/collection_online/collection_object_details.aspx?objectId=369006&partId=1. © The Trustees of the British Museum.

There is no reason that the individual in this scenario in Proverbs could not be a woman.[155] Women as much as men can be concerned with the sexual morals of the young men of the community.[156] Indeed, this is often the case. The ultimate speaker is still presumably a man, channeling the woman at the window. In any case, this introduction is cinematic, drawing the reader into the drama of the seduction to come. It may be read as the opening scene of a play over twenty-four hours, beginning on one evening, continuing through the following day (chap. 8), and completed on the next evening (chap. 9). The young man that the viewer sees is described as a simple one, a naïf, פתאים, and without a heart, but since the heart was the ancient equivalent of the mind, he is being described as mindless or stupid. The narrator goes on in 7:8, first to say that the young man is crossing over by the corner where her house is located but then goes on to say that he is heading straight for her house. Verse 9 establishes that it is dusk, evening, when the dark of night has descended.

It is not too late, however, because in 7:10 the narrator can see well enough to describe a woman dressed like a prostitute striding toward the young man. The text does not say that the woman is a prostitute, just that she is dressed like one.[157] Proverbs 7:11-12 seems to rely on what the narrator has seen previously, because they describe the woman lying in wait in the street and square and at every corner, being loud and wayward, her feet not staying at home. The word "foot," רגל, is a euphemism for genitals, so this is probably a vulgar double entendre, meaning that the woman is on the make (similarly, Ezek 16:25). The verb, "lie in wait," תארב, is from the same root, ארב, that was used to describe the gang in 1:11-14, who lie in wait for blood: נארבה. At the same time, many of the words used to describe the strange woman are also used to describe wisdom: in 1:20-21, wisdom is in the streets, בחוץ, and in the

155. Fokkelien Van Dijk-Hemmes, "Traces of Women's Texts in the Hebrew Bible," in Brenner and Van Dijk-Hemmes, *On Gendering Texts*, 57–62; Meike Heijerman, "Who Would Blame Her? The 'Strange' Woman of Proverbs 7," in *Reflections on Theology and Gender*, ed. Athalya Brenner and Fokkelein Van Dijk-Hemmes (Kampen: Kok Pharos, 1994), 21; Alice Ogden Bellis, "The Gender and Motives of the Wisdom Teacher in Proverbs 7," *BBR* 6 (1996): 79–91.

156. Bellis, "The Gender and Motives of the Wisdom Teacher," 79–91.

157. It is often assumed that prostitutes wore veils, based on the fact that Tamar donned a veil when she pretended to be a prostitute in order to trick her father-in-law Judah into having sex with her (Gen 38:14), but the reason she wore a veil was to keep Judah from recognizing her, not because it was customary attire for prostitutes. This is made clear by Rebekah's putting a veil on out of modesty in Gen 24:65 when she learns that she is about to meet Isaac for the first time.

squares, ברחבות, crying out loudly, המיה. One must be discerning to tell the difference between the two.

Proverbs 7:13 returns to what the narrator is seeing at the moment of narration: the woman grabbing and kissing the young man. We must imagine that the young man and woman are right under the narrator's window, for we now are privy to a long speech in which the woman verbally seduces the young man (7:14-20). There is more ambiguity, for the strange woman's speech is reminiscent of that of the female lover in Song of Songs who seeks her beloved (3:1-4). The spices with which she prepares her bed are also the same as those used in Song 3:6; 5:1; 14:14. These spices are expensive. They are also ambiguous: they are not only found in amatory contexts but also used to prepare the dead for burial, so again the unsuspecting youth is hooked on the expensive sensuality of the bed she has prepared, not realizing its danger.[158]

Her motives are not entirely clear. Several scholars suggest prostitution as a means of paying religious vows.[159] In this case the verb שלמתי, "paid," in 7:14 would not be intended as past completed action but modal: today I am going to fulfill/pay my vows (will have paid/fulfilled my vows). At the same time, the youth would hear it and is probably intended to hear it as completed action. It is intentionally ambiguous. He hears her words as an invitation to a feast, since the meat of the type of sacrifice she is offering, זבחי שלמים, had to be eaten on the day it was offered or on the next day (Lev 7:15-17). He may think the meal will be followed by sex. What she really means is that she is going to fulfill her vow and that he is the sacrifice.[160] On the question of why she needed to make a vow at all, Meike Heijerman suggests that it was because she has not been able to get pregnant, which in ancient Israelite society was a must for economic survival for women. She was resorting to temporary prostitution both to pay her vow and in hopes of getting pregnant, since her failure to get pregnant might have been because of some inadequacy on her husband's part.[161] Admittedly, the whole scene is a rhetorical fiction, but it only works if it is plausible.

158. Yee, *Poor Banished Children of Eve*, 156.

159. Heijerman, "Who Would Blame Her?" in *A Feminist Companion to Wisdom Literature*, ed. Athalya Brenner, FCB 9 (Sheffield: Sheffield Academic, 1995), 100–109; Karel Van der Toorn, "Female Prostitution in Payment of Vows in Ancient Israel," *JBL* 108 (1989): 193–205; Van Dijk-Hemmes, "Traces of Women's Texts in the Hebrew Bible," 60–61; Yee, *Poor Banished Children of Eve*, 155.

160. Heijerman, "Who Would Blame Her?," 100–109.

161. Ibid.

In 7:21-23, the narrator informs us that the young man has fallen for the woman's seductive speech/smooth talk. The noun לֶקַח, teaching, the word used in the first colon, is also used of the teaching of the wise (1:5; 4:2; 9:9; 16:21, 33). Thus, the wise and the strange woman compete for the attention of the young. Verses 21-23 describe what is about to happen in metaphorical terms as animal slaughter. This is deeply ironic since her statement that she has paid her vows suggests the possibility that she has had an animal sacrificed, of which a portion is available for a communal meal. Only, it appears that the young man, on one level, is the meal. Perhaps the woman intends to get money from the young man, but there are limits to how much she can get without revealing her own guilt. Alternately, the narrator may be concerned that the husband will come home prematurely, with the result that the young man's goose will be cooked. Or perhaps the concern is simply that he will develop an unsavory reputation, but that has hardly proved to be terribly detrimental to young men in more recent times. We may also ask whether there were ancient cases of venereal disease that could be in the background here. If the woman is Folly, seducing the young man from YHWH, then the venereal disease is the moral rot that will result.

Proverbs 7:24-27 is another exordium, concluding the chapter, this time addressed to a plural audience, to listen and avoid the ways of the strange woman for they lead to death and Sheol. Just as the gang in 1:12 say that they are going to swallow their victims like Sheol, here the house of the strange woman is said to lead there. If the narrator was focusing only on the story just told we would wonder whether the concern was about death as a result of violent revenge, illness, or moral death due to bad reputation or some combination. These final verses suggest that the strange woman in chapter 7 is not a mere woman, or at least can be read on two levels: as a human and as a personification of abstract Folly, just as the character in 8:1–9:12 is personified Wisdom and the one in 9:13-18 is personified Folly. Perhaps the strangeness of the story is intended to indicate the foolishness of giving in to Folly of any sort. Because the primary audience was young men, and since wisdom was traditionally associated with the feminine in the ancient Near East, it seemed only natural to the sages to paint its opposite, Folly, as a seductive woman. The fact that 8:1 begins with Wisdom's call to virtue is additional support for this identification.

In the introduction we discussed the difficulties this polarization of the feminine as very good and very bad causes modern readers, both women and men. It reminds me of a poem by Henry Wadsworth Longfellow I was told as a child,

There was a little girl,
Who had a little curl,
  Right in the middle of her forehead.
When she was good,
  she was very, very good,
  But when she was bad, she was horrid.

Although there is no sexuality explicit in the Longfellow poem, it is not a far jump from his seemingly innocent words to the suggestion that the feminine is inherently divine (asexually or otherwise) or demonic (usually with sexuality included). Men, on the other hand, are often allowed a full range of human behavior with a "boys will be boys" shrug, though this attitude may be changing.

The Introduction of Woman Wisdom (8:1-21)

Proverbs 8:1-21 is the first half of a long speech by Wisdom that can be seen as the positive parallel to the seduction story of the preceding chapter. It begins with three verses of introduction, starting off with a rhetorical question: does not Wisdom call and her parallel figure, understanding, raise her voice? The answer to the rhetorical question is, Yes, of course. Verses 2-3 detail the extent to which Wisdom/understanding makes her voice heard. Interestingly, like Folly, her negative counterpart, Wisdom is out in the public square. She is at the city gate. The word for "gate," שַׁעַר, is used of large public gates, like city gates or the gates of the temple in Jerusalem, not the gates to a residential building. The distinction between the strange/other woman in chapter 7 and Wisdom/understanding in chapter 8 is not that one is inside and the other outside; rather, the distinction is that the strange woman operates in the evening under cover of darkness on a presumably obscure street, whereas Wisdom/understanding's *modus operandi* is in broad daylight and at the public square where business is conducted. This is consistent with her human counterpart, the strong woman/wife in 31:10-31,[162] who is depicted as conducting all kinds of business, including seeking wool and flax (31:12), bringing food from far away (31:14), buying real estate (31:16), etc. These activities would be hard to do sequestered in her home. The portrait of this woman suggests that at least elite women could go about freely in the city during daylight hours, just as Woman Wisdom is described as doing.

---

162. See discussion at 31:10-31. For the translation, see Translation Matters on Strong Woman/Wife (Capable Wife), אֵשֶׁת־חַיִל, at 12:4.

Prov 8:1-21

¹Does not wisdom call,
   and does not understanding raise
      her voice?
²On the heights, beside the way,
   at the crossroads she takes her
      stand;
³beside the gates in front of the
      town,
   at the entrance of the portals she
      cries out:
⁴"To you, O people, I call,
   and my cry is to all that live.
⁵O simple ones, learn prudence;
   acquire intelligence, you who lack
      it.
⁶Hear, for I will speak noble things,
   and from my lips will come what
      is right;
⁷for my mouth will utter truth;
   wickedness is an abomination to
      my lips.
⁸All the words of my mouth are
      righteous;
   there is nothing twisted or crooked
      in them.
⁹They are all straight to one who
      understands
   and right to those who find
      knowledge.
¹⁰Take my instruction instead of silver,
   and knowledge rather than choice
      gold;

The Call of Woman Wisdom— Proverbs 8

Woman Wisdom[163] initiates her teaching early in the book of Proverbs. She cries out and raises her voice at the busy city gates (1:20-21) and rebukes people directly. Readers might be disconcerted by this enigmatic scene in which wisdom is personified as engaging in human affairs and speaking assertively to the people at the gates. Woman Wisdom, whose name has exactly the same form as the Hebrew word for "wisdom," חכמה, confidently shares her teachings with humans in a new and surprising way. Fortunately, her mysterious identity becomes clearer in the course of the book of Proverbs even though she appears infrequently, only whenever she wishes to connect with humans.

In contrast to the earlier direct depiction of Woman Wisdom, chapter 3 praises Woman Wisdom indirectly in its description of her rare magnificence. She is portrayed

---

163. The contemporary analysis of personified Wisdom can be largely summarized by four theories about her identity: Woman Wisdom was purely a literary personification; she was a hypostasis of YHWH; she was an *ummānu*, a type of Mesopotamian sage; or she was one of the ancient Near Eastern goddesses, such as Astarte, Ma'at, or Isis. The available evidence does not permit us to explain her origin(s) and identity based solely on one particular precursor.

¹¹for wisdom is better than jewels,
  and all that you may desire cannot
    compare with her.
¹²I, wisdom, live with prudence,
  and I attain knowledge and
    discretion.
¹³The fear of the LORD is hatred of
    evil.
Pride and arrogance and the way of
  evil
  and perverted speech I hate.
¹⁴I have good advice and sound
    wisdom;
  I have insight, I have strength.
¹⁵By me kings reign,
  and rulers decree what is just;

¹⁶by me rulers rule,
  and nobles, all who govern
    rightly.
¹⁷I love those who love me,
  and those who seek me diligently
    find me.
¹⁸Riches and honor are with me,
  enduring wealth and prosperity.
¹⁹My fruit is better than gold, even
    fine gold,
  and my yield than choice silver.
²⁰I walk in the way of righteousness,
  along the paths of justice,
²¹endowing with wealth those who
    love me,
  and filling their treasuries.

as even more precious than jewels, as is also noted by another admirer of wisdom in a different book of the Hebrew Bible (see Job 28). This implies that humans, including the author of this book, are well aware of how invaluable she is and feel obligated to praise her. In the midst of a passage of ornate praise, the narrator explicitly states that the Lord founded the earth via Woman Wisdom (3:19-20), which implies that she was deeply involved in God's creation. This is a crucial clue to her identity, and readers would like to hear more about this than just a couple of verses.

The wise Woman Wisdom knows our hearts—and now she tells her story. The second time she speaks, in chapter 8, is the crux of the discourse on her identity. She again cries aloud at the city gates, but this time she proceeds to offer a grand history, not only of herself, but also of the universe. With great clarity, she identifies herself as the first act of God (8:22) and, more astonishingly, asserts that she was with God when God established the heavens and the earth (8:30). She was created first of all the creatures and then, truly and faithfully, rejoiced beside God during the process of creation. She assisted God; her role was to remain in God's inhabited world and to delight in the human race.

Hence, Woman Wisdom is both God's creature and a cocreator of the world (8:30-31). Her twofold identity and liminal nature enables her to mediate between heaven and earth. She praises herself as originating from the divine authority and ardently tries to bequeath wisdom from above. At the city gates, a symbol of liminal space and human culture, she demands attention and even becomes furious when people ignore her call (1:23-27).[164] She shouts loudly in the public space—her audience is not limited to a few. Yet, the human race has the choice either to accept or to reject Woman Wisdom. Only those who recognize her divine knowledge are able to embrace truth in their lives.[165]

Sehee Kim

Wisdom Personified as Woman Exonerated—Proverbs 8

The Wisdom figure of Proverbs 8 starkly contrasts with the loose woman who precedes her and furthermore proves to be a vindication of woman who has suffered from the "Eve complex." Held liable for the fall of man, woman has since acquired the role of subordinate evildoer, responsible for the inherent evil in all humanity. Wisdom personified now stands at the crossroads beside the gates in front of the town and makes a call not just to men but to "all that live." Unlike the loose woman whose path leads to Sheol, Wisdom's call at the crossroads represents the option to choose the path between good and evil (8:4).

Men would gather at the city gates to conduct business and legal proceedings (see Ruth 4:1-12; 2 Sam 15:1-5; Job 29:7-25); yet there Wisdom personified stands, also suggestive of her authority to speak in places among society. In an illustration of her authenticity, she speaks of noble things and rejects wickedness as an abomination to her lips in 8:6-7. Wisdom speaks in the first person, a pattern similar to that of the "I am the Lord your God" of the Old Testament and the "I am" sayings of Jesus in the New Testament (see Gen 26:24; Exod 6:7; Lev 11:45; John 6:35; 8:12; 14:6), perhaps a play on her divine nature. As Geraldine Baumann puts it: "The Wisdom Figure in Proverbs 1–9 is

164. Michael V. Fox, "Ideas of Wisdom in Proverbs 1–9," *JBL* 116 (1997): 631.
165. Raymond C. Van Leeuwen, "Proverbs," in *The New Interpreter's Bible: A Commentary in Twelve Volumes*, ed. Leander E. Keck et al. (Nashville: Abingdon, 1994), 90–91.

described as a figure close to YHWH because her words and idioms resemble YHWH speech."[166] If by now there remains any doubt, in the next ten verses (8:22-31), Wisdom lays out the authority by which she stands in her call. Having been created or birthed by God is rather ambiguous, but either case is suggestive that she is the child of God, thus having some part in the divine nature of God.

What is clear is that she exists before and is present at the formation of the world, beside God like a master worker in the making of the heavens and the earth. Wisdom, furthermore, is transcendent, which serves as an indication that she is not a distant phenomenon but active in the world. It is my contention then,

that woman did not assume the responsibility for the fall of man, nor was she to be subordinate and become the embodiment of evil. Active in the world and active in humanity, at the crossroad to the supposed fall of man stood Wisdom personified; not enticing but offering an opportunity. Eve does not give rise to inherent evil. Instead, there is free will, the capacity to choose good or evil. Humanity then takes on the individual responsibility for the freedom to be human and the pursuit or lack thereof of a relationship with the Divine. Wisdom Personified and Woman Exonerated means the twenty-first-century woman can now live without limits—free to simply be.

Beverly A. Reddy

Beginning in 8:4 is Wisdom's speech, which continues throughout the entire chapter. Verses 4-11 describe the integrity of Wisdom's words. Wisdom's first declaration is that her speech is addressed to people/all that live (NRSV), though the original Hebrew really says to men, אישים/ sons of humanity, בני אדם, and the context does make it clear that a male audience is the primary focus. In 8:5 the audience is narrowed to the naive, פתאים, and dolts (fools; כסילים),[167] with the intention that they may develop prudence (ערמה) and a discerning heart/mind (לב),[168] respectively. Proverbs 8:6 describes Wisdom's words as noble, נגידים. This is the only time the word נגידים is used abstractly in the Bible. Otherwise it is used to describe noble men. It is clear from the parallel word, מישרים, what is upright, straight, pleasing, just, that here it must mean noble words. Verse 7 continues in similar fashion with the less common word חך,

---

166. Baumann, "A Figure with Many Facets," 55.
167. See Translation Matters on Dolt/Chump/Oaf/Inept (Fool), כסיל, at 1:22.
168. See Translation Matters on Heart, לב, at 2:2.

palate or gums, for mouth, and the antithetical statement that corruption (wickedness)[169] is an abomination[170] to Wisdom/understanding's lips.

In 8:8a, Wisdom/understanding's words are spoken in or with what is ethical, right, just, normal, or in better English, they are spoken ethically or justly.[171] There is nothing twisted or crooked in, with, or about her words (8:8b). It is not just that her words are true but that the intention of her words is also right and just. That is why 8:9 goes on to declare that to the person who truly is understanding—they are straight, נכחים, and they are right, pleasing (ישרים)[172] to someone who is in the process of finding knowledge. The section dealing with the integrity of Wisdom's speech concludes in 8:10-11. Here Wisdom again issues an order to those who listen to her. This is the second "better than/more than" proverb in Proverbs. The first was in 3:14-15 and reiterates the theme that Wisdom is superior to wealth; 3:14-15 and 8:10-11 are paraphrases of each other, forming a grand *inclusio*, partly echoed in 31:10. The item at the beginning of each of the first three cola is the thing that is better than the matter at the end of the cola. Then, the pattern is reversed in the final colon. In addition, there is a progression from one colon to the next, so that gold is better than silver, jewels better than choice gold, and all that you can desire is better than jewels. Similarly, knowledge is better than discipline (instruction)[173] and wisdom is better than knowledge.

Proverbs 8:12-14 focuses on Wisdom's character traits. In 8:12a, she dwells with or in prudence, ערמה.[174] In 8:12b the two terms, "knowledge" and "discretion," are often found in parallel, but here there is no conjunction between them. The second term is plural (מזמות) and sometimes refers to the evil devices of humans. Since the following verse speaks of Wisdom's hatred of evil, it is possible that this colon refers to her knowledge of the (secret evil) plans humans harbor. This suggests that Wisdom is ever present, monitoring evil plans. In 8:13 the fear of

169. See Translation Matters on Corrupt[ion]/Unscrupulous/Reprehensible (Wicked[ness]), רשע/רשעים, at 2:22.

170. See discussion of the term "abomination" at 3:32.

171. See Translation Matters on Just/Integrity/Honesty (Righteous[ness]), צדקה/צדיק/צדק, at 1:2, on צדק, which occurs in vv. 8, 15, 16, as just, rightly (righteousness).

172. See Translation Matters on Upstanding/Straight/Straightforward (Upright), ישר/ישרים, at 2:7.

173. See Translation Matters on Discipline/Chastening/Correction (Instruction), מוסר, at 1:2.

174. See Translation Matters on Prudent/Prudence (Clever[ness]), ערמה and ערום, at 1:4.

YHWH[175] is equated with hatred of evil, שנאת רע. Before it was equated with the knowledge of God (1:7, 29; 2:5, 10). Hatred of evil is then further specified as pride, גאה, a word that occurs only here in the Bible, and a related word used more frequently in a positive sense, גאון, here translated as arrogance. (See Excursus on Women's Sins 1: Arrogance at 3:8.) In 8:14, Wisdom claims the positive qualities of good advice or counsel, עצה, and sound wisdom, תושיה, a technical term of Wisdom literature. She directly says she is insight or understanding, בינה. Wisdom concludes by stating that she has the quality of valor or strength, גבורה. For a similar combination of qualities attributed to the Deity, see Job 12:13.

Proverbs 8:15-16 deals with governance. The first colon of each verse might seem to simply be stating the divine right of monarchs to rule, but the second colon of each verse says something more subtle: when rulers enact statutes that are just, when they govern well, it is through the power of Wisdom that they are acting. Related to this is the royal execution of justice through divine Wisdom. (See 1 Kgs 3:28 and 10:9.) Kings, like other humans, are exhorted to train to be wise, but even with training, the spark of wisdom is considered to be divine.

Proverbs 8:17-21 states that Wisdom confers wealth. Lest this chapter seem to be about only high philosophical matters, this section brings it back down to the practical realm. The verb translated by NRSV to seek diligently, שחר, certainly has this meaning, and, in this context, it is probably the primary one, but a secondary meaning is to seek early. Young minds are most able to grasp instruction and build their lives on it.

The first word in 8:18 for riches or wealth, עשר, is the generic word, whereas the word in the second colon, הון, is used primarily in Wisdom literature. Honor or splendor, כבוד, is often paired with עשר (3:16; 22:4). (See the Excursus on Honor and Shame at 3:35.)

The final word in this line, צדקה, normally means integrity (righteousness),[176] but in this context, parallel to words describing material wealth, it seems to have a financial meaning. Verse 19 contains a "better than" proverb, though here the second line does not have the more valuable comparison, since normally gold is considered more valuable than silver. Even though wisdom does confer wealth and honor, her fruit is better than these things. Verse 20 returns to the imagery of paths and roads. Wisdom walks in the way of צדקה, the word that normally

---

175. See discussion of this phrase at 1:7.
176. See Translation Matters on Just/Integrity/Honesty (Righteous[ness]), צדקה/ צדק/צדיק/צדק, at 1:2.

means integrity but that at the end of 8:18 seems to mean something like prosperity. By repeating the word here, so close to its unusual use in 8:18, the significance may be to tie the meanings together as an ethical prosperity. That the word has its more common meaning here is made clear by the parallel term in the second colon, משפט, justice. The final verse in this section, 8:21, returns to the theme of Wisdom making those who love her wealthy. The term used for wealth in the first colon, יש, is used in this way only here. It is typically a particle of existence, meaning there is/are.

Wisdom's Speech Describing Her Part in Creation (8:22-36)

Proverbs 8:22-31 continues Wisdom's speech, begun in 8:1-21. In this famous section of her speech she establishes the primacy of her role in creation. The verb used in 8:22 is not the common verb for "create," ברא, as is used in Genesis 1:1, but rather קנה, which usually means acquire, but is used of God originating the heavens and the earth in Genesis 14:19 and 22.

Traces of Personified Wisdom in Early Christian Literature— Proverbs 8:22–36

Apart from the wider literary context of Proverbs 1–9, the personification of wisdom in Proverbs 8 attracted much attention in the first century CE. Of utmost importance was Proverbs' depiction of Wisdom as God's confidante, who existed "in the beginning," even before God created any primordial entities (vv. 22–31). In light of this passage, ancient interpreters understood the first-person plural forms of Genesis 1:26 as referring to God and his cocreator, Wisdom,[177] authorizing the female figure's divine status and her powerful role in the creation of the universe. In turn, the Jewish wisdom tradition developed various theological ideas about Wisdom, depicting her as God's breath, emanation, image, power, and spirit; the source of life; and an instructor of wisdom and knowledge who descends into the world to enlighten humanity.[178] No doubt, early Christians inherited these ideas, yet the ways in which they conceptualized Wisdom are much more diverse than one might imagine.

One of the trajectories that took shape in the beginning of Christianity is an understanding that Jesus is Wisdom incarnate.

177. Gen 1:26 reads, "let *us* make humankind in *our* image, according to *our* likeness."
178. Prov 8:12-36; Sir 24:1-22; Wis 5–10; also Bar 3:9–4:4; 1 En 42:1-2.

Prov 8:22-36

²²The LORD created me at the beginning of his work, the first of his acts of long ago.
²³Ages ago I was set up, at the first, before the beginning of the earth.
²⁴When there were no depths I was brought forth, when there were no springs abounding with water.
²⁵Before the mountains had been shaped, before the hills, I was brought forth—
²⁶when he had not yet made earth and fields, or the world's first bits of soil.
²⁷When he established the heavens, I was there, when he drew a circle on the face of the deep,
²⁸when he made firm the skies above, when he established the fountains of the deep,

---

Adapted from contemporaneous Hellenistic Jewish thought (e.g., Philo) is the idea that Sophia (σοφία, "wisdom" in Greek) can be identified with the Word (Logos, λόγος) by which God created the whole universe and through which God mediates between the heavens and this world.[179] Different traces of this incorporation of Sophia, Logos, and Jesus are found in Luke 10:21-22 and Matthew 11:25-26,[180] the Johannine Prologue (John 1:1-5),[181] and some of the Pauline epistles. For instance, an early form of Christology preserved in Philippians 2 mirrors the salvific patterns of heavenly Sophia, presenting Christ as the one who preexisted and was coeval with God. First Corinthians also notes that "Christ Jesus . . . became for us σοφία from God" (1:30), and this wisdom existed "before the ages" (2:7). Unlike Paul, however, who finds the manifestation of Sophia in Jesus' suffering and death, his Corinthian audience, including female prophets, engross themselves in different aspects of Sophia, focusing on her roles as the source of life

---

179. See Daniel Boyarin, "The Gospel of the Memra: Jewish Binitarianism and the Prologue to John," *HTR* 94 (2001): 244–84.

180. From the so-called Q source. See Elisabeth Schüssler Fiorenza, *Jesus: Miriam's Child, Sophia's Prophet; Critical Issues in Feminist Christology* (New York: Continuum, 1994), 133–61.

181. Eldon Jay Epp, "Wisdom, Torah, Word: The Johannine Prologue and the Purpose of the Fourth Gospel," in *Current Issues in Biblical and Patristic Interpretation: Studies in Honor of Merrill C. Tenney Presented by His Former Students*, ed. Gerald F. Hawthorne (Grand Rapids, MI: Eerdmans, 1974), 130.

Prov 8:22-36 (cont.)

²⁹when he assigned to the sea its
limit,
  so that the waters might not
      transgress his command,
when he marked out the foundations
      of the earth,
³⁰then I was beside him, like a
    master worker;
and I was daily his delight,
  rejoicing before him always,
³¹rejoicing in his inhabited world
  and delighting in the human
      race.

³²"And now, my children, listen to me:
  happy are those who keep my
     ways.
³³Hear instruction and be wise,
  and do not neglect it.
³⁴Happy is the one who listens to me,
  watching daily at my gates,
  waiting beside my doors.
³⁵For whoever finds me finds life
  and obtains favor from the Lord;
³⁶but those who miss me injure
    themselves;
  all who hate me love death."

and an empowering principle that makes all of them wise, powerful, and glorious.[182] Nevertheless, the feminine images and roles of Sophia seem to be overshadowed by the kyriarchal Adam-Christ typology, as Paul sees the last Adam, Christ, as a life-giving spirit, in whom "all will be made alive" (15:22, 45).

Early Christian understandings of the personified Wisdom became more diversified between the second and fourth centuries CE. The Nag Hammadi codices contain several mythical stories that present different interpretations of Sophia in their radical retellings of the creation story in Genesis.[183] These writings distinguish the female Sophia from the male Christ and hypostasize her different attributes into various female figures, sometimes by amalgamating the characteristics of Sophia and Eve.[184] For instance, the *Apocryphon of John* casts Pronoia, the divine Mother(-Father) in the heavenly realm,[185] in a role most similar to Wisdom in

182. 1 Cor 4:8-12; 12:1-11; compare Prov 8:32-36; Wis 7:22-28; 10:21.

183. See, e.g., the *Apocryphon of John* (NHC II.1; III.1; IV.1), the *Hypostasis of the Archons* (II.4), *On the Origin of the Word* (II.5; XIII.2).

184. E.g., Pronoia, Epinoia, Pistis Sophia, Sophia, Zoe, Eve, Norea, and so on.

185. Pronoia is androgynous by nature, though she is constantly referred to with the female pronoun. Due to her androgynous identity (the Mother-Father), she is described with a variety of gendered images, such as the divine Mother (female), the first Human (male), the holy Spirit (male), the triple power (female), and so on.

Proverbs; Pronoia is the first to come forth, and she "became the womb for everything because she is prior to them all" (NHC 2.1.5).[186] In addition, to save humanity from the grip of the wicked rulers,[187] Pronoia descends to this earthly realm. Using her powers (e.g., Christ, the Spirit of Life), she enlightens humans and leads them into eternal life, which clearly corresponds to the instructive and salvific roles of Wisdom in the Jewish wisdom tradition.[188]

The kyriarchal ethos of traditional Christianity has long undermined the powerful images of Wisdom in Proverbs. Nevertheless, from personified Sophia in Hellenistic Jewish literature to Pronoia in early Christianity, the colorful traces of Wisdom invite us to reclaim her life-giving power in contemporary theological conversations. Her transformative roles in creation, revelation, and redemption are much needed in today's world—a world that seems more broken, polluted, and unjust than ever.

Eunyung Lim

TRANSLATION MATTERS

In 8:23, "I was set up," נִסַּכְתִּי (*nissaktî*), from נסך, occurs only here in the *Niphal*, a passive verb pattern. Its one other occurrence is in the *Qal* verb pattern in Psalm 2:6, where it refers to installing a king. Another possibility is to revocalize as a *Niphal* from סכך, meaning "was woven," i.e., "was formed": נְסַכֹּתִי (*nĕsakkōtî*, BHS; see Ps 139:13). Perhaps both verbs were intended to be heard as a play on words.

Although this section is evocative of the prologue to the Gospel of John ("In the beginning was the Word [Logos], and the Word was with God, and the Word was God"; see also Col 1:15-20 and Heb 1:1-3), there are significant differences.

---

186. Pronoia is "the first [power which was] before all of them . . . and it was she who praised [the Father], because thanks to him she had come forth. This is the first thought, his image; she became the womb of everything for it is she who is prior to them all."

187. By contrast, Sophia in the *Apocryphon of John* is integrated with the figure of Eve in Genesis. While Sophia's status as a female deity is maintained and she possesses the life-giving spirit ("Zoe"), she violates the rule of the divine world by producing her son, Yaldabaoth, without her male consort's consent. As Yaldabaoth becomes the God of this world and is full of lustful desires, injustice, and ignorance, Sophia's transgression, echoing Eve's decision to eat the forbidden fruit, signals the rupture between the heavenly realm and this earthly world.

188. E.g., Prov 3:17; 8:33-36; Wis 8:17.

Wisdom is portrayed as a *personification* of a divine attribute in Prov-
erbs, as if one gave life and personality to the abstract quality of justice;
God is still depicted *creating* divine Wisdom at the beginning of creation.
Proverbs; John 1:1-18; Colossians 1:15-20; and Hebrews 1:13 all arguably
depict Wisdom/Word (*Logos*)/Christ as the agent through whom God
created the world (see below for discussion of Prov 8:30). All except for
John depict Wisdom/*Logos*/Christ as the firstborn of creation, where
Logos in John 1:1-4 is not created at all but is generally understood to be
coequal with God, though was not always interpreted as such before
Nicaea.[189] In Proverbs, however, Wisdom is a personified figure, whereas
in Colossians 1:15-20 and in Hebrews 1:1-3, Jesus is the image of God.
The similarities and differences may be easier to see in a table.

Text	First Born	Agent of Creation	Personification	Image of God	Equal to God
Prov 8:22-31	X	X	X		
Col 1:15-20	X	X		X	
Heb 1:1-3	X	X		X	
John 1:1-18		X			X

189. The Jewish philosopher Philo is willing to have the Logos referred to as God,
but only when *Theos* is anarthrous; any reference to *Theos* without a definite article
is a reference to the Logos, but not to God.

> It is the true God that is meant by the use of the article, the expression being, "I am the
> God (*ho Theos*)"; but when the word is used incorrectly [that is, more figuratively], it is put
> without the article, the expression being, "He who was seen by thee in the place," not of
> the God (*tou Theou*), but simply "of God" (*Theou*); and what he here calls God is his most
> ancient word. (*On Dreams* 1.39.1.229-30 in *The Works of Philo*, trans. C. D. Younge [Peabody,
> MA: Hendrickson, 1993], 385.)

Philo even says that the Logos is a second god (*Questions and Answers on Genesis*
2, 62). Before the Council of Nicaea, everyone followed the Logos theory of Philo
as expressed in Christian terms by Origen. He used the same distinction that Philo
made; God the Father was The God, *ho theos* with the definite article, while the Logos
was merely *theos*, God as a courtesy title. Origen was a subordinationist, the Logos
was God, but only insofar as he directed all of his attention to God. (*Commentary on
the Gospel of John: Books 1–10; 2, 17–18*, trans. Ronald E. Heine [Washington, DC: The
Catholic University of America Press, 1989], 99.) This was consistent with his Philonic
stance. Deviating just enough from Philo to allow the Logos to be incarnate, Origen
kept the rest of Philo's distinctions—Jesus was not quite God. (Unpublished paper
presented at 2017 Mid-Atlantic Regional SBL by Jeff Nicoll.)

Proverbs 8:24-25 is particularly interesting because the verb, חוֹלָלְתִּי, found in each of these verses, means to be brought forth from the womb and thus is presumably a feminine image of God, or at the least God is being depicted as a midwife. Verses 26-31 establish the breadth of Wisdom's presence in God's creative activity, from the micro level of dust to the macro level of sky and the deep. Verse 28 reflects the ancient belief that there was a half-spherical dome over the earth, the firmament, רָקִיע, which separated the waters above the earth from those under the earth (Gen 1:6). Proverbs 8:29 in similar fashion indicates the way in which God kept the sea within its prescribed space. A third colon in this verse, as emended to match the LXX, has God strengthening the foundations of the earth.

TRANSLATION MATTERS

In 8:29, חֻקּוֹ (*ḥuqo*) from חקק means to cut in, inscribe, but this is not how foundations were laid. Reading with the LXX and emending slightly (changing the ו to a ז and revocalizing) to חַזְּקוֹ (*ḥazzeqô*, with LXX and BHS), the colon becomes, "when he strengthened the foundations of the earth."

After this lengthy build-up, in 8:30-31 Wisdom says that she was beside God. The MT can be understood to mean that she was growing up.

TRANSLATION MATTERS

In 8:30, NRSV has emended the MT אָמוֹן (*'āmôn*) to אֹמֵן (*'ōmman*), but this is not necessary. The MT can be understood as an infinitive absolute, meaning growing up.[190]

---

190. Michael V. Fox, *Proverbs 1–9: A New Translation with Introduction and Commentary*, AB 18A (New York: Doubleday, 2000), 287. See also Crawford H. Toy, *A Critical and Exegetical Commentary on the Book of Proverbs*, ICC (New York: Scribner's Sons, 1899), 177–79, and Peter Schäfer, *Mirror of His Beauty: Feminine Images of God from the Bible to the Early Kabbalah* (Princeton, NJ: Princeton University Press, 2002), 23–28.

This fits in well with the remaining cola of the verse. God delighted, שעשעים, in her, as a parent would take pleasure in a maturing child, and Wisdom rejoiced, משחקת, before God always, as a daughter would do who was the apple of her parent's eye. Verse 31 indicates that the specific nature of Wisdom's joy is in humanity. Here Wisdom appears to be separate from God and may represent the blossoming of human understanding.

Proverbs 8:32-36 returns to the first part of chapter 8 and recounts Wisdom's call for a response. Verse 32 is one of several beatitude-like proverbs (see also 3:13; 8:34; 14:21; 16:20; 28:14; 29:18). A better translation than NRSV's "happy" might be "blissful."[191] Proverbs 8:33 could be paraphrased: "Accept discipline[192] to become wise. Don't avoid it." Following 8:32, the point is, to put it in modern parlance, "no pain, no gain." Verse 34 is another blissful proverb, this one spelling out what it means to listen. The details here are temporal and geographical: daily watching at Wisdom's gates is the recipe. Physical exercise for a few minutes once or twice a week won't do the job. Neither will it be the case with the attainment of wisdom. Verses 35-36 bring the section to a conclusion. Those who find Wisdom find life itself and divine favor. The chapter ends on an antithetical note: Those who miss the mark of wisdom, the same verbal root used for sin, חטא, do grave injury to themselves. By the same token, those who hate Wisdom, love death.

Wisdom's and Folly's Banquets (9:1-18)

Proverbs 9:1-18 concludes the first part of Proverbs with an exquisitely expressed choice between two ways: Wisdom and Folly. Chapter 7 opens dramatically with the seduction of the foolish young man on the first evening; chapter 8 shows Wisdom's reply and claim to authority, stated in the bright day; finally, chapter 9 completes the cinematic arc by showing Wisdom and Folly at the end of the second day. Verses 1-6 focus on Wisdom's banquet, and verses 13-18 on Folly's. The two passages are structurally parallel, as is indicated in the translation that follows.

Proverbs 9:1-3 describes Wisdom's setting and preparations for a banquet and that she cries out. On one level, the house that Wisdom has built is understood as a physical structure, albeit a metaphorical one, since it is the place where she hosts a banquet. On another level, houses

---

191. See Translation Matters on Blissful (Happy), אשרי, 3:13.

192. See Translation Matters on Discipline/Chastening/Correction (Instruction), מוסר, at 1:2.

Prov 9:1-18

¹<u>Wisdom</u> has built her **house**,	A	⁵"Come, eat of my **bread**	F
she has hewn her seven pillars.		and drink of the wine I have mixed.	
²She has slaughtered her animals,		⁶Lay aside immaturity, and <u>live</u>,	G
she has mixed her wine,	B	and walk in the way of insight."	
she has also set her table.		⁷Whoever corrects a scoffer wins abuse;	
³She has sent out her servant-girls,		whoever rebukes the wicked gets hurt.	
she **calls**	C	⁸A scoffer who is rebuked will only hate you;	
from the **highest places in the town,**	D	the wise, when rebuked, will love you.	
⁴**"You that are simple, turn in here!"**	E		
To those without sense she says,			

in Proverbs represent family. The number seven is a number of completion in Hebrew. A house with seven columns (9:1b) would have been a grand house and its seven pillars signaled its perfection. Verse 2 gives us a glimpse into the preparations. The ancient Hebrews were not wealthy. They did not eat meat except on special occasions when they had an animal slaughtered. Wisdom is depicted as a wealthy woman with meat to serve at her banquet. She also mixes her wine, probably with spices (see Song 8:2), making a tasty drink for her guests.

TRANSLATION MATTERS

In 9:1, as in 1:20-33, the word for Wisdom is plural, חכמות, rather than the regular singular, חכמה.[193] The verb and possessive pronoun on the direct object associated with it are both feminine singular, so the word must be a kind of plural of majesty, like the Hebrew word for God, *Elohim*.

Also in 9:1, with a slight emendation of a ח (*ḥêt*) to a ה (*hê*) and a revocalization, MT's חָצְבָה (*ḥāṣĕbâ*) can be read as הִצִּיבָה (*hiṣîbâ*), a *Hiphil* verb pattern from נצב, meaning to set up, which is a more reasonable meaning for columns than hew out.[194]

193. See Translation Matters on Wisdom, חכמה, at 1:1.
194. Fox, *Proverbs 1–9*, 296–97.

Prov 9:1-18 (cont.)

[9]Give instruction to the wise, and they will become wiser still; teach the righteous and they will gain in learning. [10]The fear of the LORD is the beginning of wisdom, and the knowledge of the Holy One is insight. [11]For by me your days will be multiplied, and years will be added to your life. [12]If you are wise, you are wise for yourself; if you scoff, you alone will bear it. [13]The <u>foolish woman</u> is loud; she is ignorant and knows nothing.

[14]She sits at the door of her **house,** A'
on a seat at the **high places of the town,** D'
[15]calling to those who pass by, C'
who are going straight on their way, E'
[16]**"You who are simple, turn in here!"**
And to those without sense she says,
[17]"Stolen water is sweet, F'
and **bread** eaten in secret is pleasant."
[18]But they do not know that the <u>dead</u> are there, G'
that her guests are in the depths of Sheol.

After these preparations are complete, Wisdom sets her table. Finally, she sends her young women, i.e., her servant girls, to call out from the heights of the town. Again, the fact that she has servants to send on this errand shows her wealth. Their announcement of her invitation recalls her own crying out to young men throughout the town in 8:1-3.

Proverbs 9:4-6 comprises the invitation to her banquet. Wisdom has a special fondness for the simple, naive, humble people, פתי, for they are the first ones invited to turn aside (9:4a). The verb is often used of turning aside to a bad path, but in the context, it is clearly used in the opposite sense; they are to turn aside from the foolish path they are on to come to Wisdom's house. Wisdom addresses herself (through her servant girls) to those lacking heart/mind.[195] They are in much the same category as the simple ones, not malicious, just not very bright. The bread and mixed wine that Wisdom commands her invitees to eat and drink are metaphors for the spiritual substance she offers. This section concludes with an adjuration to the simple and mindless to forsake simplemindedness, פתאים, so that they might live, to walk straight, אשרו, on the path of understanding, בינה.

Proverbs 9:7-10 seems to be a later insertion with instructions for the teacher. Verses 7-8 deal with some of the hazards of the teaching profes-

---

195. See Translation Matters on the Heart, לב, at 2:2.

sion. (See the introduction, on the social setting of Proverbs, for a discussion of the evidence relating to the question of whether and to what degree women may have been teachers in ancient Judah.) Those who try to admonish a scoffer or scorner, לץ, will receive dishonor (קלון, 9:7a). Similarly, the one who rebukes the corrupt individual (wicked)[196] will end up with a stained character, מום. The word means physical blemish but, in parallel with קלון, seems to represent the shame created by the repulse of the student. Verse 8 continues along the same lines. Proverbs 9:8a admonishes not to bother disciplining a scoffer at all, because such a person will only hate you. Proverbs 9:8b provides the antithesis: the wise, who might not seem to need to be rebuked in the first place, are eager to improve and thus prefer teachers who give them constructive criticism. Thus, 9:9 similarly indicates that those who are on the path to wisdom will become wiser still when they are taught; in the same way, the just (righteous)[197] will become more learned when they are instructed. Verse 10 brings this short interruption to a close with a couplet that is reminiscent of 1:7.

This suggests the possibility that this was the original ending for chapters 1–9. Proverbs 9:11 could be the end of wisdom's speech in 9:4-6. The emphasis on lengthening of days and years being added to one's life fits in very well with 9:6.

Proverbs 9:12 seems to be a later addition, though the word "scoff" makes it somewhat compatible with 9:7-10; however, the focus is different. It is also not clear what it means to be wise for oneself versus bearing one's scoffing alone, except that wisdom is a positive trait and scoffing a negative one that ultimately attaches to one's character in a negative way.

Proverbs 9:13-18 describes the banquet of the woman of folly (אשת כסילות). She is the opposite of Wisdom (9:1). This woman is foolish in the sense that she is ignorant (כסילות),[198] simple-minded (פתיות), and does not know anything, but, interestingly, her folly is not of the worst sort, אולת. Throughout the remainder of the book of Proverbs where the English word "Folly" is used, it is translating אולת, the worst sort of foolishness that is based on corruption, rather than the type that is a result primarily of ignorance (כסיל), found here.

---

196. See Translation Matters on Corrupt[ion]/Unscrupulous/Reprehensible (Wicked[ness]), רשע/רשעים, at 2:22.

197. See Translation Matters on Just/Integrity/Honesty (Righteous[ness]), צדקה/צדק/צדיק, at 1:2.

198. See Translation Matters on Dolt/Chump/Oaf/Inept (Fool), כסיל, at 1:22.

Note that she is simple-minded, while Wisdom summons the simple, פתי, as her guests because they need her. Folly is loud and boisterous (המיה, see also 7:11). There are some parallels between Wisdom and Folly: both have houses (9:1, 14), can be found in the heights of the town (8:2; 9:3, 14), and call to passers-by (8:4; 9:4-5, 15).

It is also interesting to note that Wisdom and Folly both seem to own homes. This is consistent with the picture painted in 31:16, in which the strong woman/wife (capable wife)[199] buys real estate. Although Wisdom, at least, is depicted as an elite woman, Folly may be pictured with less lofty social status. Nevertheless, she has a home. This may have been possible, even if she is not wealthy, because after the exile, most of the elite Judahites were taken into exile, leaving the poorer people behind, who we may presume took over the land and became de facto owners in the generations while the elite were gone. It may even be that Folly is imagined as one of those left behind who had developed different ways of living during the intervening years and thus were considered strange, both ethnically and sexually.

Today, it is not so different. The wealthy often do not have any idea how the poorer strata of society manage their affairs. The poor seem strange to the elites, with their high rates of single-parent families, usually headed by a woman, drug use, etc., though these realities now impinge on much of the middle class as well.

Folly's words in 9:16 are an almost direct quotation of Wisdom's in 9:4:

> "You that are simple, turn in here!"
> To those without sense she says.

Of course, what Folly says to her audience is quite different from what Wisdom says. Whereas Wisdom invites her audience to come, eat, and drink (openly) in 9:5, Folly's invitation in 9:17 must be imagined as whispered. Strangely, she only proffers water, not mixed wine like Wisdom has on offer, but because her water is stolen, she says it is sweet. Similarly, the claim she makes for her bread is that it is bread of utmost secrecy and is thus tasty. It is eaten in secret, presumably because it too has been pilfered and therefore cannot be eaten in the open. The section closes on a somber note. The invitees don't know that the guests at Folly's banquet are the shades, רפאים, who inhabit the underworld where the dead go. In chapter 7, Folly carefully baits a trap for a young man; in chapter 9, she brazenly bids for all who ignore Wisdom's call. In both cases, the end is the same.

---

199. See Translation Matters on Strong Woman/Wife (Capable Wife), אשת־חיל, at 12:4.

Part 2
Proverbs 10:1–22:16

Two Collections: One Marked by Antithetical Parallelism, the Other by Focus on the Royal Court

Introduction

Chapters 10–29 are the core of Proverbs, comprising parts 2 and 3, which are further broken down into smaller segments. The first impression is that part 2, Proverbs 10:1–22:16, represents the conservative character often thought to pervade Proverbs. It is in this collection where we find several of the sayings about quarrelsome and contentious wives (19:13; 21:9, 19). Yet by framing sections 2 through 4b with the depiction of divine Wisdom (part 1), on the one hand, and the teaching of Lemuel's mother to her son (part 4c) and the acrostic poem in praise of the Woman of Strength (Capable Wife)[1] in part 5, on the other, the negative stereotypes are undercut. Although chapter 10 has the superscription, "The Proverbs of Solomon," few of the proverbs in this collection are attributable to Solomon. (See the introduction, on author and date, for a discussion of this issue.) Unlike chapters 1–9 and

---

1. See Translation Matters on Strong Woman/Wife (Capable Wife), אשת־חיל, at 12:4.

31, which are made up primarily of longer literary units directed to the immature son (child),[2] this material is made up of short sayings. While 1–9 and 31 are primarily intended for urban elites, the proverbs in this section reflect both urban and rural origins, elite and folk traditions. This section is full of antithetical parallelism, where the second colon of a verse says the opposite (in some) sense of the first one.

Part 2a
A Collection Marked by Antithetic Parallelism
(10:1–15:33)

YHWH Upholds the Just, but Diligence Helps (10:1-5)

Proverbs 10:1-5 introduce the cluster and the Solomonic collection. They have a chiastic pattern: ABCB'A', emphasizing the central message of the cluster of proverbs: YHWH upholds the just (righteous).[3] The B-B' lines of the structure speak to the importance of hard work and integrity (righteousness) and the A-A' lines tie the whole package together with the key word "wise son" (child, בֵּן).[4] A wise son recognizes the importance of hard work and integrity but also understands that ultimately it is God who upholds the just. Such a child makes both mother and father happy. This was especially true in the ancient world when children were parents' pension plans and social security rolled into one. Life tended to be short for both men and women: for men due to war and other types of hostility and for women due to childbirth. In the preexilic period, if women outlived their husbands, then it was especially important that their sons be in an economic position to take care of them, since in many cases an older woman was in no position to fend for herself due to a combination of economic and legal restrictions on how she could earn a living and the simple limitations of age, especially in a largely agricultural economy. By the time Proverbs came into final form, women's rights to own property seem to have become greater, judging from 31:16 and extrabiblical sources, and their ability to inherit seems to have expanded, judging in part from

2. See Translation Matters on Son (Child), בֵּן, at 1:8.
3. See Translation Matters on Just/Integrity/Honesty (Righteous[ness]), צדקה/צדיק/צדק, at 1:2.
4. See Translation Matters on Son (Child), בֵּן, at 1:8.

Prov 10:1-5

¹The proverbs of Solomon
A wise child makes a glad father,　A
　　but a foolish child is a mother's
　　　　grief.
²Treasures gained by wickedness do
　　not profit,　　　　　　　　B
　　but righteousness delivers from
　　　　death.
³The Lord does not let the righteous
　　go hungry,　　　　　　　　C
but he thwarts the craving of the
　　wicked.
⁴A slack hand causes
　　poverty,　　　　　　　　　B'
　　but the hand of the diligent makes
　　　　rich.
⁵A child who gathers in summer is
　　prudent,　　　　　　　　　A'
　　but a child who sleeps in harvest
　　　　brings shame.

concerns about Jewish men marrying foreign women (see Ezra 9–10; Neh 13:23-27). Nevertheless, the importance of children, and especially sons, to the economic welfare of parents reflects a peasant reality that did not change much over the centuries.

TRANSLATION MATTERS

The nouns in 10:4 are not marked as subject or object, and thus the line can be read as NRSV translates it, or as the converse: poverty causes a slack hand.

A כסיל, a dolt, a (fool[ish]) son, could be disastrous, whereas a wise, industrious one, a boon. The cluster focuses on the relationship of diligence/laziness and wealth/poverty. NRSV translates 10:4a, "A slack hand causes poverty"; the phrase may also be translated as, "Poverty causes a slack hand." It is possible that the saying was intended to have a double meaning, even though the primary meaning was likely that laziness results in poverty. The attitude of the sages toward wealth and poverty was not as simplistic as is sometimes thought. Diligence was certainly considered meritorious, and sloth, immoral and stupid. This cluster asserts that God takes care of the just (see also 15:6). Other proverbs, however, indicate ambivalence toward wealth. There are warnings against greed (21:26) and against relying over much on wealth (11:4, 28). Also, God cares for the poor (3:34).

Attitudes today are just as varied. From one extreme of those who think that all social ills are a result of individual responsibility or failure thereof to the other extreme who would deny individuals responsibility and blame society for the problems of ethnic minorities and the poor, opinions cross the board. Although many commentators suggest that the writers and/or editors of the book of Proverbs were on the conservative end of the spectrum, a closer and more nuanced reading of the proverbs, paying attention to the contrasts and positioning of the contradictory sayings on wealth and poverty, can produce a more sophisticated reading. It is important not to cherry-pick the proverbs to get a desired result but to look at all of the proverbs on various subjects and to see them in their contexts in the book as a whole before making a judgment on the perspective of the sages.

Integrity Is the Foundation of True Security (10:6-11)

Another chiastic structure can be seen in this cluster (ABCB'A'). Whereas 10:1-5 focuses primarily on the importance of diligence, the emphasis in 10:6-11 is on integrity. This can be seen from 10:9 (C), the center of the chiastic structure:

> Whoever walks in integrity walks securely,
>> but whoever follows crooked (perverse) ways[5] will be found out.

That integrity requires the entire human body is spelled out in each line of this cluster. It begins with the statement that blessings are on the head of the just (righteous)[6] and its antithesis that the mouth of the corrupt (wicked)[7] conceals violence. This second colon may be understood grammatically in addition to NRSV's rendering as violence covers (better: coats) the mouth of the corrupt. Both meanings may have been understood. The corrupt (wicked) try and often succeed in concealing the violence that their mouths speak, but to discerning eyes their mouths are coated in violence, like too much makeup badly applied. Verse 6 is paralleled by the last line, 10:11, which shares the identical second colon. The first colon states the opposite, that the mouth of the just (righteous) is a fountain of life. Given the dry conditions of ancient Palestine, the metaphor of a fountain of life is a rich one. Verse 7 continues with a second antithesis, that the memory of the just (righteous) is a blessing, whereas the name, i.e., the reputation, of the corrupt (wicked) will rot. The third antithesis is in 10:8: those who are wise of heart/mind[8] will obey command(ment)s. The translation "commandments" in 10:8 as opposed to "commands" suggests divine commands, but the Hebrew is more inclusive than this. לֵב is really closer

---

5. The word translated as "perverse," עקשׁ, literally means twisted.

6. See Translation Matters on Just/Integrity/Honesty (Righteous[ness]), צדקה/צדיק/צדק, at 1:2.

7. See Translation Matters on Corrupt/Unscrupulous/Reprehensible (Wicked), רשׁע/רשׁעים, at 2:22.

8. See Translation Matters on the Heart, לֵב, at 2:2.

Prov 10:6-11

⁶Blessings are on the head of the **righteous**,
but the **mouth** of the **wicked conceals violence**.
⁷The memory of the **righteous** is a blessing,   A
but the name of the wicked will rot.
⁸The wise of heart will heed commandments,   B
but a babbling fool will come to ruin.

⁹Whoever walks in integrity walks securely,   C
but whoever follows perverse ways will be found out.
¹⁰Whoever winks the eye causes trouble,   B'
but the one who rebukes boldly makes peace.
¹¹The **mouth** of the **righteous** is a fountain of life,   A'
but the **mouth of the wicked conceals violence**.

---

to "mind" than "heart." It is a matter not simply of intelligence, however, but of a combination of intelligence and prudence, for which we do not have a perfect English word. The contrast with the loose-lipped (blabbering) jerk (fool)[9] seems to be that one who is constantly spreading unsavory gossip will not be able to hear command(ment)s.

In 10:10 the antitheses are reversed and the description of the evil person leads, followed by that of the good person. The idea of eye winking as a cause of pain (10:10) is paralleled in 6:13 and Sirach 27:22. The one who rebukes boldly (implicitly, using the lips), following NRSV and LXX, in many circumstances serves the wrongdoer and society better than one who winks at the offense. The one who rebukes boldly makes peace, in the deepest sense of peace—not as evidenced in the immediate lack of tension, but by removing the injustice that makes true peace impossible. Rebuking boldly sometimes seems more difficult for women than men, but it does not require loud words or strident tone; rather, the truth spoken clearly, thoughtfully, and, if possible, compassionately, carries great weight. (See Women's Sins 1: Arrogance, at 3:8.)

TRANSLATION MATTERS

The NRSV translation of 10:10b is taken from the LXX rather than the MT; the LXX reads: ὁ δὲ ἐλέγχων μετὰ παρρησίας εἰρηνοποιεῖ ("but the one who reproves with confidence makes peace").

The MT says literally: that the foolish (אֱוִיל) of lips will be cast down or away. (See below for discussion.)

---

9. See Translation Matters on Jerk/Schmuck/Folly (Fool/Folly), אֱוִיל/אִוֶּלֶת, at 1:7.

TRANSLATION MATTERS

The nouns in 10:11 are not marked as subject or object, and thus the line can be read as NRSV translates it, "the mouth of the corrupt (wicked) conceals violence," or "violence covers (כסה) the mouth of the corrupt (wicked)."

The Wages of Justice Lead to Life (10:12-18)

This cluster of proverbs is marked by an *inclusio* in 10:12 and 10:18:

> ¹²Hatred stirs up strife,
>   but love **covers** [תכסה] all offenses.
> ¹⁸Lying lips **conceal** [תכסה] hatred,
>   and whoever utters slander is a fool.

As was the case in 10:6b and 10:11b, 10:18 could also mean that hatred covers lying lips, i.e., that the hatred that motivates a person's speech covers their lips like bad makeup. Makeup when applied properly is not discernible and subtly enhances the face. Badly applied makeup is obvious, obscuring the natural beauty rather than enhancing it and, in the worst cases, is downright grotesque. A person may think that their hatred is not obvious, but over time it will be written all over their face and it will become distorted in very sad ways. Both meanings of the proverb may have been intended and heard. A person may try to and often successfully hide unsavory motivations, but at least some of the time discerning individuals can read them on their faces. Thus, the second part of 10:18 follows: whoever utters slander is a jerk (fool).[10] In the middle of this cluster is 10:15:

> The wealth of the rich is their fortress;
>   the poverty of the poor is their ruin.

This verse would seem to be a long way from the concerns of 10:12 and 10:18, but it reminds the reader that material wealth and its absence was and is important to one's spiritual well-being. The second colon may have a slightly different nuance than the way NRSV renders it. The word translated as "ruin," מחתה, can mean ruin, but this is not its first meaning. The most common definition is terror or the object of terror. What this means is not that poverty is the ruin of the poor but rather that

10. See Translation Matters on Jerk/Schmuck/Folly (Fool/Folly), אויל/אולת, at 1:7.

Prov 10:12-18

¹²Hatred stirs up strife,
  but love covers all offenses.
¹³On the lips of one who has
    understanding wisdom is found,
  but a rod is for the back of one
    who lacks sense.
¹⁴The wise lay up knowledge,
  but the babbling of a fool brings
    ruin near.
¹⁵The wealth of the rich is their
    fortress;

the poverty of the poor is their ruin.
¹⁶The wage of the righteous leads to
  life,
  the gain of the wicked to sin.
¹⁷Whoever heeds instruction is on the
    path to life,
  but one who rejects a rebuke
    goes astray.
¹⁸Lying lips conceal hatred,
  and whoever utters slander is a
    fool.

poverty causes terror, because when one is on the verge of starvation or otherwise *in extremis*, it is difficult not to be in fear of one's life. These are statements of fact, but compare 10:29, which suggests that the way of YHWH is the (true) stronghold and that doing evil rather than poverty is the true source of terror, and 18:11, which begins like 10:15 and then undercuts the colon by saying that it is (only) in his imagination!

The verses surrounding 10:15 also bear on its meaning. Verse 14 ends with the warning that the mouthing off (babbling) of jerks brings ruin (or terror) near (using the exact same word as in 10:15, מחתה). Just as the rich find security in their wealth and the poor experience terror for lack of means (10:15), so also the wise store treasure, צפן, in the form of knowledge, while the jerk (fool) runs his mouth, resulting in ruin or at least terror that he will soon be ruined.

Like 10:14, 10:16 begins with the advice that the wage (or more literally the deeds or output) of the just leads to life. Life here does not mean eternal life but rather a long life on planet earth. The second colon states the antithesis, that the gain of the corrupt (wicked)[11] leads to sin, but given the parallelism, sin here is meant to be understood as leading to the opposite of a long happy life, i.e., to an early grave.

Thus, 10:15, which states the morally neutral fact that the wealth of the rich is their security and the poverty of the poor, their terror, is placed in the context of proverbs that make it clear that the only way to gain wealth that will lead to a long and happy life is to do it honestly and

11. See Translation Matters on Corrupt[ion]/Unscrupulous/Reprehensible (Wicked[ness]), רשע/רשעים, at 2:22.

wisely. This does not mean, however, that all poor people have become poor because they are dishonest or unwise. Verse 17 focuses on what kind of behavior leads to long life or its opposite with another proverb of a similar type, suggesting that whoever listens to instruction will live long and whoever rejects a rebuke will go astray. As indicated above, this is parallel to 10:13 in the chiastic structure.

Having seen how 10:13-17 fit together, the only remaining question is how 10:12-18 works thematically. Verse 12 focuses on the problem of hatred and the strife it stirs up, and verse 18 on the specific problem of slander, a result of hatred, which the author says is the action of a dolt (fool).[12] Since the behavior of jerks is mentioned explicitly in 10:14 and implicitly in 10:13 and 10:17, it seems that the editor has brought these verses together to indicate that the corrupt generally and all kinds of fools in particular behave in such a way as to bring economic ruin and an early grave upon themselves. The wise and just (righteous),[13] on the other hand, live in a manner that results in wealth and long life. That life is more complicated than this is indicated by at least one way of reading 10:15, that the wealthy's fortress is an illusion. In addition, if the poor are just, their wage will lead to life, and if the wealthy are evil, theirs will lead in the opposite direction (10:16). What this meant in practical terms is not clear, but the sages were not abstract philosophers; they understood life in concrete, though highly moral, terms.

The Prudent/Just/Wise Speak Little, but Their Words Are Silver (10:19-22)

This cluster of proverbs is held together by words for speech and speaking (דברים, "words, speech," 10:19; לשון, "tongue," 10:20; שפתי, "lips," 10:21) and words describing the just (righteous)[14] (צדיק, 10:20-21) and prudent (משכיל, 10:19) as well as the opposite, the corrupt (wicked; רשעים)[15] and jerks (foolish; אוילים)[16] in 10:20-21. It links with the last

---

12. See Translation Matters on Dolt/Chump/Oaf/Inept (Fool), כסיל, at 1:22.

13. See Translation Matters on Just/Integrity/Honesty (Righteous[ness]), צדקה/צדיק/צדק, at 1:2.

14. See Translation Matters on Just/Integrity/Honesty (Righteous[ness]), צדקה/צדיק/צדק, at 1:2.

15. See Translation Matters on Corrupt[ion]/Unscrupulous/Reprehensible (Wicked[ness]), רשע/רשעים, at 2:22.

16. See Translation Matters on Jerk/Schmuck/Folly (Fool/Folly), אויל/אולת, at 1:7.

Prov 10:19-22

¹⁹When words are many, transgression is not lacking, but the prudent are restrained in speech. ²⁰The tongue of the righteous is choice silver; the mind of the wicked is of little worth. ²¹The lips of the righteous feed many, but fools die for lack of sense. ²²The blessing of the LORD makes rich, and he adds no sorrow with it.

cluster, which also has the word "lips" (שפה, 10:13, 18) and the related words "babbling" (פי־אויל, 10:14, literally, mouth of jerks) and "slander" (דבה, 10:18), as well as words for wise/just (נבון, חכמים, צדיק, 10:13, 14, 16), and jerks again (אוילים, 10:13, 14, 16, 18). Thus, the core concept here—that the prudent/just/wise speak little, but what they do say, which is refined, valuable, and contributes to the general welfare—relates backward to the kind of person who tends to become wealthy and constitutes wealth in itself.

TRANSLATION MATTERS

The Hebrew עצב in 10:22 means "pain," "hurt," or "toil," not "sorrow." The idea that God would add sorrow to a blessing does not seem plausible. Why would the author of the proverb have set up such a straw man only to knock it down? There is a similar issue in the King James Version of Genesis 3:16, where this word is translated as "sorrow": "I will greatly multiply thy sorrow and thy conception; in *sorrow* [עצב] thou shalt bring forth children" (emphasis mine). The KJV translation is preferable to the NRSV, which reads "I will greatly increase your pangs in childbearing; in pain you shall bring forth children," because it does not include the idea of labor pains. The Hebrew word הריון that the KJV translates as "conception" refers to the beginning of the childbearing process, not the end, and thus childbearing pangs is impossible, as Carol Meyers points out.[17] Still, the word "sorrow" in both cola of the KJV is unfortunate. The Hebrew words both come from the same root and both have a primary meaning of toil, especially agricultural toil, tinged with the oppressiveness of harsh physical labor. Thus, "and toil adds nothing to it" is to be preferred to the NRSV translation of Proverbs 10:22 on multiple grounds.

17. Carol L. Meyers, *Discovering Eve: Ancient Israelite Women in Context* (New York: Oxford University Press, 1988), 99–103.

The first colon of the last line in this cluster, 10:22, "the blessing of YHWH makes rich," is a reminder that ultimately no human effort, whether just behavior, wisdom, or toil, is sufficient to make one rich. Without God's blessing, the proverb asserts, our labor is in vain. The NRSV translation of the second colon of this line, "and he adds no sorrow with it," is implausible (see Translation Matters). The alternative "and toil adds nothing to it" is preferable. Given the praise of diligence in 10:1-5, it is not possible that this is a put-down of all hard work. The point may simply be that from an ultimate perspective we have what we have in large measure because of the gifts we have received from others: our parents, our teachers, our culture, and those from other cultures and other times who have contributed to our wealth. Our efforts are very small in comparison. People who are fortunate in their material well-being should not become arrogant.

You Just Can't Get Good Help (10:23-28)

The beginning of this cluster is marked by another chiastic structure pivoting around the lazy employee (10:26). Words indicating mostly positive emotions (sport, pleasure, desire) but also one negative one (dread) are found in the opening and closing lines. The B and B' lines focus on longevity or lack thereof. The central line is concerned with lazy employees, who are irritants to their employers and whose behavior is compared to strong vinegar on the teeth or smoke in the eyes. The opening line contrasts the behavior and attitudes of dolts (fools)[18] and the wise. Dolts carry out evil plots (wrong, זמה) as if they were games. What this suggests is that even though dolts are not as bad as jerks, in that they are mainly inept and stupid, they are still morally deficient and can actively do harm. The antithesis is that those with understanding derive genuine pleasure from wise conduct. The cluster ends on a similar note, that the hope of the just (righteous)[19] ends in gladness and the expectations of the corrupt come to nothing. In the context, lazy employees are a variety of fools, who will not survive for long, regardless of their motivations.

---

18. See Translation Matters on Dolt/Chump/Oaf/Inept (Fool), כסיל, at 1:22.
19. See Translation Matters on Just/Integrity/Honesty (Righteous[ness]), צדקה/צדק/צדיק, at 1:2.

²³Doing wrong is like sport to a fool,   A
but wise conduct is pleasure to a
person of understanding.
²⁴What the wicked dread will come
upon them,
but the desire of the righteous will
be granted.
²⁵When the tempest passes, the
wicked are no more,   B
but the righteous are established
forever.

²⁶Like vinegar to the teeth, and
smoke to the eyes,   C
so are the lazy to their
employers.
²⁷The fear of the LORD prolongs life,   B'
but the years of the wicked will be
short.
²⁸The hope of the righteous ends in
gladness,   A'
but the expectation of the wicked
comes to nothing.

A Short Couplet on the Longevity of the Upright[20]/Demise of Evildoers (10:29-30)

These two lines continue the focus on the longevity of the just (righteous)[21] seen in the preceding cluster, 10:23-28, and may have been inserted at this point for this reason. Verse 29 provides a counterweight to 10:15, which asserts that the wealth of the rich is his stronghold.

A Couplet on the Mouth/Tongue/Lips of the Just and the Wicked (10:31-32)

This cluster of two verses is unified by the words "mouth" and "lips." Verse 32 suggests an innate knowledge of the acceptable and duplicitous (perverse)[22] on the part of the just (righteous)[23] and the corrupt (wicked),[24] respectively, which is of course prerequisite to bringing forth wisdom as described in 10:31. These verses relate back to references to the mouth, tongue, lips, babbling, and speech in 10:8, 13, 18, 19, 20, and 21.

20. See Translation Matters on Upstanding/Straight/Straightforward (Upright), ישר/ישרים at 2:7.
21. See Translation Matters on Just/Integrity/Honesty (Righteous[ness]), צדקה/צדיק/צדק, at 1:2.
22. See Translation Matters on Duplicitously (Perversely), תהפכות, at 2:12.
23. See Translation Matters on Just/Integrity/Honesty (Righteous[ness]), צדקה/צדיק/צדק, at 1:2.
24. See Translation Matters on Corrupt[ion]/Unscrupulous/Reprehensible (Wicked[ness]), רשע/רשעים, at 2:22.

Prov 10:29-32

²⁹The way of the Lᴏʀᴅ is a stronghold
 for the upright,
 but destruction for evildoers.
³⁰The righteous will never be removed,
 but the wicked will not remain in
 the land.
³¹The mouth of the righteous brings

forth wisdom,
 but the perverse tongue will be
 cut off.
³²The lips of the righteous know what
 is acceptable,
 but the mouth of the wicked what
 is perverse.

The Rescue of the Just/the Destruction of the Corrupt (11:1-14)

The cluster is bound together by the theme, stated in the central verses, 11:7-8, that the just (righteous)²⁵ are rescued, while the hopes and dreams of the corrupt (wicked)²⁶ are dashed. Proverbs 11:1 is a fitting introduction to this cluster, as well as the next, in which fair trade is a major theme. Balances in the ancient world could be made false by using a slightly smaller stone for weighing the goods sold and a slightly larger one for the silver (or whatever currency) with which the customer was paying for the goods. The idea that false balances are an abomination²⁷ but true weights are God's delight can be extended to suggest that dishonest dealings in business are loathed by God but honest ones give God delight. Based on 31:13-14, 16, and 24, at the time this material was added to the collection, at least wealthy women such as the strong woman/ wife (capable wife)²⁸ were engaging in business.

Proverbs 11:2 speaks for the first time in the Solomonic collection (10:1–22:16) of pride, זדון, in the sense of insolence or presumption, not healthy pride (which women sometimes lack; see Excursus on Women's Sins 1: Arrogance, at 3.8). Healthy pride does not lead to disgrace. Although women can be insolent and presumptuous (and when they are this attitude can lead them into disgrace even faster than it does men, for whom it is almost expected), the more common failing is a lack of healthy pride. It is the lack of healthy pride that sometimes leads to presumption and insolence as ersatz substitutes.

25. See Translation Matters on Just/Integrity/Honesty (Righteous[ness]), צדקה/ צדיק/צדק, at 1:2.
26. See Translation Matters on Corrupt[ion]/Unscrupulous/Reprehensible (Wicked[ness]), רשע/רשעים, at 2:22.
27. See discussion of the term "abomination" at 3:32.
28. See Translation Matters on Strong Woman/Wife (Capable Wife), אשת־חיל, at 12:4.

¹A false balance is an abomination to the LORD,
  but an accurate weight is his delight.
²When pride comes, then comes disgrace;
  but wisdom is with the humble.
³The integrity of the upright guides them,
  but the crookedness of the treacherous destroys them.
⁴Riches do not profit in the day of wrath,
  but righteousness delivers from death.
⁵The righteousness of the blameless keeps their ways straight,
  but the wicked fall by their own wickedness.
⁶The righteousness of the upright saves them,
  but the treacherous are taken captive by their schemes.
⁷When the wicked die, their hope perishes,
  and the expectation of the godless comes to nothing.

⁸The righteous are delivered from trouble,
  and the wicked get into it instead.
⁹With their mouths the godless would destroy their neighbors,
  but by knowledge the righteous are delivered.
¹⁰When it goes well with the righteous, the city rejoices;
  and when the wicked perish, there is jubilation.
¹¹By the blessing of the upright a city is exalted,
  but it is overthrown by the mouth of the wicked.
¹²Whoever belittles another lacks sense,
  but an intelligent person remains silent.
¹³A gossip goes about telling secrets,
  but one who is trustworthy in spirit keeps a confidence.
¹⁴Where there is no guidance, a nation falls,
  but in an abundance of counselors there is safety.

A Study in Contrasts

In reading passages on wisdom in the book of Proverbs one is often startled by contrasts. Proverbs 11:2 and Proverbs 11:16 are two such passages. Though footnotes reveal that some verses are missing in Syriac versions, the first passage, "When pride comes, then comes disgrace, but wisdom is with the humble" (v. 2), is in direct contrast to the later passage, "A gracious woman gets honor, but she who hates virtue is covered with shame, the timid become destitute, but the aggressive gain riches" (v. 16).

Who is prideful? Who is wise? The passages are unclear. Is it the aggressive person or the humble person? If one is to consider that being a gracious woman would require interaction with guests while timidity implies not speaking up one is left with contradictions.

The context of the intervening verses reveals a tapestry of counseling insights. One is to listen to the righteous over the rich (v. 4) and not be taken in by schemes (v. 6). One is warned of gossip against a neighbor (v. 9a) and that knowledge is better than words of slander (v. 9b).

A passage from Egyptian writings may give insight: "Good speech is hidden more than emerald, (but) it may be found among the servant girls at the millstones" (*Teachings of Ptahhotep*, 58–59).

Humility in this case may be a state of poverty, not a state of being. We might be warned that we need to judge, like the proverbs say, with a fair measure and "the rich and poor have this in common, the Eternal makes them both" (Prov 22:2).

From a feminist point of view, one must look always for places not to make distinction by gender, or wealth, but listen to wisdom, whatever the source.

Rev. Charles Redden Butler, Neto

When Pride Comes, Then Comes Disgrace; but Wisdom Is with the Humble (Prov 11:2)

Many persons have said that pride goes before a fall. How interesting to offer a comparison between something as inanimate as "pride" and as concrete as a "fall." One might suppose that attributing pride to oneself is a show of arrogance and/or disdain. Disagreements abound, in this regard, since a fall may be physically felt and seen by many, while pride is only seen, felt, or managed by the individual who is its subject.

The Wisdom Writer provides a commonplace, everyday comparison in which he catapults the end product of pride. As high and lifted up as one's experience might be, the onset of pride is destined to cause a significant downfall. The logical question that one could pose is "Can one be prideful while simultaneously maintaining a state of grace?" A flurry of responses would probably run the gamut of those who absolutely agree and others who definitely and positively disagree. Pride, from a biblical perspective, suggests contemptible behavior or prodigious arrogance. Accordingly, one must attempt to reconcile this fallen state of pride with an undeserved state of grace.

There exists an obvious quandary between the appearance of pride and the subsequent "follow-up" of disgrace. Is there something about pride that specifically beckons disgrace? If grace can be treated as favor that is not deserved, what has pride to offer that grace cannot cover? One explanation might be that pride does not appear alone; it brings with it the prideful. Likewise, one cannot expect that pride will exist and thrive in a vacuum. It is accompanied by a haughty spirit, a disdainful heart and an unashamed countenance.

For countless decades, women have spoken up, shown up, and stood up simply to display a sense of pride in who we are. In some circles, this behavior has been regarded as signs of arrogance, contempt, and/or disdain. Likewise, it has been met with disgrace and open rejection. In spite of what we may or may not have encountered, we have remained undaunted and determined in our undeniable quest to stand tall and be counted. We have

learned from the challenges and developed a level of astuteness that has been rewarded by unmerited favor from on High. How thankful we are for the grace that has continued to shield us in our own selves. As we have continued to move forward, we have become stronger and wiser.

The humility that we now possess, we own because of the many times that we have "fallen" and yet been restored, "pushed out" and yet been invited back in, and "cast aside" while creating a beat to a different drum to which we have marched. As women of faith, we have collectively arrived at a point where we are proud to have displayed grace through the heat of our adversity. Whether viewed as pride or humility, we know the difference between the two and we are confident and satisfied with this distinction.

Glenda Hodges

The second colon of 11:2, that wisdom is with the humble (or modest), is the other side of the coin of the first. The main theme of this cluster is stated in 11:3-4. Verse 3 is filled with geometric images. It contrasts the integrity, i.e., the wholeness as in whole numbers (the integers 1, 2, 3, etc.),[29] of the upstanding (upright),[30] literally the straight and level, with the crookedness or moral deviousness of the treacherous. Those with integrity are whole, undivided individuals who act based on their principles. Although principles can be difficult to apply in real life situations,

29. See Translation Matters on Integrity/Whole/Complete (Blameless), תם, at 2:7.
30. See Translation Matters on Upstanding/Straight/Straightforward (Upright), ישר/ישרים, at 2:7.

persons of integrity have a strong sense of what is right and strive to apply their principles to whatever dilemmas confront them. In contrast, the treacherous act in crooked, twisted ways because they have no clear principles other than self-aggrandizement and so zigzag through life. This often gets them nowhere and sometimes destroys them. In the same way that insolent pride can lead to one's own disgrace, so crookedness ultimately can destroy the crooked.

Excursus on Tricksters in the Hebrew Bible

This raises an issue that needs to be considered here. In the Hebrew Bible there are many stories of tricksters, individuals who do not have the full access to power that would normally be expected and thus have to use their intelligence and scheme to do things that, if there were a level playing field, would be considered unjust.

Jacob is the leading example of a male trickster, especially in the way he responds to his father-in-law Laban, who did not treat him fairly with respect to his two wives Rachel and Leah (Gen 29–31). Among female tricksters are Moses' sister Miriam, who, when Pharaoh's daughter asks for a nurse to take care of baby Moses, runs and gets Moses' own mother, whom Pharaoh's daughter then (we assume) pays to be the wet nurse to her own son without knowing that she is his mother (Exod 2:7). Rachel steals the family "gods" when the family leaves her father Laban's compound. Then, when he comes searching for them, she is sitting on them on the saddle of her camel and claims to have the "way of women" and cannot get up to be searched, a raunchy female hoot of a story. We'll never know whether she was telling a fib or not, but Laban wasn't going to investigate any further (Gen 31:19). The greatest story is that of Tamar, Judah's daughter-in-law, in Genesis 38 in which she has to pretend to be a prostitute and seduce him in order to get justice, since he would not allow her to marry his last son, which legally he was bound to do. When he finds out what happened, he declares that she was more righteous/just than he was. So, although these stories do involve lack of full disclosure, they are hardly crooked in the negative sense of the word. There is a difference between twisting the law due to greediness and twisting it to get what one needs and justly deserves to survive.

Proverbs 11:4 returns explicitly to the theme of wealth discussed in 10:2-6, 15-16, 22. Whereas 10:2a simply states that riches gained through corrupt behavior will not bring profit, 11:4a asserts that riches, regardless of how they may have been acquired, are of no value in the day of wrath. This day is not a final judgment day but any day of terrible disaster. Both 10:2b and 11:4b assert that integrity (righteousness) delivers from death. The only thing that can help in a day of terrible disaster is one's character. If we care about others, then we will do what we can to help those who are in worse conditions than we are, and in turn our reputation for such behavior will mean that those who know us and are able to do so will do what they can to help us.

TRANSLATION MATTERS

In 11:6, the NRSV has emended וּבְהַוַּת (desire/chasm/destruction) to וּבָהֹת, their schemes.

Verses 5-6 exhibit two antithetically parallel lines:

(A) **The integrity** (צדקת) of *the blameless* (תמים) <u>**keeps their ways straight**</u>
   (B) *The wicked* <u>fall</u> *by their own wickedness*
(A') **The integrity** (צדקת) **of the** *upright* <u>**saves them**</u>
   (B') *The treacherous* <u>are taken captive</u> *by their schemes*

The parallelism is both grammatical and semantic, as indicated by the underlined, italicized, and bold type. The Hebrew word translated as schemes, הות, has a triple meaning: (evil) "desire," "chasm" (a figure for destruction), and "word." The idea, then, is that people who think they can get ahead by taking advantage of others (evil desires) and who use words destructively will become captive to their own schemes and fall by them into a chasm of destruction.[31] The good character of those with integrity, on the other hand, will keep them on the straight path of success and will keep them safe. These proverbs do not say how this happens, and certainly people with integrity do not always fare well, but in the ideal world, the community protects those who maintain the public good because their great value to society is understood.

---

31. John Kselman, "Ambiguity and Wordplay in Proverbs XI," *VT* 52 (2002): 545–47.

TRANSLATION MATTERS

In 11:7, the NRSV emended the Hebrew אונים to אוילים, "jerks" (fools), based on the Greek ἀσεβῶν, "godless," but the focus on financial matters in this section suggests that the MT is superior. אונים means generative power or wealth. The colon then means that the hope (of the corrupt) in their human power or wealth will come to nothing.

As indicated above, 11:7-8 states the theme of this cluster, that the just survive while the corrupt die, their hopes dashed, their behavior having gotten them into the mess that brought them down. This last aspect of these verses, stated in 11:8b, echoes 11:5b and 6b, reinforcing the theme. Verse 8 says something more specific than the general theme, however. No sooner has a just person been delivered from trouble than a corrupt individual falls into the vacuum left waiting for a victim. The just do sometimes get snared by trouble, but they will be delivered, according to this proverb, while the corrupt will then walk right into the trouble left waiting for them. The godless, irreligious, or profane slander (חנף) people (11:9a), but the remedy is knowledge (דעת, 11:9b). If a person has built up a strong reputation as a good, honest, and trustworthy person, then people will be less likely to believe lies spread by the corrupt about them. Lies can still destroy a person, but a strong reputation does represent the best defense. When things go well for a person who is known in the community as a just individual, then the whole community feels good about the individual's success (11:10a), while the death of a known villain causes the community to rejoice.

The blessing of the upstanding uplifts the entire city (11:11a). In the context of the following colon, the blessing would seem to be oral, prayers for the prosperity and welfare of the city but perhaps also honest speech in business dealings as well as responding to the lies of the corrupt. The second colon (11:11b) says that, in contrast, a city can be overthrown by the mouth of the corrupt. As suggested explicitly in 11:9, and perhaps alluded to implicitly here in 11:10a, when the mouth of the godless slanders a neighbor, the defense is the knowledge of just people, who bless the community by their principled stands against those who tell lies.

Proverbs 11:11 connects with the following three verses, all of which deal with speech, and especially with 11:14, which again deals explicitly with the communal. Verse 12 describes a person who despises someone and is open and vocal about it, as opposed to someone who spreads lies about another (11:9a); this person is said to be lacking heart, and, since heart is closer to our concept of mind plus conscience,[32] the proverb is asserting that such a person is a combination of heartless, thoughtless, imprudent, and just plain stupid. We might say that such a person doesn't have the sense that they were born with. The second colon may be understood in two ways. First, a smart person knows that there is no advantage in indulging in such verbalizing of one's negative thoughts about others. It may boost a weak ego, but in the long run it does more harm to the person who is putting someone down than the person who is being put down, because most people will soon realize that the judgment of the one constantly criticizing others is not reliable. Alternately, the smart person will remain silent when insulted. Some affronts are too petty for a response. Verse 13 is similar, but here, instead of talking about one's own negative attitudes about someone, the talk is a secret that was meant to be held in confidence that instead is being passed on as gossip. The noun is stronger than "gossip"; רכיל really means "slanderer" or "informant." Keeping confidences is what a trustworthy individual does. Although the proverb does not explicitly describe the consequences, it is fair to assume that, just as in the proverb in the previous verse, it was considered stupid to be a gossip and worse yet to be an informant, because passing on secrets may give a temporary high, but once a person is known as a gossip or an informant, little information will be shared and a negative label will have been attached to his or her name. Verse 14 speaks to the issue of verbal counsel to the nation rather than to individuals. Without guidance, the nation falls. The antithesis is that when there is an abundance of (hopefully independent-minded) counselors there is safety. (See also 29:18.)

Rewards and Punishments (11:15-31)

This long cluster of proverbs is about rewards and punishments. Of the eighteen proverbs, six are explicitly about financial matters. The second and the ninth involve feminine images (11:16 and 11:22), the second of which has received a great deal of discussion concerning its meaning.

---

32. See Translation Matters on the Heart, לֵב, at 2:2.

Prov 11:15-31

¹⁵To guarantee loans for a stranger brings trouble,
but there is safety in refusing to do so.
¹⁶A gracious woman gets honor,
but she who hates virtue is covered with shame.
The timid become destitute,
but the aggressive gain riches.
¹⁷Those who are kind reward themselves,
but the cruel do themselves harm.
¹⁸The wicked earn no real gain,
but those who sow righteousness get a true reward.
¹⁹Whoever is steadfast in righteousness will live,
but whoever pursues evil will die.
²⁰Crooked minds are an abomination to the Lord,
but those of blameless ways are his delight.
²¹Be assured, the wicked will not go unpunished,
but those who are righteous will escape.
²²Like a gold ring in a pig's snout

TRANSLATION MATTERS

In 11:16, the NRSV is translating loosely from the Greek LXX rather than the MT, which reads instead:

A shapely (gracious) woman gets honor,
but aggressive men gain riches,

omitting

but she who hates virtue is covered with shame.
The timid become destitute.

These last two lines would more accurately be translated:

But she who hates justice is a throne of disgrace
The indolent will become destitute.

Looking at the first part of the LXX text, it seems clear that the LXX translators interpreted חן positively, so that the contrast is between the honor of the gracious woman and the disgrace (shame) of the woman lacking virtue. This could have been an expansion of the MT, in which case the MT would have contrasted the honorable woman with the greedy man. However, the second phrase added in the LXX, "the indolent (timid) becomes destitute," is interpreted by the NRSV positively or at least neutrally rather than negatively. The Greek word in the LXX, which is translated as "timid" by NRSV here, is ὀκνηροί, "idle" or "indolent," i.e., lazy, which has a different connotation from timid. This colon, if understood as "the indolent becomes destitute," makes a good foundation for the second colon to provide the antithesis: "but the aggressive gain riches."

is a beautiful woman without good
sense.
²³The desire of the righteous ends
only in good;
the expectation of the wicked in
wrath.
²⁴Some give freely, yet grow all the
richer;
others withhold what is due, and
only suffer want.
²⁵A generous person will be
enriched,
and one who gives water will get
water.
²⁶The people curse those who hold
back grain,
but a blessing is on the head of
those who sell it.

²⁷Whoever diligently seeks good
seeks favor,
but evil comes to the one who
searches for it.
²⁸Those who trust in their riches will
wither,
but the righteous will flourish like
green leaves.
²⁹Those who trouble their households
will inherit wind,
and the fool will be servant to the
wise.
³⁰The fruit of the righteous is a tree
of life,
but violence takes lives away.
³¹If the righteous are repaid on earth,
how much more the wicked and
the sinner!

The proverb in 11:16 contains the first feminine image in the cluster, asserting that a woman who is gracious, i.e., attractive and charming, gets (and keeps) honor. If we follow the longer version based on the LXX with the NRSV, 11:16ab offers a contrast between a (merely?) elegant, gracious woman (חן, see 31:30 for a negative view) and a woman with a bad reputation. Proverbs 11:16cd presents a contrast between the lazy individual and the aggressive. In the MT the contrast is between the gracious woman and the aggressive man. Both types of individuals in the MT are successful, but as the following proverbs indicate, their success may be limited.

Whichever set of contrasts we go with, the one in the MT or the one in the LXX (which the NRSV follows), we have the picture of a gracious woman, i.e., an elegant, beautiful, charming individual. This is, of course, a stereotype, just as the bad woman and the aggressive man are stereotypes, but stereotypes are not fiction; they are based on popular perceptions of an amalgamation of many real people. We all know these individuals. The fact that from ancient Judah to contemporary North America, we understand the gracious woman, bad woman, and aggressive man tropes, even if we don't agree with the cultural valuations, indicates that there is something inherent in human nature that does not change quickly or easily. Gracious women do succeed more easily than ugly, awkward ones do, and they are not necessarily shallow people. Tall, handsome, aggressive men often succeed more than we like, unless they are particularly inept in the way they go about their pursuits. The point here is to acknowledge the reality but at the same time to suggest that their success may be less than we might think. It was the sort of advice my parents gave me when I was a teenager and envied the success of some of my peers. They were right, of course, even though I didn't appreciate the advice at the time and did not give it to my daughters.

In 11:17a and 18b, the kind ones who sow justice (righteousness)[33] achieve real rewards and are contrasted with the cruel and corrupt (wicked),[34] who, despite appearance, harm themselves. Verses 19-21 then continue the contrast between the eventual destruction of the unethical (wicked; here רע, rather than the more common רשע, both of which NRSV sometimes translates as "wicked") and the reward of the steadfast.

We come finally to 11:22, the central verse of this cluster and the central theme: what appears beautiful and highly attractive at first glance may be horrible and to be avoided because of its inner qualities. In the case of a human being, this is the person's values. In the case of a business proposition, it is how it will affect other people. Is it likely to benefit the community or be exploitative? Most commentators assume that 11:22— "Like a gold ring in a pig's snout is a beautiful woman without good sense"—does not really fit into this cluster. The proverb is not comparing a woman with a pig, however; rather, her beauty is being compared with a gold ring in an inappropriate place. The ludicrous image of a gold ring in a pig's snout, an animal who wallows in filth, is meant to convey the equally horrific image of a woman, but ultimately any person or thing, concrete or abstract, that is attractive in appearance but that actually acts like a pig, i.e., lolling about in the mire. What can this have to do with the cluster of proverbs about reward and punishment in general and finance in particular? Each of the negative practices described in the preceding proverbs in this cluster can be read as gold rings in a pig's snout; their gleam may at first beckon but in the long run will drag a person into the mire. This verse is therefore the hinge of this cluster, emphasizing the differences between appearance and reality. Verse 23 follows verse 22 well, for 23 indicates that what the just want results in good, whereas

---

33. For the meaning of צדיק, צדק, צדקה in vv. 18, 21, 23, 28, 30, 31, see Translation Matters on Just/Integrity/Honesty (Righteous[ness]), צדיק/צדק/צדקה, at 1:2.

34. See Translation Matters on Corrupt[ion]/Unscrupulous/Reprehensible (Wicked[ness]), רשע/רשעים, at 2:22.

what the corrupt expect leads to wrath. When people do not consider the effects of their behavior on others, when they grab the gold ring without regard to its consequences, the result will be a lot of angry people. It is not a good way to make friends and influence people. Verse 24 says that some people give freely and yet they grow even richer, while others do not pay what they owe, yet it is they paradoxically who are lacking. Those who are generous are well loved in the community; business flows their way and they prosper. Those who cheat or are miserly often end up less well off than if they had been more generous. And even if they are not found out, there is more to happiness than great wealth. Verse 25 says it again: the generous are enriched and those who give water get water. The generous may be compared to the gracious woman who receives honor, while the aggressive and greedy achieve only barren riches.

Proverbs 11:26 gives a specific example: the people do not like it when the distributor holds back grain (reading between the lines), waiting to sell it later when prices rise, even though the time of need is now. The distributor is not a small farmer but someone who has control of the market, like Joseph in Egypt (Gen 42:6), Sihon (Deut 2:28), or the large agribusinesses in Amos 8:5-6. The proverb asserts that there will be a blessing on the head of the distributor who sells it at the time of need, going against personal interest. We may assume that even though the demand was high, circumstances were such that people were not in a position to pay a high price at the time. Perhaps there had been a drought and people's crops had not come in, thus triggering the unusual need for the distribution and the lack of resources with which to pay a high price for it. Verse 27 returns to the more general, stating that whoever seeks (to do what is) good diligently and early is seeking goodwill (from the community), but bad things come to the one who seeks evil.

The image of a green tree is introduced in 11:28. People who trust in their wealth will wither, but the just will flourish like the healthy green leaves of a tree. Wealth certainly would appear to be a gold ring, but putting too much trust in it is not life affirming. Wealth in and of itself is not bad, but putting ultimate trust in it is not smart. Verse 29 may be focused on a son seeking an inheritance. (Unless there were no sons, usually daughters could not inherit [see Num 27:8].) People who cause trouble for their households, the proverb predicts, will inherit the wind, i.e., nothing. Such shortsighted individuals, literally servants of dolts (fools),[35] may end up serving wiser contenders for the household wealth.

---

35. See Translation Matters on Jerk/Schmuck/Folly (Fool/Folly), אוֹיל/אוִלֹת, at 1:7.

TRANSLATION MATTERS

In 11:30, the NRSV emends חכם, "wise," to חמס, "violence," based on the LXX.

Proverbs 11:30 returns to the tree image—this time, the tree of life—saying that the fruit of the just is like (the fruit of) such a tree. The MT says: "the wise [חכם] take lives [נפשות] away," in the sense of understanding souls (see Translation Matters, 29:10).[36] The cluster ends in 11:31 with the statement that if the just are repaid on earth, how much more will the corrupt and sinners be. This proverb is in tension with one interpretation of 11:16, which indicates that charming women and aggressive men gain riches, but is consistent with the interpretation that the whole section is contrasting the search for honor and a good reputation in the community with the search for material gain.

On Discipline and Stupidity (12:1-7)

This cluster focuses on discipline and stupidity. Since in its original context the audience was primarily boys and young men, the central verse in this cluster, which is about the importance of the right wife, is a key component. Proverbs 12:1 speaks of the value of discipline (מוסר),[37] as in being corrected or reprimanded, as the following parallel antithetical colon makes clear. The statement that anyone who resents being rebuked is stupid (בער, literally a brute) is a strong statement but is meant to drive home the point that, without painful correction, we do not learn. Even the gentlest correction is somewhat painful, but some methods are harder to take than others and some more effective than others.

The aphorism "No pain, no gain" came into contemporary usage when, in 1982, the actress Jane Fonda created a set of workout videos in which this was a motto she used. It caught on and has become ubiquitous in the fitness industry and throughout sports ever since. Though it can be overdone, leading to counterproductive results, there is truth in the aphorism. Nevertheless, no one should ever be subjected to any form of nonconsensual pain.[38]

---

36. Daniel C. Snell, " 'Taking Souls' in Proverbs XI, 30," *VT* 33 (1983): 362–65.

37. See Translation Matters on Discipline/Chastening/Correction (Instruction), מוסר, at 1:2.

38. This can be a little tricky in situations where there is an imbalance of power, as in athletic coaching relationships, where the coach may feel that he or she needs

Prov 12:1-7

¹Whoever loves discipline loves knowledge,
but those who hate to be rebuked are stupid.

²The good obtain favor from the LORD,
but those who devise evil he condemns.

³No one finds security by wickedness,
but the root of the righteous will never be moved.

⁴A good wife is the crown of her husband,
but she who brings shame is like rottenness in his bones.

⁵The thoughts of the righteous are just;
the advice of the wicked is treacherous.

⁶The words of the wicked are a deadly ambush,
but the speech of the upright delivers them.

⁷The wicked are overthrown and are no more,
but the house of the righteous will stand.

Proverbs 12:2 says that a good person gains God's approval while God will condemn a person of evil devices or practices. The Hebrew noun devices, מזמות, itself is neutral, gaining its negativity only from the context (a man of devices he condemns). Verse 3 similarly states that a person is not established through corruption (wickedness),[39] but that the root of a just (righteous)[40] individual cannot be shaken (compare 11:28, 30). The verb translated as "established" means to be fixed concretely, as in a house, but also metaphorically of a person; in addition, it has moral senses, to be steadfast and prepared. The root in the second colon evokes the image of a tree that, being deeply rooted, cannot be shaken. It is similar to other biblical texts such as Jeremiah 17:8-9. The song "We/I Shall Not Be Moved," used in many protest movements, including both labor and civil rights, is based on these passages.[41]

---

to push the athlete beyond what is comfortable in order for the athlete to perform at the highest level, but the athlete must ultimately be in control of the relationship and know when to draw the line. With minors this is especially difficult and requires the involvement of parents, who need to have the kind of relationships with their children in which they really can know what is going on, which is unfortunately not always the case.

39. See Translation Matters on Corrupt[ion]/Unscrupulous/Reprehensible (Wicked[ness]), רשע/רשעים, at 2:22.

40. For the meaning of צדיקים in 12:3, 5, 7, see Translation Matters on Just/Integrity/Honesty (Righteous[ness]), צדיק/צדק/צדקה, at 1:2.

41. "I Shall Not Be Moved," Wikipedia, https://en.wikipedia.org/wiki/I_Shall_Not_Be_Moved.

TRANSLATION MATTERS

Strong Woman/Wife (Good/Capable Wife), אֵשֶׁת־חַיִל; חַיִל alone can mean "strength," "efficiency," "wealth," and "army." In the context of the two Proverbs passages where it is found (12:4; 31:10), only the last possibility does not fit. The simplest and most obvious translation for the phrase, however, is "a woman of strength" or "a strong woman," the more natural English translation. NRSV's translation of the Hebrew אֵשֶׁת־חַיִל as "a good/capable wife" is a modest improvement over the RSV's "good wife" and KJV's "virtuous woman," which follows the LXX, since חַיִל does mean efficiency as well as strength. The same word is used in Hebrew for "woman" and "wife," so either translation is possible. Interestingly, Michael Fox, who is hardly a feminist, translates the phrase as "a woman of strength," in his Anchor Bible commentary.[42]

Proverbs 12:4 focuses on the importance of the choice of wife for a young man. This is the first time in Proverbs the term אֵשֶׁת־חַיִל, "woman of strength" or "strong woman," is used. The other instance is in 31:10. A woman who was strong in mind and personal values was a man's crown. She was probably strong in body as well because even for a woman with servants there was physical work that needed to be done. Drawing on 31:10-31, we can see that she was also efficient in running her household and multiple small business operations, and as a result, if she was not already wealthy, she became wealthy. Calling a woman a man's crown is not to trivialize her, though it makes us uncomfortable today. A crown was a sign of dignity, like a signet ring. Nevertheless, the woman's value is clearly seen in terms of her relationship with her husband. The audience was primarily young men and the proverb serves as advice on whom to marry. The opposite of the woman of strength (capable wife) was the one who brought shame to her husband. Although the proverb is not explicit, the most obvious way, given the sexualized context of Proverbs, would be sexual immorality (see Hos 1–3). The contrast between the woman of strength's husband who can proudly wear his figurative crown in the open and the disgraceful woman's husband who will bear his disgrace privately in emotional turmoil, the "rottenness in his bones," is probably intended. The contrast may go beyond the sexual, however, to criticize the trivial woman, who is at least a private exasperation and cannot bring out her husband's virtues. She may also

---

42. Michael V. Fox, *Proverbs 10–31: A New Translation with Introduction and Commentary*, AB 18B (New Haven: Yale University Press, 2009), 888.

mismanage the family estate and the children, bringing public disgrace on her husband as well as herself. A young man who sought and found a woman of strength for his mate was smart. One who chose a woman who turned out to bring disgrace to him and his house was not at all smart. Today, people with ethical sensitivity looking for mates should be seeking individuals with strength of mind and personal values, who will be in sync with them in the short and long run, rather than humiliating them and bringing them to economic ruin. One could rewrite 12:4 as:

> A strong, just mate is a spouse's pride
>> A disgraceful one is like rottenness in the bones.

Proverbs 12:5 is general: the plans of the just are justice, but the advice of the corrupt (wicked)[43] is deceptive or treacherous. There may be two points here: try to be among the first group rather than the second, and do not listen to advice from people known to fall into the second category. Verse 6 follows naturally from 12:5b; the words of the corrupt create deadly (metaphorical) ambushes, but the mouth of the upstanding (upright)[44] will deliver them. Several proverbs in this collection state that the just will be able to escape the traps of the corrupt (10:2b; 11:6a, 8a, 9b; 12:21). Since the pronoun "them" is ambiguous, it could refer to others that the upstanding save, even though there are no antecedents other than the upstanding themselves nearby. Verse 7 rounds out this cluster with the declaration that the corrupt will be overthrown and eliminated, while the house of the just will stand.

Work Matters (12:8-12)

This small cluster, dealing primarily with work matters, opens with a general statement in 12:8, saying that a person will be praised for being sensible but scorned for a mind that distorts reality. People who do not see reality clearly are not as sensible as people who do. One must have a good grasp of the situation before one can make good decisions. The proverb does not suggest that these qualities are innate; the implicit notion is that they can be acquired (in the first case) and shed (in the second) through education.

43. See Translation Matters on Corrupt[ion]/Unscrupulous/Reprehensible (Wicked[ness]), רשע/רשעים, at 2:22.
44. See Translation Matters on Upstanding/Straight/Straightforward (Upright), ישר/ישרים, at 2:7.

Prov 12:8-12

⁸One is commended for good sense,

but a perverse mind is despised.

⁹Better to be despised and have a servant,

than to be self-important and lack food.

¹⁰The righteous know the needs of their animals,

but the mercy of the wicked is cruel.

¹¹Those who till their land will have plenty of food,

but those who follow worthless pursuits have no sense.

¹²The wicked covet the proceeds of wickedness,

but the root of the righteous bears fruit.

TRANSLATION MATTERS

In 12:8, "perverse" is not the best translation for נעוה, which comes from a root meaning to bend or twist but does not necessarily mean anything sexual, which is what the term "perverse" tends to connote. "Twisted" may be better.

TRANSLATION MATTERS

In 12:9, NRSV's "despised" is unnecessarily harsh. "Lightly esteemed" or "lowly" are also possible.

Also in 12:9, "have a servant," ועבד, would be rendered better as "be a servant to oneself." The Hebrew allows either translation. Alternately, a slight emendation of MT's ועבד to ועבור results in a colon that reads as follows: "Better to be lowly and have sustenance than to be self-important and lack food" (BHS).

Proverbs 12:9 does not say why the person in the first colon is despised or just lightly esteemed, but it is clearly a preferable condition to work for oneself or have a servant than not to have food, regardless of reputation. The person in the second colon may be lacking food because of negative character traits, which may have affected his or her standing in the community. Perhaps the individual in the first colon is lightly esteemed due to low social class or because the individual does not parade his or her wealth, while the person in the second colon is obnoxious due to ostentation. This verse raises the issue that if it is not easy to tell how much wealth people have, it is not easy to determine whether God has rewarded the wise/diligent/just and the corrupt (wicked)[45] appropriately.[46] (See also 13:7.)

Proverbs 12:10 states that the just (righteous)[47] know the needs and desires of their animals. The Hebrew translated as "needs" is נפש, traditionally translated as "soul" but that means at its core "neck" or "gullet (esophagus)." This suggests a narrow interpretation of sustenance. The word also means the whole being, though, and thus the proverb can be interpreted more broadly as well. The proverb does not distinguish between compassion for the animals and maximizing the animals' usefulness to the human owner. The second colon, however, which sarcastically says that even the mercies of the corrupt are cruel, suggests that at least part of the motivation is humanitarian.

It is quite interesting to find this proverb in the collection dealing with animal welfare. One would not have guessed that such a saying would be here among the aphorisms about wealth and poverty, success and sexuality. The ancient Hebrews were poor people; they did not own many animals, but the animals they did own, we can imagine, were important to them. They were, of course, utilitarian in that they helped them with farm chores and in some cases provided milk, eggs, wool, or transportation, but we can also suppose that they became part of the family and bonded with the family members.

Proverbs 12:11 deals with diligence. The two halves of the line must be read together, with the thought of each colon completing the other one. Those who sensibly till their land will be satiated, but people who foolishly fritter away their time on vain pursuits will not have enough to eat.

This small cluster is concluded with 12:12, which states that corrupt people desire what will turn out to be a trap, while the root of the just gives (fruit).

---

45. See Translation Matters on Corrupt[ion]/Unscrupulous/Reprehensible (Wicked[ness]), רשע/רשעים, at 2:22.

46. Peter T. H. Hatton, *Contradiction in the Book of Proverbs: The Deep Waters of Counsel*, SOTSMS (Hampshire: Ashgate, 2008), 110.

47. For the meaning of צדיק, צדיקים in 12:10, 12, see Translation Matters on Just/Integrity/Honesty (Righteous[ness]), צדיק/צדק/צדקה, at 1:2.

TRANSLATION MATTERS

In biblical Hebrew, מצוד normally means "trap" (e.g., Job 19:6; Eccl 7:26). The NRSV rendering, "proceeds," assumes that the corrupt (wicked) are desiring the results of the hunt of the unethical (wickedness).[48]

On Speech (12:13-28)

This cluster of proverbs deals mostly with speech. It begins in 12:13 with a proverb that connects backward to the previous cluster with its image of a net. The trap that is set by the transgression of the lips of people of ill will may ensnare them, but it is also dangerous for others. The second colon of the proverb, however, asserts that the just (righteous)[49] escape from trouble. Verse 14 also connects backward, as it lauds the manual labor in its second colon, but its first colon is focused on the fruit of the mouth as filling a person with good things. If these good things are understood concretely, then it might seem that the kind of fruit that is involved here is some sort of professional speech. On the other hand, the proverb could simply be saying that those who speak honestly are better at business than their dishonest counterparts and will thus find that their larders stay fuller than those of their dishonest counterparts. (See Excursus on Women's Sins 3: Dishonesty, at 6:6-19.)

TRANSLATION MATTERS

In 12:13, the Hebrew בפשע שפתים מוקש רע is ambiguous; it states that through the transgression of the lips either a vicious trap or a trap of an unethical (evil)[50] person (or both due to wordplay) results. Implied is that the transgressor is ensnared.

48. See Translation Matters on Unethical (Evil/Bad/Wicked), רע/רעים, at 4:14. NRSV's translation of "wickedness" here assumes that the Hebrew noun is abstract, but the natural reading is rather that it refers to individuals.

49. See Translation Matters on Just/Integrity/Honesty (Righteous[ness]), צדקה/צדיק/צדק, at 1:2.

50. See Translation Matters on Unethical (Evil/Bad/Wicked), רע/רעים, at 4:14.

Prov 12:13-28

¹³The evil are ensnared by the
   transgression of their lips,
   but the righteous escape from
      trouble.
¹⁴From the fruit of the mouth one is
   filled with good things,
   and manual labor has its reward.
¹⁵Fools think their own way is right,
   but the wise listen to advice.
¹⁶Fools show their anger at once,
   but the prudent ignore an insult.
¹⁷Whoever speaks the truth gives
   honest evidence,

but a false witness speaks
   deceitfully.
¹⁸Rash words are like sword thrusts,
   but the tongue of the wise brings
      healing.
¹⁹Truthful lips endure forever,
   but a lying tongue lasts only a
      moment.
²⁰Deceit is in the mind of those who
   plan evil,
   but those who counsel peace
      have joy.
²¹No harm happens to the righteous,

Proverbs 12:15-16 deal with the opposing ways of the jerks (foolish)[51] and wise or prudent. Verse 15 says that the wise listen to advice while jerks pay attention only to their own ideas. Verse 16 continues, indicating that on the same day that the jerk becomes angry, the anger is broadcast, whereas the sensible person ignores (literally covers) an insult.

TRANSLATION MATTERS

In 12:17 the NRSV, which usually translates צדק as "righteous" (as in 12:13, 21, 26), here renders it as "honest evidence," which is a good translation.

Proverbs 12:17 moves into the judicial realm. This proverb is definitional: a truthful witness gives honest testimony and a false one speaks dishonestly. The point is that it is critical to cultivate honesty as a reflex. The verb פוח literally means "breathe." One who breathes, יפיח, truth declares honest evidence, צדק.[52] This way, when called upon to testify, one will automatically tell the truth, and the judge and jury will have every reason to believe the testimony given. Verse 18 focuses on rash,

51. See Translation Matters on Jerk/Schmuck/Folly (Fool/Folly), אויל/אולת, at 1:7.
52. See Translation Matters on Just/Integrity/Honesty (Righteous[ness]), צדקה/צדק/צדיק, at 1:2.

but the wicked are filled with trouble.

[22]Lying lips are an abomination to the LORD,

but those who act faithfully are his delight.

[23]One who is clever conceals knowledge,

but the mind of a fool broadcasts folly.

[24]The hand of the diligent will rule,

while the lazy will be put to forced labor.

[25]Anxiety weighs down the human heart,

but a good word cheers it up.

[26]The righteous gives good advice to friends,

but the way of the wicked leads astray.

[27]The lazy do not roast their game,

but the diligent obtain precious wealth.

[28]In the path of righteousness there is life,

in walking its path there is no death.

thoughtless words, which are compared with sword thrusts. In contrast, the tongue of the wise is said to be healing. The word מרפא, "healing," involves a pun. It plays on the roots for healing, רפא, and soft, רפה. A soft, gentle word is healing.[53] In 12:19 the comparison is between truthful lips and a lying tongue. The former are said to endure while the latter last only a moment. Either the body parts represent the speech that endures or quickly fades, or they stand for the persons who speak. True words endure and people who speak them also endure because they are internally consistent. Dishonesty is in the heart/mind[54] of those who plan evil, but those who counsel peace—Hebrew שלום, a word meaning completeness, soundness, welfare, and peace—will experience joy (12:20). The just experience no harm, but the corrupt (wicked)[55] are filled with trouble (12:21). This is one of those ideal truths, which stand in tension with proverbs such as 11:16. Lying lips are called an abomination[56] to YHWH, and, by contrast, those who "do" faithfulness are God's delight (12:22). But unguarded speech is not recommended; the prudent (clever)[57] person

53. Fox, *Proverbs 10–31*, 556.

54. See Translation Matters on the Heart, לב, at 2:2.

55. See Translation Matters on Corrupt[ion]/Unscrupulous/Reprehensible (Wicked[ness]), רשעים/רשע, at 2:22.

56. See discussion of the term "abomination" at 3:32.

57. See Translation Matters on Prudence/Prudent (Clever[ness]), ערמה and ערום, at 1:4.

knows that it is often smart to conceal one's knowledge; in contrast, a dolt's (fool's)[58] heart/mind[59] proclaims foolishness (12:23).[60]

The proverb in 12:24, which focuses on diligence and laziness, does not seem to fit very well in this cluster; it would fit much better in the last one on work. It may have been put here because רמיה, lazy, has a synonym meaning "deceit,"[61] which would fit in with 12:20 and 12:22. Verse 25 is similarly possibly misplaced, but the second colon may connect to speech: a well-chosen word can comfort the anxious.

TRANSLATION MATTERS

The Hebrew in the first part of 12:26 is obscure. It can be revocalized in several different minor ways and made to make sense, but none are obviously the correct solution to the puzzle. The NRSV's translation is based on the Syriac.

Verse 26 as emended can be translated as follows:

> The just will be released from trouble,
> but the way of the corrupt leads astray.

The point of comparison is now that if/when the just do get into trouble, presumably caused by the corrupt, they will be released, by their own wisdom, the community, or God, but the way of the corrupt leads (themselves) astray. This is in tension with 11:5: the integrity (righteousness)[62] of the forthright (blameless)[63] makes their way straight, i.e., smooth and successful.

TRANSLATION MATTERS

The Hebrew word חרוץ, at the end of the second colon in 12:27, has a synonym meaning "gold." The NRSV translation "diligent" does not work grammatically in Hebrew, because יקר, ("obtain," NRSV), is not a transitive verb; the Hebrew makes sense when it is translated rather as an adjective: "but the wealth of the uncommon individual is gold," where יקר is modifying the individual (uncommon, rare).

---

58. See Translation Matters on Dolt/Chump/Oaf/Inept (Fool), כסיל, at 1:22.
59. See Translation Matters on the Heart, לב, at 2:2.
60. See Translation Matters on Jerk/Schmuck/Folly (Fool/Folly), אויל/אולת, at 1:7.
61. Both meanings are possible.
62. See Translation Matters on Just/Integrity/Honesty (Righteous[ness]), צדקה/צדיק/צדק, at 1:2.
63. See Translation Matters on Integrity/Whole/Complete (Blameless), תם, at 2:7.

In the first colon of 12:27, the lazy person has apparently hunted, a metaphor for the various exploitative schemes the individual has engaged in, but such a one will not be allowed to roast the results of the hunt. The word רְמִיָּה, "lazy," has a synonym meaning "deceit," which would fit in with 12:20, 22, and 24. In the second colon the last word חָרוּץ can mean both "diligent" and "gold." Both meanings may have been heard. Combining the meanings of deceit and laziness in the first colon and diligent and gold in the second and translating the second line from the Hebrew, we get the following:

> The deceitful sluggard will not roast his game,
>> but the wealth of the uncommon individual is pure gold/
>>> diligence.

The lazy individual who tries to get rich through deceit will not get to enjoy the spoils, but the person who is diligent will be rewarded with gold, the most stable and secure form of wealth, one that does not need any cooking or preserving. It does not rust or go bad. This proverb does not involve speech, but it does touch on deception and the results of deceptive behavior, a topic discussed in 12:17, 19, 20, 22, and especially 24, where laziness is included as a concern.

TRANSLATION MATTERS

The Hebrew of the first two words of 12:28 says, "the path of the path," and seems highly unlikely, although no satisfactory emendation is obvious. Probably the best choice is מְשׁוּבָה, "apostasy," based loosely on the LXX, μνησικάκων, "vengeful" (BHS).

In the final colon, "there is no death": although the particle is a negative, it is better to emend אַל, "not," to אֶל, "to," based on many manuscripts and versions, including the LXX (BHS).

The final proverb in this cluster, 12:28, is a general one, but it picks up the theme of the path discussed in 11:15 and 11:26. As emended, it reads:

> In the path of integrity there is life,
>> the way of apostasy leads to death.

The life and death spoken of here are probably to be understood not as eternal but as temporal. Living in a just way leads to a long life on the earth, while doing things displeasing to God shortens one's life span according to the proverb.

Contrast Between Wise Child and Everyone Else (13:1-6)

Proverbs 13:1 is a reminder that the original audience of many of the proverbs is young enough to be under a parent's tutelage. The son (child)[64] is expected to listen to the parent's discipline, unlike the scoffer who doesn't take kindly to a rebuke. This proverb is similar to 12:1. The Hebrew בן חכם מוסר אב, which reads, "a wise son—a father's discipline," can also be understood to mean that a child is the product of the discipline received, just as we say, "Like father, like son; like mother, like daughter." The starkness of the nominal sentence syntactical structure in which there is no explicit form of the verb "to be," a standard feature of classical Hebrew, makes the point strongly. Verses 2-4 form a subunit within this cluster, dealing with speech.

TRANSLATION MATTERS

In 13:1, NRSV emends the Hebrew אב, "father," to אהב, "loves," but this is not necessary. The MT is preferable. "A wise child—a father's discipline,"[65] can be translated, "A wise child pays attention to a father's discipline," assuming the verb from the second colon is to be understood with the first colon as well.

In 13:2 NRSV understands the Hebrew word טוב, an adjective meaning "good," as referring both to the person who is subject of the sentence and to the object of the verb "eat." This is possible. The antithetical line is more closely related than the translation indicates. The word NRSV translates as "desire," נפש, which is traditionally translated "soul," here means desire in the sense of appetite, but with an undertone of the original meaning of the word, neck or gullet (esophagus), from which was derived the meaning breath, life, and soul but also desire, appetite, and passion. So here it is the treacherous hunger for wrongdoing, including injurious language. Implied is that through their treachery they hope to eat.

Proverbs 13:3 returns to the theme of the value of keeping one's mouth shut (see above 10:14, 19; 11:13; 12:23; the theme will also occur in 15:2, 28; 17:27-28; 21:23). Verse 3 is connected to 13:2 with the word נפש, here

---

64. See Translation Matters on Son (Child), בן, at 1:8.
65. See Translation Matters on Discipline/Chastening/Correction (Instruction), מוסר, at 1:2.

Prov 13:1-6

¹A wise child loves discipline,
but a scoffer does not listen to
rebuke.
²From the fruit of their words good
persons eat good things,
but the desire of the treacherous
is for wrongdoing.
³Those who guard their mouths
preserve their lives;
those who open wide their lips
come to ruin.

⁴The appetite of the lazy craves, and
gets nothing,
while the appetite of the diligent is
richly supplied.
⁵The righteous hate falsehood,
but the wicked act shamefully and
disgracefully.
⁶Righteousness guards one whose
way is upright,
but sin overthrows the
wicked.

translated as "life" (but may hark back to its alternate meanings), for discretion is urged as a matter of life and death. The verb used in the second colon, פשק, is not the usual one for opening the lips. The only other occurrence of this verb in the Hebrew Bible is in Ezekiel 16:25, where it is used of Jerusalem spreading her legs to passers-by. Thus, it may have coarse connotations here. The word "appetite" in 13:4 is again נפש. The verb used of craving here, מתאוה, is one that can refer to any bodily desire, for food, water, or sex. It sometimes has negative connotations (see 21:26, of a covetous man; and 24:2, of desiring evil companionship), so the proverb may be both criticizing the person's sloth and the nature of the desires.

The antithesis of the sluggard with an inappropriate appetite is the diligent individual whose appetite is richly rewarded (13:4b). The proverb says that these people will grow fat. In a time of limited resources, what was called fatness (perhaps not obesity as we know it) was a sign of prosperity. It is unlikely that anyone in ancient Israel was what we would call obese. One exception comes to mind: the Moabite king Eglon had enough belly fat that the hilt of Ehud's knife that killed him was supposedly hidden by it, though that story may have been exaggerated (Judg 3:17, 21). Verse 5 returns to the theme of speech, as the first colon says that the just (righteous)[66] hate a false word. The antithesis is that the corrupt (wicked)[67] smell bad/are ashamed and act disgracefully/

66. See Translation Matters on Just/Integrity/Honesty (Righteous[ness]), צדקה/צדיק/צדק, at 1:2.
67. See Translation Matters on Corrupt[ion]/Unscrupulous/Reprehensible (Wicked[ness]), רשע/רשעים, at 2:22.

are disgraced. The first verb, יבאיש, means to have a bad smell, but it is a pun on יביש, meaning to be ashamed. The two words sound essentially identical. The second colon then means that the corrupt act in such a way as to cause a bad smell and generally in a disgraceful manner, and as a result they are shamed and disgraced. It is implicit, then, that the just who hate false words will gain the opposite of what the wicked people get, which is a good reputation.

TRANSLATION MATTERS

The NRSV translation of the second colon of 13:6 is possible grammatically and semantically, but parallelism suggests that the subject and verb be reversed: "but corruption (wickedness) overthrows sin," where sin represents sinners, just as in the first colon, "the integrity of the way," is understood to refer to the upright person.

This cluster is concluded with a proverb that links with the preceding cluster with the root "integrity, completeness," תם,[68] and the word "corruption" (wicked) רשעה (13:6). In this sentence abstract nouns are used to represent classes of people. Parallelism suggests the following literal translation: integrity guards the completeness/integrity (uprightness)[69] of the way, and corruption overthrows sin. The classes of people represented by the abstracts are, in the first line, those who walk the walk of integrity and, in the second line, sinners, so the meaning is that integrity guards those who walk the walk and corruption overthrows sinners. According to this proverb, there is an abstract quality of integrity in line with which humans should walk, as many other proverbs make clear, but that also will guard the path of those who are persons of integrity. Although the Hebrew Bible is not generally dualistic, this proverb is moving in that direction with the concept of abstract corruption (wickedness) overthrowing sinners. It is very close to "the devil made me do it," though of course the authors of the proverbs would not let a sinner get off with such an excuse.

---

68. See Translation Matters on Integrity/Whole/Complete (Blameless), תם, at 2:7.
69. See Translation Matters on Upstanding/Straight/Straightforward (Upright), ישר/ישרים, at 2:7.

Excursus on Feminist Views on Dualism

Feminist theologians have opposed traditional Western theological dualist thinking, which pits good versus evil, the body versus the spirit, supernatural versus natural, etc. These dualisms are not evenly weighted; one is better than the other, so good is better than evil; the spirit is better than the body; the supernatural is superior to the natural. This dualistic way of thinking also affected Christian anthropology, with the male being considered more rational, active, and autonomous, and therefore better than the female, who was viewed as more emotional, intuitive, and passive. Feminist theologians opposed these various dualisms, at first trying to downplay gender differences, but later affirming at least some biological differences and coming to celebrate a multipolar world with multiple differences interacting interdependently.[70]

On Wealth and Poverty (13:7-11)

This small cluster focuses primarily on wealth and poverty and the attitudes that are conducive toward these states. The opening proverb in 13:7 can be read two ways. It can be read, as NRSV reads it, as focusing on people who hold themselves out as being rich when they actually have very little. The proverb may not necessarily be condemning people who hide their wealth, as this could be thought of as a sign of modesty. On the other hand, if it is motivated by a desire not to provide for the poor, then it would not be a good thing. Another way of reading this proverb is to understand the *Hithpa'el* verb forms, which are usually reflexive, as follows:

> Some make themselves rich, but have nothing,
> others make themselves poor, yet have great wealth.

Read this way, the proverb would be suggesting that those who have become rich illicitly or without wisdom will end up with nothing, and those who have become poor in order to help others will end up with great wealth. This last sentiment is in line with 11:24-25.

---

70. Marie Giblin, "Dualism," in *Dictionary of Feminist Theologies*, ed. Letty M. Russell and J. Shannon Clarkson (Louisville: Westminster John Knox Press, 1996), 74.

Prov 13:7-11

⁷Some pretend to be rich, yet have nothing;
  others pretend to be poor, yet have great wealth.
⁸Wealth is a ransom for a person's life,
  but the poor get no threats.
⁹The light of the righteous rejoices,
  but the lamp of the wicked goes out.
¹⁰By insolence the heedless make strife,
  but wisdom is with those who take advice.
¹¹Wealth hastily gotten will dwindle,
  but those who gather little by little will increase it.

TRANSLATION MATTERS

The verb שמע in 13:8, translated as "get," literally means "hear" or "heed"; גערה means "rebuke" rather than "threat."

Verse 8 begins with the wealthy person for whom wealth can be used as a ransom to pay for a loss that has been caused to another, who otherwise would exact vengeance. The second colon states that the poor do not hear or heed rebukes. This does not seem to have much to do with the first colon, which is why NRSV has read גערה as "threat" (of blackmail) for which ransom would need to be paid, but this is a stretch.

TRANSLATION MATTERS

The root שמח usually means "rejoice," "be glad," as the NRSV translates it at 13:9, but in this case there is another archaic usage, "to shine."[71] The verb is thus a pun, meaning both "shines" and "rejoices."

Proverbs 13:9 uses light imagery, the lights standing for individuals' lives, and a pun: the light of the just (righteous) shines, as the just (righteous)[72] person rejoices; meanwhile the lamp of the corrupt

---

71. Fox, *Proverbs 10–31*, 564.
72. See Translation Matters on Just/Integrity/Honesty (Righteous[ness]), צדקה/צדק/צדיק, at 1:2.

(wicked)[73] goes out. In 13:10 the contrast is between the vain, heedless person who arrogantly causes contention and those who wisely seek counsel from several advisers, who, it is implied, can bring about peaceful resolution to problems. (See Excursus on Women's Sins 1: Arrogance at 3:8.) In the context of proverbs on wealth and poverty, it is likely that those who seek advice are also more likely to make wise business decisions than those who arrogantly think they know it all and stir up strife in their families and communities. The cluster concludes with a proverb dealing with wealth acquisition. The contrast here is between wealth quickly acquired and that attained little by little, by hand.

TRANSLATION MATTERS

The MT of 13:11 says either that wealth from a breath will dwindle or that wealth will dwindle to less than a vapor. In the first case, wealth that has been quickly acquired will not last, and, in the second, wealth will become virtually nonexistent. The problem with the first reading is its awkwardness in Hebrew; thus, many translations, including the NRSV, have emended from מהבל, from nothing, to מבהל, hastily gotten (BHS).

The Teaching of the Wise is a Fountain of Life (13:12-19)

This cluster is framed by 13:12 and 13:19, which speak of deferred and realized hopes/desires, but the core primarily deals with discipline (instruction).[74] The opening proverb states an obvious fact, that when hopes are drawn out, we are miserable. Some desires are trivial and the wait for their fulfillment should be borne patiently, but others are of a different character. The antithesis of the first colon is that a fulfilled desire is a tree of life (see Gen 2:9, 3:22, 24), i.e., it is life giving.

The main theme of this cluster is introduced in 13:13-14: the importance of education. In the first colon of 13:13 the second verb is a pun. The Hebrew word חבל has two roots, the first one meaning to bind or pledge and the second one to act corruptly or ruinously. The meanings here are, first, the one NRSV presents, that "Those who despise the word *bring destruction* on themselves," and, second, that they have a pledge taken from them, i.e., that they incur a debt. This second meaning fits in

---

73. See Translation Matters on Corrupt[ion]/Unscrupulous/Reprehensible (Wicked[ness]), רשע/רשעים, at 2:22.

74. See Translation Matters on Discipline/Chastening/Correction (Instruction), מוסר, at 1:2.

¹²Hope deferred makes the heart sick,
　but a desire fulfilled is a tree of life.
¹³Those who despise the word bring destruction on themselves,
　but those who respect the commandment will be rewarded.
¹⁴The teaching of the wise is a fountain of life,
　so that one may avoid the snares of death.
¹⁵Good sense wins favor,
but the way of the faithless is their ruin.
¹⁶The clever do all things intelligently,
　but the fool displays folly.
¹⁷A bad messenger brings trouble,
　but a faithful envoy, healing.
¹⁸Poverty and disgrace are for the one who ignores instruction,
　but one who heeds reproof is honored.
¹⁹A desire realized is sweet to the soul,
　but to turn away from evil is an abomination to fools.

well with the second colon, which says that those who fear or are in awe of the command(ment), order, or precept (not necessarily a divine commandment) will be repaid. So those who have the improper emotional attitude of scorn for the word lose something financially, which has to be repaid, and, ultimately, they are destroyed. Those who have a high regard for the command(ment) will get something back for their proper attitude of respect. This fits in with the preceding proverb that focuses on deferred and realized dreams. The student who has the right attitude toward the word will be rewarded, though the proverb does not say how long the student will have to wait.

The thought of 13:13 continues in 13:14 with the statement that the teaching of the wise is like a water fountain, which will have the effect of turning the person who pays attention to it away from the lures put into traps, but figuratively the traps or snares are death itself. Verses 15-16, at the middle of this cluster, speak of good sense and its opposite. Proverbs 13:15a states that people who have good sense and thus act sensibly win approval from the community. The antithesis of this statement in 13:15b is that the path of the treacherous leads to their own destruction. Verse 16 follows these insights up with the statements that prudent (clever)[75] individuals do everything with knowledge, while dolts (fools)[76] put their folly[77] on display. Reading each colon into the other, the

75. See Translation Matters on Prudent/Prudence (Clever[ness]), ערמה and ערום, at 1:4.
76. See Translation Matters on Dolt/Chump/Oaf/Inept (Fool), כסיל, at 1:22.
77. See Translation Matters on Jerk/Schmuck/Folly (Fool/Folly), אויל/אולת, at 1:7.

prudent person speaks and acts with knowledge and the dolt displays folly (verbally) as well as through deeds. Verse 17 might seem unrelated to the surrounding proverbs, but it may be that a messenger required a relatively high level of education. In any case, a messenger who is not simply bad, i.e., incompetent, brings trouble if he mangles even an important detail, but a corrupt (wicked)[78] one can bring disaster. On the other hand, a trustworthy envoy produces just the opposite—healing, in the figurative sense.

Proverbs 13:18 brings the reader back to the main theme of discipline (instruction).[79] Both poverty and shame will be the lot of one who does not pay attention to instruction in its meaning of correction, but the one who listens to such rebukes will be honored. Verse 19 concludes the cluster with a variant of the one in the opening verse of the cluster (13:12): a desire that has been satisfied is sweet. The opposite of this sweetness is the loathing that dolts feel at the thought of turning away from wrongdoing. They want the wrong things, so even if they were to be granted their wishes, they would not be sweet because what they want leads only to their own destruction (13:13a, 15b, 18a).

The Good Tend to Prosper, but Injustice Makes Some Poor (13:20-25)

This cluster opens with the advice in 13:20 that the company one keeps is important. Those who spend time with smart people tend to become smarter themselves, and those who sit around with dolts (fools)[80] are worse off for it. Verse 21 similarly suggests that trouble pursues sinners but good repays the just (righteous).[81] Verse 22 is linked with 13:21 by the word טוב, "good." This time it refers to people. The good people (who have been repaid with good things) will leave an inheritance—not just for their children, but for their grandchildren. By contrast, the wealth of sinners will be hidden away for the just (although the mechanism for this is unclear). In addition, these two verses are linked by the root for "bad." In 13:20 the verb translated "suffers harm," רעע, is denominated

---

78. See Translation Matters on Corrupt[ion]/Unscrupulous/Reprehensible (Wicked[ness]), רשע/רשעים, at 2:22.

79. See Translation Matters on Discipline/Chastening/Correction (Instruction), מוסר, at 1:2.

80. See Translation Matters on Dolt/Chump/Oaf/Inept (Fool), כסיל, at 1:22.

81. For the meaning of צדיקים (13:21) and צדיק (13:22, 25), see Translation Matters on Just/Integrity/Honesty (Righteous[ness]), צדיק/צדק/צדקה, at 1:2.

Prov 13:20-25

²⁰Whoever walks with the wise becomes wise,
but the companion of fools suffers harm.
²¹Misfortune pursues sinners,
but prosperity rewards the righteous.
²²The good leave an inheritance to their children's children,
but the sinner's wealth is laid up for the righteous.

²³The field of the poor may yield much food,
but it is swept away through injustice.
²⁴Those who spare the rod hate their children,
but those who love them are diligent to discipline them.
²⁵The righteous have enough to satisfy their appetite,
but the belly of the wicked is empty.

from the noun "misfortune" in 13:21, רעה. Verse 23, as it stands in the MT, is in tension with the many proverbs criticizing the lazy, which state or imply that this is the main cause of poverty. Here, however, is an acknowledgment that sometimes the poor get a bad deal. The term translated by NRSV as "field," ניר, is not the standard one, but rather one that means tillable, untilled, or fallow ground, ground that either needs to be tilled or that has been lying fallow for one reason or another. Presumably, the poor are working this land because it is not particularly desirable, but they must take what they can get and through hard work are able to induce the land to produce a relatively large quantity of food, not so much that they can be called rich, but large considering the quality and quantity of the land they are working. The second colon says that it is (or they are) swept away by lack of justice. This proverb is a reminder that the wealth that the just people have is not to be taken for granted as due solely to their own diligence. It is not enough to walk with the right people and to properly raise one's children. Injustice sometimes leaves people poor through no fault of their own.

TRANSLATION MATTERS

The verb rendered as "walks" in 13:20 is a *Qeré/Ketib*. The NRSV is following the *Qeré*, הלך, a participle. The *Ketib*, הלוך, is an imperative—"Go with the wise and become wise"—but it does not make for as good parallelism as the *Qeré*.[82]

---

82. On *Qeré/Ketib*, see Translation Matters at 1:27.

Excursus on Disproportion of Wealth and Poverty in the Contemporary World

In 2016, eight men owned as much of the world's wealth as the bottom half of the world's population, 3.6 billion people. And the 1,810 billionaires on Forbes's list—89 percent male—held $6.5 trillion, as much wealth as 70 percent of humanity. Who are the people who constitute the bottom half and where do they live? Eighty percent are adults living in Africa and India. They're young and likely to be single and poorly educated. Women who are poorly educated are even more likely than men to have very little wealth.[83] These extremes of wealth and poverty make it extraordinarily difficult, particularly for those at the bottom, to eke out any sort of existence for themselves and their children. They lack resources and skills; when they acquire these, they usually thrive. Microfinance coupled with skills training is making a difference, however, in some areas.[84]

The proverb in 13:24, which is well known from the English paraphrase, "spare the rod, spoil the child," is repugnant to many modern sensibilities. The basic concept of the importance of setting limits for children, of providing discipline[85] and reproof when the child has misbehaved, is not the problem. Corporal punishment, which is illegal in many classrooms and frowned on in the home now, was standard in the ancient world; there were far fewer alternatives and modern philosophical approaches were centuries away.

The second colon says that those who love their children begin early to discipline them. The cluster is rounded out with a general statement saying that the just eat enough to satisfy their appetites, but the corrupt (wicked)[86] will have empty stomachs. This proverb links with the one in

83. Emily Peck, "These 8 Men Have as Much Money as Half the World," *Huffington Post*, January 16, 2017, https://www.huffingtonpost.com/entry/income-inequality-oxfam_us_58792e6ee4b0b3c7a7b13616.

84. Rathiranee Yogendrarajah, "The Impact of Micro Credit on Women Empowerment," *International Journal of Research in Commerce, Economics & Management* 2 (2012), https://papers.ssrn.com/sol3/papers.cfm?abstract_id=2431565.

85. See Translation Matters on Discipline/Chastening/Correction (Instruction), מוסר, at 1:2.

86. See Translation Matters on Corrupt[ion]/Unscrupulous/Reprehensible (Wicked[ness]), רשע/רשעים, at 2:22.

13:23, as the words for "have enough" and for "food" in 13:23 are from the same root, אכל.

Contrast Between the Wise and Foolish Women (14:1-3)

The short cluster, 14:1-3, which opens chapter 14, is bound together by vocabulary: wise (חכמות, 14:1; חכמים, 14:3) and jerks (foolish; אולת, 14:1)/ Folly (אויל, 14:3).[87] However the first colon in 14:1 is read, it has to do with a wise woman (or Wisdom) building her house (compare 9:1-18 for the earlier contrast between Wisdom and Folly), "house" meaning not primarily the physical structure but being a figure for the family and the household operations. The phrase "house of the/my mother" (as opposed to house of the father) occurs in Ruth 1:8 (בית אמה) and Song 3:4; 8:2 (בית אמי).

The mother's house was apparently the women's compound where the mother and her children lived together. When there was more than one wife, each wife had her own house.[88] The term "father's house" could be used in the sense of lineage but also may have referred to a physical space. The arrangement was not usually of women-headed households, as in the contemporary world, but of extended families in which the men and women had separate domains.

TRANSLATION MATTERS

In 14:1, the Hebrew חכמות נשים, "the wise ones of women," or "wisest of women," followed by the singular verb בנתה, "builds," is difficult. Claudia Camp reads the phrase as "the wisdom (of women),"[89] but it is necessary to revocalize the first word from חַכְמוֹת to חָכְמוֹת, "wisdom," and preferable to omit the second word altogether to provide better parallelism.

---

87. See Translation Matters on Dolt/Chump/Oaf/Inept (Fool), כסיל, at 1:22 and on Jerk/Schmuck/Folly (Fool/Folly), אויל/אולת, at 1:7.

88. Cynthia R. Chapman, *The House of the Mother: The Social Roles of Maternal Kin in Biblical Hebrew Narrative and Poetry* (New Haven: Yale University Press, 2016).

89. Claudia V. Camp, *Wisdom and the Feminine in the Book of Proverbs*, BLS 11 (Sheffield: Almond Press, 1985), 192.

[1]The wise woman builds her
house,
but the foolish tears it down with
her own hands.
[2]Those who walk uprightly fear the
LORD,

but one who is devious in conduct
despises him.
[3]The talk of fools is a rod for their
backs,
but the lips of the wise preserve
them.

The Wise Woman Builds Her House—Proverbs 14:1

In the discussion of good versus evil, sometimes, a woman's virtue is couched in the center. In terms of social position, a woman's place is within the margins and the categories created by gender, racial, sexual, and economic oppressions—as they are byproducts of patriarchy, industrialization, and other tools of supremacy.[90] Proverbs 14:1 situates womanist principles of grounding, foundation, work, and interdependence through the lens of the covert binary of the text, construction versus demolition; it reads like a rubric of wisdom and folly as it juxtaposes opportunity, agency, and group dynamics.

The "wise woman" begins the dialectic of virtue with its counter "folly." Tools for the construction of houses for "wise women" may vary due to culture, access to material,

levels of oppression, and consciousness; dimensions of the house need not be mentioned; in as much as work is done to construct—opportunity, foundation for genders. The "foolish" are a select group that tear down foundations, fortitude, and wisdom. Moreover, the metaphoric demolition of the house is preceded by missed opportunity, lack of agency, or oppression. Simply put, the "foolish" do not ascribe to proverbial truths.

The underpinnings of womanist grouping amalgamate to community, interdependence, and self-care foundations. In the context of community, buildings are often attributed to the establishment of substance and something planned. When we consider the foundations of planning, we think of following the plans that God has set before us. Often, we take the role of self-constructionists whereby

90. bell hooks, "Choosing the Margin as a Space of Radical Openness," in *The Feminist Standpoint Theory Reader: Intellectual and Political Controversies*, ed. Sandra Harding (New York: Routledge, 2001), 153–59.

our motivations, thoughts, and drive push us away from God's vision for our lives and separate us from the path laid before us. The journey is not a singular one, and this is where wisdom comes into play. It takes spiritual rootedness and an understanding of who we are as God's children that equips us to follow God's blueprint and thus create God's intended "houses."

The work of wise women is not to anticipate or counteract the work of the foolish but to share material resources, emotional support, and our connection to the Divine in a way that makes allies. The disjunction in attraction is the pathology of independent thought. If one reasons that God has an intended plan and wise women follow the plan, then, the inverse becomes apparent: foolish women are independent and believe in their own sense of self. This is a fallible truth in that the work of wisdom in "every woman" is to acknowledge how dependence on God leads to interdependence among God's people through discovery of personal agency and opportunity that gathers allies, produces new streams of consciousness, and is declarative of personal faith and commitment to relationship with God and God's peoples; the inverse makes us allies to patriarchy, oppression, racism, and sexism and is folly.

Alexandrea Rich

Proverbs 14:2 consists of two cola, each of which are nominal sentences in which either phrase can be considered to be the subject or the predicate nominative. Thus, the proverbs can be read either as:

> The one who walks in the straightness of his (ways) (is) a fearer of YHWH,
> but one whose way is crooked (is) one who despises him.

or

> The one who fears YHWH is the one who walks in the uprightness of his (ways),
> but one who despises him is one whose ways are crooked.

The first version says that people who exhibit certain types of behavior have corollary attitudes toward God. You can tell a tree by the fruit it produces. The second version says that the attitudes people have predict their behavior. These are two sides of the same coin, but we hear and experience them in subtly different ways. According to various proverbs, walking on the straight path tends to lead to success in life. This in turn, it could be argued, makes it easier to have a positive attitude toward God. Contrariwise, someone whose ways are crooked, perhaps because of not having been brought up well, will not be very successful and thus will be more likely to have a negative attitude toward God. The opposite perspective is that people who begin with the right attitude toward God, however it may have been gained—though Proverbs certainly suggests that training in youth is important—will tend toward the correct behavior.

TRANSLATION MATTERS

The NRSV's emendation in 14:3 of MT's גאוה, "pride, haughtiness," to גוה, "back," based on 10:13 is not necessary. MT makes sense: "The talk of fools is a rod of haughtiness."

The last proverb in this cluster, 14:3, in the NRSV translation suggests that what jerks say is a rod for their own backs. They say stupid things that boomerang in such a way as to beat themselves up. This type of fool is not just inept; he is someone we would label as a troublemaker, so this kind of proverb provides psychological relief to people who must put up with such people.

The antithesis is that what the wise say tends to guard them from adversity. The first colon in the MT says that the speech of jerks is a rod of haughtiness. Haughtiness does hurt the person who throws such sticks outward, as they sometimes boomerang, but the sticks also hurt others. The second colon of the proverb, however, asserts that the lips of the wise will preserve them, implicitly, from jerks' arrogant rods. (See the Excursus on Women's Sins 1: Arrogance, at 3:8.)

The Importance of True and Wise Speech (14:4-9)

This cluster consists of a series of antitheses; it opens with the proverb in 14:4 that speaks of the importance of oxen and, by extension, of resources. Because the word בר can mean either "grain" or "clean," as in empty, this proverb can mean either that the crib is empty or that there is a crib of grain. In either case, and the two meanings may have been intended as a pun, the contrast is between no grain or, at most, a single crib of grain, on the one hand, and abundance of crops, on the other, which result from the use of oxen that helped the ancient farmer plow the fields. Verse 5 moves to the main theme of this cluster, speech. This proverb would seem to be simply defining terms, but the point is

---

Prov 14:4-9

⁴Where there are no oxen, there is
no grain;
abundant crops come by the
strength of the ox.
⁵A faithful witness does not lie,
but a false witness breathes out
lies.
⁶A scoffer seeks wisdom in vain,
but knowledge is easy for one

who understands.
⁷Leave the presence of a fool,
for there you do not find words of
knowledge.
⁸It is the wisdom of the clever to
understand where they go,
but the folly of fools misleads.
⁹Fools mock at the guilt offering,
but the upright enjoy God's favor.

---

that faithful witnesses never lie. They can be counted on always to tell the truth. They bring a steady foundation to justice as the oxen are the foundation of the farm. Similarly, false witnesses exhale lies with every breath. It is part of their character.

Proverbs 14:6-7 deals with scoffers and dolts (fools).⁹¹ Compared with the arrogant scoffer, to the discerning, knowledge is easy. (See the Excursus on the Sins of Women 1: Arrogance, at 3:8.) The scoffer who tries to turn to wisdom is out of luck. The habitually corrupt scoffers will not be able to find it within themselves, and the wise will be too suspicious of them to teach them (see 1:28). On the other hand, the second colon in 14:6 states the antithesis that those who build a foundation of understanding find it relatively easy to gain further knowledge. The mind and spirit are trained for the activity.

TRANSLATION MATTERS

The Hebrew למנגד does not mean "from the presence of," as NRSV renders it in 14:7, but rather "opposite, in front of." Thus, the line probably means, "Go into the presence of a dolt (fool), and . . ."

Verse 7, as understood by NRSV, indicates that one should run from the presence of a dolt (fool; כסיל) because no knowledgeable words will be found there. If the preposition is understood differently, the proverb says, rather, "If you go in front of a dolt, you'll find no words of knowledge." The two approaches amount to the same thing.

---

91. See Translation Matters on Dolt/Chump/Oaf/Inept (Fool), כסיל, at 1:22.

Proverbs 14:8-9 again provides opposing pictures of the prudent (clever)[92] person and the stupid, foolish one. The wisdom of the prudent lies in their discernment of the correct paths. The folly[93] of dolts is described here as deceit, deceptiveness, or craftiness. Simply acting without having done the discernment necessary to determine the right course of action will result in an inconsistent pattern of behavior at best and, because, lacking any other principle, we will tend to act on what seems to promise short-term self-aggrandizement, behavior that is often crafty or deceptive. The first colon of 14:9 is difficult. The subject is plural and the verb is singular, but this is not unheard of in classical Hebrew. The most difficult part is the object of the verb, which can mean guilt, the feeling of guilt, or a guilt offering (see Lev 5:14–6:7; 7:1-6), whether restitution for sin or the sacrificial offering itself. It is possible that jerks (fools)[94] might mock the concept of their own guilt, thinking themselves above the law; in this case they would not feel guilt. It is also possible that they might avoid paying restitution when they have injured someone. The latter understanding may make the best sense of the MT in the context of the second colon, where the Hebrew says that among the upstanding (upright)[95] there is favor, i.e., they treat each other in such a way that they enjoy each other's regard. This verse connects with 14:6, for the words "scoffer" and "mock" share the same Hebrew root, ליץ. It also connects with 14:8, where both use the same root for folly, אול.

Paths, Choices, and Consequences (14:10-14)

This proverbial cluster contains an unusual amount of emotional content with the words for heart/mind, לב,[96] and joy, שמחה, at the beginning and in 14:13 near the end of the cluster. This emotional content is interspersed with proverbs dealing with the consequences of actions, suggesting that the emotions depicted are the results of good or bad choices. The first colon of the opening proverb, 14:10, says what seems obvious enough, that a person's (own) heart/mind knows that individual's own bitterness. Some interpret the colon to mean that only the bitter person

---

92. See Translation Matters on Prudent/Prudence (Clever[ness]), ערמה and ערום, at 1:4.

93. See Translation Matters on Jerk/Schmuck/Folly (Fool/Folly), אויל/אולת, at 1:7.

94. See Translation Matters on Dolt/Chump/Oaf/Inept (Fool), כסיל, at 1:22.

95. See Translation Matters on Upstanding/Straight/Straightforward (Upright), ישר/ישרים, at 2:7.

96. See Translation Matters on the Heart, לב, at 2:2.

¹⁰The heart knows its own bitterness,
and no stranger shares its joy.
¹¹The house of the wicked is
destroyed,
but the tent of the upright flourishes.
¹²There is a way that seems right to a
person,

but its end is the way to death.
¹³Even in laughter the heart is sad,
and the end of joy is grief.
¹⁴The perverse get what their ways
deserve,
and the good, what their deeds
deserve.

understands his or her own bitterness. Certainly, those who are bitter are likely to understand their bitterness better than others. The colon probably just means that although we may sympathize with others' problems and their bitterness in the face of them, we can never totally empathize with them. The second colon asserts that a stranger will not share in one's joy. Again, on the face of it, this seems obvious. Those who know us, our family and close friends, are the ones with whom we expect to share our joy. The two cola combined may be suggesting, however, that no one can really share either our bitterness or our joy. In the context of the other proverbs in this cluster, this opening proverb may be suggesting that one should choose one's ways carefully because individuals must live with the consequences of the choices, including the emotional impact, which no one can help them with, cannot even fully fathom.

Proverbs 14:11 presents the apparent paradox that the solid house of the corrupt (wicked)[97] is wiped out, but the much flimsier tent of the upright shows buds or sprouts and thus flourishes. The image conjures up that of a tree, and since the abode represented the family, the modern reader can picture the family tree with many branches. Thus, the rich may revel in their great houses, but they can be swept away, leaving them with nothing; and if the houses stand, they do not represent the true wealth of wisdom. The tent may more easily be blown down, but the wisdom within it remains.

In 14:12, the word "seems" is not in the Hebrew, but some linking verb is required by the Hebrew syntax, and in the context of the second colon, "seems" is most appropriate. This proverb acknowledges that it is not always easy to discern which road is the best one to take. There are

97. See Translation Matters on Corrupt[ion]/Unscrupulous/Reprehensible (Wicked[ness]), רשע/רשעים, at 2:22.

times when a seemingly pleasant road is ahead, but when the end of that seemingly pleasant road appears, it turns out that one is confronted only with paths leading to bad places. There's no turning back. In the context of the final proverb in this cluster, this proverb is probably to be read to mean not just that it is not easy to discern which road is the right one to take but that bad people pick easy roads, roads that take advantage of others, thinking only of what will make their own lives comfortable, not seeing the consequences for themselves (or perhaps even for others) down the road. This is connected to 14:10; the paths chosen may seem to lead to prosperity and happiness, but they conceal bitterness if not chosen correctly with wisdom. If 14:13 is read in the context of 14:12, then it is easy to see how even in laughter the heart is sad. If one has made poor choices in life, then one may find momentary diversions in which laughter can lighten the mood, but underneath the heart is still sad.

Of course, even outside the immediate context of the other proverbs, it is often true that when people are suffering from depression, whether of the clinical variety or as a result of circumstances, they may find that laughter is the best medicine for a time, but the underlying sadness will still be there in most cases.

The second half of this proverb says that (an artificial) joy leads to sadness (based on incorrect values). Again, reading this thought in the context of the surrounding proverbs, it could mean that the kind of joy that a person who has made poor choices will experience is mere mirth or gaiety rather than something deeper. Perhaps it is even the emotion that results from a temporary financial gain through a deceptive business practice. The proverb could be asserting in the context that such mirth will turn to sadness. Outside the context it could be saying simply that after a really good party there is the inevitable let-down. The final proverb in this cluster, 14:14, returns to the road metaphor and the concept of just deserts. This time the phrase used of the bad guys is an unusual one, לב סוג, "faithless or backsliding heart/mind." As with other words that NRSV translates as "perverse," I prefer to avoid this rendering due to its sexual connotations. Such a one will be requited based on the roads taken (or presumably not taken). The antithesis is that good individuals likewise will be repaid based on their deeds.

The Simple and the Prudent, the Wise and the Foolish (14:15-18)

This cluster is bound together by an *inclusio* in 14:15 and 14:18: singular and plural forms of "simple" or, in this context, naive or gullible

Prov 14:15-18

¹⁵The simple believe everything,
but the clever consider their steps.
¹⁶The wise are cautious and turn
away from evil,
but the fool throws off restraint
and is careless.

¹⁷One who is quick-tempered acts
foolishly,
and the schemer is hated.
¹⁸The simple are adorned with folly,
but the clever are crowned with
knowledge.

(פתי, 14:15; פתאים, 14:18) and prudent (clever, ערום, 14:15; ערומים, 14:18).[98] In the intervening verses is the usual word for the wise (חכם) and standard words for the dolt (fool; כסיל)[99] and folly (אולת).[100] The opening proverb states that the simple are uniformly credulous rather than discerning what is true and false. The prudent, on the other hand, weigh what is said so that they can discern which steps to take. Wise people are wary and thus are cautious and turn from רע, evil, misery, injury, or anything negative (14:16a). Precisely how to interpret this depends on the following colon (14:16b). The opposite of the cautious, wise individual is the dolt. The verbs in this colon can be understood in two ways. The individual arrogantly refuses to be careful (מתעבר) and is trusting, i.e., complacent (בוטח, see Isa 32:9). This second verb can also mean "falls," a rare homonym occurring clearly only in Jeremiah 12:5.[101] With this reading of the second colon, the first colon then means that the wise are cautious and avoid what they discern to be trouble; the dolt arrogantly refuses to be careful, is unfazed by the risks, and thus falls. Another possible reading of מתעבר is that the dolt gets angry. This creates another pun that adds to the richness of the meaning: The wise person is cautious and avoids unnecessary conflict, while the arrogant dolt gets angry, throws off restraint, (gets into unnecessary conflict), and falls. From a feminist perspective this tends to be truer of young men than young women.

98. See Translation Matters on Prudent/Prudence (Clever[ness]), ערמה and ערום, at 1:4.
99. See Translation Matters on Dolt/Chump/Oaf/Inept (Fool), כסיל, at 1:22.
100. See Translation Matters on Jerk/Schmuck/Folly (Fool/Folly), אויל/אולת, at 1:7.
101. HALOT, 120b. See Jer 12:5.

Excursus on Women's Sins 4: Anger

Anger is one of the traditional seven deadly sins. Women tend to be socialized more than men not to express anger. It has been the focus of much feminist theological discussion.[102] Like arrogance, the male's greater propensity to anger may have a physical basis in his larger production of testosterone. (See Excursus on Women's Sins 1: Arrogance, at 3:8.) Interestingly, research shows that women and men both experience and express anger very similarly.[103] So our perception that men express their anger more freely and comfortably than women do is likely to come from the fact that men often have greater power (economic, political, and physical) whether at work or at home. Thus, they are often in positions where they can afford to express their anger more than women are. This is not absolute, however. We have images of the irate powerful male executive but not of the lower-status angry salesman.

The question remains whether anger is ever good, whether it is simply neutral depending on how it is expressed, or whether it is always bad. Anger as an emotion is healthy. It is what alerts us to injustice, whether done to ourselves or to others. Expression of anger in the form of yelling or any other sudden outburst or even in ongoing hostility is seldom productive and it tends to poison our own inner selves.

One of the most important things that the mindfulness movement teaches is awareness of each moment. At the instant anger is triggered, a small part of the brain called the amygdala goes into action, along with the hippocampus and the prefrontal cortex. If we allow these parts of our brain just to react mindlessly, reflexively, then we will go into a state of acute hyperarousal, which will prepare us almost instantaneously for fight or flight. But we can also pause, be mindful of how we are responding to the trigger, and determine if we are actually in danger, if we really need to respond angrily to the situation. In most cases, there is a smarter way to handle the provocation. This takes training, but we can change our brains; the neuroplasticity of the brain throughout our lives has been established. Ultimately, whoever learns this technique will be more effective, and thus more successful, than people who fly off the handle, even if they

---

102. See Carolyn Osiek, *Beyond Anger: On Being a Feminist in the Church* (New York: Paulist, 1986); Kathleen Fischer, *Transforming Fire: Women Using Anger Creatively* (New York: Paulist, 1999); Carol Tavris, *Anger: The Misunderstood Emotion*, rev. ed. (New York: Simon & Schuster, 1989); Beverly Wildung Harrison, "The Power of Anger in the Work of Love," *USQR* 36 (1981): 41–57.

103. Tavris, *Anger*, 179–202.

are tolerated because of the power they exercise. People "lose points" when they have tantrums. In addition, we will be healthier, happier, and live longer.[104]

Proverbs 14:17 follows up the concern in 14:16 with the way anger can lead to problems. Those with short fuses act foolishly, but the individual with schemes, the one who has carefully rather than quickly devised plans, is hated. Schemes are not always evil, but, in the context, these schemes are not good ones.

TRANSLATION MATTERS

In 14:18, NRSV emends the MT נָחֲלוּ, "inherits," to נֶחֱלוּ, "are adorned," which is unnecessary.

The concluding proverb in the cluster, 14:18, returns to the vocabulary of the opening proverb; the MT says that the naive individuals inherit folly.[105] They are not intrinsically bad people, but their lack of knowledge predisposes them to foolishness; they do not know how to avoid it. A pun between the MT נָחֲלוּ, (*nāḥălû*) "inherit," and NRSV's emendation נֶחֱלוּ, (*neḥĕlû*) "are adorned," is possible. The two words are identical except for the vowels and even those are similar, the last one being identical, the middle one being super short in נֶחֱלוּ, and the first one being the only one that is significantly different. If this is correct, then the colon asserts that the simple will inherit folly and be adorned with it. The second colon provides the antithesis, that the prudent people wear knowledge as their crowns. They do not simply inherit it because of their condition. They work hard to attain it and then wear it proudly as royalty wear crowns.

---

104. See Jon Kabat-Zinn, *Full Catastrophe Living: Using the Wisdom of Your Body and Mind to Face Stress, Pain, and Illness*, rev. ed. (New York: Bantam, 2013); Louis Cozolino, *The Neuroscience of Human Relationships: Attachment and the Developing Social Brain*, 2nd ed. (New York: W. W. Norton & Company, 2014).

105. See Translation Matters on Jerk/Schmuck/Folly (Fool/Folly), אויל/אולת, at 1:7.

Attitudes toward the Rich and the Poor (14:19-22)

This proverbial cluster is bound together by an *inclusio* of the words for "good" and "bad" (evil) in 14:19 (רעים; טובים) and 14:22 (רע; טוב).[106] The middle two proverbs focus on economic inequality. Verse 19 opens with a statement asserting that unethical people (the evil)[107] will (eventually) prostrate themselves before good people, and the corrupt (wicked)[108] at the gates of the just (righteous).[109] The word for "gate," שער, is used of large public gates, like city gates or the gates of the temple in Jerusalem, not the gates to a residential building. Thus, the area inside the city gate was the place where the wicked were brought to justice. Perhaps they might bow down before the gates of the temple as well, acknowledging their guilt, since the vocabulary of the proverb includes both words for good and bad (evil) and just and corrupt. Verses 20 and 21 deal with economic inequality, 14:20 stating an objective but sad reality. Many people tend to distance themselves from the poor, even their neighbors, because the poor are always in need. Contrariwise, the rich always have many "friends," because of the hope that the rich will be able to be of some benefit. Verse 21 follows up with a critique of the first colon of verse 20. People who hate their neighbors, in this context, especially their poor neighbors, are labelled sinners. In the context of 14:19 they will be judged at the gates of the just. By contrast, those who are compassionate to the poor are called blissful, blessed, fortunate, or happy.[110]

This contrasts with the proverbs that criticize the sluggards whose laziness leads to poverty. This proverb does not directly refute this notion, because people could still have gotten into poverty through lack of diligence, and the proverb writer still urges compassionate treatment of them. At the very least, there is a tension between this proverb and the many that suggest the cause of poverty is lack of diligence.

The final verse in this cluster, 14:22, returns to the language of good and evil from 14:19 with a rhetorical question: Don't those who plan evil wander hopelessly in physical confusion that represents moral confusion so that they err? On the other hand, what the second colon literally says is that

---

106. See Translation Matters on Unethical (Evil/Bad/Wicked), רע/רעים, at 4:14. Here, for the sake of parallelism, "bad" is preferred to "unethical."

107. See the discussion of רעים at 4:14.

108. See Translation Matters on Corrupt[ion]/Unscrupulous/Reprehensible (Wicked[ness]), רשע/רשעים, at 2:22.

109. See Translation Matters on Just/Integrity/Honesty (Righteous[ness]), צדקה/ צדיק/צדק, at 1:2.

110. See Translation Matters on Blissful (Happy), אשרי, at 3:13.

Prov 14:19-22

¹⁹The evil bow down before the good,	²¹Those who despise their neighbors are sinners,
the wicked at the gates of the righteous.	but happy are those who are kind to the poor.
²⁰The poor are disliked even by their neighbors,	²²Do they not err that plan evil?
but the rich have many friends.	Those who plan good find loyalty and faithfulness.

those who plan good (are) kindness (loyalty)[111] and faithfulness. The verb "to be" is implicit rather than explicit in the Hebrew. We might say that they are the epitome of these qualities or they embody these qualities. In the context of the first colon, it is also implied that they do not wander about aimlessly. They plan good and well and walk down a straight, smooth path of success. The sages were aware that life does not always go smoothly, but they believed that planning and good intentions generally pay off, and, even when they don't, they are better than the alternative. And kindness is repaid both in practical terms and in the acquisition of wisdom.

Consequences of Wise and Perfidious (Foolish) Behavior (14:23-27)

This small cluster focuses rather broadly on the various consequences of wise and foolish behavior. Verse 23 begins with the results of difficult, painful work—abundance or profit. The antithesis is that a word of the lips, that is mere talk without action, will bring poverty. The talk without the walk will bring no lasting results.

TRANSLATION MATTERS

In 14:24, NRSV emends עשרם, "their wealth," to ערמם, "their prudence (wisdom)."[112] I prefer to reserve the gloss "wisdom" for words related to the root חכם. In addition, NRSV emends אולת, "folly," to לוית, "garland," probably necessary to avoid the tautology, the folly of fools is folly. LXX reads διατριβή, "wearing away" or "pastime," which is not helpful.

---

111. See Translation Matters on Kindness/Mercy (Loyalty), חסד, at 2:8. The Hebrew חסד is best understood as mercy or kindness rather than loyalty (NRSV).

112. See Translation Matters on Prudent/Prudence (Clever[ness]), ערמה and ערום, at 1:4.

Prov 14:23-27

²³In all toil there is profit,
    but mere talk leads only to poverty.
²⁴The crown of the wise is their
        wisdom,
    but folly is the garland of fools.
²⁵A truthful witness saves lives,
    but one who utters lies is a
        betrayer.

²⁶In the fear of the Lᴏʀᴅ one has
        strong confidence,
    and one's children will have a
        refuge.
²⁷The fear of the Lᴏʀᴅ is a fountain
        of life,
    so that one may avoid the snares
        of death.

Proverbs 14:24 follows this thought with the assertion in the MT that the crown of the wise is their wealth. In the context of 14:23, this makes sense. The wise are willing to work hard, painfully hard, and as a result will become wealthy. The NRSV's emendation, "their prudence (wisdom)," is possible and makes for good parallelism with folly in the second colon. The second colon, as emended by NRSV, suggests that the parallel to the prudence of the wise worn as their crown is the folly that jerks (the foolish)[113] will wear as their wreath or garland. This is a much simpler, more humble ornament than a crown, as befits the foolish wearer. Perhaps if the text is not emended, it could be understood that wisdom leads to wealth, but folly leads merely to more folly.

Proverbs 14:25 moves into the judicial realm. In a capital case, a truthful witness could be the difference between life and death; such a person saves innocent individuals who have been falsely accused as well as future victims of guilty defendants. The second part of the proverb says that one who breathes out lies is (the epitome of) deceptiveness or treachery. (One is reminded of the elders in the story of Susanna in the Additions to the Book of Daniel.) Implicitly, this sort of person can cost people their lives. The movie *Marshall*, about an early case in which Thurgood Marshall, later a Supreme Court justice, was involved is an all too real reminder of the potential deadly effects of false testimony, particularly in a matter of illicit sex.[114]

The proverbs in 14:26-27 can refer back to the initial ones in this cluster in 14:23-24, and to the preceding one in 14:25. When one has the appropriate fear of and reverence for the divine, one can move forward with

113. See Translation Matters on Jerk/Schmuck/Folly (Fool/Folly), אויל/אולת, at 1:7.
114. See Lily Rothman, "What to Know about the Real Case That Inspired the Movie *Marshall*," October 17, 2017, http://time.com/4972645/marshall-movie-true-story/.

28The glory of a king is a multitude of people;
without people a prince is ruined.
29Whoever is slow to anger has great understanding,
but one who has a hasty temper exalts folly.
30A tranquil mind gives life to the flesh,
but passion makes the bones rot.
31Those who oppress the poor insult their Maker,
but those who are kind to the needy honor him.

32The wicked are overthrown by their evildoing,
but the righteous find a refuge in their integrity.
33Wisdom is at home in the mind of one who has understanding,
but it is not known in the heart of fools.
34Righteousness exalts a nation,
but sin is a reproach to any people.
35A servant who deals wisely has the king's favor,
but his wrath falls on one who acts shamefully.

strong trust and confidence. One will have worked hard to make provision for oneself and one's family, and one will have sought knowledge on which to build one's life, and one will have been an honest witness when called into court. For all these reasons one's children will have a refuge to which to go in times of trouble. Verse 27 uses the metaphor of a fountain of life. It is not immediately obvious how a fountain of life helps avoid the snares of death, other than thirst in the hot, dry climate of ancient Israel, but this specific snare was dire enough perhaps to be a stand-in for all others. A life lived in the fear of YHWH,[115] with Wisdom, made death, while inevitable, nothing to dread.

Behavior Befitting a King (14:28-35)

This large cluster of proverbs has an *inclusio* in 14:28 and 14:35 with the word "king." The intervening proverbs can be understood as relating to royal behavior, as well as more generally to the moral behavior of citizens, though the proverb in the final verse specifically focuses on what a presumably royal servant must do to get the king's favor (or wrath). The opening proverb (14:28) asserts that a king's glory is in the large number of people under his rule, while—without people—a prince is all washed up. Thus, a ruler had best rule wisely so that the people are content and

---

115. See discussion of this phrase at 1:7.

international relations are handled adroitly as well. In 14:29, "slow to anger" renders the idiom "long of nostrils," ארך אפים, as opposed to wide, flared nostrils. Similarly, being short of spirit, breath, or wind means being short tempered; the result of the latter is that folly[116] is exalted. Along similar lines, a pun in 14:30 speaks of a tranquil mind, this adjective translating the MT's מרפא, while the Hebrew evokes an identical sounding word, meaning calm, taken from the root רפה, denoting soft or gentle. Thus, the proverb asserts the mind-body connection, that a healthy, calm mind is life-giving for the flesh. The second half of the proverb says that passion, but not all passion, is unhealthy. The Hebrew קנאה refers in an unfavorable sense to jealousy or anger. It can be used positively, but in the context the word has a negative connotation. Such jealousy or anger results in bones rotting or decaying. So whereas inner calmness produces life for the entire body, jealousy and anger, which are exhibited outwardly, result in interior rot and decay. (See Excursus on Women's Sins 4: Anger, at 14:16.)

In the context of this cluster beginning and ending with proverbs dealing with kings, it seems likely that 14:31 was intended by the editors to be read as instructions to a ruling official. Rulers who oppress the poor or deal tyrannically with them are insulting the one who created both of them, i.e., the poor and the oppressor, for the same God made both, though the pronoun "their" is ambiguous. On the other hand, people who show kindness to the poor are honoring God.

TRANSLATION MATTERS

In 14:32, MT במותו, "in his death," is emended by NRSV with LXX and Syriac to בתומו, "in his integrity." The מ and ת were apparently switched.

Proverbs 14:32 is a good follow-up to 14:31, for this proverb, though a general one, in this context provides the consequences of oppressive behavior. The corrupt (wicked)[117] will be punished violently for their wrongdoing, but the just (righteous)[118] will be able to seek refuge in their own integrity. Exactly what this meant on a practical level is not clear.

---

116. See Translation Matters on Jerk/Schmuck/Folly (Fool/Folly), אויל/אולת, at 1:7.

117. See Translation Matters on Corrupt[ion]/Unscrupulous/Reprehensible (Wicked[ness]), רשע/רשעים, at 2:22.

118. See Translation Matters on Just/Integrity/Honesty (Righteous[ness]), צדקה/צדיק/צדק, at 1:2.

TRANSLATION MATTERS

In 14:33, the NRSV adds the negative, "not," following the LXX and the Syriac, but it is probably unnecessary.

Proverbs 14:33 begins with an unsurprising statement, that wisdom is comfortably at rest in those who have understanding, but the second colon, as it stands in the MT, requires reflection. It says that it is known in the heart or midst of dolts (fools).[119] The pronoun seems to refer to wisdom. The colon could mean that, even among the dull, stupid, foolish people, wisdom makes herself known—they just don't pay attention. Alternately, or at the same time, the colon could mean that, in a mixed crowd of dull, stupid, foolish and smart people, the stupidity of the foolish will make the wisdom of the smart people all the more obvious. Or, alternatively, as NRSV emends, perhaps the colon needs a negative.

Proverbs 14:34 states a standard concept, that integrity exalts a nation. The second colon is more interesting because the first word, חסד, usually means kindness, but then the second colon would mean that sin is kindness to any people, which cannot be correct. A rare homonym found in Leviticus 20:17 meaning "disgrace" provides the necessary sense of reproach or disgrace. The final proverb in this cluster, 14:35, focuses on how a servant must act to win a king's favor: he must behave sensibly, prudently, wisely. The antithesis is that the king will be angry with one who acts in a shameful manner. The proverb addresses both royal servants (and would-be servants) on how to stay in the king's favor and also the king, as it implies the value of royal reward of good behavior and rebuke of poor performance.

The Nature of the Tongue (15:1-4)

The proverbs in 15:1-4 deal primarily with speech. Verses 1-2 are a pair. The better known 15:1 takes a personal tone, while 15:2 suggests the unproductivity of rough words. The word for "folly" here is from the root meaning not just ineptitude but moral depravity.[120] Verse 3 is a YHWH saying. It asserts that YHWH's eyes are everywhere, keeping an

---

119. See Translation Matters on Dolt/Chump/Oaf/Inept (Fool), כסיל, at 1:22.
120. See Translation Matters on Jerk/Schmuck/Folly (Fool/Folly), אויל/אולת, at 1:7.

¹A soft answer turns away wrath,
 but a harsh word stirs up
  anger.
²The tongue of the wise dispenses
  knowledge,
 but the mouths of fools pour out
  folly.

³The eyes of the LORD are in every
  place,
 keeping watch on the evil and the
  good.
⁴A gentle tongue is a tree of life,
 but perverseness in it breaks the
  spirit.

eye on everyone, the good and bad (evil) alike.[121] The speech we choose does not vanish once our words have been uttered but is remembered. The final proverb in this cluster, 15:4, returns to the theme of the opening proverb in the cluster, gentle speech. As in 12:18, the word מרפא, healing, involves a pun. It plays on the roots for "healing," רפא, and "soft, gentle," רפה. A soft, gentle word is healing.[122]

No Pain, No Gain (15:5-12)

This proverbial cluster focuses on discipline (instruction),[123] the benefits to those who accept it and the consequences to those who do not. Verse 5 states that a jerk (fool; אויל)[124] spurns fatherly discipline, while one who listens to reproof becomes prudent, able to handle life's situations well. There is no generic word in Hebrew for "parent," only gender-specific words for "father" and "mother." It seems clear from proverbs that include mothers as part of the instruction team that mothers, as well as fathers, taught. Thus, it is possible that just as Hebrew "son" sometimes does mean "child," "father" may in some contexts mean "parent."[125] Verse 6 is a good follow-up of verse 5, for it asserts that the houses of the just (righteous)[126] have much wealth, but the income of the corrupt

121. See Translation Matters on Unethical (Evil/Bad/Wicked), רע/רעים, at 4:14. As in 14:19, the translation "bad" is used for reasons of parallelism.

122. Fox, *Proverbs 10–31*, 590.

123. See Translation Matters on Discipline/Chastening/Correction (Instruction), מוסר, at 1:2.

124. See Translation Matters on Jerk/Schmuck/Folly (Fool/Folly), אויל/אולת, at 1:7.

125. See Translation Matters on Father/Parent/Ancestor at 1:8.

126. See Translation Matters on Just/Integrity/Honesty (Righteous[ness]), צדקה/צדיק/צדק, at 1:2.

Prov 15:5-12

⁵A fool despises a parent's instruction,
  but the one who heeds
    admonition is prudent.
⁶In the house of the righteous there is
  much treasure,
  but trouble befalls the income of
    the wicked.
⁷The lips of the wise spread
  knowledge;
  not so the minds of fools.
⁸The sacrifice of the wicked is an
  abomination to the LORD,
  but the prayer of the upright is his
    delight.

⁹The way of the wicked is an
  abomination to the LORD,
  but he loves the one who pursues
    righteousness.
¹⁰There is severe discipline for one
  who forsakes the way,
  but one who hates a rebuke will
    die.
¹¹Sheol and Abaddon lie open before
  the LORD,
  how much more human hearts!
¹²Scoffers do not like to be
  rebuked;
  they will not go to the wise.

(wicked)[127] involves calamity. The just accept parental discipline and thus can handle life's affairs prudently to gain and maintain or increase wealth. Jerks (fools) do not heed discipline and often fall into corrupt ways of earning a living, which result in calamity. The third proverb (15:7) in this tightly knit group says that the lips of the wise spread or scatter knowledge like seeds; the antithesis may involve a pun on the two meanings of כן: the dolts (fools)[128] are not right, true, honest (כן used adjectivally); and they are not so (כן used adverbially), i.e., they do not scatter knowledge (from the first colon).

Proverbs 15:8-9 are two YHWH proverbs. Verse 8 asserts that the sacrifice offered by the corrupt is loathed by YHWH; the antithesis is that the prayer of the upstanding is God's delight. This is not a put-down of the sacrificial cult. Each colon needs to be read in view of the other, so that the meaning is that God loves the prayer and sacrifice of the upright but loathes the prayer and sacrifice of the corrupt. Verse 9 broadens the focus from worship to everyday life. The life of the corrupt is loathed by YHWH, but God loves whoever pursues integrity. Verses 10-12 return to the main theme of the cluster: discipline and its consequences. Verse 10 suggests that one who forsakes the correct path will experience a harsh

127. See Translation Matters on Corrupt[ion]/Unscrupulous/Reprehensible (Wicked[ness]), רשע/רשעים, at 2:22.
128. See Translation Matters on Dolt/Chump/Oaf/Inept (Fool), כסיל, at 1:22.

discipline, for the consequences can be disastrous. The second colon spells out the consequences explicitly. A student who hates to be reprimanded and thus does not learn how to stay on the path will ultimately wander into paths that lead to death. Verse 11 follows up with two words for the underworld where the dead were understood to dwell, both of which are in front of God, i.e., God sees them. The second colon suggests that God knows human hearts/minds[129] even more than the underworld. People should behave correctly, because God knows even what is inside of them. The final proverb in this cluster, 15:12, states that scoffers don't like to be chided, and as a result they will not go to the wise from whom they would get instruction but also rebuke.

What Makes for Happiness and Unhappiness (15:13-18)

This cluster focuses on what makes for happiness and unhappiness. It opens with a proverbial pair in 15:13-14, in which the word for heart/mind[130] occurs three times. Verse 13 states that a joyful heart shows on the face, while through an emotional injury to the heart/mind a stricken spirit results. Although the first colon speaks of an outer condition (a smiling face) and the second colon of an inward condition (a broken spirit), the smiling face reflects an inner disposition and the broken spirit is also reflected in the person's countenance. Verse 14 follows up on verse 13 with the word for heart/mind being repeated, but here the focus shifts to a more intellectual plane. Those who have understanding seek knowledge, but the mouths of dolts (fools)[131] graze on folly.[132] Combined with 15:13, the hint is that having the kind of understanding that leads to the search for knowledge aids in developing a joyful heart/mind. Similarly, those who graze on folly are opening themselves up for emotional injuries.

Proverbs 15:15-17 expresses the notion that in matters important to God, the poor may be in a better state than the rich. Verse 15 states that all the days of the poor are difficult, but in spite of this objective external circumstance, a good heart/mind can make life a continual feast. Verse 16 asserts that it is better to have a small amount of wealth with the right attitude, i.e., the fear of YHWH,[133] than to have much wealth and trouble

---

129. See Translation Matters on the Heart, לֵב, at 2:2.
130. See Translation Matters on the Heart, לֵב, at 2:2.
131. See Translation Matters on Dolt/Chump/Oaf/Inept (Fool), כְּסִיל, at 1:22.
132. See Translation Matters on Jerk/Schmuck/Folly (Fool/Folly), אֱוִיל/אִוֶּלֶת, at 1:7.
133. See discussion of this phrase at 1:7.

Prov 15:13-18

¹³A glad heart makes a cheerful countenance,
but by sorrow of heart the spirit is broken.
¹⁴The mind of one who has understanding seeks knowledge,
but the mouths of fools feed on folly.
¹⁵All the days of the poor are hard,
but a cheerful heart has a continual feast.

¹⁶Better is a little with the fear of the LORD
than great treasure and trouble with it.
¹⁷Better is a dinner of vegetables where love is
than a fatted ox and hatred with it.
¹⁸Those who are hot-tempered stir up strife,
but those who are slow to anger calm contention.

along with it. This proverb makes it clear that although there may be a general correlation between piety and wealth, it is not absolute. Verse 17 continues the line of thought with a focus on food. It uses the same "better than" language as in 15:16. This proverb states that a simple vegetable-based dinner served with love is preferable to the fatted ox when hatred is a side dish. The proverbial cluster concludes with a return to anodyne advice in 15:18, which states that the hot-tempered stir up or engage in strife, but people who are slow to anger allay contention. They make life more pleasant for everyone. (See Excursus on Women's Sins 4: Anger, at 14:16.)

Wisdom Brings Gladness; Folly Brings Joy to No Sensible Person (15:19-23)

This proverbial cluster includes emotional, moral, and intellectual vocabulary. The cluster begins in 15:19 with the image of the path/highway, which is picked up in 15:21. The language of emotion is seen in verses 20 (ישמח, "glad"; בוזה, "despise"), 21, and 23 (שמחה, "joy"; טוב, "good"). Moral language is found in verses 19 (עצל, "lazy"; ישרים, "upstanding [upright]")[134] and 20 (כסיל, "fool[ish]," as in inept).[135] Intellectual

134. See Translation Matters on Upstanding/Straight/Straightforward (Upright), ישר/ישרים, at 2:7.
135. See Translation Matters on Dolt/Chump/Oaf/Inept (Fool), כסיל, at 1:22.

Prov 15:19-23

¹⁹The way of the lazy is overgrown
with thorns,
but the path of the upright is a
level highway.
²⁰A wise child makes a glad father,
but the foolish despise their
mothers.
²¹Folly is a joy to one who has no
sense,

but a person of understanding
walks straight ahead.
²²Without counsel, plans go wrong,
but with many advisers they
succeed.
²³To make an apt answer is a joy to
anyone,
and a word in season, how good
it is!

vocabulary is seen in verses 21 (אולת, "folly" [as in morally deficient];[136] תבונה, "understanding"), 22 (סוד, "counsel"; יועצים, "advisers"), and 23 (מענה, "answer"; דבר, "word"). The cluster begins with the assertion that the path of the lazy is a briar hedge (15:19). This image suggests that the lazy are not going to make much progress, because they are not willing to clear the hedge, which would be difficult due to the briars. The second colon indicates that the path of the upright is a smooth highway, an unobstructed path on which passage is easy. The implication may be that the upstanding experience such smooth passage because they deal justly with people. This may mean that the briar hedge that the lazy encounter is a result of their get-rich-quick schemes that defraud their neighbors and lead ultimately to their paths becoming overgrown with briar hedges, making movement difficult.

Verses 20-21 are a proverb pair, with 15:21 connecting back to 15:19. Proverbs 15:20a is a repetition of 10:1a, but instead of the second colon saying that a wise son (child)[137] in some way gladdens a mother, this time we get the antithesis, that dull, stupid, foolish individuals hate their mothers (and thus make them very sad). Verse 21 says that folly[138] is a joy to the one who lacks heart/mind,[139] but someone who has understanding walks straight. This second type of individual is the kind who brings joy to parents; the first type is the sort of individual who hates mother (and father) and gives them grief rather than joy. Verses 22-23 are another

136. See Translation Matters on Jerk/Schmuck/Folly (Fool/Folly), אויל/אולת, at 1:7.
137. See Translation Matters on Son (Child), בן, at 1:8.
138. See Translation Matters on Jerk/Schmuck/Folly (Fool/Folly), אויל/אולת, at 1:7.
139. See Translation Matters on the Heart, לב, at 2:2.

proverb pair that conclude this cluster. Verse 22 suggests that without advice, plans can be frustrated, but there is wisdom in the thoughts of many advisers. In verse 23, the word "apt" in the NRSV translation is not in the Hebrew. NRSV is assuming that the two cola are parallel, but the meaning could be:

> To make an answer is a joy to anyone,
>> but a word in season, how good it is.

In the context of 15:22, the point might be that anybody can enjoy mouthing off, but someone who has sought counsel from friends and family will be able to provide a perceptive word when it is critically needed. A word in season is a very well-known cliché for a timely remark.

Life for the Wise and Just; Sheol for the Rest (15:24-27)

This short cluster is marked by a weak *inclusio* formed by words from the root חיה, "to live": חיים, "life," in 15:24 and יחיה, "live," in 15:27. The middle two proverbs are YHWH proverbs. Verse 24 opens the cluster with the general statement that life's path for those with insight (משכיל, "wise") has an upward movement to avoid Sheol below. The upward movement does not imply heaven but is best understood as referring to the earthly path. Verse 25 is more specific: God will pull down the house of those who lift themselves up. (See the Excursus on Women's Sins 1: Arrogance, at 3:8.) In contrast to those who are on the path of life leading upward, the arrogant, who may think themselves heading upward, are not. Since the second colon of the proverb is usually related to the first, the implication is that the arrogant think the widow is so irrelevant that the stone marking the boundary between their properties can be moved without anyone noticing. It is true that widows, women without husbands or grown sons to defend them in court, were vulnerable to this sort of abuse, but the proverb proclaims that God maintains their boundaries. The second YHWH proverb in this cluster, 15:26, states that YHWH loathes the schemes of an evil person; the antithesis is that gracious, pleasant words are pure. We are not surprised at the first half of the proverb, but the idea that words that are merely gracious and pleasant are considered pure is somewhat startling. Verse 27 states explicitly what was implied in 15:25: people who get their income unjustly will stir up trouble for their houses; on the other hand, individuals who hate gifts, meaning bribes, will live.

Prov 15:24-27

²⁴For the wise the path of life leads upward,
  in order to avoid Sheol below.
²⁵The LORD tears down the house of the proud,
  but maintains the widow's boundaries.

²⁶Evil plans are an abomination to the LORD,
  but gracious words are pure.
²⁷Those who are greedy for unjust gain make trouble for their households,
  but those who hate bribes will live.

Open to Discipline, the Just Humbly Fear YHWH (15:28-33)

This cluster is rich in the language of speech (all verses) and hearing/heeding (15:29-32). It also includes many references to body parts: heart/mind[140] (15:28, 30), eyes (15:30), body (15:30), and ear (15:31). Discipline (instruction)[141] and the reproof that goes with it is also a theme (15:31-32). There are two YHWH sayings (15:29 and 33). Verse 28 asserts that the just (righteous)[142] think before answering, whereas the mouth of the corrupt (wicked)[143] just spews words out carelessly. Such thought on the part of the just protects both their own interests and those of others with whom they are associated. It is all too easy to divulge a secret if one does not stop to think. The corrupt may be careful not to divulge their own schemes, if secrecy is in their own interest, but they will not be so careful about other people's interests, and because they may not have developed the habit of caution, they may even end up spilling the beans on their own plans.

Proverbs 15:29 is a YHWH proverb, which states that YHWH is far from the corrupt (wicked) but that God does hear the prayer of the just. This suggests that God does not hear the prayer of the corrupt, given God's remoteness from them. Verse 30 talks about two things that can make a huge difference in one's disposition. The first is meeting someone with bright eyes. The eyes are the most expressive feature of the face and communicate a great deal about a person's inner disposition. A smile

140. See Translation Matters on the Heart, לֵב, at 2:2.
141. See Translation Matters on Discipline/Chastening/Correction (Instruction), מוּסָר, at 1:2.
142. See Translation Matters on Just/Integrity/Honesty (Righteous[ness]), צְדָקָה/צַדִּיק/צֶדֶק, at 1:2.
143. See Translation Matters on Corrupt[ion]/Unscrupulous/Reprehensible (Wicked[ness]), רְשָׁעִים/רֶשַׁע, at 2:22.

²⁸The mind of the righteous ponders how to answer,
but the mouth of the wicked pours out evil.
²⁹The Lᴏʀᴅ is far from the wicked,
but he hears the prayer of the righteous.
³⁰The light of the eyes rejoices the heart,
and good news refreshes the body.

³¹The ear that heeds wholesome admonition
will lodge among the wise.
³²Those who ignore instruction despise themselves,
but those who heed admonition gain understanding.
³³The fear of the Lᴏʀᴅ is instruction in wisdom,
and humility goes before honor.

can be faked, but not bright smiling eyes. Good news too can lift the whole body, especially if the news allays a concern about a loved one or a matter of deep import. In the context of the preceding proverb, when a just individual has been worried about something of deep importance, such an individual may have prayed, and, according to the previous proverb, the prayers will have been heard. We are reminded of Hannah, who prayed to God that she might become pregnant and her prayer was answered (1 Sam 1:1–2:10). If a good report is then heard, the relief is combined with gratitude for the answered prayers. Of course, prayers are not always answered. The good do not always prosper. Consider Job.

Verses 31-32 are a proverb pair focused on discipline. Verse 31 indicates that the person whose ear has paid attention to correction will abide with the wise. On the other hand, people who avoid it despise themselves, because those who listen to correction acquire a heart/mind. The final proverb of this cluster, and of the first half of the Solomonic collection (10:1–15:33), 15:33, begins with a nominal sentence: the fear of YHWH[144] (is/equals) instruction in wisdom. The two halves of the equation can equally well be placed on either side of the equals sign. If one has a proper awe and respect for God one will be instructed in wisdom. Similarly, the first virtue learned in wisdom instruction is the fear of YHWH. Nevertheless, the fear of YHWH comes first. This proverbial statement reflects on those in 15:31-32. The second colon of 15:33 states that just as the fear of YHWH comes first in the first colon, humility comes before honor, which is a necessary attitude if one is going to heed admonition and correction and ultimately develop wisdom.

144. See discussion of this phrase at 1:7.

Part 2b

A Courtly/Royal Collection (16:1–22:16)

One Proposes; God Disposes (16:1-9)

Proverbs 16 opens the second half of the Solomonic collection (16:1–22:16) with a cluster in which all but one proverb is a YHWH proverb. An *inclusio* in 16:1 and 16:9 binds the cluster together:

> ¹The plans [מערכי] of the **mind** [לב] belong to **mortals** [אדם]
>   but the answer of the tongue is from the **Lord** [יהוה].
> ⁹The **human mind** [לב אדם] plans [יחשב] the way,
>   but the **Lord** [יהוה] directs the steps.

Moreover, לב, mind/heart,[145] occurs in 16:5, where NRSV translates "arrogant"; the Hebrew is "exalted of heart" (גבה־לב). In addition to the words forming the *inclusio*, four key words are repeated several times in the cluster: "way" (דרך, 16:2, 7, 9), "answer/purpose" (מענה, 16:1, 4), two forms of the root "to plan" (חשב, 16:1, 3, 9), and "all/every" (כל, 16:2, 4, 5). Both proverbs are stating the same thing. In the first, human plans must conform to God's word (however we describe our plans, God's law supervenes); in the second, we can set out on a planned journey, but God will determine our arrival.

Proverbs 16:2b-3 expands on 16:1-2a and speaks to the problem of self-deception. We justify our intentions (all our ways are pure), but there may be a less noble purpose within that God (who weighs the spirit) knows. Verse 3 literally says "roll" (גל) your work to God. The verb גלל is used of rolling stones off wells or onto caves. This proverb does not mean to expect God to do all the work but rather to partner with God, to follow the principles of wisdom and integrity (righteousness).[146] Then one's plans and work will endure.

Proverbs 16:4 is a theologically difficult proverb for contemporary readers, asserting as it does that God has made corrupt (wicked people)[147] for a day of trouble (the Hebrew lacks the definite article). Whether the day of trouble is an ordinary day or judgment day, the problem remains.

145. See Translation Matters on the Heart, לב, at 2:2.
146. See Translation Matters on Just/Integrity/Honesty (Righteous[ness]), צדקה/צדיק/צדק, at 1:2.
147. See Translation Matters on Corrupt[ion]/Unscrupulous/Reprehensible (Wicked[ness]), רשעים/רשע, at 2:22.

Prov 16:1-9

¹The plans of the mind belong to mortals,
but the answer of the tongue is from the LORD.
²All one's ways may be pure in one's own eyes,
but the LORD weighs the spirit.
³Commit your work to the LORD,
and your plans will be established.
⁴The LORD has made everything for its purpose,
even the wicked for the day of trouble.
⁵All those who are arrogant are an abomination to the LORD;

be assured, they will not go unpunished.
⁶By loyalty and faithfulness iniquity is atoned for,
and by the fear of the LORD one avoids evil.
⁷When the ways of people please the LORD,
he causes even their enemies to be at peace with them.
⁸Better is a little with righteousness.
than large income with injustice.
⁹The human mind plans the way,
but the LORD directs the steps.

The proverb does not necessarily need to be read as an assertion of predestination, that God has made some people corrupt from the outset. It could be and probably is simply saying that some people will choose to be corrupt, and God has set things up in such a way that they will be punished for their crimes. (See Jer 18.)

Proverbs 16:5 focuses on a kind of attitude that God particularly loathes: the arrogant, which the proverb assures the reader will not get off without punishment. (See the Excursus on Women's Sins 1: Arrogance, at 3:8.) Verse 6 provides a good follow-up, suggesting that iniquity may be atoned by kindness (loyalty)[148] and faithfulness; it also indicates that one avoids evil in the first place by the proper attitude of fear of YHWH.[149] Verse 7 says that when God is pleased with human ways, God causes even their enemies to make peace with them. Verse 8, the only non-YHWH proverb in the cluster, is a good follow-up to 16:7. It is one of the "better than" proverbs: it is better to be just and poor than rich and unjust. This proverb indicates a positive attitude toward the poor and subverts the conservative admonitions that seem to focus on gain. The final proverb in the cluster, 16:9, completes the *inclusio* opened in 16:1.

---

148. See Translation Matters on Kindness/Mercy (Loyalty), חסד, at 2:8. The Hebrew חסד is best understood as mercy or kindness rather than loyalty (NRSV).
149. See discussion of this phrase at 1:7.

Instructions for the King and his Servants (16:10-15)

This cluster of proverbs focuses on the king. It opens in 16:10 with a statement establishing the king as a divine agent: on the king's lips is divination, קֶסֶם, a word that is usually used disparagingly but here is used in a positive sense. The second colon can be read either descriptively (as in the NRSV translation) or prescriptively: let his mouth not act faithlessly against justice. Verse 11 is the only proverb in this cluster that does not speak explicitly about the king, but its focus on weights and scales in the midst of royally oriented proverbs implies the king's responsibility, as divine agent, for the administration of justice both in the marketplace and in the court. Verse 12 follows up with its assertion that kings (should) loathe evildoing by themselves or others, since the throne is established through integrity (righteousness).[150] On the positive side, 16:13 states that a king's delight is or ought to be honest (righteous) lips and that he loves (or should love) those who speak uprightly, i.e., honestly. This is directed both at kings and at royal servants. Verse 14 indicates what happens when a king becomes angry with one of his servants: there will be messengers of death, indicating the unpredictability of the objects of the king's wrath that can consume more victims than the initial one. Thus, the second colon advises a wise courtier to pacify it. Ending on a positive note, contrasting with the messengers of death in 16:14, 16:15 enthusiastically compares the light of a king's face to life itself and his favor to the spring rains that were essential to the harvest maturing and there being food on the table.

Wisdom Is Better Than Gold or Military Might (16:16-33)

This long cluster opens with a "better than" proverb in 16:16 that states a central theme of the book of Proverbs, the incalculable value not simply of wisdom and understanding but also of the journey of acquiring them, which is better than precious metals. Verse 17 was marked by the Masoretic scribes as the midpoint of the book of Proverbs and thus is a significant proverb. A highway, מְסִלָּה, was a raised major public road outside of a city that, like today, made for smooth, relatively easy travel. The path taken by the upstanding (upright),[151] the straight (one), avoids

---

150. See Translation Matters on Just/Integrity/Honesty (Righteous[ness]), צְדָקָה/ צַדִּיק/צֶדֶק, at 1:2.

151. See Translation Matters on Upstanding/Straight/Straightforward (Upright), יָשָׁר/יְשָׁרִים, at 2:7.

Prov 16:10-15

¹⁰Inspired decisions are on the lips of a king;
his mouth does not sin in judgment.
¹¹Honest balances and scales are the LORD's;
all the weights in the bag are his work.
¹²It is an abomination to kings to do evil,
for the throne is established by righteousness.

¹³Righteous lips are the delight of a king,
and he loves those who speak what is right.
¹⁴A king's wrath is a messenger of death,
and whoever is wise will appease it.
¹⁵In the light of a king's face there is life,
and his favor is like the clouds that bring the spring rain.

trouble. People who guard their road from dangers will be safeguarding their lives. One such danger is made explicit in the next very well-known proverb in 16:18. Arrogant pride makes us careless, unaware of our weaknesses and insensitive to our neighbors. When one harbors an arrogant spirit, a fall is bound to occur, sooner or later, in one sphere of life or another. (See Excursus on Women's Sins 1: Arrogance, at 3:8.)

TRANSLATION MATTERS

Although the NRSV translation in 16:16 is in line with most, נבחר, a *Niphal* participle, can also be translated as an adjective modifying "understanding," with the sense of choice or fine, really true understanding. This would seem to be a preferable way of rendering the colon, since the verbal meaning of choosing is already found in the phrase "to get" at the beginning of the colon.

TRANSLATION MATTERS

In 16:19, NRSV is reading the *Ketib*, עניים, "poor, needy." The *Qeré* is ענוים, "afflicted, oppressed, poor." The difference in the Hebrew is only one consonant, and the difference in meaning is only nuance, but it may be an important nuance.[152]

152. On *Qeré/Ketib*, see Translation Matters at 1:27.

¹⁶How much better to get wisdom than gold!

To get understanding is to be chosen rather than silver.

¹⁷The highway of the upright avoids evil;

those who guard their way preserve their lives.

¹⁸Pride goes before destruction, and a haughty spirit before a fall.

¹⁹It is better to be of a lowly spirit among the poor

than to divide the spoil with the proud.

²⁰Those who are attentive to a matter will prosper,

and happy are those who trust in the LORD.

²¹The wise of heart is called perceptive,

and pleasant speech increases persuasiveness.

²²Wisdom is a fountain of life to one who has it,

but folly is the punishment of fools.

²³The mind of the wise makes their speech judicious,

and adds persuasiveness to their lips.

²⁴Pleasant words are like a honeycomb,

Verse 19 states the corollary of verse 18 in another "better than" proverb: better to be humble amid the oppressed poor (reading with the MT *Qeré*) than rich among the proud. (See Excursus on Women's Sins 1: Arrogance, at 3:8.)

The phrase "divide the spoil" may suggest ill-gotten gains, especially in view of the MT *Qeré* in the first colon that emphasizes the oppressed nature of the poor. Verse 20 is multivalent. People who pay attention to a matter, whether it be a word of instruction or a business matter, will do well. Discipline of whatever kind pays off. The second line is parallel: those who trust in God are blissful (happy).[153] The two cola are not framed as either/or. One can develop discipline in various spheres of life as well as trust in YHWH. Nevertheless, trusting in God was considered the most important virtue. It does not make the first unnecessary but undergirds it.

Proverbs 16:21 and 16:23-24 have a common theme of speech. Verse 21 opens the subcluster of 16:21-24 with the perception that the wise of heart/mind[154] either are now or will come to be called perceptive, discerning, astute. They have the openness to learning that will lead to this characteristic. The second colon of this proverb says that people with sweet or pleasant speech will add to teaching, meaning their ability

---

153. See Translation Matters on Blissful (Happy), אשרי, at 3:13.

154. See Translation Matters on the Heart, לב, at 2:2.

sweetness to the soul and health to the body.

25Sometimes there is a way that seems to be right,
but in the end it is the way to death.

26The appetite of workers works for them;
their hunger urges them on.

27Scoundrels concoct evil,
and their speech is like a scorching fire.

28A perverse person spreads strife,
and a whisperer separates close friends.

29The violent entice their neighbors, and lead them in a way that is not good.

30One who winks the eyes plans perverse things;
one who compresses the lips brings evil to pass.

31Gray hair is a crown of glory;
it is gained in a righteous life.

32One who is slow to anger is better than the mighty,
and one whose temper is controlled than one who captures a city.

33The lot is cast into the lap,
but the decision is the LORD's alone.

to teach others. So, the first colon seems to focus on a student and the second on a teacher. Verse 22, although it does not say anything directly about speech, refers back to verse 21 because of their common vocabulary of wisdom. So, the wise of heart/mind from 16:21, who is or will be called perceptive, is on the way to prudence or insight (שכל, wisdom), which is called a fountain of life, a common image for the sustaining power of the divine in the Bible. (See Ps 36:9; Prov 10:11; 13:14; 14:27; Jer 2:13; Joel 3:18; Rev 7:17.) The antithesis can be understood variously. The NRSV and other translations treat מוסר as "punishment." The word מוסר fundamentally means discipline, education, so the colon can also mean that the kind of "education" that jerks (fools) provide to others, as opposed to what the wise offer, is folly. Both words come from the same root.[155] Listening to fools is foolhardy. Both senses of the colon may be intended. Verse 23 returns explicitly to the theme of speech and reverses the phrase found in 16:21. Instead of the wise of heart/mind, here we get the heart/mind of the wise. The sagacious mind results in judicious speech. The second half of the proverb is very similar to 16:21b; such a mind makes the person more persuasive when teaching. Finally, 16:24 asserts the advantages of pleasant speech, which is compared to

---

155. See Translation Matters on Jerk/Schmuck/Folly (Fool/Folly), אויל/אולת, at 1:7.

honeycomb; such speech is sweetness to the נפש, appetite (soul),[156] and health to the body (bones).

Proverbs 16:25-30 form a subcluster within the larger cluster, dealing with the behavior of bad people. Verse 25 is identical to 14:12. In this context it introduces the following proverbs dealing with the people who choose paths that lead to unpleasant ends. The root for "workers" and "works," עמל, also means "suffers." The picture is of very low-level workers working long hours for low pay, building a building or tilling a field. They must work in order to eat. Either the proverb is out of place or the editors have placed it here with the suggestion that such workers tend to seek shortcuts to success. It could relate back to 16:19, which says that it is better to be humble among the oppressed than to divide the spoils among the arrogant. The following four proverbs specify various forms of negative behavior. The first of these, 16:27, states that scoundrels, איש בליעל, concoct (כרה, "dig," as in dig a pit) trouble; the second colon describes how they do this: through fiery hot words. Verse 28 names two more types of wrongdoers: the duplicitous (perverse)[157] person who openly spreads contentiousness and the backbiter whose quiet whisperings behind the scenes break up friendships. The third proverb in this group, 16:29, is concerned with violent people who try to seduce their neighbors to join them in their violence. One thinks back here to 16:26 and the struggling worker who might be vulnerable to such enticement. The second colon of this proverb says simply but powerfully that leading people in this way is not good. We think here of contemporary conmen (and women), especially politicians who seduce the people by promising one thing and delivering the opposite, but also businesspeople who advertise one thing but market shoddy products that do not live up to what is claimed in the ads and sometimes are downright dangerous to people's health and safety. The final proverb, 16:30, suggests that the ancient authors of the proverbs understood body language. Winking or squinting of the eyes was associated with planning vicious (perverse) schemes, especially speech, and pinching the mouth was associated with an attitude of determination to bring an evil plot to fulfillment.

Proverbs 16:31 attests to an age that revered the wisdom that comes with having lived well for a long time. In a time when many were not lucky enough to live that long due to high maternal mortality rates in childbirth and men dying in war and other hostilities as well as the

156. See Translation Matters on Soul/Neck/Person/Desire, נפש, at 2:10. The best meaning here is appetite.

157. See Translation Matters on Duplicitously (Perversely), תהפכות, at 2:12.

ravages of disease and famine, a head of gray hair was a thing to be proud of, not to be covered up with dye. Verse 32 uses military imagery to praise self-restraint; it suggests both the strength it takes to master one's temper and the power of one whose disposition is under control. Verse 33 is reminiscent of 16:1 in its focus on divine sovereignty. Casting lots was like drawing straws. Stones were thrown into a person's lap to make a decision. The result was believed to come from God. It need not be confined to divination; casting lots is a metaphor for choice as in Caesar's *alea iacta est* on crossing the Rubicon. He decided to cross, the dice were thrown, but the final fate was in the hands of the gods.[158]

Tests and Rewards (17:1-9)

Chapter 17 is apparently an unstructured collection of proverbs; it begins with a "better than" proverb. The comparison is between dry bread, i.e., bread without dipping sauce such as oil or vinegar, and a communal sacrificial meal, זבח. The ancient Hebrews were, for the most part, poor people who did not eat meat regularly. When they did, at least before Josiah's reformation in the seventh century, it was as part of a sacrificial ceremony. Even after the Deuteronomic reform that permitted profane slaughter, eating meat was only done on a regular basis by the wealthy. The proverb asserts that it is better to have even dry bread and quiet than meat along with strife. Although not subversive in the sense of contrasting the just poor with the unjust rich, it does place serenity above riches. Verse 2 is probably addressed to children who are likely to inherit rather than to slaves, who if they act wisely may inherit a portion of the estate. They are warned not to disappoint their parents, or else they will lose their standing in the house and part of their inheritance to enterprising servants.

Proverbs 17:3 suggests that just as precious metals are put into furnaces at high heat so that the impurities may be burned off, so God puts us into tough situations to rid us of our impurities and tests us to see if there is anything precious left after we have been through the fire (see Isa 48:10). This notion of the usefulness of suffering is one that has been questioned by womanist theologian Delores Williams, since in North American culture it is usually women of color who do the greatest amount of suffering and it is not clear what the benefits of it are.[159] On

158. Suetonius, *Vita Divi Iuli* (Perseus Digital Library, 0121), http://www.perseus.tufts .edu/hopper/text?doc=Perseus%3Atext%3A1999.02.0061%3Alife%3Djul.%3Achapter %3D32%3Asection%3D1.

159. Delores Williams, *Sisters in the Wilderness: The Challenge of God-Talk* (Maryknoll, NY: Orbis Books, 1993), 161–67.

Prov 17:1-9

¹Better is a dry morsel with quiet
  than a house full of feasting with
    strife.
²A slave who deals wisely will
    rule over a child who acts
    shamefully,
  and will share the inheritance as
    one of the family.
³The crucible is for silver, and the
    furnace is for gold,
  but the LORD tests the heart.
⁴An evildoer listens to wicked lips;
  and a liar gives heed to a
    mischievous tongue.
⁵Those who mock the poor insult their
    Maker;

those who are glad at calamity will
    not go unpunished.
⁶Grandchildren are the crown of the
    aged,
  and the glory of children is their
    parents.
⁷Fine speech is not becoming to a
    fool;
  still less is false speech to a ruler.
⁸A bribe is like a magic stone in the
    eyes of those who give it;
  wherever they turn they prosper.
⁹One who forgives an affront fosters
    friendship,
  but one who dwells on disputes
    will alienate a friend.

the other hand, Emilie Townes believes that suffering can lead to a new vision and thus to new hope.[160]

TRANSLATION MATTERS

In 17:4 NRSV translates the verb מֵזִין as "heed," a *Hiphil* participle from אזן; the verb can also be analyzed as being a *Hiphil* participle from זון, meaning "nourish," creating a pun that cannot be reproduced in English.

The understanding of 17:4 depends on the interpretation of the verb in the second colon; it could be derived from two different roots, "hear/heed," אזן, and "nourish," זון, creating a pun. The second colon says that the abstract quality of lying, which may stand for a lying person, nourishes a tongue of desire or destruction or hears/heeds it. With two meanings for the verb and two for the final noun, there are multiple meanings for the colon and

160. Emilie M. Townes, *In a Blaze of Glory: Womanist Spirituality as Social Witness* (Nashville: Abingdon, 1995), 139. See also M. Shawn Copeland, "'Wading through Many Sorrows': Toward a Theology of Suffering in Womanist Perspective," in *A Troubling in My Soul: Womanist Perspectives on Evil and Suffering*, ed. Emilie Townes (Maryknoll, NY: Orbis Books, 1994), 124.

the whole proverb. A tongue of desire could represent appetite. Thus, liars nourish their appetites by listening to the lips of troublemakers (from the first colon), hoping to bring home some quick gains. Looking at it another way, the abstract quality of deception nourishes a destructive tongue, the same tongue that is listened to in the first colon. With the verb in the second colon meaning hear/heed, the tongue is again a tongue both of desire and of destruction. Just as the one who does bad things pays attention to the one with troublemaking lips, so a liar listens to/heeds a tongue of destruction in the sense of destroying others, and both unknowingly are listening to/heeding a tongue that will lead to their own destruction.

Verse 5 deals with bad attitudes. People who deride the poor insult the one who made them (see 14:31). People who find pleasure in other people's disasters will not get away with their silent gloating. Whether the calamities people experience are self-inflicted or come through no fault of their own, which in most cases we have no way of knowing, and we certainly rarely know the whole story, we should pity them rather than feel joy at their suffering. To do anything else suggests that we believe that whatever level of prosperity we enjoy is solely a result of our efforts and that our good fortune is totally secure, neither of which is ever the case.

Proverbs 17:6 speaks to the interconnection between generations. There is little that seniors take more pride in than their grandchildren, especially if those children show interest in their grandparents. Not so obviously, but no less accurately, the glory of children is their forebears (Hebrew אב can mean ancestor) who laid the foundation on which the children stand, even though they usually do not appreciate this when they are young.

Proverbs 17:7 contrasts what is appropriate and/or attractive for an impious, presumptuous, and ignoble fool (נבל; *nabal*)[161] and a generous, noble person or ruler. Certainly, fine speech is not appropriate to presumptuous individuals, who often sound ridiculous because they do not know the subtle nuances of the words they are employing and, using the alternative meaning of יתר, babble incoherently. Similarly, but more so, false speech is not attractive in a ruler.

TRANSLATION MATTERS

The word יתר in 17:7, rendered as "fine" by NRSV, can also mean "excessive."

---

161. For a discussion of the three kinds of fools in Proverbs, see Translation Matters on Jerk/Schmuck/Folly (Fool/Folly), אויל/אולת, at 1:7.

Proverbs 17:8 gives the perspective of people who are bribe givers; in their own eyes such gifts are like magic that opens doors of prosperity for them. Although the proverb does not explicitly condemn bribes, often when proverbs use the phrase "in the eyes of," the suggestion is that the human perception does not comport with reality. Verse 9 begins by stating that people who can forgive an injury care about their relationship with the person who has affronted them, but someone who dwells on it by repeating it will separate as enemies.

The Bad Behavior of Dolts (17:10-16)

This cluster is bound together by the *inclusio* in 17:10 and 17:16. Both verses deal with dolts (fools; כסיל),[162] who are prone to the kinds of bad behavior described in 17:11-15. Proverbs 17:10 opens with the statement that a verbal rebuke is felt more deeply by a person of discernment than one hundred physical blows is felt by a dolt. This is hyperbole, since one hundred blows might kill the poor fool. Verse 11 can be read two ways: the subject could be evil people (NRSV) or rebellious people, since the noun can be understood as abstract or concrete. In the second colon, if the first alternative is chosen, the messenger may be being sent against the evil people, as NRSV translates, or against the rebellion to put it down. Verse 12 returns to the theme of folly[163] in a paradoxical comparison: it is less dangerous to encounter an enraged mother bear than to become involved with a dolt. Verse 13 asserts that the houses of the ungrateful will experience unremitting trouble. No one can lose a reputation for ingratitude. Verse 14 is concerned with the uncontrollability of wrath compared to the splashing of spilled water; better to never start. Verse 15 describes two judicial practices that are equally loathsome to God: legally justifying the guilty (wicked)[164] and condemning the just (righteous).[165]

162. See Translation Matters on Dolt/Chump/Oaf/Inept (Fool), כסיל, at 1:22.
163. See Translation Matters on Jerk/Schmuck/Folly (Fool/Folly), אויל/אולת, at 1:7.
164. See Translation Matters on Corrupt[ion]/Unscrupulous/Reprehensible (Wicked[ness]), רשע/רשעים, at 2:22. In this context, the needed meaning is a person who is guilty of a crime.
165. See Translation Matters on Just/Integrity/Honesty (Righteous[ness]), צדקה/צדק/צדיק, at 1:2.

¹⁰A rebuke strikes deeper into a
  discerning person
  than a hundred blows into a fool.
¹¹Evil people seek only rebellion,
  but a cruel messenger will be sent
  against them.
¹²Better to meet a she-bear robbed of
  its cubs
  than to confront a fool immersed
  in folly.
¹³Evil will not depart from the house
  of one who returns evil for good.

¹⁴The beginning of strife is like letting
  out water;
  so stop before the quarrel breaks
  out.
¹⁵One who justifies the wicked and one
  who condemns the righteous
  are both alike an abomination to
  the LORD.
¹⁶Why should fools have a price in
  hand
  to buy wisdom, when they have
  no mind to learn?

The cluster ends with 17:16, which asks why dolts should try to buy wisdom when they don't have the disposition to learn anyway.

On Friends and Neighbors (17:17-20)

This small proverbial cluster begins with a focus on friendship. The last two proverbs can be viewed as relating to this theme, even though they can also be understood more broadly. The first proverb in this group, 17:17, can be read a number of ways. The first colon is telling us that a true friend is there for us, come what may. The verb אהב, "love," covers a wide range of meanings, from the relationship between husband and wife to that between a servant and master. In the second colon, the sage may be distinguishing the brother (אח), but also kin more broadly, from the friend or may be suggesting that they are both available in rough times. This is the meaning the NRSV translation has captured.

TRANSLATION MATTERS

In 17:19, מגביה פתחו does not mean "high threshold," as translated by NRSV, but rather high opening or entrance.

The last word in 17:19 is the verb שבר, which means simply "break, crash." "Bones" is not in the Hebrew.

Prov 17:17-20

¹⁷A friend loves at all times,
and kinsfolk are born to share
adversity.
¹⁸It is senseless to give a pledge,
to become surety for a neighbor.
¹⁹One who loves transgression loves
strife;

one who builds a high
threshold invites broken
bones.
²⁰The crooked of mind do not
prosper,
and the perverse of tongue fall
into calamity.

Excursus on Female Friendship in the Hebrew Bible

There are few stories of female friendship in the Hebrew Bible. The story of Ruth and Naomi is a lead example, but they are from different generations so are not peers. Still, they cooperate to achieve mutually important goals, the younger woman helping the older one. Similarly, the sisters Rachel and Leah, though competitive in their desire to have the maximum number of children, which was important in their culture to produce as many workers as possible for the farm and to provide financial security in old age, still worked together at times (Gen 6:14-18). It is not clear what the relationships between the handmaids of Rachel, Leah, and Sarah, and their "mistresses" was intended to be. All we really know that they did was bear children when their "mistress" was not able to do so. The relationship between Sarah and Hagar was fraught and ended with Hagar and her son by Abraham, Ishmael, exiled in the wilderness (Gen 16, 21). On contemporary female friendship, see Marilyn Yalom and Theresa Donovan Brown, *The Social Sex: A History of Female Friendship.*[166]

It is true that close friends sometimes become as close or closer than blood relatives do, though the latter often show up in a crisis. In spite of or because of this high valuation of friendship, 17:18 does not think it wise to give surety for the loan of a friend/neighbor. The Hebrew for the

---

166. Marilyn Yalom and Theresa Donovan Brown, *The Social Sex: A History of Female Friendship* (New York: HarperPerennial, 2015).

neighbor, רַע, is the same as the word for "friend" in 17:17. As Polonius says to his son in Hamlet (1.3.75–77):

> Neither a borrower nor a lender be,
> For loan oft loses both itself and friend,
> And borrowing dulls the edge of husbandry.

In the context of advice on friendship, the first colon of 17:19 can be read to mean that people who love to talk about injuries that have been done to them are people who love contention. Alternately, people who love to hurt others certainly love strife. The second colon says that one whose opening or doorway is high is seeking a crash or break, encouraging someone to trip. In the context of the following proverb where those with duplicitous tongues (perverse of tongue) are referenced, it is possible that the word "opening" can mean mouth here and the idea is that someone who has an arrogant mouth invites a crash. (See Excursus on Women's Sins 1: Arrogance, at 3:8.) Verse 20 completes this group with the statement that the crooked of mind don't find good and the duplicitous (perverse)[167] fall into trouble. This was not the kind of adversity that kinfolk were born to help their relatives with. There is no implication that family is required to bail family out of the sorts of problems that result from crookedness of mind or duplicity of tongue, though family often tries to do so with limited success.

Foolish Children Cause Much Trouble to Their Parents (17:21-25)

This cluster is marked by an *inclusio* in 17:21 and 17:25:

> [21]The one who **begets** [ילד] a fool [כסיל] gets trouble;
>   the <u>parent</u> [אבי] of a fool [נבל] has no joy.
> [25]*Foolish* [כסיל] children are a grief to their <u>father</u> [אבי]
>   and bitterness to her who **bore** [ילד] them.

The cluster opens with a proverb about the grief caused to parents by foolhardy children. The NRSV translates אבי, which normally means "father of," in 17:21, 25 as "parent of," in part because the verb beget/give birth, ילד, occurs in a masculine form, "begets," what the father does, in 17:21 and a feminine form, "bore," what the mother does, in 17:25. As in 17:25,

---

167. See Translation Matters on Duplicitous (Perverse), תהפכות, at 2:12. The parallel term, עקש, means twisted and occurs several times in Proverbs.

²¹The one who begets a fool gets
        trouble;
    the parent of a fool has no joy.
²²A cheerful heart is a good medicine,
    but a downcast spirit dries up the
        bones.
²³The wicked accept a concealed bribe
    to pervert the ways of justice.

²⁴The discerning person looks to
        wisdom,
    but the eyes of a fool to the ends
        of the earth.
²⁵Foolish children are a grief to their
        father
    and bitterness to her who bore
        them.

this proverb is apparently specifically describing the way in which foolish children ("inept" [כסיל] in 17:21a and "presumptuous" [נבל] in 17:21b[168]) bring trouble to their mothers and fathers. (See 10:1 and 15:19.)

Proverbs 17:22 contrasts with 17:21, describing the positive effects of a joyful heart (the same adjective is used at the end of 17:21 and the beginning of 17:22). The antithesis of this well-known reality is that a stricken spirit dries up the bones, perhaps an ancient way of describing creaky joints (see 15:13) or just a metaphorical way of portraying the weariness of aging. In the context of this cluster and right in the heart of it, 17:23 describes one of the ways that an adult child may act like a dolt and thus cause grief to parents: accepting a concealed gift, i.e., a bribe, with the intention of perverting justice. Some gifts to officials were considered acceptable, but not if they were intended to pervert justice. Verse 24 returns explicitly to the theme of foolish behavior and this time its opposite. For the discerning person, wisdom is nearby, but the dolt is looking in the distance, not aware that wisdom is close to home. The final proverb in the cluster, 17:25, reiterates the opening message, that foolish offspring cause vexation and bitterness to mothers and fathers, specifically naming both parents.

Outrageous Judicial Behavior and the Value of Brevity (17:26-28)

Proverbs 17:27-28 obviously go together and relate back to 17:23, but 17:26 fits in with what follows only if the problem for which the noble

---

168. For the three words used in Proverbs, see Translation Matters on Jerk/ Schmuck/Folly (Fool/Folly), אויל/אולת, at 1:7. See also Translation Matters on Dolt/ Chump/Oaf/Inept (Fool), כסיל, at 1:22.

Prov 17:26-28

26To impose a fine on the innocent is not right, or to flog the noble for their integrity.
27One who spares words is knowledgeable;

one who is cool in spirit has understanding.
28Even fools who keep silent are considered wise; when they close their lips, they are deemed intelligent.

is flogged has something to do with speech. It says fining the innocent (צדיק)[169] is not good, nor is smiting the noble for their uprightness. Perhaps, in the context of 17:27-28, the concern is with people of noble character being fined or even flogged for saying true but inconvenient things.

Proverbs 17:27 states the paradox that people who speak sparingly (appear to) know a lot and those with cool spirits (seem to) have understanding. Similarly, 17:28 asserts that even jerks (fools)[170] will be considered wise if they can manage to shut their mouths.

Speech and Bad Behavior (18:1-9)

This cluster focuses on speech and negative behavior. Some of the proverbs focus on speech explicitly; others do so implicitly. Verse 1 has two possible interpretations, depending on the reading of the Hebrew; either the loner pursues his own desire or seeks pretexts to show contempt for others. The verb in the second colon seems to mean to burst out in anger, as in 17:14. The colon therefore may mean getting angry at all who have sound judgment. The sages value community; this proverb would then make clear their disdain for isolated individuals. There is a wordplay between verses 1 and 2. In the MT of 18:1b, the recluse bursts out in anger (יתגלע from the root גלע, see Translation Matters), while in 18:2b the dolt (fool)[171] expresses himself (התגלות from the root גלה).

169. See Translation Matters on Just/Integrity/Honesty (Righteous[ness]), צדקה/צדיק/צדק, at 1:2.
170. See Translation Matters on Jerk/Schmuck/Folly (Fool/Folly), אויל/אולת, at 1:7.
171. See Translation Matters on Dolt/Chump/Oaf/Inept (Fool), כסיל, at 1:22.

Prov 18:1-9

¹The one who lives alone is self-
indulgent,
showing contempt for all who
have sound judgment.
²A fool takes no pleasure in
understanding,
but only in expressing personal
opinion.
³When wickedness comes, contempt
comes also;
and with dishonor comes
disgrace.
⁴The words of the mouth are deep
waters;
the fountain of wisdom is a
gushing stream.

⁵It is not right to be partial to the
guilty,
or to subvert the innocent in
judgment.
⁶A fool's lips bring strife,
and a fool's mouth invites a
flogging.
⁷The mouths of fools are their ruin,
and their lips a snare to
themselves.
⁸The words of a whisperer are like
delicious morsels;
they go down into the inner parts
of the body.
⁹One who is slack in work
is close kin to a vandal.

TRANSLATION MATTERS

If the MT's reading of תאוה, "desire," in 18:1 is correct, then the recluse pursues only (the individual's own) desire. If the LXX is correct (προφάσεις), then the Hebrew reading would be תאנה, "pretext," and the meaning would be that the recluse seeks a pretext to do what is described in the following colon. "Showing contempt for," יתגלע, seems to mean to burst out in anger, as in 17:14.

TRANSLATION MATTERS

In 18:3, the NRSV unnecessarily emends MT רָשָׁע, corrupt ("wicked"),[172] to רֶשַׁע, corruption ("wickedness").

The word rendered as "disgrace," חרפה, here is better translated as "reproach," since disgrace is a synonym for dishonor and the meaning needed is a consequence of dishonor, not a synonym.

172. See Translation Matters on Corrupt[ion]/Unscrupulous/Reprehensible (Wicked[ness]), רשע/רשעים, at 2:22.

Proverbs 18:3 asserts that just as the proverbs in 18:1-2 pair the recluse and the dolt, so contempt, whether for the corrupt or by the corrupt, comes when a corrupt person enters the scene (following the MT rather than the NRSV's emended text). Similarly, with dishonor comes reproach.

Proverbs 18:4 begins with an enigmatic statement that human words are deep waters. It is not clear whether this is positive or negative or just that words require care in use and have significance beyond our knowledge. The second colon compares the fountain of wisdom to a gushing stream, which is a perpetually fed stream. Verse 5 asserts that it is not good to favor the guilty or subvert the innocent (צדיק)[173] in judgment. It is not clear in what sense it is not good—not good for individuals, for society, for the judge who makes such partial decisions, or for all of the above (see 27:23). Verse 6 returns to the theme of the dolt from 18:2 and contention from 18:1, 3. What a dolt says leads to quarrels and is so incendiary that it can lead to blows. (See Excursus on Women's Sins 2: Violence, at 6:16-19.) Verse 7 is a good follow-up to verse 6. It suggests that the mouths of dolts bring their own destruction, not just that of others. In 18:8, the movement is from outward speech to the gossip or slanderer whose words are delicacies that go down into the inner recesses of the belly, where we may understand they settle and do their dirty work. Verse 9 is not explicitly or even implicitly about speech, but it is about a ne'er-do-well, a sluggard. The passivity of such a person is described as kin to people who actively destroy the work of others.

Security and Humility (18:10-15)

Proverbs 18:10-15 forms a cluster with the intertwined themes of security and humility. Verses 10-12 contrast the absolute security provided the just (righteous)[174] and the humble by YHWH's name with the delusional dependence of the rich on their wealth. Verses 13-15 appear to be separate comments on the rudeness of interruption (akin to folly), the relative difficulty of recovering from a spiritual/emotional/mental distress compared to disease (see 15:13), and the advantage of listening in the pursuit of knowledge (see also 15:14). The connection to arrogance and humility is tenuous, unless all the condemned behaviors (not merely

173. See Translation Matters on Just/Integrity/Honesty (Righteous[ness]), צדקה/ צדיק/צדק, at 1:2.

174. See Translation Matters on Just/Integrity/Honesty (Righteous[ness]), צדקה/ צדיק/צדק, at 1:2.

Prov 18:10-15

¹⁰The name of the LORD is a strong
      tower;
   the righteous run into it and are
      safe.
¹¹The wealth of the rich is their strong
      city;
   in their imagination it is like a high
      wall.
¹²Before destruction one's heart is
      haughty,
   but humility goes before honor.

¹³If one gives answer before
      hearing,
   it is folly and shame.
¹⁴The human spirit will endure
      sickness;
   but a broken spirit—who can
      bear?
¹⁵An intelligent mind acquires
      knowledge,
   and the ear of the wise seeks
      knowledge.

15:13) are associated with arrogance. (See Excursus on Women's Sins 1: Arrogance, at 3:8.)

Judicial Issues (18:16-19)

This small proverbial cluster focuses on judicial matters. Verse 16 deals with gifts. Bribes were a fact of life in the ancient world, much more so than they are openly today in the modern West. In the context of 18:17, however, 18:16 may appear in a different light. If the gift giver is trying to influence a judge, then the gift is not a good thing. Verse 17 states another objective fact. The first person who states a case often seems persuasive, but when the other person in the case has the opportunity to ask questions, the perspective frequently changes. This proverb, then, implies the importance of giving all sides the opportunity to state what they know and ask questions. This may be related back to 18:13. Verse 18 describes another judicial procedure in which a lot or stone is thrown to decide certain types of cases. It has the advantage of being immune to bribery. The final proverb in this cluster, 18:19, compares the dispute resulting from an injury to a relative or ally to the strength of a city or castle bars. The implication is not to cross such a person.

Finding Friends through Speech (18:20-24)

This cluster deals with finding various kinds of relationships through speech. Verses 20-21 are a proverb pair. The metaphorical produce of the mouth/tongue/lips satisfies not only the listeners who eat its fruit but also the speaker. Since both life and death are within its power (18:21),

Prov 18:16-24

[16]A gift opens doors;
it gives access to the great.
[17]The one who first states a case
seems right,
until the other comes and cross-
examines.
[18]Casting the lot puts an end to
disputes
and decides between powerful
contenders.
[19]An ally offended is stronger than a
city;
such quarreling is like the bars of
a castle.
[20]From the fruit of the mouth one's

stomach is satisfied;
the yield of the lips brings
satisfaction.
[21]Death and life are in the power of
the tongue,
and those who love it will eat its
fruits.
[22]He who finds a wife finds a good
thing,
and obtains favor from the LORD.
[23]The poor use entreaties,
but the rich answer roughly.
[24]Some friends play at friendship
but a true friend sticks closer than
one's nearest kin.

however, people need to be careful how they speak, whether in a judicial setting (looking back to 18:15-19) or in ordinary speech (looking forward to seeking). At the center of this cluster is a proverb (18:22) that restates a central theme of chapters 1–9 and 31: the importance for a young man of finding a (good) wife, although this proverb does not use a modifier. This verse, and 18:24, seem unconnected to the theme of speech in the surrounding proverbs. Perhaps the advice is to find both a wife and a true friend (18:24) using honest speech. Verse 23 no doubt describes the way things were (and are); the poor had/have no choice but to ask for help, and the rich often treat the poor harshly. The proverb is intended not as mere description but as a critique that will elicit better behavior from the rich.

On Wealth and Poverty (19:1-10)

This proverbial cluster deals with wealth and poverty and related topics. It begins in 19:1 with a "better than" proverb. As the proverb stands in the MT, it compares a poor person who walks in integrity with a dolt (fool)[175] who has a crooked (perverse)[176] tongue. The Syriac and the similar proverb in 28:6 instead compare the honest poor person with the

175. See Translation Matters on Dolt/Chump/Oaf/Inept (Fool), כסיל, at 1:22.
176. The word translated as "perverse," עקש, literally means twisted.

Prov 19:1-10

¹Better the poor walking in integrity
    than one perverse of speech who
        is a fool.
²Desire without knowledge is not
    good,
    and one who moves too hurriedly
        misses the way.
³One's own folly leads to ruin,
    yet the heart rages against the
        LORD.
⁴Wealth brings many friends,
    but the poor are left friendless.
⁵A false witness will not go
    unpunished,
    and a liar will not escape.
⁶Many seek the favor of the
    generous,

and everyone is a friend to a giver
    of gifts.
⁷If the poor are hated even by their kin,
    how much more are they shunned
        by their friends!
When they call after them, they are
    not there.
⁸To get wisdom is to love oneself;
    to keep understanding is to
        prosper.
⁹A false witness will not go
    unpunished,
    and the liar will perish.
¹⁰It is not fitting for a fool to live in
    luxury,
    much less for a slave to rule over
        princes.

duplicitous rich one, which is more what we expect: better to be poor yet honest than rich but deceitful. Yet, the proverb may not be in error as it stands. People who intentionally twist their speech usually do so to get rich quickly by taking advantage of others, and they often get away with it for a while, but from the perspective of the sages they are dolts. Their wealth is ephemeral; it will not last, for their twisted ways will be found out, not to mention that they will be constantly anxious. Many proverbs implicitly blame poverty on laziness (13:4; 19:15, 24; 20:4; 21:25; 26:15). This one agrees with many of the other "better than" proverbs in inverting the relative value of wealth and poverty.

Verse 2 expands on walking with integrity: without knowledge, desire (literally appetite [נפש]) is not good; 19:2b warns that when we move too fast we miss the path. Together the two cola suggest that knowledge and thoughtful deliberation are necessary to travel life's road successfully. Desire is not bad, but we must not act on impulses without first considering how best to satisfy them, else we may be like the dolt in 19:1. The road motif continues in 19:3 with a proverb that states that human folly[177] leads to ruin, but (because humans do not understand this) we rail against God for our misfortune.

177. See Translation Matters on Jerk/Schmuck/Folly (Fool/Folly), אויל/אולת, at 1:7.

Proverbs 19:4 returns to the main theme of wealth and poverty. Money makes "friends," not real intimate friends, but people who suck up to the rich, either hoping for handouts or just wanting their social status to rub off on them. Unfortunately, the poor have the opposite problem. Their neediness often sends all but the truest friends far away from them because people have their own troubles and don't want to be bothered with someone else's. Verse 5 ties in with verse 1 (deceitful of tongue) since it deals with negative speech: false witness and lying. People who engage in this type of behavior will be punished (see 14:5). Verses 6-7 again return to the theme of wealth and are like 19:4, though more explicit. Generous gift-givers will have lots of friends seeking their favor, but are they genuine friends? Verse 7 asserts that the poor are abandoned by family and friends. This is surely an exaggeration, but the contrast between the rich, who have many friends and would-be friends, and the very poor, whose circle of family and friends is much smaller, is perhaps accurate. In contrast to the advantages of wealth and the disadvantages of poverty, 19:8 states that acquiring wisdom is (the best way) to love oneself; likewise, guarding understanding is (the ideal way) to prosper. See Excursus on Women's Sins 5: Self-Abnegation and Self-Love at the end of this section.

Proverbs 19:9 is almost identical to 19:5, except that in 19:9 the punishment is specified as death. Finally, 19:10 asserts that it is not appropriate for a dolt to live in luxury, and it is even worse for a slave to rule over princes. Dolts behave(d) in such a way as to drive wealth away. Similarly, the sages did not think servants had the wisdom to rule over others.

Excursus on Women's Sins 5: Self-Abnegation and Self-Love

Self-love is related to pride and arrogance (see the Excursus on Women's Sins 1: Arrogance, at 3:8). Just as women tend to be acculturated not to express their anger (see Excursus on Women's Sins 4: Anger, at 14:16), we are similarly taught in many ways not to love ourselves, perhaps especially our bodies.[178] Perfect, beautiful women's bodies are used to sell everything from cars to detergent. Women feel that they cannot measure up to the ideal.[179] On a psychological level, we are also taught to deny ourselves, to give in, to take care of others, but not ourselves. In

---

178. See Wioleta Polinsky, "Dangerous Bodies: Women's Nakedness and Theology," *JFSR* 16 (2000): 45–62.

179. See Michelle Mary Lelwica, "Spreading the Religion of Thinness from California to Calcutta: A Critical Feminist Postcolonial Analysis," *JFSR* 25 (2009): 19–41.

part this probably arises from the biological fact that women are the ones who bear children, but this fact need not dominate every facet of our lives. Healthy self-love involves both self-care and the choice of how to give of ourselves to others.

A note of caution: as contemporary Westerners in an individualistically oriented society our notions of selfhood are different from those in group-oriented societies such as the biblical world or in much of the developing world today.

In these societies, the sense of a healthy self is much more identified with the group than in developed countries.[180]

In whatever culture women find themselves, it is necessary to deal with the cultural codes that dictate gender roles, and in many cases, in order to love ourselves, we may have to resist some of those codes and actively work to change them. This is hard work and is done most effectively in solidarity with other like-minded individuals.

Macrocluster: On Moral Qualities and Education (19:11–20:4)

On Prudence, Anger, and Wives (19:11-14)

This small proverbial cluster is part of a macrocluster, 19:11–20:4, concerning moral qualities and the education required to develop them. Proverbs 19:11-14 has two foci: (1) anger and favor and (2) domestic happiness. The cluster is bound together by an *inclusio* in 19:11 and 19:14, which is obscured by the English translation:

> [11]Those with good **sense** [שכל] are slow to anger,
>   and it is their glory to overlook an offense.
> [14]House and wealth are inherited from parents,
>   but a **prudent** [משכלת from the root שכל] wife is from the LORD.

Proverbs 19:11 opens with a standard concept of the sages that it is prudent to be slow to anger and glorious to overlook an offense presumably done against oneself. Verse 12 is also about anger, but not ordinary anger. It compares royal anger to the roar of a lion, without passing judgment one way or the other, though in the context it may be urging royal restraint. On the other hand, it indicates that the king's favor is like the

180. Boyung Lee, "Caring-Self and Women's Self-Esteem: A Feminist's Reflection on Pastoral Care and Religious Education of Korean-American Women," *Pastoral Psychology* 54 (2006): 337–53.

Prov 19:11-14

¹¹Those with good sense are slow to anger,
and it is their glory to overlook an offense.
¹²A king's anger is like the growling of a lion,
but his favor is like dew on the grass.

¹³A stupid child is ruin to a father,
and a wife's quarreling is a continual dripping of rain.
¹⁴House and wealth are inherited from parents,
but a prudent wife is from the LORD.

dew on the grass. In a dry climate that did not experience much rain, at least not in the summer dry season, the morning dew was a refreshing moisture. Thus, the proverb may also be contrasting the king's anger, which was episodic, with his favor, which was more constant.

TRANSLATION MATTERS

Usually NRSV translates אב as "parent," but perhaps because it wants to translate אשה in 19:13b as "wife," rather than spouse, it retains the more traditional "father" here.

Given the NRSV's usual generic rendering of the language of "parent" and "child" (for father, אב, and son, בן), it is interesting that the translators did not go the next step to render אשה, "wife," as "spouse" in 19:13, 14. (See Translation Matters on Father/Parent/Ancestor at 1:8.)

Verses 13-14 both deal with wives. The sages were focused on qualities in wives, since their audience is young men, but there is no reason not to extend the proverb to both sexes, since today's audience is persons of all ages and genders. Nevertheless, we may bridle at this characterization of wives as quarrelsome, even if it is not necessarily intended to be true of all wives. (See Excursus on Women's Sins 4: Anger, at 14:16.)

At the same time, we should note that in 26:21, we find a different form of the same word used of a man: איש מדונים! One difference is that the Hebrew word אשה can mean either wife or woman, and in the context of 19:13 wife is meant. איש rarely means husband. בעל, literally "lord" or "master," is the usual word for husband in Hebrew. Nevertheless, it is important to note that men are frequently counseled not to be quarrelsome. (See the discussion and note at 21:9, 19.)

Proverbs 19:13b could be understood to be a result of relationships where one party held or holds a disproportionate amount of the economic, political, and/or social power. In such cases the party with less power, usually the wife, was or is likely to come across as or actually be quarrelsome, especially if the husband uses his greater power imperiously. Most of the time persons in power do not fully understand how imperiously they are acting and the effects of their behavior on those around them. They are so accustomed to the status quo that they cannot imagine any other scenario. This is captured perfectly in the 2016 film *Hidden Figures* in which the white boss declares, "Despite what you may think, I have nothing against y'all." Dorothy Vaughn then responds with perfect equanimity, "I know you probably believe that."

Proverbs 19:14 declares that although you may be able to inherit wealth, a good partner is a divine gift, so at least this cluster ends on a somewhat positive note with regard to attitudes toward wives. If the compilers of the proverbs were trying to recontextualize the troublesome proverbs like 19:13 in such a way as to blunt their negative force, they did so with some success here by ending the section with a positive saying about the value of a good partner.

Be Kind and Don't Be Lazy, Ill-Tempered, or a Liar (19:15-24)

This long cluster focuses loosely on education and the various qualities it seeks to engender or root out. It is bound together by an *inclusio* in 19:15 and 19:24:

> [15]**Laziness** [עצלה] brings on deep sleep;
>   an **idle person** will suffer hunger.
> [24]The **lazy person** [עצל] buries a hand in the dish,
>   and will not even bring it back to the mouth.

Proverbs 19:15-16 contrasts laziness, both economic and moral, with its opposite. Inattention will bring hunger and death; following the commandments, life. Verses 17-18 both refer to long-term benefits of actions taken in the present. Kindness to the poor (who are treated sympathetically) will (eventually) be repaid by YHWH; and patient discipline of a child will prevent him from going wrong.

In 19:18, if the conjunction is read temporally, as NRSV does, then the meaning is that children can and should be molded while they are young. To neglect to do this is the equivalent of trying to kill them. It can also be read causatively, "because there is hope." Sometimes it may not be obvious that efforts will pay off, but the proverb asserts that they will.

Prov 19:15-24

¹⁵Laziness brings on deep sleep;
  an idle person will suffer hunger.
¹⁶Those who keep the commandment
  will live;
  those who are heedless of their
  ways will die.
¹⁷Whoever is kind to the poor lends to
  the LORD,
  and will be repaid in full.
¹⁸Discipline your children while there
  is hope;
  do not set your heart on their
  destruction.
¹⁹A violent tempered person will pay
  the penalty;
  if you effect a rescue, you will only
  have to do it again.
²⁰Listen to advice and accept
instruction,
  that you may gain wisdom for the
  future.
²¹The human mind may devise many
  plans,
  but it is the purpose of the LORD
  that will be established.
²²What is desirable in a person is
  loyalty,
  and it is better to be poor than a
  liar.
²³The fear of the LORD is life indeed;
  filled with it one rests secure
  and suffers no harm.
²⁴The lazy person buries a hand in
  the dish,
  and will not even bring it back to
  the mouth.

TRANSLATION MATTERS

In 19:18, NRSV is reading the כי conjunction temporally, "while" (there is hope), but it can also be read causatively, "because" (there is hope).

Proverbs 19:19 is one of a number of proverbs that criticize people who are quick-tempered. Juxtaposed to the advice given in 19:18, this proverb suggests that there is no point in bailing out adults who were badly brought up, for this will not help them learn their lesson; they will only do it again. This seems to be an ancient version of tough love, as well as conserving one's resources.

Proverbs 19:20 returns again to the explicit theme of education, this time addressed to the recipient of the process. Verse 21 links with verse 20 with the words for advice (עצה, 19:20) and purpose (עצת, 19:21) from the same Hebrew root. Verse 21 is not a suggestion that humans should not plan but rather a reminder of God's ultimate sovereignty over everything (see 16:1, 9).

TRANSLATION MATTERS

A more natural translation than NRSV's "what is desirable in a person" is "a person's desire," in the sense of greed. The translators were confused by the following word, חסד, which they rendered as "loyalty." In the context, the rare meaning of חסד, "disgrace," as in 14:34, is a possibility.

Proverbs 19:22 is difficult because of the way the two cola fit together and the question of whether חסד should be understood in its usual meaning of kindness or its unusual meaning of disgrace. The proverb may have been a verbal riddle, with multiple possible meanings. The proverb works well if it is translated as follows:

> A person's greed is disgrace,
>   and it is better to be poor than a liar.

The implication would be that greed leads to lying, which in turn leads to disgrace. It is better to be poor but honest than greedy, dishonest, and ultimately in disgrace. Verse 23 follows verse 22 well, for it asserts that the fear of YHWH[181] is life or leads to life; when one is filled with this quality, one's desires can be filled and one need not worry about being visited by any trouble. Finally, we are back to 19:24 and the lazy person who is sarcastically said to be so indolent that a hand is put in a dish (of food) but no energy can be found to bring it to the mouth to eat. This is especially true in education.

Education for the Scoffers and Dolts[182] (19:25–20:1)

This proverbial cluster continues the focus on education but with a special concentration on the scoffer, לץ, and related terms. The scoffing root occurs in 19:25 and 20:1, forming an *inclusio*, but it also occurs in 19:28-29. The cluster begins in 19:25 with the statement that striking a scoffer (generally assumed to be not improvable) will have the effect of teaching the simple to be at least prudent enough to avoid such a beating. A mere word of reprimand to the discerning, on the other hand, is sufficient for them to acquire knowledge. What the Hebrew says in 19:26 is impersonal: one who does violence to a father chases away a mother. This gives the impression of the behavior of a violent criminal

---

181. See discussion of this phrase at 1:7.
182. See Translation Matters on Dolt/Chump/Oaf/Inept (Fool), כסיל, at 1:22.

[25]Strike a scoffer, and the simple will learn prudence;
reprove the intelligent, and they will gain knowledge.
[26]Those who do violence to their father and chase away their mother
are children who cause shame and bring reproach.
[27]Cease straying, my child, from the words of knowledge,
in order that you may hear instruction.

[28]A worthless witness mocks at justice,
and the mouth of the wicked devours iniquity.
[29]Condemnation is ready for scoffers,
and flogging for the backs of fools.

[20:1]Wine is a mocker, strong drink a brawler,
and whoever is led astray by it is not wise.

who has fallen upon the family home, but depending on the interpretation of the problematic 19:27, it could also refer to a dramatic rejection of their teaching. The second colon thus comes as a shock when it turns out that it is a son (child)[183] who is responsible and is therefore labeled as one who brings not just disaster on the house but shame and reproach. This is likely the kind of child who was a scoffer as a student. The MT of 19:27 would have been intended ironically. Verse 28 picks up the root from which the word "scoffer" in the first and last verses of this cluster is taken: a corrupt witness mocks or scoffs at justice. In the second colon, the sages explain that the corrupt (wicked)[184] swallow iniquity, and, having internalized it thoroughly, they spit it back out when it is time for them to serve as witnesses (see 14:5). Verse 29 relates to the first verse in this cluster, 19:25, which speaks of the effects of striking a scoffer or the simple. The MT speaks of שפטים, judgments, and the judgments in question in the context are surely some sort of beating, since the word is parallel with מהלמות, "blows," in the next colon.

The final proverb in this cluster, in 20:1, changes gears somewhat and personifies wine as a scoffer or mocker and strong drink as a boisterous individual; it asserts that those who are led into error by strong drink are not wise. This is a proverb intended for the ears of those who want to be wise and thus are being told to be careful how much they drink.

183. See Translation Matters on Son (Child), בן, at 1:8.
184. See Translation Matters on Corrupt[ion]/Unscrupulous/Reprehensible (Wicked[ness]), רשע/רשעים, at 2:22.

TRANSLATION MATTERS

The MT of 19:27 is difficult but not impossible. What it says is:

> Cease, my son, heeding instruction,
>   (cease) going astray from the words of knowledge.

NRSV has inverted the predicates of the cola in order to make sense out of the line, but it is not clear that the Hebrew syntax works the way it is translated.

On Anger and Laziness (20:2-4)

These three proverbs bring the macrocluster of 19:11–20:4 to a close. Proverbs 20:2a is very similar to 19:12, but the second colon is different. Whereas 19:12 contrasts the king's favor with his anger, here the king's servants are warned not to provoke his anger. Verse 3 moves on to say that it is honorable not to get into a dispute in general, but jerks (fools)[185] just tend to quarrel. Combined with 19:11 and 19:19, the theme of anger is at the beginning, middle, and end of this macrocluster. (See Excursus on Women's Sins 4: Anger, at 14:16.) The final proverb, in 20:4, on laziness, picks up from two centrally located ones, in 19:15 and 19:24. This one is more specific in its sarcastic attack on the lazy character; if you cannot even figure out when the harvest will be, how can you handle any of life's more subtle challenges?

On Discerning What Is in the Human Heart/Mind (20:5-13)

This cluster deals primarily with what is in the human heart/mind[186] and how these qualities may be discerned. If verses 5 and 6 are taken together, they are a comment on the difficulty in correctly assessing the motives of our friends, our acquaintances, or (looking forward to the regal verses 20:8-9) our subjects (see also 18:4). Verse 7 begins by saying that the just (righteous)[187] walk continually in integrity and follows with the observation that the children who come after them are blissful or fortunate (happy).[188] In the context of the surrounding

---

185. See Translation Matters on Jerk/Schmuck/Folly (Fool/Folly), אויל/אולת, at 1:7.
186. See Translation Matters on the Heart, לב, at 2:2.
187. See Translation Matters on Just/Integrity/Honesty (Righteous[ness]), צדקה/צדיק/צדק, at 1:2.
188. See Translation Matters on Blissful (Happy), אשרי, at 3:13.

²The dread anger of a king is like the growling of a lion;
anyone who provokes him to anger forfeits life itself.
³It is honorable to refrain from strife, but every fool is quick to quarrel.
⁴The lazy person does not plow in season;
harvest comes, and there is nothing to be found.
⁵The purposes in the human mind are like deep water,
but the intelligent will draw them out.
⁶Many proclaim themselves loyal, but who can find one worthy of trust?
⁷The righteous walk in integrity— happy are the children who follow them!

⁸A king who sits on the throne of judgment
winnows all evil with his eyes.
⁹Who can say, "I have made my heart clean;
I am pure from my sin"?
¹⁰Diverse weights and diverse measures
are both alike an abomination to the LORD.
¹¹Even children make themselves known by their acts,
by whether what they do is pure and right.
¹²The hearing ear and the seeing eye—
the LORD has made them both.
¹³Do not love sleep, or else you will come to poverty;
open your eyes, and you will have plenty of bread.

proverbs, perhaps the meaning can be narrowed to the idea that the children learn how to be trustworthy (20:6) and do what is pure and right (20:11). The purposes of the just are visible, because they do not lie or deceive; their integrity is easy to discern, even by a child, who is deeply fortunate to follow such role models. Verse 8 returns to the theme of discernment. Winnowing involved throwing the harvested grain up into the air so that the wind could separate the grain from the chaff, allowing the wind to blow the lighter chaff away. The king's penetrating gaze similarly reveals hidden human purposes and blows away the evildoers. Verse 9, following up on verse 8, as a rhetorical question, makes it clear that no human can discern all evil and no human is perfect. Yet this is not to say that humans are inherently evil, for 20:7 states that the just do walk in integrity. Verse 10 is one of several proverbs that condemn false weights used in trade. Perhaps this proverb is in this cluster because it is not easy to discern the falseness of the weights or of people.

Proverbs 20:11 returns again to the theme of how a person's merit is discerned. This proverb asserts that even children are known by their behavior. Although the *Hithpa'el* of the verb נכר usually means to feign, in this case the context suggests the reflexive meaning of the NRSV translation. The assertion in 20:12 of the divine craftsmanship of the hearing ear and seeing eye suggests that humans should use these sense organs to discern good and evil among other humans and that if human beings can perceive these qualities, how much more God can do so. Verse 13 picks up on the word "eye" and advocates keeping the eyes open rather than sleeping, to avoid poverty and hunger (see 19:15, 24).

Truth or Consequences (20:14-19)

The proverbial cluster in 20:14-19 deals primarily with business transactions, and most of the proverbs involve the lips, mouth, and/or speech, explicitly or implicitly. Talking down the price of some merchandise as in 20:14 is very common; it is not good business in the long run, according to the sages. People prefer to do business on a regular basis with honest buyers and sellers. Verse 15 compares gold and many precious stones, which are worth more than the gold and stones alone, with knowledgeable speech, which is said to be a precious artifact. In the context of 20:14, knowledgeable lips can discern and reply to the dishonesty of the buyer who says, "bad, bad," but it could also represent a different form of a "better than" proverb, knowledge is better than gemstones. Compare 3:15; 8:11; and 31:10.

Proverbs 20:16 is one of several proverbs that advises against giving surety, ערב, for a loan (6:1; 11:15). In this case, the advice is not to do it for a stranger, for you can already hear the judge seizing and giving away your coat. Verse 17 follows up on this advice with a proverb that involves a play on words with the word for "surety" in 20:16. In 20:17 bread gained through duplicity or, alternately, a steady diet of falsehood, in either case reminiscent of 20:14, is said to be sweet, ערב, at first, but later the one who eats it will end up with a mouth full of gravel. Verse 18 begins with general counsel regarding taking advice when making plans and then moves to the more specific arena of war, where it is perhaps even more critical to get as much good advice as possible. The final proverb in this cluster, 20:19, picks up on the wordplay in 19:16-17 in its advice not to associate (תתערב) with the babbler.

¹⁴"Bad, bad," says the buyer,
   then goes away and boasts.
¹⁵There is gold, and abundance of
   costly stones;
   but the lips informed by knowledge
   are a precious jewel.
¹⁶Take the garment of one who has
   given surety for a stranger;
   seize the pledge given as surety
   for foreigners.

¹⁷Bread gained by deceit is sweet,
   but afterward the mouth will be full
   of gravel.
¹⁸Plans are established by taking
   advice;
   wage war by following wise
   guidance.
¹⁹A gossip reveals secrets;
   therefore do not associate with a
   babbler.

Conduct and Consequences (20:20-30)

This long cluster, 20:20-30, dealing mostly with acts and consequences, begins in 20:20 with a warning to children concerning their estates. Verse 21 may involve a pun of the two Hebrew readings of the verb in the first colon, meaning "quickly acquired" and "gotten by greed." The result will be death and the loss, ironically, of a future. Proverbs 20:21 may be concerned with a similar problem as the one described in 19:26, in which the parents have been driven away from the family estate. Verse 22 is a good follow-up to 20:20-21, for in the context it may be advising parents who have been cursed by their children and/or forced to give up the family estate prematurely not to seek vengeance but to let God do it for them. This is one of three "do not say" proverbs. The others are 3:28 and 24:29.

TRANSLATION MATTERS

In 20:21, NRSV is reading the *Qeré*, מבהלת, "acquired." The *Ketib*, מבחלת, "gotten by greed," is also possible, and both meanings may have been heard, creating a pun.[189]

189. On *Qeré/Ketib*, see Translation Matters at 1:27.

Prov 20:20-30

²⁰If you curse father or mother,
    your lamp will go out in utter
        darkness.
²¹An estate quickly acquired in the
        beginning
    will not be blessed in the end.
²²Do not say, "I will repay evil";
    wait for the Lord, and he will help
        you.
²³Differing weights are an
        abomination to the Lord,
    and false scales are not good.
²⁴All our steps are ordered by the
        Lord;
    how then can we understand our
        own ways?
²⁵It is a snare for one to say rashly, "It
    is holy,"
and begin to reflect only after
    making a vow.
²⁶A wise king winnows the wicked,
    and drives the wheel over them.
²⁷The human spirit is the lamp of the
    Lord,
    searching every inmost part.
²⁸Loyalty and faithfulness preserve
        the king,
    and his throne is upheld by
        righteousness.
²⁹The glory of youths is their strength,
    but the beauty of the aged is their
        gray hair.
³⁰Blows that wound cleanse away
        evil;
    beatings make clean the
        innermost parts.

Proverbs 20:23 is one of several proverbs that assert that differing, and thus unjust weights, and the false scales that go along with them are an abomination[190] to God and just plain not good (see 16:11 and 20:10). Verses 21-23 could also be read as a series of contrasts; you may get some pleasure in despising your parents, but it will recoil on you; a rich beginning (possibly unjustly obtained) is no guarantee of the end; taking matters in your own hands may in fact violate God's purposes; and the temporary benefit of deceptive commercial practices will result in God's punishment.

Verse 24, like several other proverbs, asserts that human steps are from God, so the sages ask how we can understand our own ways. This might seem a counsel of despair, of total fatalism or predestination, except for the many proverbs that place a high value on human planning and taking counsel before acting (see 16:1, 9; 19:21; and 21:1-2). God is ultimately in charge, and all of our plans are subject to God's approval, tweaking, and even radical reworking. We should plan and work but

190. See discussion of the term "abomination" at 3:32.

be humble about our role in the grand scheme of things. Verse 25 could be restated by the modern proverb, look before you leap. Verse 26 introduces the king into this cluster with agricultural imagery, though the actual order of events is reversed, for the wheel was driven over the grain to separate the wheat from the chaff (the threshing process) and then it was winnowed. Both the threshing and winnowing aspect of the process are used as metaphors of punishment (see 20:8). Verse 27 uses an unusual word, נשמה, which means "breath." The idea is that God illuminates every part of us that our breath reaches; both God and the king may probe us by that light.

TRANSLATION MATTERS

In 20:28, MT has חסד, "kindness." NRSV is following the LXX, with its reading of the Hebrew צדק as "integrity/righteousness."[191]

Proverbs 20:28 returns to the king. There are various ways of reading the proverb, but if the MT is followed with its reading of "kindness" in the second colon instead of "integrity,"[192] following the LXX, then "kindness [loyalty]"[193] and "faithfulness" in the first colon may be understood as divine guardians, and "kindness [righteousness]" in the second colon as royal kindness to the king's subjects (see 20:6-7). Verse 29 praises both the strength of youth and the gray hair of the mature. More emphasis is given by the sages to the glories of gray hair than to the beauty of young strength, but here at least they tip their hat to the attractiveness of the latter. As NRSV has translated the proverb, with the conjunction "but," the aged still are valued more, but the conjunction in Hebrew may be translated as either "but" or "and." Nevertheless, the sages did value gray hair more than youthful strength, just as the contemporary era has reversed this perspective.

---

191. See Translation Matters on Just/Integrity/Honesty (Righteous[ness]), צדקה/צדיק/צדק, at 1:2.

192. See Translation Matters on Just/Integrity/Honesty (Righteous[ness]), צדקה/צדיק/צדק, at 1:2.

193. See Translation Matters on Kindness/Mercy (Loyalty), חסד, at 2:8. The Hebrew חסד is best understood as mercy or kindness rather than loyalty (NRSV).

TRANSLATION MATTERS

In 20:30, MT בְּרֻע, a prepositional phrase with the object, "evil," is awkward. With a slight repointing to בְּרֵעַ, changing the object to "mind," the colon makes more sense and is more parallel with the following colon: Blows that wound cleanse the mind. (Compare the use of רֵעַ in Ps 139:2).[194]

Proverbs 20:30 is one of several proverbs that exhibit the sages' certainty that corporal punishment had a salutary effect on the moral development of young people. (See discussion at 13:24.)

Macrocluster: Of Diligence and Idleness and Nagging Wives (21:1-19)

YHWH Weighs the Heart/Mind; Consequences Follow (21:1-8)

Chapter 21 as a whole appears to be a macrocluster with different kinds of sayings arranged chiastically:

A YHWH sayings (21:1-3)

   B diligence (21:5)

      C nagging wife (21:9)

      C' nagging wife (21:19)

   B' laziness (21:25)

A' YHWH sayings (21:30-31)

The cluster of 21:1-8 is marked by repetition of key words: דרך, "way" (21:2 [MT], 8); ישר, "right" (21:2, 8); לב, "heart/mind" (21:1, 2, 4);[195] forms of the verb עשה, "to do" (21:3, 7); and משפט, "justice" (21:3, 7). Proverbs 21:1-2 closely resembles 16:1-2. In both chapters the first verse focuses on God's ultimate control and the second notes that although we may all see ourselves as in the right, God is the ultimate judge. In 16:1 it was mortal plans that were subject to God's decision; in 21:1, even the king's heart/mind is a stream of water in God's hand, such as was used for irrigation, that God could turn in whatever direction God choses.

194. Michael V. Fox, *Proverbs 10–31: A New Translation with Introduction and Commentary*, AB 18B (New Haven: Yale University Press, 2009), 678–79.
195. See Translation Matters on the Heart, לב, at 2:2.

Prov 21:1-8

¹The king's heart is a stream of water
   in the hand of the Lᴏʀᴅ;
he turns it wherever he will.
²All deeds are right in the sight of the
      doer,
   but the Lᴏʀᴅ weighs the heart.
³To do righteousness and justice
   is more acceptable to the Lᴏʀᴅ
      than sacrifice.
⁴Haughty eyes and a proud heart—
   the lamp of the wicked—are sin.
⁵The plans of the diligent lead surely
   to abundance,

but everyone who is hasty comes
   only to want.
⁶The getting of treasures by a lying
      tongue
   is a fleeting vapor and a snare of
      death.
⁷The violence of the wicked will
   sweep them away,
   because they refuse to do what
      is just.
⁸The way of the guilty is crooked,
   but the conduct of the pure is
      right.

TRANSLATION MATTERS

In 21:2, NRSV is reading MT דרך, "ways," as "deeds," in the sense that one's ways represent one's character, but the more literal "way" works fine here.

Proverbs 21:2 is almost identical to 16:2. Proverbs 21:3 states that doing integrity/justice (righteousness)[196] is more pleasing to God than religious ceremonies. This does not negate the value of ceremonies, just relativizes their merits.

The idea in 21:4 is that the corrupt (wicked)[197] use arrogant (literally high) eyes and a proud (literally wide) heart/mind as the only lamp with which to discern the correct path; the sages state that these attitudes in themselves constitute sin, but, clearly, they also lead to choosing incorrect paths, which leads to further sin. (See Excursus on Women's Sins 1: Arrogance, at 3:8.) Verse 5 contrasts diligence with hastiness.

---

196. See Translation Matters on Just/Integrity/Honesty (Righteous[ness]), צדקה/צדיק/צדק, at 1:2.

197. See Translation Matters on Corrupt[ion]/Unscrupulous/Reprehensible (Wicked[ness]), רשע/רשעים, at 2:22.

TRANSLATION MATTERS

In the first colon of 21:6 we have a case where emending the vocalization so that the MT matches the LXX is helpful. פֹּעַל, (*pō'ēl*), "making of" (LXX), rather than פָּעַל (*pō'al*), "getting of" (MT), as the first colon (BHS), will now match the participle (fleeting) in the second colon.

In the second colon of 21:6, NRSV emends מבקשי, "seekers of," to מוקשי, "snares of." But a simpler emendation to the singular, "seeker of," מבקש, solves the syntactical problem (BHS).

In 21:7, if the MT יְגוֹרֵם from גרר ("drag away") is slightly revocalized to יְגוּרֵם, from the root גור, it would mean that their violence will attack them.

Proverbs 21:6 represents a progression from 21:5. Haste is problematic, but lying can get you killed. Following the minor emendations suggested in Translation Matters, one who acquires treasures through lying is a fleeting vapor and is seeking death. Verse 7 continues the progression, now focusing on violence and the refusal to do justice. The opening word, שׁד, can mean violence/havoc as social sin, or it can mean the ruin experienced as a result of the social sin. The verb in the first colon means that their violence/ruin will drag them away like fish in a fishing net. If the verb is slightly revocalized (see Translation Matters), it means that their violence/ruin will attack them. Since the two verbs sound so much alike, the author might have intended both meanings as wordplay.[198]

TRANSLATION MATTERS

In 21:8, NRSV translates וָזָר as "guilty," based on a hypothetical Arabic etymology, but its validity is doubtful. Either the word should be viewed as a dittography of the following word, זַךְ, whose consonants are nearly identical, or it should be translated as "a stranger," so that the colon as a whole reads: "the way of a man who is a stranger is winding."[199] NRSV translates הפכפך as "crooked," and forms of this verb usually do mean something negative, but in the context of this proverb a more neutral translation is in order: "winding."

198. Fox, *Proverbs 10–31*, 682.
199. Ibid.

Proverbs 21:8, as it stands in the MT, says:

> The way of a man-and-a-stranger [may appear] winding,
>   but his conduct [may be] pure, right.

A stranger may appear to do things differently from what we expect;
nevertheless, the conduct of such a person may be perfectly pure and
right. If the word "stranger" is a dittography (a mistaken repetition by
the copyist), as seems likely, then the proverb simply says the same
thing, applied to all people. There are people who do things differently,
in circuitous ways, but sometimes they surprise us and, assuming they
are not doing anything crooked in a moral sense, they get there faster
than those who seem to be walking on the straight path. It is wise not
to be quick to judge. That is God's business. This forms a contrasting
parallel to 16:2 and 21:2, which argue that even though we think we are
on the straight path, God might judge otherwise.

On the Testy, Greedy, and Corrupt, and Scoffers, Bribers, and Hedonists (21:9-19)

The cluster 21:9-19, the second cluster in the macrocluster, is bound
together by the *inclusio* of the sayings regarding the difficulty of living
with a contentious wife. (On the factors that might make a wife contentious, see the discussion on quarrelsome wives at 19:13.) Modern readers
may read this as "spouse" rather than "wife," even though the original
author certainly intended "wife." Within the cluster, there is a wide
diversity of sayings.

TRANSLATION MATTERS

In 21:9 and 21:19, NRSV translates אשה literally as "wife," when it translates the
term for son inclusively as "child" in other places. Although it is not precisely
parallel, by much the same inclusive logic, אשה could be translated as "spouse."

Proverbs 21:9 is similar to 19:13, which compares living with a contentious wife to a leaky roof, only this time the beleaguered spouse has
sought refuge on (or been banished to) a corner of the roof. Ancient Israelite houses were typically one-story buildings with flat roofs surrounded
by a parapet (small wall) to prevent falls, reached by an external staircase.

Prov 21:9-19

⁹It is better to live in a corner of the housetop
than in a house shared with a contentious wife.
¹⁰The souls of the wicked desire evil;
their neighbors find no mercy in their eyes.
¹¹When a scoffer is punished, the simple become wiser;
when the wise are instructed, they increase in knowledge.
¹²The Righteous One observes the house of the wicked;
he casts the wicked down to ruin.
¹³If you close your ear to the cry of the poor,
you will cry out and not be heard.
¹⁴A gift in secret averts anger;

and a concealed bribe in the bosom, strong wrath.
¹⁵When justice is done, it is a joy to the righteous,
but dismay to evildoers.
¹⁶Whoever wanders from the way of understanding
will rest in the assembly of the dead.
¹⁷Whoever loves pleasure will suffer want;
whoever loves wine and oil will not be rich.
¹⁸The wicked is a ransom for the righteous,
and the faithless for the upright.
¹⁹It is better to live in a desert land
than with a contentious and fretful wife.

In ancient Israel and in the Middle East today people used their roofs for a variety of purposes. Although these sayings concerning contentious wives are troublesome, it should be kept in mind that balancing the five such sayings are nineteen proverbs dealing with quarreling and strife that are surely focused on men rather than women.[200]

Verse 10 says that the corrupt (wicked)[201] are so focused on their desire for evil that they will not even show kindness to their neighbors. Proverbs 21:11a is like 19:25a, only there the simple person learned from observing a scoffer receive a beating, whereas here the simple individual becomes wiser from observing a scoffer receive any sort of punishment. The second part of this proverb says that when a wise person is taught, that individual attains further knowledge.

200. The passages are 3:30; 10:12; 13:10; 15:18; 16:28; 17:1, 14, 19; 18:6, 19; 20:3; 22:10; 23:29; 26:4, 20, 21; 28:25; 29:22; and 30:33. They utilize three words for the concept of strife/quarreling: ריב, מדון, and מצה.

201. See Translation Matters on Corrupt[ion]/Unscrupulous/Reprehensible (Wicked[ness]), רשע/רשעים, at 2:22.

Verse 12 is problematic because nowhere else in Proverbs is the term צַדִּיק, just (righteous)[202] used as an epithet of God. On the other hand, it seems unlikely that a human would be presented as casting the corrupt to ruin, although perhaps this could be said of a just judge. Verse 13 asserts that people who stop up their ears to the plight of the needy will discover that their own cries for help will not be heard. Although the passive voice of the verb in the second colon leaves the subject ambiguous, it also suggests that no one will answer, neither humans nor God.

Verse 14 is generally understood to be about bribes and this may be right, but the fact that the gifts are given to deal with anger suggests that a broader context than a business transaction may be involved. If someone has done something, inadvertent or not, that has upset a neighbor, whether geographical, social, or business, and desires to get back on a good footing with said individual, a gift given quietly without it being made public may be the best route.

TRANSLATION MATTERS

In 21:15, the NRSV translates the active infinitive as a passive, "is done," but the active works better: "Doing justice is a joy to the just (righteous)."[203]

Reading the infinitive in 21:15 as active rather than passive, this proverb states that doing justice is a joy for the just, but it is terror to evildoers. The reason is that when people do justice, it is not merely the workings of the judicial system that catch criminals up in its wake, but it is the working out in the broader social milieu of a just order, which is the last thing that evildoers want to see. The idea of the ransom (כֹּפֶר) in 21:18 is of a payment to buy someone's release from trouble. (See 6:35, where the Hebrew כפר is translated as "compensation," and Isa 43:3, where God offers Cyrus other nations as a ransom for returning Israel from exile.)

Verse 19 brings us back to the contentious and this time irritating wife or spouse. Such a housemate has gone from being worse than a leaky roof (19:13) to being worse than living on a corner of that roof (20:9), to

202. See Translation Matters on Just/Integrity/Honesty (Righteous[ness]), צדקה/צדק/צדיק, at 1:2.
203. See Translation Matters on Just/Integrity/Honesty (Righteous[ness]), צדקה/צדק/צדיק, at 1:2.

now being forced out of the house altogether and living in the wilderness! The typical house was small, from one to four rooms, so, unlike modern Western homes, except for urban row houses, there was not much room in the house to escape if one's housemate was not pleasant. Nevertheless, it does take two to tango.

The Nature of the Wise and the Wicked (21:20-31)

The proverbial cluster in 20:21-31 comprises five subunits or mini-clusters: 20-22, 23-24, 25-26, 27-29, and 30-31. The first subunit, 21:20-22, "The Wise, Mightier Than Swords; Justice and Kindness as Treasures," deals with the wise (21:20, 22), who are by context (21:21) also the just (righteous). Verse 20 says that precious treasure or stored goods, which can refer to gold and silver but in this context refers to food, stay in the abode of the wise, but a dolt (fool)[204] individual swallows it all. Verse 21 states that integrity (righteousness) and kindness will achieve life and honor. Verse 22 comments that wisdom is sometimes mightier than the sword (or other similar entities). One is reminded of the story of the wise woman of Abel of Beth-Maacah who saved her city from destruction (1 Sam 20:15-22), the stories of Esther and Judith in the books of the same names, and that of Joshua and Jericho.

TRANSLATION MATTERS

In 21:21, the MT has צדקה, "integrity (righteousness)," in the second colon as well as the first, but LXX does not have it and it seems better to omit it as a dittography, as NRSV does, and substitute "honor."[205]

The next subunit, 21:23-24, "Restraint of Tongues Avoids Trouble Typical of the Arrogant," begins in verse 23 by stating a common proverbial theme: the importance of guarding the tongue in order to stay out of trouble. Some wordplay here is not apparent in the English translation. What the Hebrew says is:

204. See Translation Matters on Dolt/Chump/Oaf/Inept (Fool), כסיל, at 1:22.
205. See Translation Matters on Just/Integrity/Honesty (Righteous[ness]), צדקה/צדיק/צדק, at 1:2.

[The Wise, Mightier than Swords; Justice and Kindness as Treasures]

²⁰Precious treasure remains in the
house of the wise,
but the fool devours it.
²¹Whoever pursues righteousness
and kindness
will find life and honor.
²²One wise person went up against a
city of warriors
and brought down the stronghold
in which they trusted.

[Restraint of Tongue Avoids Trouble Typical of the Arrogant]

²³To watch over mouth and tongue
is to keep out of trouble.
²⁴The proud, haughty person, named
"Scoffer,"
acts with arrogant pride.

[The Lazy Lust; the Corrupt Covet; the Just Are Generous]

²⁵The craving of the lazy person is fatal,
for lazy hands refuse to labor.
²⁶All day long the wicked covet,

Guarding (or one who guards) one's mouth and tongue
(is) guarding (or one who guards) one's self/neck.

The word נפש means everything from self to person to desire, but at its most basic level it means neck.[206] If one keeps one's trap closed, one will not allow anything down one's throat, and one will protect oneself from the damage caused by speaking impulsively. More graphically, an unguarded mouth could lead to the speaker getting it in the neck. Verse 24 continues the thought with a specific version of the kind of people who should not open their mouths: the arrogant scoffer. (See Excursus on Women's Sins 1: Arrogance, at 3:8.)

Proverbs 21:25-26, the next subunit, "The Lazy Lust; the Corrupt Covet; the Just Are Gracious," is a couplet because both involve the word "crave/covet," אוה. NRSV interprets the first colon of 20:25 to mean that the cravings of the lazy person kill that person, for such a person is busy consuming rather than producing. Lazy individuals' desire not to work would also do the job, which is what the second colon says, i.e., that their hands refuse to work. Proverbs 20:26a suggests that the corrupt ("wicked,"[207] reading with LXX and NRSV) covet all day. The second colon does not initially seem to relate to it, but it is stating a paradox. The corrupt covet and thus are not generous, but according to 21:25, their

---

206. See Translation Matters on Soul/Neck/Person/Desire, נפש, at 2:10.

207. See Translation Matters on Corrupt[ion]/Unscrupulous/Reprehensible (Wicked[ness]), רשע/רשעים, at 2:22.

but the righteous give and do not
hold back.
**[Corrupt Sacrifices, False
Witnesses, Bold-Faced Lies
versus the Upstanding]**
²⁷The sacrifice of the wicked is an
abomination;
how much more when brought
with evil intent.
²⁸A false witness will perish,
but a good listener will testify
successfully.

²⁹The wicked put on a bold face,
but the upright give thought to
their ways.
**[Not Even Wisdom Can Avail
against YHWH; Victory Belongs to
YHWH]**
³⁰No wisdom, no understanding, no
counsel,
can avail against the Lord.
³¹The horse is made ready for the
day of battle,
but the victory belongs to the Lord.

desire kills them. The just don't hold back when it comes time to give. Although this proverb does not say it explicitly, the implication is that their desires are satisfied. The greedy never have time for wisdom, while the generous, who make time for others, have room for it.

Proverbs 21:27-29, "Corrupt Sacrifices, False Witnesses, Bold-Faced Lies versus the Upstanding," is held together by the word "corrupt" in verses 27 and 29 and the fact that the three verses all focus on various ways the corrupt do their evil deeds. Verse 27 complains about their sacrifices, that they are loathsome (presumably to YHWH, as in 15:8), more so if they are brought with an (evil) scheme. Verse 28 is concerned with false witnesses and their antithesis, individuals who listen (carefully) and then speak victoriously. Whether this means that they listen to the false testimony, see through it, and can win the case for the side of the innocent or that they listen carefully in the first place so that when it comes time to present evidence they can do it in an accurate and persuasive manner and thus be successful is not clear. Verse 29 can be read as a continuation of verse 28. The wicked (false witnesses of 20:28) put on bold faces (to try to cover up their lies), but the upstanding (upright)²⁰⁸ understand their ways and see through the facade.

Proverbs 21:30-31, "Not Even Wisdom Can Avail against YHWH; Victory Belongs to YHWH," is the last subunit in the cluster, containing two

---

208. See Translation Matters on Upstanding/Straight/Straightforward (Upright), ישׁר/ישׁרים, at 2:7.

proverbs highlighting divine sovereignty. Verse 30 is a reminder of the necessity of humility. Though the sages are in favor of wisdom (חכמה), understanding (תבונה), and counsel (עצה) before God, it is as if they did not exist. Verse 31 puts this in a specific military context. The horse may be ready for battle, but no matter how prepared we are for battle or anything else in life, God is in charge. (See 16:1, 9 and 21:1.)

On Wealth, Poverty, and Morality (22:1-16)

Proverbs 22:1-16 is the final section in the Solomonic collection; it is a macrocluster with an introductory verse expressing a "better than" comparison (22:1) and two small clusters, 22:2-5 and 22:6-16, which in turn have yet smaller subunits or miniclusters. The macrocluster is marked by an *inclusio* in 22:2 and 22:16. They use the same word for rich, עשיר, but different words for poor (רש, 22:2; דל, 22:16). Proverbs 22:1 opens the macrocluster with the statement that reputation and honor are better than wealth. Verses 2-5, "On Wealth and Poverty," have a parallel arrangement of themes as marked above, with the A and A' verses emphasizing the role of YHWH and B and B' verses emphasizing caution. Verse 2, following immediately after 22:1 and taken together with it, is an especially strong reminder to the rich of the importance of humility. To the poor, this proverb is a reminder of their equal worth. Although laziness may lead to poverty, this proverb makes it clear that poverty was not considered direct evidence of laziness. Verse 3 moves on to make a distinction between the prudent (clever),[209] who avoid trouble, and the simple-minded, who stumble into the midst of it. Verse 4 deals explicitly with what is implied in verse 2, humility. This proverb asserts that the consequence or reward for humility and fear of YHWH[210] is wealth, honor, and life, a heady combination. It does not encourage seeking these three as primary goals; they are byproducts of the virtues that one is to learn through moral education. Verse 5 says that just as the simple walk right into trouble, which prudent individuals avoid (22:3), so thorns and traps are in the way of the crooked (or on the crooked way),[211] from which those who guard themselves will stay far away. Whether they should stay far from the thorns and traps or from the devious people or from

209. See Translation Matters on Prudent/Prudence (Clever[ness]), ערמה and ערום, at 1:4.
210. See discussion of this phrase at 1:7.
211. The word translated as "perverse," עקש, literally means twisted.

Prov 22:1-16

[The Value of Reputation over Wealth]

¹A good name is to be chosen rather than great riches,

and favor is better than silver or gold.

[On Wealth and Poverty]

²The rich and the poor have this in common: A

the LORD is the maker of them all.

³The clever see danger and hide;   B

but the simple go on, and suffer for it.

⁴The reward for humility and fear of the LORD   A'

is riches and honor and life.

⁵Thorns and snares are in the way of the perverse;   B'

the cautious will keep far from them.

[On Moral Education, Wealth, and Poverty]

⁶Train children in the right way,

and when old, they will not stray.

⁷The rich rule over the poor,

and the borrower is the slave of the lender.

⁸Whoever sows injustice will reap calamity,

and the rod of anger will fail.

⁹Those who are generous are blessed,

both is not clear. Whereas the simple will be impoverished by their lack of foresight, the devious will be discomfited temporarily by the thorns and put out of business for good by the traps. The cautious will continue down their straight paths unharmed.

TRANSLATION MATTERS

Proverbs 22:11 is textually difficult. Many emendations have been offered, but none are compelling. The gist of it is clear as it stands in the MT.

The cluster in 22:6-16, "On Moral Education, Wealth, and Poverty," is marked by a quadruple *inclusio*:

⁶Train *children* [נער] in the right way,

and when old, they will not stray (from it [ממנה]).

⁷The **rich** [עשיר] rule over the <u>poor</u> [רשים],

and the borrower is the slave of the lender.

¹⁵Folly is bound up in the heart of a *boy* [נער],

but the rod of discipline drives it far away (from him [ממנו]).

for they share their bread with the
poor.

[On Speech]

¹⁰Drive out a scoffer, and strife goes
out;
quarreling and abuse will cease.

¹¹Those who love a pure heart and
are gracious in speech
will have the king as a friend.

¹²The eyes of the Lᴏʀᴅ keep watch
over knowledge,
but he overthrows the words of
the faithless.

¹³The lazy person says, "There is a
lion outside!

I shall be killed in the streets!"

¹⁴The mouth of a loose woman is a
deep pit;
he with whom the Lᴏʀᴅ is angry
falls into it.

**[The Folly of Oppressing the
Poor]**

¹⁵Folly is bound up in the heart of a
boy,
but the rod of discipline drives it
far away.

¹⁶Oppressing the poor in order to
enrich oneself,
and giving to the rich, will lead
only to loss.

¹⁶Oppressing the <u>poor</u> [דל] in order to enrich oneself,
and giving to the **rich** [עשיר], will lead only to loss.

These verses give an idea of the key themes in the cluster: moral education, wealth, and poverty. Verse 6 begins with education. The sages were aware of the malleability of the youthful mind, that this was the easiest and best time to instill in a person the moral values that they viewed as essential to a successful life and that if these values were inculcated early, they would tend to stay with the individual for life, though of course this was and is not guaranteed. Verse 7 states a fact of economic life: in many ways the rich rule over the poor and those who have to borrow will tend to be the slaves of the lenders. In ancient Israel, debt was the leading cause of actual slavery, because when a debtor could not pay a debt on time, the individual was often sold into slavery to pay off the debt.²¹² Verse 8 is difficult. The agricultural imagery in the first colon is not problematic, but it is not clear what the rod of anger refers to. Usually שבט in Proverbs refers to an instrument of punishment, but that does not seem suitable here. In other contexts, it can mean an instrument of war (2 Sam 8:14; 23:21) or a stick used for threshing (Isa 28:27). Perhaps the

212. John J. Collins, *Introduction to the Hebrew Bible*, 2nd ed. (Minneapolis: Fortress Press, 2014), 135.

meaning here is that the force employed by the unjust will not suffice. In 22:9 the Hebrew expression טוב־עין, "good of eye," means generous. Unlike those who sow injustice in 22:8, the generous who give of their bread to the poor will be blessed, presumably by God and the community.

Proverbs 22:10-14 is a minicluster on the theme of speech. In 22:10 the hearer/reader is admonished to drive out the scoffer; the result will be that strife will also exit, and quarreling of a legal sort and dishonor will also cease. In 22:11 the king seeks associates who value a pure heart/ mind and speak graciously. Verse 12 asserts that God guards knowledge and overthrows the words of the faithless. The parallelism implies that God guards knowledge in the form of wise words and discredits treacherous words. Verse 13 ridicules the idle by depicting them coming up with a particularly creative excuse not to go outside to work: there's a lion out there; I will be murdered! Finally, 22:14 mentions strange/ foreign/(loose) women[213] for the first time since Proverbs 1–9, this time in the plural. Their speech is said to be a deep pit, suggesting hunting imagery. Men who are denounced by God will fall into this pit according to the proverb. There is not enough context to determine the nature of the women in this proverb, whether prostitutes, adulterers, foreigners, or symbols of folly.

Although one of the proverbs in this cluster appears to be preexilic in that it speaks of the king (22:11), most could be postexilic. In that context, it seems most likely that the זרות, foreign/strange women, are those who were left behind at the time of the Babylonian exile and who are viewed as different by the higher-class returnees. They are not foreign necessarily in the sense that they come from a neighboring country like Moab, Edom, or Ammon, though this is also possible, but they could simply be viewed as foreign because after two generations of separation from their upper-class sisters, they have become quite different, and they were already somewhat different before the exile in that it was the wealthy who were taken away and the poor who were allowed to remain at home.

The last two verses in the Solomonic collection, 22:15-16, "The Folly of Oppressing the Poor," close the small and large clusters. Verse 15 is one of many proverbs that advise corporal punishment for children. In this case the reason is to get rid of folly. Today the rod may be reinterpreted as the noncorporal discipline of study. (See discussion at 13:24.) One

---

213. See Translation Matters on Strange/Foreign/Alien Woman (Loose Woman, Adulteress), אשה זרה, at 2:8.

form of folly (אִוֶּלֶת)[214] is described in 22:16, though the proverb can be interpreted in multiple ways because of the ambiguity of the pronoun in the first colon (one who oppresses the poor to bring increase to him) and the lack of clarity regarding the referent of the final noun in the second colon (one who gives to the rich surely for loss):

1) oppressing the poor will enrich the poor; giving to the rich will impoverish the giver

2) oppressing the poor will enrich the oppressor; giving to the rich will impoverish the rich

3) oppressing the poor will enrich the poor; giving to the rich will impoverish the rich

4) oppressing the poor will enrich the oppressor; giving to the rich will impoverish the giver

Although the third interpretation is not parallel in terms of the reading of the ambiguous elements, it does have the advantage of going against expectation in both cola. Oppressing the poor would be expected to enrich the oppressor; giving to the rich (in the form of a bribe or to curry favor) would be expected to enrich the donor. This proverb is a riddle that forces the reader to think about which interpretation is best.

Freedom from Harm, Abuse, and Exploitation: A Reflection on Proverbs 22:16

Daniel Holtzclaw, a former patrol officer for the Oklahoma Police Department, was sentenced on December 10, 2015, to 263 years after being convicted of raping and assaulting black women in low-income neighborhoods. Holtzclaw, who is half white and half Asian, was convicted of eighteen of the thirty-six counts, which included four separate counts of first-degree rape. Why were these women so vulnerable to Holtzclaw's attacks? Officer Holtzclaw knew that it was safe to prey on the poor black women, who face three different types of marginalization: being poor, being black, and being women. In fact, even two years later Asian American conservative pundit Michelle Malkin leads a crusade to overturn the charges and dismiss the surmounting evidence and the thirteen black women's testimonies.

214. See Translation Matters on Jerk/Schmuck/Folly (Fool/Folly), אֱוִיל/אִוֶּלֶת, at 1:7.

In Proverbs 22:16, "Oppressing the poor in order to enrich oneself, and giving to the rich, will lead only to loss." If one ignores the class dimension of racism and sexism, they will fail to understand how to unravel these evils most efficiently. The fact is that there is much exploitation of the creative energy of black women for capitalistic gains from which they do not benefit. Capitalism requires a driving engine, and that engine is the exploitation of black bodies or other marginalized bodies who can work for cheaper rates than their actual value. This exploitation encourages public policies that are patronizing and inductive toward perpetual poverty.

This all leads to an atmosphere that produced the results at the end of 2017 when several wealthy powerful men were held accountable for sexually abusing white women. Nevertheless, individuals such as Robert Kelly, an R&B singer, and Supreme Court Justice Clarence Thomas go unscathed because their victims are black women. So, it is clear why Holtzclaw felt comfortable raping many poor and vulnerable black women; it is because too many individuals wickedly find it perfectly acceptable to oppress, harm, mutilate, and violate black bodies.

Proverbs 22:16 proved itself faithful for Holtzclaw who, despite pundits like Malkin's attempt to overturn the conviction, is currently serving a 263-year sentence. But what about those who continue to exploit vulnerable groups for their selfish gain? How about those who are seemingly getting away with abuse and exploitation? These individuals must encounter justice, but who are the justice bearers? The truth-tellers? The people who know that oppressing the vulnerable to please yourself or to enrich yourself is both abominable and deplorable? To remain silent when seeing anyone being exploited is to be complicit in the oppression of all marginalized people.

How can we work toward ending the problem of rape culture, gender pay gaps, mass incarceration, sexual abuse, and other issues? How can we use our agency and our ability to ensure that people who harm others are held responsible? This is a heavenly mandate for all the faithful daughters and sons of God.

Lawrence W. Rodgers

Part 3

Proverbs 22:17–29:27

International Wisdom and the Hezekian Collection

Introduction

Part 3 is divided into three sections: (a) 22:17–24:22; (b) 24:23-34; and (c) 25:1–29:27. Part 3a, "The words of the wise," so called from its introductory colon, has significant parallels with the twelfth-century BCE or earlier Egyptian wisdom literature, *The Instruction of Amenemope*. Proverbs 22:20 speaks of thirty sayings and Amenemope's work has thirty chapters. There are many similarities between the proverbs in this section and Amenemope's *Instruction*. The narrator of Amenemope is a royal official and scribe. The words of the wise contains material appropriate for young men intended for royal service.

Part 3b, "These also are the sayings of the wise," is similar to 3a but seems to be intended for a more general audience and is dependent on other foreign sources. Both 3a and 3b contain instructions and directions for living, sometimes adding explanations in the second half of the verse. Although 3a and 3b show signs of dependence on foreign wisdom, they do not slavishly imitate it but creatively adapt it, adding their own thoughts and perspectives.

213

Part 3c, "These are other proverbs of Solomon that the officials of King Hezekiah of Judah copied," includes material that was presumably collected and edited by scribes in Hezekiah's court. Hezekiah was king of Israel from late eighth to early seventh century BCE. Proverbs 25:1–26:28 has some sequences that are thematically organized, while chapter 27 ends with instructions that run for several verses. Proverbs 28:1–29:27 return to the antithetical parallel sayings that were typical of part 2a, the collection of Solomonic proverbs in 10:1–15:33, suggesting literary shaping.[1]

Part 3a

A Free Adaptation of the Egyptian Wisdom Text, The Instruction of Amenemope *(22:17–24:22)*

Because of the length of this material, it is divided up into three sections for ease of use. Each section is commented on before the next section of text is presented.

Maxims for the Good Life, Part 1 (22:17–23:11)

Proverbs 22:17–23:11 constitutes the first section of part 3a of Proverbs 22:17–24:22, "the words of the wise," maxims mostly in the form of imperatives. It begins with an exordium in 22:17-21, which is very similar to the prologue to the parent's work in 5:1. Verse 17 instructs the listeners to hear the sage's words and to apply their minds to the teaching (literally knowledge). Then the motivation is given. Proverbs 22:18a says that it will be pleasant if/when you keep them in your belly, i.e., deeply rooted within. If you store them there, then the result is described in 22:18b: they will be ready on your lips, together. They will be so much a part of you that, when needed, they are easily and effortlessly summoned in their entirety, not piecemeal. The author is making all of this known to the addressee very personally so that he (in the original case) might trust in YHWH (22:19). Learning to live wisely and become aware of the consequences of such a mode of living engenders trust in

---

1. Katherine M. Hayes, *Proverbs*, New Collegeville Bible Commentary 18 (Collegeville, MN: Liturgical Press, 2013), 93.

¹⁷The words of the wise:
Incline your ear and hear my words,
   and apply your mind to my
      teaching;
¹⁸for it will be pleasant if you keep
   them within you,
   if all of them are ready on your lips.
¹⁹So that your trust may be in the
   L<small>ORD</small>,
   I have made them known to you
   today—yes, to you.
²⁰Have I not written for you thirty
   sayings

of admonition and knowledge,
²¹to show you what is right and true,
   so that you may give a true
      answer to those who sent
      you?

²²Do not rob the poor because they
   are poor,
   or crush the afflicted at the gate;
²³for the L<small>ORD</small> pleads their cause
   and despoils of life those who
      despoil them.
²⁴Make no friends with those given to
   anger,

God. Proverbs 22:20-21 is in the form of a rhetorical question and speaks of thirty sayings, the same number as chapters in Amenemope's work. Although scholars disagree on exactly how to divide up this part of Proverbs (22:17–23:11), it does divide into roughly thirty maxims. Verse 21 again gives the motivation, to reveal to the reader(s)/audience the truth so that they may return a true, i.e., accurate, response to the ones who sent them; with this verse the context of these proverbs is shown; we are to imagine emissaries sent to receive accurate information. Without modern snail mail, e-mail, phones, and other communication devices, the importance of messengers who could convey precisely what the sender intended and the answer received was very great. The ability to listen carefully, to read body language, to read between the lines, and to pick up various hidden cues all no doubt came into play, even if a written message was sent and received.

    Proverbs 22:22-23 begins the list of maxims with the exhortation not to steal from the poor even though they are vulnerable, as God is on their side, will plead their case legally (at the gate, the place where legal cases took place), and will avenge their cause, robbing those who rob the poor. Verse 23a invokes the *lex talionis* (law of retaliation), an eye for an eye, etc., but it might appear to be going much further, since taking the life of the one who robs the poor would seem disproportionate. The logic was, however, that robbing the poor left them without enough sustenance to live and in effect was murder. Verses 24-25 repeat the caution given in a number of Proverbs, as well as in Amenemope. Verses 26-27 strongly

Prov 22:17–23:11 (cont.)

and do not associate with
hotheads,
²⁵or you may learn their ways
and entangle yourself in a snare.
²⁶Do not be one of those who give
pledges,
who become surety for debts.
²⁷If you have nothing with which to pay,
why should your bed be taken
from under you?
²⁸Do not remove the ancient
landmark
that your ancestors set up.

²⁹Do you see those who are skillful in
their work?
They will serve kings;
they will not serve common people.

²³﹕¹When you sit down to eat with a
ruler,
observe carefully what is before
you,
²and put a knife to your throat
if you have a big appetite.
³Do not desire the ruler's delicacies,
for they are deceptive food.

recommend against the practice of giving surety for debts (20:16; 27:13). Verse 28 commands that ancient boundary markers not be moved; it was a kind of theft to move markers (see 15:25). Verse 29 is a rhetorical question. Its function is to encourage the young to perfect their skills so that they will be able to advance to the royal court rather than to remain among the ordinary folk. Proverbs 23:1-3 warns those who are eating in the presence of an official not to display a big appetite. The food may be delicious now, but eating too much will show the eater's lack of self-restraint. Verses 4-5 deal with a different appetite: desire for wealth. Although Proverbs has no problem with money, and no use for laziness, here it counsels against overexertion in the pursuit of riches. This proverb recognizes how ephemeral money can be. Seeking it too diligently makes it disappear. Verses 6-8 return to the subject of food. "Stingy" translates Hebrew "evil of eye" (see 22:9). The circumstances under which the guest is in the home of the stingy are not clear, but the advice is to avoid the occasion if possible. The guest will vomit the food (metaphorically) from indigestion due to the uncomfortable atmosphere. Any pleasant words the guest has said will be wasted because the host was so focused on the cost of the meal. Verse 9 says not to bother speaking in the ears of a dolt (fool),[2] for such an individual will just scorn your insights. Verses 10-11 are similar to 22:28 but more specific in that they mention orphans and say that their redeemer (presumably God), who will plead their legal case, is strong. A redeemer was the next of kin who

2. See Translation Matters on Dolt/Chump/Oaf/Inept (Fool), כסיל, at 1:22.

⁴Do not wear yourself out to get rich;
  be wise enough to desist.
⁵When your eyes light upon it, it is
    gone;
  for suddenly it takes wings to itself,
    flying like an eagle toward
      heaven.
⁶Do not eat the bread of the stingy;
  do not desire their delicacies;
⁷for like a hair in the throat, so are
    they.
  "Eat and drink!" they say to you;
  but they do not mean it.

⁸You will vomit up the little you have
    eaten,
  and you will waste your pleasant
    words.
⁹Do not speak in the hearing of a fool,
  who will only despise the wisdom
    of your words.
¹⁰Do not remove an ancient landmark
  or encroach on the fields of
    orphans,
¹¹for their redeemer is strong;
  he will plead their cause against
    you.

had the responsibility to redeem family land if it was threatened with seizure to pay off debts or a person if threatened to be sold into slavery for the same reason. God was the ultimate redeemer.

TRANSLATION MATTERS

Along with many commentators, NRSV has rearranged and emended the first part of 22:17. MT has, "Incline your ear and hear the words of the wise." LXX has added ἐμὸν λόγον, "my word," making a double direct object, but without a conjunction, to the phrase "these are the words of the wise." The title in 24:23, "These (words) also (are) of the wise," suggests that the phrase in 22:17, "the words of the wise," is a misplaced title, as NRSV indicates by placing it before the couplet, and that the phrase, "my word" (NRSV reads as "my words"), which is parallel to "my knowledge (teaching)" at the end of the colon, has fallen out by haplography (inadvertent omission of a repeated phrase). Proverbs 22:17 would now read as:

The words of the wise:
Incline your ear and hear my word [note the singular],
and apply your mind to my teaching;

Maxims for the Good Life, Continued (23:12-35)

Proverbs 23:12–24:22 is the second section of the sayings of the wise (part 3a), but these come from other international sources besides Amenemope. As in the first section of 3a, this section begins with an introduction, 23:12-14, in which there is an exhortation to be attentive to

Prov 23:12-35

¹²Apply your mind to instruction
and your ear to words of
knowledge.
¹³Do not withhold discipline from your
children;
if you beat them with a rod, they
will not die.
¹⁴If you beat them with the rod,
you will save their lives from
Sheol.
¹⁵My child, if your heart is wise,
my heart too will be glad.

¹⁶My soul will rejoice
when your lips speak what is right.
¹⁷Do not let your heart envy sinners,
but always continue in the fear of
the LORD.
¹⁸Surely there is a future,
and your hope will not be cut off.

¹⁹Hear, my child, and be wise,
and direct your mind in the way.
²⁰Do not be among winebibbers,
or among gluttonous eaters of
meat;

instruction and knowledge, and then to discipline one's own children in the form of corporal punishment. The perspective was that beating foolishness and immorality out of children would result in their not dying through their wanton behavior; thus, such punishment was thought to save them from themselves. In modern terms, we can interpret the rod as moral discipline. (See discussion of corporal punishment at 13:24.) In 23:15-16 the parent speaks directly to the child, expressing the joy that the parent will feel if the child becomes wise and speaks correctly. The two organs mentioned are the heart/mind[3] (of both parent and child in 23:15), and the kidneys (of the parent in 23:16), associated with emotions. Even today, children, at least up to a certain age, want to please their parents. Verses 17-18 counsel against envying sinners (presumably their ill-gotten gains). Instead, the addressee is admonished to envy the fear of YHWH,[4] or to be more parallel and more sensible, those who have this reverence. Verse 18 is difficult, because the word translated as "future" can mean so many things in Hebrew, but the gist of it seems clear enough, that the one who has the proper respect for the divine has hope for a good outcome (unlike sinners and their ill-gotten gains).

Proverbs 23:19-21 begins with an introductory exhortation to the child and then moves to specifics in 23:20-21. Verses 22-25 deal with the lifelong relationship between the parents and child. Verse 23 is absent from LXX and breaks up the logical progression. Verse 24 expresses the same gen-

3. See Translation Matters on the Heart, לֵב, at 2:2.
4. See discussion of this phrase at 1:7.

²¹for the drunkard and the glutton will
    come to poverty,
    and drowsiness will clothe them
      with rags.

²²Listen to your father who begot you,
    and do not despise your mother
      when she is old.
²³Buy truth, and do not sell it;
    buy wisdom, instruction, and
      understanding.
²⁴The father of the righteous will
    greatly rejoice;

he who begets a wise son will be
    glad in him.
²⁵Let your father and mother be glad;
    let her who bore you rejoice.

²⁶My child, give me your heart,
    and let your eyes observe my
      ways.
²⁷For a prostitute is a deep pit;
    an adulteress is a narrow well.
²⁸She lies in wait like a robber
    and increases the number of the
      faithless.

eral sentiment as 23:15-16, the delight parents feel when their children are just (righteous)[5] and wise. Verse 25 has a jussive verb form (let X do Y), which implicitly instructs children to make sure that their parents are able to rejoice.

TRANSLATION MATTERS

In 23:26, NRSV follows the *Ketib*, תרצנה. The *Qeré* is תצרנה from נצר.[6] The meaning would then be "delight in" rather than "observe."

In 23:27, MT זונה, "prostitute," in the first colon should perhaps be emended to זרה, "stranger, foreigner," based on the LXX ἀλλότριος, "another," which is parallel to נכריה, "foreign, alien woman," in the next colon and which LXX translates with the same word as the parallel term in the first colon.[7]

Proverbs 23:26-28 again begins with a preamble, this time for the child to give the parent his or her heart/mind[8] and then asks that the child delight in (*Qeré*) or observe or keep (*Ketib*) the parent's ways.

---

5. See Translation Matters on Just/Integrity/Honesty (Righteous[ness]), צדקה/צדק/צדיק, at 1:2.

6. On *Qeré/Ketib*, see Translation Matters at 1:27.

7. See Translation Matters on Strange/Foreign/Alien Woman (Loose Woman/Adulteress), אשה זרה, at 2:16.

8. See Translation Matters on the Heart, לב, at 2:2.

Prov 23:12-35 (cont.)

²⁹Who has woe? Who has sorrow?
  Who has strife? Who has
    complaining?
Who has wounds without cause?
  Who has redness of eyes?
³⁰Those who linger late over wine,
  those who keep trying mixed
    wines.
³¹Do not look at wine when it is red,
  when it sparkles in the cup
  and goes down smoothly.
³²At the last it bites like a serpent,
  and stings like an adder.

³³Your eyes will see strange things,
  and your mind utter perverse
    things.
³⁴You will be like one who lies down
  in the midst of the sea,
  like one who lies on the top of a
    mast.
³⁵"They struck me," you will say, "but I
    was not hurt;
  they beat me, but I did not
    feel it.
When shall I awake?
  I will seek another drink."

Verse 27 then asserts that a prostitute (MT) or a strange woman (LXX) is a deep pit and a foreign or alien woman[9] (not NRSV's "adulteress") is a narrow well. Association with such women will result in one ending up at the bottom of such structures (figuratively speaking). The consequence will be more traitors (to their marriage vows). Such a woman, according to 23:28, actively lies in wait, as a bandit. Although consorting with prostitutes was not illegal, the sages believed that it was immoral and dangerous. (For a discussion of the issues of this woman, see Part 1.) Proverbs 23:29-35 warns the reader about the dangers of excessive drinking. It begins in 23:29 with a series of rhetorical questions regarding the morning after. The wounds without cause are not real wounds; it is just that the hangover makes the drunkard feel as if there had been a fight. The answer is in 23:30: people who stay up late drinking. Verse 31 in effect says not to let the pretty red color of wine or its sparkle (literally it gives its eye) or the fact that wine goes down smoothly fool you. The reasons are then given in 23:32-35: in contrast with its smoothness while being consumed, its aftereffects are like a serpent's bite (23:32); this poison is partly that the drunkard will see and say duplicitous (perverse) things[10] (23:33) and partly that the hangover will feel like seasickness (23:34); and finally, the drunk feels all beat up but remembers no pain (23:35a, as in 23:29). Worse yet, the poor alcoholic can't wait to get over the hangover and find another drink (23:35b).

9. See Translation Matters on Foreign/Alien Woman, נכריה, at 2:16.
10. See Translation Matters on Duplicitous (Perverse), תהפכות, at 2:12.

The Sayings of the Wise, Continued (24:1-22)

Proverbs 24:1-22 continues the second section of the sayings of the wise. Verses 1-2 advise one not to envy or desire to be with the unethical (literally men of evil/injury/trouble/mischief [wicked], רעה) because their minds imagine havoc and their lips speak trouble, עמל, being a word that means both trouble for others and trouble for oneself. These verses are a prequel for 24:3-4. In contrast to being associated with or envying the rich, our energies should be focused on building our house, primarily the family, with wisdom, understanding, and knowledge (9:1). Verses 5-6 reflect the modern sentiment that the pen is mightier than the sword. Verse 7 pivots from the wise to the foolish. It does not mean that jerks (fools; אויל)[11] literally do not open their mouths in the gate (the place where legal proceedings took place). Rather, it means either that they should not, for their foolishness will be revealed for what it is, or perhaps they will not be allowed to speak because their former performance has shown them to be untrustworthy witnesses. Verses 8-9 continue the focus on jerks, saying in 24:8 that one who plans evil will get labeled as a mischief-maker, literally a master of schemes, and in 24:9 that the devising of folly (same root as used for jerks), i.e., devising dangerous schemes, is sin(ful) and that the scoffer, here equated with the jerk, is loathed by everyone. So, the addressee is implicitly warned: don't be a jerk, and if it's too late for that, at least stay away from other jerks.

Proverbs 24:10-12 address the urgency of helping those who are in distress and not making excuses for failure to do so. God knows and repays according to our deeds (24:12). Verses 13-14 say that just as honey is sweet to the taste, so wisdom is to the נפש, appetite and life.[12] Verses 15-16 suggest the futility of doing harm to the just, for even though they may fall numerous times (seven is the number of completeness), they will get back up on their feet, while evil people stumble in distress and do not get up again. Verses 17-18 advise against *Schadenfreude*, that smug enjoyment of one's enemies' suffering, for God will see it and not be pleased. Verses 19-20 counsel the addressee(s) to be neither irritated at nor envious of the unethical (evil)[13] or corrupt (wicked),[14] even if they are prosperous now, because they do not have a future (see 23:18).

---

11. See Translation Matters on Jerk/Schmuck/Folly (Fool/Folly), אויל/אולת, at 1:7.
12. See Translation Matters on Soul/Neck/Person/Desire, נפש, at 2:10.
13. See Translation Matters on Unethical (Evil/Bad/Wicked), רע/רעים, at 4:14.
14. See Translation Matters on Corrupt/Unscrupulous/Reprehensible (Wicked), רשע/רשעים, at 2:22.

Prov 24:1-22

¹Do not envy the wicked,
  nor desire to be with them;
²for their minds devise violence,
  and their lips talk of mischief.

³By wisdom a house is built,
  and by understanding it is
    established;
⁴by knowledge the rooms are filled
  with all precious and pleasant
    riches.
⁵Wise warriors are mightier than
  strong ones,
  and those who have knowledge
    than those who have
    strength;
⁶for by wise guidance you can wage
  your war,
  and in abundance of counselors
    there is victory.
⁷Wisdom is too high for fools;
  in the gate they do not open their
    mouths.

⁸Whoever plans to do evil
  will be called a mischief-maker.
⁹The devising of folly is sin,
  and the scoffer is an abomination
    to all.

¹⁰If you faint in the day of adversity,
  your strength being small;
¹¹if you hold back from rescuing
    those taken away to
    death,
  those who go staggering to the
    slaughter;
¹²if you say, "Look, we did not know
    this"—
  does not he who weighs the heart
    perceive it?
Does not he who keeps watch over
  your soul know it?
And will he not repay all according
  to their deeds?

¹³My child, eat honey, for it is good,

TRANSLATION MATTERS

In 24:21, the NRSV is emending the MT's עם־שׁונים אל־תתערב, "do not intermingle with those who change," to שׁניהם אל־תתעבר, "do not anger either of them" (by disobeying them), which matches the LXX. (See 14:16 and 20:2 for the use of the verb.)

Verses 21-22 conclude part 3a with the admonition to fear YHWH and the king and not to anger them, since suddenly they can cause disaster that no one can comprehend. (On fear of YHWH,[15] see 16:6; 19:23; 22:4; 23:17; 29:25; and 31:30.)

15. See discussion of this phrase at 1:7.

and the drippings of the
honeycomb are sweet to
your taste.
¹⁴Know that wisdom is such to your
soul;
if you find it, you will find a
future,
and your hope will not be cut off.

¹⁵Do not lie in wait like an outlaw
against the home of the
righteous;
do no violence to the place where
the righteous live;
¹⁶for though they fall seven times,
they will rise again;
but the wicked are overthrown by
calamity.

¹⁷Do not rejoice when your enemies
fall,
and do not let your heart be glad
when they stumble,
¹⁸or else the LORD will see it and be
displeased,
and turn away his anger from them.

¹⁹Do not fret because of evildoers.
Do not envy the wicked;
²⁰for the evil have no future;
the lamp of the wicked will go out.

²¹My child, fear the LORD and the king,
and do not disobey either of them;
²²for disaster comes from them
suddenly,
and who knows the ruin that both
can bring?

Part 3b

A Small Collection of Miscellaneous Proverbs (24:23-34)

More Sayings of the Wise (24:23-34)

Proverbs 24:23-34, part 3b, is a short section appended to part 3a, 22:17–24:22, as indicated by the heading, "These also are sayings of the wise." Verses 23b-26 deal with judicial matters. Verse 23b literally says that recognizing a face in/while judging is not good. One should judge as if everyone were strangers. Following up on this, 24:24 can be translated, "Whoever says to the guilty (wicked),[16] 'you are innocent,' will be cursed," etc. In 24:25, the word "guilty" does not occur; it is assumed from the preceding verse. Just as 24:24 indicates human disapproval of judges' partiality, 24:25 expresses divine approval of judicial integrity. Verse 26 includes honest speech more generally, but in the context the

---

16. See Translation Matters on Corrupt[ion]/Unscrupulous/Reprehensible (Wicked[ness]), רשע/רשעים, at 2:22.

Prov 24:23-34

²³These also are sayings of the wise:

Partiality in judging is not good.
²⁴Whoever says to the wicked, "You
  are innocent,"
    will be cursed by peoples,
      abhorred by nations;
²⁵but those who rebuke the wicked
    will have delight,
    and a good blessing will come
      upon them.
²⁶One who gives an honest answer
    gives a kiss on the lips.

²⁷Prepare your work outside,
    get everything ready for you in the
      field;
    and after that build your house.

²⁸Do not be a witness against your
      neighbor without cause,
    and do not deceive with your lips.

²⁹Do not say, "I will do to others as
      they have done to me;
    I will pay them back for what they
      have done."
³⁰I passed by the field of one who
      was lazy,
    by the vineyard of a stupid
      person;
³¹and see, it was all overgrown with
      thorns;
    the ground was covered with
      nettles,
    and its stone wall was broken
      down.
³²Then I saw and considered it;
    I looked and received instruction.
³³A little sleep, a little slumber,
    a little folding of the hands to rest,
³⁴and poverty will come upon you like
      a robber,
    and want, like an armed warrior.

focus is still on judicial speech. The phrase שפתים ישק, kiss on the lips, is unusual in this nonromantic context but clearly indicates approval. Verse 27 deals with priorities. We can live without a house by living in a tent or living with a relative; we cannot live without food. Verse 28 returns to the judicial setting with its admonition not to be a witness against your neighbor for no reason (24:28a) or to use your lips to deceive. (See Excursus on Women's Sins 3: Dishonesty, at 6:16-19.) Verse 29 abandons the law of revenge. This ancient principle may have made sense in lawless times, but once the community could handle matters of justice, it was no longer appropriate for individuals to avenge themselves.

Proverbs 24:30-34 contains an anecdote. The author has passed by a field of a sluggard and concludes that all it takes is a little (extra) sleep and relaxation, and poverty will arrive like a robber. This may seem extreme, but the author no doubt was (1) trying to instill a strong work ethic; (2) aware of the way that, if one does not do the work when it needs to be done in a regular and consistent manner, it has a way of getting beyond the ability to catch up with it; and (3) survival itself could be an arduous race.

Part 3c

A Collection with a Courtly/Royal Focus (25:1–29:27)

Instructions for Members of a Royal Court (25:1-27)

Proverbs 25:1-27 is the beginning of part 3c of Proverbs ("These are other proverbs of Solomon that the officials of King Hezekiah of Judah copied"), the Hezekian collection, which runs from 25:1 to 29:27. The Hebrew title of this collection suggests that the scribes in Hezekiah's royal court not only copied these proverbs but also selected and edited them. Proverbs 25:2-27 may constitute a small wisdom collection, written as advice to young courtiers. The two main sections deal with the courtier's relationship to the ruler (25:2-15) and behaviors to be avoided (25:16-27).

An *inclusio* marks the beginning and end of the collection, underscoring the theme of the collection:

> [2b]but the **glory** of kings is to *search* things out.
> [27b]but to *search* out **difficult** things is **glorious** [see Translation
> Matters].

Proverbs 25:2-5 opens the collection with matters related to the royal court. Verse 2 differentiates God and the king, but the real point of the combined proverbs in 25:2-3 is that both are inscrutable. In 25:4-5, the metaphor of smelting is used. Silver was heated to a high temperature so that the impurities could be poured off. The remaining pure silver was poured into a mold to make a vessel, instrument, or weapon (see 17:3). Similarly, 25:5 says that the corrupt (wicked)[17] must be removed from the royal presence so that the throne may be established in integrity (righteousness).[18]

Proverbs 25:6-7b is addressed to low-level court officials, who might tend to push themselves forward, thinking that this would advance their career; the sages suggest this sets them up for humiliation. Proverbs 25:7c-10 deals with disputes that can end up harming you and your reputation. Verses 11-12 continue the focus on speech with a complex metaphorical comparison. A word aptly spoken is like (tiny) apples of gold in a silver carving (25:11; see 15:23), and a wise rebuke is even more valuable, like a solid gold earring (25:12; see 10:10). Verse 13 speaks of

---

17. See Translation Matters on Corrupt[ion]/Unscrupulous/Reprehensible (Wicked[ness]), רשע/רשעים, at 2:22.

18. See Translation Matters on Just/Integrity/Honesty (Righteous[ness]), צדקה/צדק/צדיק, at 1:2.

Prov 25:1-27

[Advice to Courtiers]

¹These are other proverbs of
Solomon that the officials
of King Hezekiah of Judah
copied.
²It is the glory of God to conceal
things,
but the glory of kings is to search
things out.
³Like the heavens for height, like the
earth for depth,
so the mind of kings is
unsearchable.
⁴Take away the dross from the silver,
and the smith has material for a
vessel;
⁵take away the wicked from the
presence of the king,

and his throne will be established
in righteousness.
⁶Do not put yourself forward in the
king's presence
or stand in the place of the great;
⁷for it is better to be told, "Come up
here,"
than to be put lower in the
presence of a noble.

What your eyes have seen
⁸do not hastily bring into court;
for what will you do in the end,
when your neighbor puts you to
shame?
⁹Argue your case with your neighbor
directly,
and do not disclose another's
secret;

harvest time, which, being in what is called summer, would be a time when it was dry[19] and the wetness of snow would be a welcome relief to the harvesters, even though it was highly unlikely. Equally refreshing to the spirit were faithful messengers to those who sent them (see 22:21). Verse 14 compares the disappointment of an anticipated gift that did not come to clouds that fail their promise. The word for "clouds," נשיאים, has a homonym that means princes, so there is wordplay in the proverb. It says:

Princes/clouds and hot air, and rain—not; one who boasts of a gift of falsehood.

Verse 15 uses strong contrasting imagery in its articulation of a common theme: the power of patience and gentle speech. The verb in the first colon, יפתה, can mean anything from persuade to seduce to deceive.

Proverbs 25:16-27 is the second cluster in this collection. It is marked by an *inclusio*:

¹⁶ᵃIf you have found **honey**, *eat* only enough for you
²⁷ᵃIt is not good to *eat* much **honey**

19. Frank S. Frick, "Palestine, Climate of," in *ABD*.

¹⁰or else someone who hears you will
bring shame upon you,
and your ill repute will have no end.

¹¹A word fitly spoken
is like apples of gold in a setting
of silver.
¹²Like a gold ring or an ornament of
gold
is a wise rebuke to a listening ear.
¹³Like the cold of snow in the time of
harvest
are faithful messengers to those
who send them;
they refresh the spirit of their
masters.
¹⁴Like clouds and wind without rain
is one who boasts of a gift never
given.

¹⁵With patience a ruler may be
persuaded,
and a soft tongue can break
bones.

[Behaviors to Be Avoided]

¹⁶If you have found honey, eat only
enough for you,
or else, having too much, you will
vomit it.
¹⁷Let your foot be seldom in your
neighbor's house,
otherwise the neighbor will become
weary of you and hate you.
¹⁸Like a war club, a sword, or a sharp
arrow
is one who bears false witness
against a neighbor.
¹⁹Like a bad tooth or a lame foot

Verses 16-17 caution against too much of a good thing, whether it be of sweets or of visiting one's neighbor. In the former case, the body will regurgitate the excess, and, in the latter, one's neighbor will come to hate the visitor as an unwanted intruder. Verse 18 begins a series of four proverbs in 25:18-20, each of which begins with a metaphor and describes some form of despicable behavior. Verse 18 compares false testimony with deadly weapons of war. Verse 19 compares putting confidence in a person who deals treacherously in a time of distress to a bad tooth or lame leg. Not only are bad teeth and legs unable to do the essential jobs we need them to do for us, but they positively get in the way.

TRANSLATION MATTERS

In 25:20, NRSV follows the LXX, which does not include the first colon of the MT, "one who removes clothes on a cold day" (perhaps referring to removing someone else's clothes). The Hebrew of the first line that the NRSV translates literally means "vinegar on natron (see below) [is] a singer of songs upon a bad heart."

Prov 25:1-27 (cont.)

is trust in a faithless person in
time of trouble.
²⁰Like vinegar on a wound
is one who sings songs to a heavy
heart.
Like a moth in clothing or a worm in
wood,
sorrow gnaws at the human heart.
²¹If your enemies are hungry, give
them bread to eat;
and if they are thirsty, give them
water to drink;
²²for you will heap coals of fire on
their heads,
and the Lᴏʀᴅ will reward you.

²³The north wind produces rain,
and a backbiting tongue, angry
looks.
²⁴It is better to live in a corner of the
housetop
than in a house shared with a
contentious wife.
²⁵Like cold water to a thirsty soul,
so is good news from a far country.
²⁶Like a muddied spring or a polluted
fountain
are the righteous who give way
before the wicked.
²⁷It is not good to eat much honey,
or to seek honor on top of honor.

In Proverbs 25:20a, natron is sodium bicarbonate, better known as baking soda. When it is mixed with vinegar (acetic acid), the two fizz violently. Carbonic acid is formed, which quickly breaks down into carbon dioxide and water. The fizzing may be suggestive of the irritation that happy songs can cause for the depressed.

Verses 21-22 are well-known advice to feed and provide drink for your enemies when they are hungry and thirsty, since Paul quotes from the LXX version of it in Romans 12:20-21 (ἐὰν πεινᾷ ὁ ἐχθρός σου, ψώμιζε αὐτόν· ἐὰν διψᾷ, πότιζε αὐτόν· τοῦτο γὰρ ποιῶν ἄνθρακας πυρὸς σωρεύσεις ἐπὶ τὴν κεφαλὴν αὐτοῦ; "if your enemies are hungry, feed them; if they are thirsty, give them something to drink; for by doing this you will heap burning coals on their heads"). In the context, the heaped-up coals are probably coals of humiliation.

Verse 23 returns to weather imagery, with wordplay. The north (wind), צפון, is from the root צפן, to hide, pointing forward to the backbiting, hidden (סתר) tongue. Verse 24 is a duplicate of 21:9. (See the discussion there.) Proverbs 25:25 is like 25:13; good news from a great distance took a long time to arrive and was thus that much more refreshing when it finally arrived, like cold water in a hot, dry climate. Verse 26 realistically acknowledges that sometimes the just (righteous)²⁰ do give way

20. See Translation Matters on Just/Integrity/Honesty (Righteous[ness]), צדקה/צדק/צדיק, at 1:2.

before the corrupt, and, when they do, it is as bad as a precious spring or fountain being destroyed. The proverb does not mean, however, that the giving way is necessarily permanent (24:16).

TRANSLATION MATTERS

The MT of the last colon of 25:27 is difficult. What it seems to say is "the investigation of their honor is honor," but Glendon Bryce argues that there is a play on words between the two instances of כבוד, the first meaning "difficult things," so that the colon should be translated, "but to search out difficult things is glorious."[21]

On Inept Dolts (25:28–26:12)

Proverbs 25:28–26:12 focuses on the dolt (fool; כסיל)[22] with eleven references in twelve verses. These people are said not to restrain their spirits, so that when something happens, they immediately let their innermost feelings break forth; they are compared to a city without a wall that has been broken through (25:28). Although the wall protects the city from outside attack and self-restraint protects individuals (and society) from the ill-effects of spilling their guts, the point seems to be that lack of self-control can be just as deadly as a breached city wall.

Proverbs 26:1 begins with weather imagery. Although snow and rain might be pleasant during the hot, dry summer season, they are not fitting and would disrupt the harvest (contrast 25:13). Honoring a dolt is similarly not fitting and would be disruptive to the social fabric. Verse 2 deals with a gratuitous curse, which, like small birds, does not find a place to light and is thus ineffective. In the context, the maker of the curse is assumed to be a dolt. Verse 3 compares him with a horse and a donkey; these animals are controlled with a whip and bridle, respectively; likewise, a dolt was thought to require a rod.

Verses 4-5 are the most contradictory proverbial pair in Proverbs. Verse 4 says not to answer the dolt according to his own folly[23] or else one will become like the dolt, but verse 5 says precisely the opposite: to answer him according to his folly, because failure to do so will leave him think-

21. Glendon E. Bryce, "Another Wisdom 'Book' in Proverbs," *JBL* 91 (1972): 150.
22. See Translation Matters on Dolt/Chump/Oaf/Inept (Fool), כסיל, at 1:22.
23. See Translation Matters on Dolt/Chump/Oaf/Inept (Fool), כסיל, at 1:22.

²⁸Like a city breached, without walls,
   is one who lacks self-control.
²⁶:¹Like snow in summer or rain in
   harvest,
   so honor is not fitting for a fool.
²Like a sparrow in its flitting, like a
   swallow in its flying,
   an undeserved curse goes
   nowhere.
³A whip for the horse, a bridle for the
   donkey,
   and a rod for the back of fools.
⁴Do not answer fools according to
   their folly,
   or you will be a fool yourself.
⁵Answer fools according to their folly,
   or they will be wise in their own
   eyes.
⁶It is like cutting off one's foot and
   drinking down violence,

to send a message by a fool.
⁷The legs of a disabled person hang
   limp;
   so does a proverb in the mouth of
   a fool.
⁸It is like binding a stone in a sling
   to give honor to a fool.
⁹Like a thornbush brandished by the
   hand of a drunkard
   is a proverb in the mouth of a fool.
¹⁰Like an archer who wounds
   everybody
   is one who hires a passing fool or
   drunkard.
¹¹Like a dog that returns to its vomit
   is a fool who reverts to his folly.
¹²Do you see persons wise in their
   own eyes?
   There is more hope for fools than
   for them.

ing that he is wise. This conundrum almost kept the book of Proverbs out of the Christian canon! These two proverbs suggest the subtlety and complexity of the sages' thought. Dolts are impossible to deal with. No matter what one does, they will think they have triumphed. Verse 6 uses violent imagery to describe how ludicrous it is to send this kind of fool as a messenger. You might as well cut off your feet or drink violence, another metaphor for self-inflicted suffering derived from drinking (too much) alcohol.

This kind of fool can no more "move" a proverb than a person with paralyzed limbs is able to move her legs. This is not a criticism of the disabled. It is statement of reality. When we have disabilities, they do not make us lesser people, but they do mean there are some things we cannot do. This proverb is simply making an analogy, not criticizing anyone.

The stupid kind of fool just does not know when and how to apply the right saying, which takes wisdom (26:7). Honoring such fools increases their arrogance and puts a weapon in their hands (26:8). Verse 9 suggests that the dolt's use of a proverb will cause the random damage of a drunk waving thorns; getting too close (to correct the dolt) will result in scratches. (See 26:4-5, 7-8.) Verse 10, a textually difficult verse, as emended by NRSV, equates the hiring of dolts and drunkards with the havoc wreaked by an archer who pierces everyone with arrows. (This may remind us today of the gun violence to which random people are subjected almost casually on an all too frequent basis.)

TRANSLATION MATTERS

In 26:10, NRSV has emended the MT שֹׂכֵר (*sōkēr*), "hires," to שִׁכּוֹר (*šikkōr*), "drunkard." The MT reads: "one who hires a fool hires a passer-by."

In 26:11 the dolt repeats and admires his own foolishness. Verse 12 asserts that the only thing worse than ordinary dolts are those who think themselves wise.

On the Lazy, Quarrelsome, and False Friends (26:13-28)

This macrocluster is divided into three miniclusters.

Proverbs 26:13-16 is the first of three miniclusters within this cluster, 26:13-28. Proverbs 26:13-16 is a group of four proverbs dealing with laziness. Sluggards make ridiculous excuses (26:13), creakingly roll over in bed (26:14), and cannot even be bothered to feed themselves (26:15) but nevertheless think themselves smarter than seven (the number of completeness), who can answer tastefully (26:16). Verses 17-22 deal with quarrels. There were no domesticated dogs in ancient Israel, so grabbing a passing dog was seizing a wild animal, causing trouble for no reason, like meddling in a quarrel. (See Excursus on Women's Sins 4: Anger, at 14:16.) Careless speech is as dangerous (26:18-19) as shooting at random; a gossip (26:20-21) provokes strife. As wood is to fire, אֵשׁ (*'ēš*), so is a quarrelsome person, אִישׁ (*'îš*), to kindling strife. Verse 22 concludes the sequence with different imagery. The words spoken by a gossip are like delicacies that go down into the chambers of the belly.

Proverbs 26:23-28 is a minicluster that deals with people who pretend to be friends.

Prov 26:13-28

[On the Lazy]

[13]The lazy person says, "There is a
  lion in the road!
There is a lion in the streets!"
[14]As a door turns on its hinges,
  so does a lazy person in bed.
[15]The lazy person buries a hand in
  the dish,
  and is too tired to bring it back to
  the mouth.
[16]The lazy person is wiser in self-
  esteem
  than seven who can answer
  discreetly.

[On the Quarrelsome]

[17]Like somebody who takes a
  passing dog by the ears
is one who meddles in the quarrel
  of another.
[18]Like a maniac who shoots deadly
  firebrands and arrows,
[19]so is one who deceives a neighbor
  and says, "I am only joking!"
[20]For lack of wood the fire goes out,
  and where there is no whisperer,
  quarreling ceases.
[21]As charcoal is to hot embers and
  wood to fire,

TRANSLATION MATTERS

In the first colon of 26:23, NRSV has emended the MT כסף סיגים, "silver of dross,"
to כספסגים, "like glaze." In the second colon, NRSV has emended the MT דלקים,
"burning," to חלקים, "smooth."

The MT of the first colon of 26:23 is arguably preferable to NRSV's
emendation because the dross that is poured off after silver is refined is
of inferior quality to real silver. Glaze actually protects pottery, but the
silver dross looks superficially attractive and is not actually valuable.[24]
NRSV's emendation in the second colon seems likely, because a false
friend speaks smoothly rather than with heat. Verse 24 continues the
theme, making explicit what the metaphor in 26:23 implied: the deceit
of the false friend. Verse 25 counsels a hermeneutic of suspicion against
any seemingly gracious words spoken by an enemy, because seven (the
number of completeness) abominations[25] are inside of this person. Verse
27 does not explicitly have anything to do with false friends but, in the

---

24. Michael V. Fox, *Proverbs 10–31: A New Translation with Introduction and Commentary,* AB 18B (New Haven: Yale University Press, 2009), 800.
25. See discussion of the term "abomination" at 3:32.

so is a quarrelsome person for
kindling strife.

²²The words of a whisperer are like
delicious morsels;
they go down into the inner parts
of the body.

[On False Friends]

²³Like the glaze covering an earthen
vessel
are smooth lips with an evil heart.

²⁴An enemy dissembles in speaking
while harboring deceit within;

²⁵when an enemy speaks graciously,
do not believe it,
for there are seven abominations
concealed within;

²⁶though hatred is covered with guile,
the enemy's wickedness will be
exposed in the assembly.

²⁷Whoever digs a pit will fall into it,
and a stone will come back on the
one who starts it rolling.

²⁸A lying tongue hates its victims,
and a flattering mouth works ruin.

context, can be interpreted to refer to them. A pit was dug and branches were put on top of it as a trap for animals to fall into. The stone would come back onto the one who started it rolling because of the size of the stone. The point of both metaphors is that those who do evil will suffer the consequences themselves. Verse 28 concludes the cluster. The first colon says that a lying tongue hates those it has oppressed, and the second that a smooth mouth (echoing 26:23 if the emendation is correct) works ruin.

On Friendship (27:1-10)

Proverbs 27:1-10 continues the Hezekian collection. Verses 1-2 are linked by the verb "praise" and enjoin humility—let praise come from strangers. Verse 3 compares the anger of a jerk (fool; אויל)[26] to the weight of stone and sand; verse 4 suggests that jealousy is even worse. A stone can be lifted and sand pushed away, but this kind of fool is nearly inescapable. This is not a benign ignoramus but a real jerk.

Someone who cares about you enough to offer constructive criticism is a much more valuable friend than one who admires you silently (27:5). The criticism of a friend is well-intended, while flattery may come from an enemy (27:6; see 25:12 and 10:10). Verse 7 states a truism, that satiety breeds lack of interest, but hunger makes even food that would ordinarily

26. See Translation Matters on Dolt/Chump/Oaf/Inept (Fool), כסיל, at 1:22.

Prov 27:1-10

¹Do not boast about tomorrow,
    for you do not know what a day
        may bring.
²Let another praise you, and not your
    own mouth—
    a stranger, and not your own lips.
³A stone is heavy, and sand is weighty,
    but a fool's provocation is heavier
        than both.
⁴Wrath is cruel, anger is
        overwhelming,
    but who is able to stand before
        jealousy?
⁵Better is open rebuke
    than hidden love.
⁶Well meant are the wounds a friend
    inflicts,

    but profuse are the kisses of an
        enemy.
⁷The sated appetite spurns honey,
    but to a ravenous appetite even
        the bitter is sweet.
⁸Like a bird that strays from its nest
    is one who strays from home.
⁹Perfume and incense make the
        heart glad,
    but the soul is torn by trouble.
¹⁰Do not forsake your friend or the
        friend of your parent;
    do not go to the house of your
        kindred in the day of your
        calamity.
Better is a neighbor who is nearby
    than kindred who are far away.

be considered unappetizing appealing. Birds with young in their nests will only abandon them if the nests have been disturbed and/or there are other dangers lurking (27:8). Everyone has a place, and only extreme circumstances justify abandonment of that place. The pleasures of the senses are wonderful but are exceeded by the enjoyment of friendship; it brings the perspective of another, which is better than our own limited one, yet a friend still understands our context. This is one of the joys of having a place (see 27:8).

TRANSLATION MATTERS

In the second colon of 27:9, the MT ומתק רעהו מעצת־נפש, "the sweetness of one's friend is better than one's own counsel," is possible and works better in the context than NRSV's emendation, which follows the LXX.

Verse 10 continues the theme of friendship and also of place. Friendship is a paramount responsibility; one provides help to one's friend and even the friends of the family, and help may be more easily obtained from a neighbor (friend) than from distant relatives.

Advice for Successful Living (27:11-27)

Proverbs 27:11 appears to be a transition to a new cluster. There are echoes of earlier proverbs. Proverbs 27:12 recalls 22:3; 27:13 recalls 20:16; 27:15 recalls 19:13. (See the discussion there.) Verse 16 is difficult. The idea may be that trying to hide the contentious woman (or we may add today any contentious person) is like trying to hide wind; it can't be done. The second colon seems to involve a pun. The root for "hide," צפן, may evoke the word for "north," צפון.

TRANSLATION MATTERS

At 27:13, the MT has "foreign woman" (נכריה) rather than "foreigners," which is based on the LXX. Elsewhere NRSV translates נכריה as "adulteress."[27]

TRANSLATION MATTERS

The MT of the second colon of 27:16 is difficult. The Hebrew of 27:16a, צפניה צפן־רוח, says, "the one who hides her hides the wind." In 27:16b, NRSV's "grasp" is purely based on context; it is not in the text; a small emendation of שמן ימינו, "his right hand, oil," to שמו ימיני, "his name is Southerner," may help.[28] In either case, the two words must be connected with the verb יקרא, "one calls." The line may then be translated:

One who hides her, hides wind;
he is called Right/Southerner.

Verse 17 suggests that just as iron sharpens iron, so people sharpen each other. The word translated as "wits," פני, usually means "face" but can also mean the edge of a sword (Eccl 10:10). We hone our skills on one another. Verse 18 compares the hard, agricultural work of tending fig trees with the rather different sort of labor involved in tending to one's human master(s)/authority figures. Verse 19 suggests that we may learn something about ourselves both by looking at ourselves in a mirror (in this case water) and by interaction with another human being.

27. See Translation Matters on "Strange/Foreign Woman/Alien Woman (Loose Woman/Adulteress) זרה אשה , at 2:16.
28. Fox, *Proverbs 10–31*, 682–83.

Prov 27:11-27

¹¹Be wise, my child, and make my
heart glad,
so that I may answer whoever
reproaches me.
¹²The clever see danger and hide;
but the simple go on, and suffer
for it.
¹³Take the garment of one who has
given surety for a stranger;
seize the pledge given as surety
for foreigners.
¹⁴Whoever blesses a neighbor with a
loud voice,
rising early in the morning,
will be counted as cursing.

¹⁵A continual dripping on a rainy day
and a contentious wife are alike;
¹⁶to restrain her is to restrain the
wind
or to grasp oil in the right hand.
¹⁷Iron sharpens iron,
and one person sharpens the wits
of another.
¹⁸Anyone who tends a fig tree will eat
its fruit,
and anyone who takes care of a
master will be honored.
¹⁹Just as water reflects the face,
so one human heart reflects
another.

Verse 20 suggests that human eyes (desires) are insatiable and can lead us to destruction. Proverbs 27:21 is very similar to 17:3, but the smelting in 17:3 is tested by YHWH, not the praise of the community. Proverbs 27:22 uses the imagery of a mortar and pestle. Unlike the grain, whose husk can be separated by grinding or beating, this kind of fool, whom we might call a jerk (אויל),[29] is intractable. This is the worst sort of fool, one who is considered morally deficient, not just dumb. Foolishness won't be driven out, though other proverbs suggest that one ought still to try.

Proverbs 27:23-27 is a minicluster dealing with animal husbandry. It is also possible to read this section as dealing metaphorically with royal matters, since kings were considered to be the shepherds of their people. If read this way, this section introduces chapters 28–29, which comprise advice to rulers.[30] Whereas monetary wealth can be stolen or squandered, flocks—if they are managed well—will renew themselves naturally and will provide food and clothing for the household. Verse 23 begins with an admonition to really know the faces of your flock and put your mind to your herds. With proper attention, the flock will prosper and provide clothing, currency, and enough goat's milk to feed everyone in the house, down to the most insignificant members, the female servants!

29. See Translation Matters on Dolt/Chump/Oaf/Inept (Fool), כסיל, at 1:22.
30. Bruce V. Malchow, "A Manual for Future Monarchs," *CBQ* 47 (1985): 243–44.

²⁰Sheol and Abaddon are never
satisfied,
and human eyes are never
satisfied.
²¹The crucible is for silver, and the
furnace is for gold,
so a person is tested by being
praised.
²²Crush a fool in a mortar with a pestle
along with crushed grain,
but the folly will not be driven out.

[On Animal Husbandry]
²³Know well the condition of your
flocks,

and give attention to your herds;
²⁴for riches do not last forever,
nor a crown for all generations.
²⁵When the grass is gone, and new
growth appears,
and the herbage of the mountains
is gathered,
²⁶the lambs will provide your clothing,
and the goats the price of a field;
²⁷there will be enough goats' milk for
your food,
for the food of your household
and nourishment for your servant-
girls.

Advice to a Future King (28:1–29:27)

Law and Justice for the Poor (28:1-11)

Chapters 28–29 are often considered a separate collection or at least a subunit within the Hezekian collection (part 3c). The theme is advice for future rulers. Most of the verses are individual, two-line proverbs and most are antithetic couplets. In addition, the material has been organized using the words צדיק (just [righteous])[31] and רשע (corrupt [wicked]).[32] The word pair occurs in 28:1, 12, 28; 29:2, 16, 27, thus at the opening and closing verses and at four other verses. The subunit of chapters 28–29 can then be subdivided into the following sections: 28:1-11; 28:12-28; 29:1-15; 29:16-27.[33]

Proverbs 28:1-11 focuses on law (28:4, 7, 9) and justice (28:4) for the poor (28:3, 6, 8, 11). The well-known proverb in 28:1 is the heading for the two-chapter collection. It is a comparison of the corrupt (wicked) and the just (righteous), who are as confident as the noble lion. The Hebrew text of 28:2 is difficult, but its meaning seems to be that when

---

31. See Translation Matters on Just/Integrity/Honesty (Righteous[ness]), צדקה/ צדיק/צדק, at 1:2.
32. See Translation Matters on Corrupt[ion]/Unscrupulous/Reprehensible (Wicked[ness]), רשע/רשעים, at 2:22.
33. Malchow, "Manual," 238–40.

Prov 28:1-11

¹The wicked flee when no one
pursues,
but the righteous are as bold as
a lion.
²When a land rebels
it has many rulers;
but with an intelligent ruler
there is lasting order.
³A ruler who oppresses the poor
is a beating rain that leaves no
food.
⁴Those who forsake the law praise
the wicked,
but those who keep the law
struggle against them.
⁵The evil do not understand justice,
but those who seek the Lord
understand it completely.

there is rebellion, many rulers try to take charge, all at once and over time. When a discerning person is the ruler, however, a firmly standing order (כן, compare 11:19) will be extended in time and, by implication, rebellions will not occur.

TRANSLATION MATTERS

In 28:3, NRSV emends רש, "poor," to ראש, "head." Other possible emendations include רשע, "corrupt (wicked),"[34] following the LXX, and עשיר, "rich," in which the same consonants as corrupt (wicked) are used, but in a different order.

The MT of 28:3 says:

A poor man and oppressor of the poor,
a torrential rain and no bread.

NRSV emends the first colon so that, instead of a poor man oppressing the poor, it is a ruler, but the poor can oppress each other. It is possible that a pun is involved and both the meanings of "ruler" and "poor" are intended to be heard. Although rain is generally beneficent, if it comes too hard and fast, it will beat crops down and wash them away. Verse 4 indicates that abandoning the law—not necessarily the law of Moses, but the laws taught by parents, sages, and kings—amounts to praising the wicked; conversely, keeping it is the equivalent of actively struggling against them. Verse 5 picks up from verse 4 drawing a comparison between unethical (evil)[35]

34. See Translation Matters on Corrupt[ion]/Unscrupulous/Reprehensible (Wicked[ness]), רשע/רשעים, at 2:22.
35. See Translation Matters on Unethical (Evil/Bad/Wicked), רע/רעים, at 4:14.

⁶Better to be poor and walk in integrity
   than to be crooked in one's ways
      even though rich.
⁷Those who keep the law are wise
   children,
   but companions of gluttons shame
      their parents.
⁸One who augments wealth by
   exorbitant interest
   gathers it for another who is kind
      to the poor.

⁹When one will not listen to the law,
   even one's prayers are an
      abomination.
¹⁰Those who mislead the upright into
   evil ways
   will fall into pits of their own making,
   but the blameless will have a
      goodly inheritance.
¹¹The rich is wise in self-esteem,
   but an intelligent poor person
      sees through the pose.

people and those who seek YHWH. The former do not understand משפט, a word that means various things depending on the context, but here is best translated broadly and abstractly as "justice." The latter understand it completely. The pronoun is not in the Hebrew but is necessary in English because the point is not that those who seek YHWH understand everything but rather that they understand everything relating to justice.

The first colon of 28:6 is identical to 19:1a. In the second colon, "ways" is dual. It is not clear why, unless it is to indicate that the rich man is of two minds about what way he wants to follow. Verse 7 juxtaposes children who keep the precepts of the sages with those who consort with gluttons. Verses 8-11 suggest the kind of ideal social order that should prevail when a just ruler is in charge.

Necessity of a Just Ruler Who Must Deal with the Just and the Unjust (28:12-28)

The first and last line of this cluster form an *inclusio* using the key words "just" (righteous)[36] and "corrupt" (wicked):[37]

¹²When the **righteous** triumph, there is great glory,
   but when the *wicked* prevail, people go into hiding.
²⁸When the *wicked* prevail, people go into hiding;
   but when they perish, the **righteous** increase.

36. See Translation Matters on Just/Integrity/Honesty (Righteous[ness]), צדקה/צדק/צדיק, at 1:2.
37. See Translation Matters on Corrupt[ion]/Unscrupulous/Reprehensible (Wicked[ness]), רשע/רשעים, at 2:22.

Prov 28:12-28

¹²When the righteous triumph, there
is great glory,
but when the wicked prevail,
people go into hiding.
¹³No one who conceals
transgressions will prosper,
but one who confesses and
forsakes them will obtain
mercy.
¹⁴Happy is the one who is never
without fear,
but one who is hard-hearted will
fall into calamity.
¹⁵Like a roaring lion or a charging bear
is a wicked ruler over a poor
people.
¹⁶A ruler who lacks understanding is a
cruel oppressor;
but one who hates unjust gain will
enjoy a long life.
¹⁷If someone is burdened with the
blood of another,
let that killer be a fugitive until
death;
let no one offer assistance.
¹⁸One who walks in integrity will be
safe,
but whoever follows crooked ways
will fall into the Pit.
¹⁹Anyone who tills the land will have
plenty of bread,
but one who follows worthless
pursuits will have plenty of
poverty.
²⁰The faithful will abound with
blessings,

The cluster is unified by the listing of many types of corrupt people
that the ruler was supposed to avoid being and in addition must deal
with as sovereign. Proverbs 28:12 suggests that when the just are successful, there is much glory, but when the evil stand up, then people go into
hiding, because it is dangerous to be in public; compare 28:1, in which
the corrupt are the ones fleeing. Verse 13 is the only reference in Proverbs
to confession of sin, repentance, and consequent mercy.

Verse 14 begins with a proverb in which NRSV translates אשרי as
"happy," better rendered "blissful."[38] The fear in the phrase "without
fear," מפחד, in 28:14 is not the same fear as in "fear of YHWH," יראה.[39]
Both kinds are good, but they are different. מפחד means fear in the sense
of dread. This proverb is suggesting that a regular dose of dread can be
useful. יראה is sometimes used in parallel with מפחד, showing that it can
also mean dread, but when it is coupled with YHWH, it means something more like awe and reverence, though it should be understood as
combined with the knowledge of God, with which it is also frequently
parallel in Proverbs (e.g., 1:29; 2:5), and that it is the beginning of wis-

38. See Translation Matters on Blissful (Happy), אשרי, at 3:13.
39. See discussion of this phrase at 1:7.

but one who is in a hurry to be
  rich will not go unpunished.
²¹To show partiality is not good—
  yet for a piece of bread a person
    may do wrong.
²²The miser is in a hurry to get rich
  and does not know that loss is
    sure to come.
²³Whoever rebukes a person will
  afterward find more favor
    than one who flatters with the
      tongue.
²⁴Anyone who robs father or mother
  and says, "That is no crime,"
    is partner to a thug.

²⁵The greedy person stirs up strife,
  but whoever trusts in the Lᴏʀᴅ will
    be enriched.
²⁶Those who trust in their own wits
  are fools;
  but those who walk in wisdom
    come through safely.
²⁷Whoever gives to the poor will lack
  nothing,
  but one who turns a blind eye will
    get many a curse.
²⁸When the wicked prevail, people go
  into hiding;
  but when they perish, the
    righteous increase.

dom (Prov 9:10). Since the second colon says that the hardhearted will experience calamity, perhaps one should always fear calamity and learn how to avoid it, according to the sages.

TRANSLATION MATTERS

If 28:15-16 are joined together, they make better sense:

¹⁵Like a roaring lion or a charging bear
  is a wicked ruler over a poor people;
¹⁶ᵃA ruler who lacks understanding, and a cruel oppressor;
  but one who hates unjust gain will enjoy a long life.

In 28:17, the word translated by NRSV as "death," בור, literally means "pit."

Verses 15-16 are both about rulers. Proverbs 28:15a describes wild predatory animals; 28:15b gives the first comparison: a corrupt ruler over poor people (compare 28:1, NRSV). Proverbs 28:16a then gives a second one: a ruler lacking understanding; this person will be a chief of (or great in) extortions. Proverbs 28:16b closes off the quatrain with an antithesis: someone who hates unjust gain will see a long life. Verse 17 seems to be concerned with someone who has a guilty conscience about having killed a person and is fleeing. It is not clear whether the verb in the last colon, יתמכו, means to help or to seize the guilty individual to stop the flight. Verse 18 compares those who walk in integrity with those whose two ways are twisted; the former will be saved, while the latter will fall into a pit (reading with NRSV and the Syriac). Proverbs 28:19 is a variant of 12:11. Verse 20 asserts that a person who cuts corners to get rich quick will end up poor (see 13:11). Verse 21 has been interpreted two ways: that showing partiality is not good, (1) but that it happens, even for a trifling amount, and (2) that judges should consider the circumstances and be aware that people will steal when it comes to a matter of necessities like bread. Verse 22 deals with stingy individuals (evil of eye) who are trying to get rich quick, not knowing that poverty is going to come upon them, whether because of their stinginess or haste in acquiring their money or both. Verse 23 disdains flattery. Constructive criticism is more helpful, though sincere compliments are pleasant (see 27:5-6). Verse 24 indicts children who would steal from their parents and claim that there was no crime, as the equivalent of thugs, literally איש משחית, a "man of destruction." Verse 25 first describes someone who is wide of throat, נפש, indicating greediness, with emphasis on the pleasures of the table.[40] Those who trust in YHWH will become fat, a sign in ancient Judah of prosperity. Verse 26 continues with the focus on trust. In this proverb, people who trust in their own intelligence (alone) are called dolts (fools; כסיל),[41] while those who walk in wisdom will be saved. (See Excursus on Women's Sins 1: Arrogance, at 3:8.) Verse 27 is a riddle, but the solution is clear: those who give to the poor will receive God's blessing; those who do not will be disdained by their fellow humans, as well as by God. Proverbs 28:28a is like 28:12b. Just as in 28:12b, when the corrupt rise, people hide, but here the second colon says that when they ultimately perish, the just increase.

Reflections for a Just King (29:1-16)

This cluster again contains an *inclusio* with the words "just" (righteous)[42] and "corrupt" (wicked):[43]

> [2]When the **righteous** are in authority, the people rejoice;
> but when the *wicked* rule, the people groan.

---

40. See Translation Matters on Soul/Neck/Person/Desire, נפש, at 2:10.
41. See Translation Matters on Dolt/Chump/Oaf/Inept (Fool), כסיל, at 1:22.
42. See Translation Matters on Just/Integrity/Honesty (Righteous[ness]), צדקה/צדיק/צדק, at 1:2.
43. See Translation Matters on Corrupt[ion]/Unscrupulous/Reprehensible (Wicked[ness]), רשע/רשעים, at 2:22.

Prov 29:1-16

¹One who is often reproved, yet remains stubborn,
will suddenly be broken beyond healing.
²When the righteous are in authority, the people rejoice;
but when the wicked rule, the people groan.
³A child who loves wisdom makes a parent glad,
but to keep company with prostitutes is to squander one's substance.
⁴By justice a king gives stability to the land,
but one who makes heavy exactions ruins it.
⁵Whoever flatters a neighbor
is spreading a net for the neighbor's feet.
⁶In the transgression of the evil there is a snare,
but the righteous sing and rejoice.
⁷The righteous know the rights of the poor;

¹⁶When the *wicked* are in authority, transgression increases,
but the **righteous** will look upon their downfall.

Although the general theme of advice for rulers is clear, there are many subthemes. In 29:1 one who is often reproved, who hardens his neck, is the opposite of a supple tree, which can bend with the wind; the stiff-necked individual who has not bowed to reproof will be suddenly broken. Verse 3 goes from the general to the specific, first speaking of how a child who loves wisdom delights a parent, then giving an example implicitly of one way that a child can grieve a parent: by keeping company with prostitutes, thereby wasting both money and one's sexual virility.

TRANSLATION MATTERS

In 29:4, תְּרוּמוֹת (*tĕrûmôt*), rendered by NRSV as "the one who makes heavy exactions," should either be repointed as תַּרְמִת (*tarmît*), "deceit," or understood as a variant form of deceit, derived from רום, "to be high," rather than רמה, "to deceive."[44] The word translated as "heavy exactions" really only referred to sacral donations to the temple. As emended the proverb reads:

By justice a king gives stability to the land,
but one who is deceitful destroys it.

44. Fox, *Proverbs 10–31*, 835.

Prov 29:1-16 (cont.)

the wicked have no such
understanding.

⁸Scoffers set a city aflame,
but the wise turn away wrath.

⁹If the wise go to law with fools,
there is ranting and ridicule
without relief.

¹⁰The bloodthirsty hate the blameless,
and they seek the life of the
upright.

¹¹A fool gives full vent to anger,
but the wise quietly holds it back.

¹²If a ruler listens to falsehood,
all his officials will be wicked.

¹³The poor and the oppressor have
this in common:
the Lord gives light to the eyes of
both.

¹⁴If a king judges the poor with equity,
his throne will be established
forever.

¹⁵The rod and reproof give wisdom,
but a mother is disgraced by a
neglected child.

¹⁶When the wicked are in authority,
transgression increases,
but the righteous will look upon
their downfall.

The contrast in verse 4, then, is between a king who rules justly and one who is dishonest; the former creates a situation in which the land will stand for a long time, but the latter quickly brings it down. Verse 5 speaks of the dangers of flattery, both for the flatterer and for the one who is flattered. The pronoun on the word "feet" in Hebrew is ambiguous; it can refer to both people, so the proverb is warning its audience to be on the lookout for people who might be trying to flatter them but also not to be flatterers themselves. Verse 6 is a good follow-up for 29:5, in that it makes explicit what is implied in the preceding verse, that the evil intended to ensnare the just will actually hurt themselves; meanwhile, the good folks will sing and rejoice, not at the downfall of the bad people, but because they have avoided the trap set for them by the evil individuals. Verse 7 again contrasts the just with the corrupt; the former understand the rights of the poor, while the latter know nothing broadly speaking and, in particular, they do not understand the rights of the poor. Verse 8 compares scoffers who stir up a city's tensions, while the wise do the opposite: returning wrath (to its source). Verse 9 implicitly advises the wise to avoid legal disputes with this sort of fool, the sort we think of as jerks (אויל),⁴⁵ because the proceedings will only be a mockery of law.

45. See Translation Matters on Jerk/Schmuck/Folly (Fool/Folly), אויל/אולת, at 1:7.

TRANSLATION MATTERS

Proverbs 29:10 is a proverb where one expects an antithesis. There is a way of translating it that provides one, but it involves an unusual sense of the verb in the second colon:

The bloodthirsty hate persons of integrity (the blameless)[46]
but the upstanding (upright)[47] seek to preserve their lives.

The phrase "to preserve" is not in the Hebrew but is added in the translation to clarify the sense of the verb. This would be the only time in the Hebrew Bible that the verb בקש is used this way. Ordinarily its meaning is to seek.

The idea in 29:10 would be that when the bloodthirsty go after the blameless, the upstanding would be there, ready to protect them.

Verse 11 deals with anger. The dolt (fool; כסיל)[48] lets it all out, but the wise individual holds it back. (See Excursus on Women's Sins 4: Anger, at 6:16-19.) Verse 12 places the responsibility squarely on the leader's back. If the ruler pays attention to lies, then an atmosphere is created in which the leader's servants will be corrupt. Verse 13 is an equalizing proverb. These two individuals met, as was surely the case on a regular basis in a small community. They must have seemed very different to each other, but they both had the gift of life, which is what the phrase "gives light to the eyes" essentially means.

Verse 14 speaks of the king's responsibility toward the poor, which if fulfilled would establish his dynasty forever. Verse 15 deals with discipline. In the second colon, the word translated as "neglected" means something like let loose, so the idea is that the child has not been kept properly at home and this is why the mother in particular is shamed by the behavior. The assumption seems to be that the mother had more responsibility for the young.

Proverbs 29:16, like 28:28 and 29:2a, speaks of the problems when the corrupt are in charge; in this proverb the second colon indicates that the just will see their downfall.

---

46. See Translation Matters on Integrity/Whole/Complete (Blameless), תם, at 2:7.
47. See Translation Matters on Upstanding/Straight/Straightforward (Upright), ישר/ישרים, at 2:7.
48. See Translation Matters on Dolt/Chump/Oaf/Inept (Fool), כסיל, at 1:22.

More Reflections for a King (29:17-27)

Proverbs 29:17-27 is not as unified in theme as the other clusters in chapters 28–29, as it echoes the themes in the previous three clusters and ends the collection. Proverbs 29:17 returns to the theme of discipline. Here, parents are encouraged to discipline their children and are motivated by promises both of rest at the end of the process and of delights for their soul/appetite. Wordplay is involved. On one level, as NRSV has translated, the well-disciplined child will give delight to the parents' hearts/minds.[49] On another level, such a child will provide sustenance in old age.

In 29:18, the Hebrew word translated as "prophecy" by NRSV is literally חזון, "vision," a somewhat narrower term than "prophecy." A contrast is also being made between the whole people being in disarray in the first colon and the blissful state (happiness)[50] of a single individual who keeps the law in the second colon. KJV translates the first colon, "Where there is no vision, the people perish." This verse is thus used in evangelical circles to mandate vision statements.

Verse 19 deals with discipline of slaves, who by implication are thought to respond only to a beating (see discussion at 13:24). Verse 20 is a variation on 26:12. This time the individual is quick tongued rather than wise from his or her own perspective. In both cases the person in the first colon is said to have less hope than a dolt (fool; כסיל).[51] Verse 21 again deals with the discipline of slaves.

TRANSLATION MATTERS

The last word in 29:21, מנון, is a *hapax legomenon* (a word that occurs only once) in the Bible, so it must be translated either from context or based on ancient translations or cognate languages. NRSV translates from the Vulgate. The first colon in the Hebrew is active rather than passive: "One who pampers his slave from his youth"; NRSV is presumably avoiding the masculine pronoun by the use of the passive. The second colon in the Hebrew is more ambiguous than in the NRSV; the pronoun in "he will come to a bad end" may refer to the master, to the slave, or to both.

---

49. See Translation Matters on the Heart, לב, at 2:2.
50. See Translation Matters on Blissful (Happy), אשרי, at 3:13.
51. See Translation Matters on Dolt/Chump/Oaf/Inept (Fool), כסיל, at 1:22.

¹⁷Discipline your children, and they
  will give you rest;
 they will give delight to your heart.
¹⁸Where there is no prophecy, the
  people cast off restraint,
 but happy are those who keep the
  law.
¹⁹By mere words servants are not
  disciplined,
 for though they understand, they
  will not give heed.
²⁰Do you see someone who is hasty
  in speech?
 There is more hope for a fool than
  for anyone like that.
²¹A slave pampered from childhood
 will come to a bad end.
²²One given to anger stirs up strife,
 and the hothead causes much

transgression.
²³A person's pride will bring
  humiliation,
 but one who is lowly in spirit will
  obtain honor.
²⁴To be a partner of a thief is to hate
  one's own life;
 one hears the victim's curse, but
  discloses nothing.
²⁵The fear of others lays a snare,
 but one who trusts in the Lᴏʀᴅ is
  secure.
²⁶Many seek the favor of a ruler,
 but it is from the Lᴏʀᴅ that one
  gets justice.
²⁷The unjust are an abomination to
  the righteous,
 but the upright are an abomination
  to the wicked.

Proverbs 29:22 once more deals with people who are quick tempered and implicitly warns against being such and associating with such. (See Excursus on Women's Sins 4: Anger, at 14:16.) Verse 23 contrasts the proud who will be brought low and the lowly of spirit who will attain honor. The same Hebrew root is used to describe what happens to the arrogant and the type of attitude praised in the second colon: שפל, creating a wordplay. Verse 24 describes a situation where someone has partnered in one way or another with a thief, whether through receiving stolen goods or participating in the crime more directly. Thus, when a community curse is sounded seeking information about the crime (Lev 5:1), this individual will certainly not testify, thus compounding the guilt.

Verse 25 implicitly contrasts fear of humans with fear of YHWH.[52] Those who fear humans create a trap for themselves, whereas those who fear YHWH and trust in YHWH explicitly will be secure. Verse

52. See discussion of this phrase at 1:7.

26 is a good follow-up of verse 25. This proverb is not suggesting that people should not look to human rulers for justice but is a reminder that ultimately the decision about a situation is in God's hands. Verse 27 concludes the collection with a statement about how the just and the corrupt (wicked)[53] feel about each other: each loathes the other, and this is not viewed as problematic.

53. See Translation Matters on Corrupt[ion]/Unscrupulous/Reprehensible (Wicked[ness]), רשע/רשעים, at 2:22.

Part 4
Proverbs 30:1–31:9

Foreign Wisdom and Riddles

Introduction

Part 4 includes 4a, 30:1-14 (or 30:1-9), "Sayings of an Unknown Individual, Possibly a Non-Judahite," described in Hebrew as "The words of Agur son of Jakeh, an oracle"; 4b, 30:15-33, consisting of numerical and other sayings; and 4c, 31:1-9, "The words of King Lemuel. An oracle that his mother taught him."

Agur, according to the MT, is a man of Massa (see Translation Matters below), thus not an Israelite. Whereas material in part 3 drew on Egyptian wisdom literature, here a non-Israelite author is explicitly named and included. Themes in 4a include the limitations of human wisdom, as in Job, and the importance of having enough, but not too much, so that God may be the focus of life. The numerical and other sayings in 4b are like riddles, causing the reader/hearer to reflect on the answers to the posed questions. In 4c, King Lemuel may also be a Massaite, like Agur. Structurally, 4c parallels the first nine chapters, where mostly fathers teach sons.[1] This part is significant because it incorporates the

---

1. Katherine M. Hayes, *Proverbs*, New Collegeville Bible Commentary 18 (Collegeville, MN: Liturgical Press, 2013), 111.

249

counsel of a foreign woman to her son. This is the only known wisdom text attributed solely to a woman in the ancient Near East. In addition, the fact that she is a foreign woman undercuts the negative images of the strange woman in part 1 and in Proverbs 22:14 and 23:27.[2]

There are several wise women in the Hebrew Bible, such as the wise women from Tekoa (2 Sam 14:1-3) and Abel (2 Sam 20), the Queen of Sheba who is skilled in Wisdom traditions (1 Kgs 10:1-13), and Woman Wisdom in Proverbs 1–9 and her human counterpart in 31:10-31. In addition, the wisdom book of Qohelet (Ecclesiastes) is traditionally attributed to a man, but the word "Qohelet," meaning preacher or teacher, is feminine in gender. Johanna van Wijk-Bos has speculated on the possibility that the author might be a woman, writing as if she were a man.[3] Of course, there is no way to know whether some of the biblical proverbs may have been authored by women.

4a Proverbs of an Unknown Individual, Possibly a Non-Judahite (30:1-14)

Proverbs 30:1 is very difficult but as emended confesses Agur's humility; he does not have even human understanding (30:2), much less knowledge of wisdom and the divine. He continues with a series of questions like those posed to Job in the whirlwind in Job 38 (Prov 30:4) and declares the truth and sufficiency of God's words (30:5-6). In 30:7-9 Agur asks God for two things before he dies, (1) that vanity and falsehood be removed far from him and (2) that he be neither rich nor poor but instead be given just his assigned portion of bread. Otherwise, in the former case, in his satiety, he will forget God or, in the latter case, he might steal and seize God's name. Verse 10 may be connected to 28:1-9 by the humility of the speaker; the humble person does not slander the weak, or it may be a freestanding transition. Proverbs 30:11-14 is a short poem bound together by the word "generation" at the beginning of each line, which NRSV translates as "There are those who . . ." rather than "A generation does . . ." The idea is that evil is contagious and, also,

2. Christl Maier, "Proverbs," in *Feminist Biblical Interpretation: A Compendium of Critical Commentary on the Books of the Bible and Related Literature*, ed. Luise Schottroff and Marie-Theres Wacker (Grand Rapids, MI: Eerdmans, 2012), 255–72, at 270.
3. Private e-mail communication with PowerPoint.

Prov 30:1-14

¹The words of Agur son of Jakeh. An oracle.

Thus says the man: I am weary, O God,

I am weary, O God. How can I prevail?

²Surely I am too stupid to be human; I do not have human understanding.

³I have not learned wisdom, nor have I knowledge of the holy ones.

⁴Who has ascended to heaven and come down?

Who has gathered the wind in the hollow of the hand?

Who has wrapped up the waters in a garment?

Who has established all the ends of the earth?

What is the person's name? And what is the name of the person's child? Surely you know!

⁵Every word of God proves true; he is a shield to those who take refuge in him.

⁶Do not add to his words, or else he will rebuke you, and you will be found a liar.

⁷Two things I ask of you; do not deny them to me before I die:

⁸Remove far from me falsehood and lying; give me neither poverty nor riches; feed me with the food that I need,

⁹or I shall be full, and deny you, and say, "Who is the LORD?"

that people who fail to respect their parents are the same ones who are arrogant, and these in turn are the same ones who are greedy and exploitative of the poor. (See Excursus on Women's Sins 1: Arrogance, at 3:8.)

TRANSLATION MATTERS

In the first colon of 30:1, the MT has "[man of] Massa," perhaps in Northern Arabia, rather than an oracle. In the second colon, NRSV has emended: לאיתי אל לאיתי אל ואכל, "I have wearied myself, O God, I have wearied myself, O God, How can I prevail?" The MT can be translated as: "the speech of the man to Ithiel and Ucal" (two personal names), where the first one has been written twice due to dittography (accidentally writing the same word two times) or possibly to two individuals with the same name:

The words of Agur son of Jakeh of Massa:
Thus says the man to Ithiel (to Ithiel) and to Ucal.

or I shall be poor, and steal,
and profane the name of my God.

[10]Do not slander a servant to a master,
or the servant will curse you, and
you will be held guilty.

[11]There are those who curse their
fathers
and do not bless their mothers.
[12]There are those who are pure in
their own eyes

yet are not cleansed of their
filthiness.
[13]There are those—how lofty are their
eyes,
how high their eyelids lift!—
[14]there are those whose teeth are
swords,
whose teeth are knives,
to devour the poor from off the
earth,
the needy from among mortals.

4b Numerical and Other Sayings (30:15-33)

The numerical pattern in this section of threes and fours is reminiscent of Amos' oracles in the first chapter of his book, in which he begins his indictments of the various nations with: "For three transgressions and four, I will not revoke the punishment." This material, of course, is wisdom literature rather than prophetic; here it is presenting riddles, but there is a certain bite in some of them, even though it would seem that the social setting is quite a bit later than that of Amos.

Proverbs 30:15a can be read independently or as the introduction to 30:15b-16. The leech, the word for which is grammatically feminine in Hebrew, has two sucking heads, thus the two daughters, both of whom ambiguously are either called "Give" or who cry, "Give." Proverbs 30:15b introduces a kind of riddle: three/four (things) are (never) satisfied. Verse 16 presents the solutions: Sheol always wants more people; the barren womb always wants a child, since children, especially sons, were what gave women economic and social status; the earth was always thirsty in a land with little rainfall; and fire seems greedy when it rages out of control. In 30:17 the leeches (children) of 30:15 are repaid for their lack of respect (see 30:11). Verses 18-19 describe three/four things that are too wonderful to be understood. One unresolved issue is what the four answers have in common; the first three are examples of physical motion in the air, on the ground, and on the sea, but the fourth is a metaphorical reference to the mysterious ways of intimacy. Verse 20 is clearly an addition, as it does not have the same syntax as 30:18-19, but it may have been added at this location because of the connection to sexuality. We

¹⁵The leech has two daughters;
  "Give, give," they cry.
Three things are never satisfied;
  four never say, "Enough":
¹⁶Sheol, the barren womb,
  the earth ever thirsty for water,
  and the fire that never says,
    "Enough."

¹⁷The eye that mocks a father
  and scorns to obey a mother
will be pecked out by the ravens of
    the valley
  and eaten by the vultures.

¹⁸Three things are too wonderful for
    me;
  four I do not understand:
¹⁹the way of an eagle in the sky,
  the way of a snake on a rock,

the way of a ship on the high seas,
  and the way of a man with a girl.
²⁰This is the way of an adulteress:
  she eats, and wipes her mouth,
  and says, "I have done no wrong."

²¹Under three things the earth
    trembles;
  under four it cannot bear up:
²²a slave when he becomes king,
  and a fool when glutted with food;
²³an unloved woman when she gets a
    husband,
  and a maid when she succeeds
    her mistress.

²⁴Four things on earth are small,
  yet they are exceedingly wise:
²⁵the ants are a people without
    strength,

do understand, however, all too well the way of the cheater, whether it be the man or the woman or both who are at fault.

TRANSLATION MATTERS

In 30:23, if MT תִּבָּעֵל (*tibbāʿēl*), a *Niphal*, a passive verb form meaning "to be married," is revocalized as תִּבְעַל (*tibʿal*), a *Qal*, an active verb form from another meaning of the root "to rule," the colon will provide a more sensible answer to the riddle: a hated woman gains authority (over her household).[4]

Proverbs 30:21-23 is another poetic riddle, this one dealing with matters that upset the social order. Three of them are obvious, but it is not easy to see how an unloved woman getting married would disturb the

---

4. Michael V. Fox, *Proverbs 10–31: A New Translation with Introduction and Commentary*, AB 18B (New Haven: Yale University Press, 2009), 876–77.

Prov 30:15-33 (cont.)

yet they provide their food in the summer;

[26]the badgers are a people without power,

yet they make their homes in the rocks;

[27]the locusts have no king,

yet all of them march in rank;

[28]the lizard can be grasped in the hand,

yet it is found in kings' palaces.

[29]Three things are stately in their stride;

four are stately in their gait:

[30]the lion, which is mightiest among wild animals

and does not turn back before any;

[31]the strutting rooster, the he-goat,

and a king striding before his people.

[32]If you have been foolish, exalting yourself,

or if you have been devising evil,

put your hand on your mouth.

[33]For as pressing milk produces curds,

and pressing the nose produces blood,

so pressing anger produces strife.

order of things. The emendation suggested in Translation Matters allows the colon to be read in such a way that it perhaps fits in better: a hated woman gains authority (over her household), authority that was presumably assumed to belong to the husband. The fact that she was hated, perhaps because she was not a very pleasant person or because she was domineering, would only make matters worse. Interestingly, the woman of strength/strong woman (capable wife)[5] in 31:10-31 in fact did seem to exercise quite a lot of authority over her household, and she was highly praised, thus undercutting this proverb, if the emendation is correct! Note that the root used both here and in 30:32 for "fool" is neither of the two commonly used ones in Proverbs but the one meaning presumptuous, ignoble, נבל.[6]

Proverbs 30:24-28 is also a poetic riddle, focused on small yet wise and skillful animals, from which people may learn lessons, particularly that wisdom does not lie in the hands of the mighty.

Proverbs 30:29-31 is a poetic riddle that goes in the other direction, speaking of animals and a king, bearing themselves with pride. If we imitate their example (32:33), exalting ourselves or, worse, contemplating evil, we are headed for a fall (see 16:18).

---

5. See Translation Matters on Strong Woman/Wife (Capable Wife), אשת־חיל, at 12:4.

6. For the use of all three of the roots meaning fool, see Translation Matters on Jerk/Schmuck/Folly (Fool/Folly), אויל/אולת, at 1:7.

TRANSLATION MATTERS

In 30:31, the MT אַלְקוּם (*'alqûm*) should perhaps be emended to אֶל קוּם (*'al qôm*). Reading this along without the NRSV emendation of עִמּוֹ (*'immô*), "with/against him," to עַמּוֹ (*'ammô*), "his people" (BHS), the colon now translates as: "and a king—let none stand against him."

4c The Words of King Lemuel, an Oracle That His Mother Taught Him (31:1-9)

King Lemuel, named in 31:1, is otherwise unknown. Lemuel may be from Massa of North Arabia (see Translation Matters at 30:1). Verse 2 begins the instruction with a series of mother-son terms of endearment. Verse 3 moves into the substance of the matter with the mandate not to dissipate one's strength, probably sexual virility, with women. The advice is perhaps moderated in the second colon with the phrase "those who destroy kings" or it may be that all women (except for his wife) may have been viewed by his mother as destructive of him and his monarchy.

TRANSLATION MATTERS

In 31:4, NRSV has emended MT או (*'ô*), *Ketib*, "or," אֵי (*'ê*), *Qeré*,[7] "where?" to אַוָּה (*'avâ*), "desire," but a solution that produces better parallelism is to revocalize the *Qeré* as אִי (*'î*), a negative particle. The colon then reads: "not for rulers— strong drink."[8]

Verse 4 moves to the subject of strong drink. Not all alcohol is forbidden, as wine was part of the daily fare, since pure water was not generally available. The concern was excessive drinking, which would cause the king to forget his own laws and pervert justice (31:5). Verses 6-7 go on to suggest that wine is fine for those who are on their deathbeds or in great anguish, as it is acceptable for them to forget their poverty and misery, but the king must always be alert. Verses 8-9 bring this section to a close with two verses, each of which begins with "open your mouth" ("Speak out"; NRSV), in the area of justice, as opposed to in drinking wine.

---

7. On the meaning of *Ketib/Qeré*, see Translation Matters at 1:27.
8. Fox, *Proverbs 10–31*, 886–87.

Prov 31:1-9

¹The words of King Lemuel. An oracle
    that his mother taught him:

²No, my son! No, son of my womb!
    No, son of my vows!
³Do not give your strength to women,
    your ways to those who destroy
    kings.
⁴It is not for kings, O Lemuel,
    it is not for kings to drink wine,
    or for rulers to desire strong drink;
⁵or else they will drink and forget
    what has been decreed,
    and will pervert the rights of all the
    afflicted.

⁶Give strong drink to one who is
    perishing,
    and wine to those in bitter
    distress;
⁷let them drink and forget their
    poverty,
    and remember their misery no
    more.
⁸Speak out for those who cannot
    speak,
    for the rights of all the destitute.
⁹Speak out, judge righteously,
    defend the rights of the poor and
    needy.

A Mother's Recipe for Successful Leadership (Prov 31:1-9)

Mothers of royal sons are mentioned several times in Scripture. Perhaps this is because many of the Bible's source documents were royal annals or similar official documents, or because of the high value placed on mothering in the ancient world. Mothers of royal sons include Azubah (Jehoshaphat), Nehushtah (Jehoiachin), Maacah (Absalom), Hamutal (Jehoahaz/Zedekiah), Jezebel (Jehoram), Ahinoam (Amnon), Athaliah (Ahaziah), and Bathsheba (Solomon). Yet the nature of the relationship between mother and royal son is not given much attention in these sacred texts, most likely as a result of the biblical writers' patriarchal bent. The few exceptions include the relationship between Bathsheba and Solomon and the negative influence Athaliah is supposed to have had on Ahaziah. This oracle that King Lemuel's mother taught in verses 2-9 of chapter 31 offers some insight into the mother-to-royal-son dynamic and the influence these women had on their offspring's leadership styles. Verses 2-9 and 10-31 serve as a two-part treatise on successful leadership offered by a mother to her royal son.

The first section (vv. 2-9) is a lesson on sobriety. The king is to avoid any activity that could diminish his ability to think clearly and, most important, to judge rightly. His mother establishes sobriety as a guard for the king's voice. Being levelheaded and free from distraction will enable him to use his voice of authority as a catalyst for justice. Once the king's voice of authority has been established and protected, verses 10-29 serve as a guide to strategic partnerships. A future wife was used as the example, but in the context of the chapter, the pericope can be viewed as a laundry list of characteristics the king should seek in potential partners. The creativity, business acumen, industriousness, respect, wisdom, and leadership skills described in these verses suggest a partner of high value. The mention of purple garments alludes to royalty, a queen perhaps, but ultimately a viable partner who by description could serve as an equal voice of authority.

What is evident from the few remnants of mother-to-royal-son relations in the Bible is that these mothers had a vested interest in securing the crown for their sons and creating longevity for their reign.

NaShieka Knight

Part 5

Proverbs 31:10-31

Poem on the אשת־חיל, the Strong Woman/Wife (Capable Wife)[1]

Introduction

The acrostic poem in Proverbs 31:10-31 concludes the book of Proverbs. Each line begins with the next letter of the Hebrew alphabet, א, ב, ג, etc. This famous poem, frequently used in women's day sermons in African American churches, is the source of divided opinion among African American women and more broadly among feminists of all ethnicities. Some are pleased that a woman with so many responsibilities in the business world is presented as a model woman. Christine Yoder suggests that her portrait probably reflects an amalgamation of the social roles that actual elite postexilic women exercised.[2] Some are disturbed, however, that she seems to be an impossible superwoman whose combination of virtues no real human could attain. Yoder thinks the reason the woman seems superhuman is that on one level she is

---

1. See Translation Matters on Strong Woman/Wife (Capable Wife), אשת־חיל, at 12:4.
2. Christine Roy Yoder, "The Woman of Substance (חיל אשת): A Socio-Economic Reading of Proverbs 31:10-31," *JBL* 122 (2003): 427–47.

divine Wisdom personified.[3] On the other hand many of my students tell me that she reminds them of their mothers who worked from dawn to late at night doing multiple tasks to keep the family going.

Just as Wisdom and Folly are personified in the first nine chapters, so here, the woman of strength can be viewed as fulfilling a dual role, the ideal woman and Woman Wisdom. Read this way, it is easy to see why it is difficult for humans to meet the standard she sets. Nevertheless, the fact that she is depicted as a businesswoman while also exercising other duties managing her estate is useful in contexts where women's roles are still restricted. We will return to the superwoman problem after analyzing the poem carefully.

Reading the Strong Woman as Wisdom creates a nice envelope for the book of Proverbs, with personifications of Wisdom at the beginning and end. Understood as abstract Wisdom, although the imagery is still androcentric, the point is now broader than finding a wife or even a spouse. It is to mate with Wisdom to find happiness and true success in life. Christl Maier points out that just as King Lemuel's mother's foreignness undercuts the negative image of the strange woman in Proverbs 1–9 and 22:14 and 23:27, the Strong Woman incorporates an element of the strange woman into her character, in that she does business with foreigners (31:14), subtly weakening the negativity of the strange woman imagery.[4]

Interestingly, the only other use of the phrase "the strong woman" in the Hebrew Bible is in the book of Ruth. There it is applied to a woman from Moab. Moab was not just a foreign country but one of the most hated of all alien places because the Moabites did not provide hospitality to the Hebrews when they fled Egypt, and they hired the prophet Balaam against them (Deut 23:3-5). As a result, the Moabites (and Ammonites) were never to be allowed to be part of the Israelite community. In spite of this Deuteronomic text, Ruth is depicted very positively as a strong woman (3:11) and the great-grandmother of David. The seeds of this usage, subversive also of Ezra's and Nehemiah's dictates to Israelite men to divorce their foreign wives and send them and the ethnically

---

3. Christine Roy Yoder, *Wisdom as a Woman of Substance: A Socioeconomic Reading of Proverbs 1–9 and 31:10-31*, BZAW 304 (Berlin: de Gruyter, 2001).

4. Christl Maier, "Proverbs," in *Feminist Biblical Interpretation: A Compendium of Critical Commentary on the Books of the Bible and Related Literature*, ed. Luise Schottroff and Marie-Theres Wacker (Grand Rapids, MI: Eerdmans, 2012), 255–72, at 270.

mixed children away (Ezra 9:1–10:44; Neh 13:1-3), are already present in the book of Proverbs,[5] assuming as I do that Proverbs predates Ruth.

*African Womanist Perspective
on Proverbs 31
"Abafazi, Imbokodo, a Woman
Is a Rock" Narrative*

Even though household help was available, my mom would personally lead the spring cleaning activities in the home during school holidays; when maize meal season commenced, she would wake up while it was dark and hoe the maize meal fields; on a daily basis before work commenced as a high school teacher, she supervised breakfast preparation, returning home to prepare dinner; she multitasked to fit the definition of a virtuous woman. Her life journey would symbolize the South African idiom "wathintha abafazi, wathinta imbokodo," meaning, you "touch a woman, you touch a rock."

The Oxford American Dictionary has several meanings of a rock that fit the African woman rock narrative, including "used in similes and metaphors to refer to someone or something that is extremely strong, reliable, or hard."[6] In most communities, the African woman is the matriarch of the household and monitors the home with strength and firmness; although the man is the head of the household, the woman sets the tone of how the home should be run. She may appear weak, yet her influence develops a spiritual and emotional framework that holds the family together and determines community and church engagement.

No doubt, a woman of African descent willingly works hard, expeditiously, nurturing and nourishing her family through entrepreneurial endeavors, her efforts undergirded by hands upturned in prayer, increasing her confidence in God and allowing her to continue to build on this Rock and be a woman of positive influence in her home and beyond.[7]

Sindile Dlamini

5. For a discussion of the issues of interpretation in the book of Ruth, see Alice Ogden Bellis, "Ruth," and the literature cited there, in *Helpmates, Harlots, and Heroes: Women's Stories in the Hebrew Bible*, 2nd ed. (Louisville: Westminster John Knox, 2007), 183–89.

6. Erin McKean, ed., *New Oxford American Dictionary*, 2nd ed. (New York: Oxford University Press, 2005), s.v. "rock."

7. Jane Hansen, "A Woman of Eternal Significance, in Jack Hayford, ed., *New Spirit-Filled Life Bible* (Nashville: Thomas Nelson, 1982), 840.

The Strong Woman: Noble Rock of Family and Community (31:10-31)

In 31:10 a rhetorical question is asked about the strong woman (capable wife): who can find her? The answer is not "no one," since 12:4a says that a strong woman is her husband's crown. The second colon of this verse says that her price is far beyond rubies. On one level, the price alludes to the bride-price that the groom had to pay when he got married, but what made a woman truly valuable was not how much she cost, which was based on the size of her dowry, but rather the qualities that are described in the poem. (See 3:15 and 8:11 for language in which the feminine figure is identified as Wisdom and is again better than jewels.) These qualities are what a young man had to be able to discern as he sought a mate. Even though the original poem was oriented toward young men seeking brides, it can be read today in a gender-neutral way of women seeking husbands or of same-sex pairings. And though the division of labor and the precise tasks to be done are not what are required today in the West, the character traits that are praised still are valid.

Reading Proverbs 31 through an Islamic Feminist Framework

The Islamic worldview challenges us to view our human experience within the framework of both rights and responsibilities. If we do witness that we have God-given rights as humans, then we also must witness that we have God-given responsibilities tied to each right. On the other hand, feminism propels us to think of the social structures required for women to thrive and live their best lives. It challenges us to think of the rights that we owe to women in our society. What are we responsible for providing women and girls so that they can be the most God-ordained versions of themselves?

Reading Proverbs 31 through an Islamic feminist framework, the text not only calls us to witness the inner constitution of the Noble Wife but invites us as well to examine the necessary constitution of her family and social support systems that make her nobility possible. Though much of the Scripture speaks to what the Noble Wife offers her family and community, it also teaches us what we are required to offer her. The first two things that we learn about the Noble Wife are that she is both "far more precious than jewels" (31:10) and that she is given trust by "the heart of her husband" (31:11). It is this trust that allows the Noble Wife to move as freely empowered in society. We see later that this Noble Wife takes charge as a merchant, as a landowner, as a household manager, and as

¹⁰A capable wife who can find?
　She is far more precious than
　　jewels.
¹¹The heart of her husband trusts in
　her,
　and he will have no lack of gain.
¹²She does him good, and not harm,
　all the days of her life.
¹³She seeks wool and flax,
　and works with willing hands.
¹⁴She is like the ships of the
　merchant,
　she brings her food from far away.
¹⁵She rises while it is still night

and provides food for her
　household
and tasks for her servant-girls.
¹⁶She considers a field and buys it;
　with the fruit of her hands she
　plants a vineyard.
¹⁷She girds herself with strength,
　and makes her arms strong.
¹⁸She perceives that her merchandise
　is profitable.
　Her lamp does not go out at night.
¹⁹She puts her hands to the distaff,
　and her hands hold the spindle.
²⁰She opens her hand to the poor,

a mother, and she is trusted to do so by her husband. She is trusted to manage the money and the estate. She considers land and she buys it (31:16). She has her own business; it is *her own* merchandise that earns her profit (31:18). She not only earns her own money but keeps it and spends it how she sees best.

For the Noble Wife to be at her best, we are required to provide her with a clear field of authority; she must be trusted to manage the domicile, the estate, the children, and all the resources she wishes to acquire and manage as well. Therefore, *she* can open her home to the needy, give charity with her own earnings, and practice God-led stewardship over the land around her as we are all called to do. Denying the woman this trust, freedom, and support denies her the opportunity to fully serve God.

In this passage, we also read that her children and husband love her and support her emotionally. They praise her for her work (31:28) and see to her happiness. No mother performs well in a loveless environment, without praise and support, or without emotional nourishment. In all her dignity and virtue, the Noble Wife needs to know that her work matters and is sustenance to her family. Thus, we are responsible for giving emotional support to the women in our families as well.

The chapter ends with a final instruction. We are *required* to "give her a share in the fruit." This instruction is not to be taken lightly. Only by giving women the support to grow *and enjoy* the fruits of our labor can we achieve the level of Nobility described in Proverbs 31.

Niciah Petrovic

Prov 31:10-31 (cont.)

and reaches out her hands to the
needy.

²¹She is not afraid for her household
when it snows,
for all her household are clothed
in crimson.

²²She makes herself coverings;
her clothing is fine linen and purple.

²³Her husband is known in the city
gates,
taking his seat among the elders
of the land.

²⁴She makes linen garments and
sells them;
she supplies the merchant with
sashes.

²⁵Strength and dignity are her clothing,
and she laughs at the time to
come.

²⁶She opens her mouth with wisdom,

and the teaching of kindness is on
her tongue.

²⁷She looks well to the ways of her
household,
and does not eat the bread of
idleness.

²⁸Her children rise up and call her
happy;
her husband too, and he praises
her:

²⁹"Many women have done excellently,
but you surpass them all."

³⁰Charm is deceitful, and beauty is
vain,
but a woman who fears the LORD
is to be praised.

³¹Give her a share in the fruit of her
hands,
and let her works praise her in the
city gates.

The woman of strength is trustworthy (31:11) and brings in booty (NRSV "gain") and the husband will have no lack of gain (as a result). Whether he trusts her because she brings home the bacon or is "supportive" is unclear. The word booty, שלל, usually has military connotations, showing that she is truly a woman of strength. The word means the spoils of war, garments, gold, silver, flocks, and even slaves, including women, though we hope based on verse 12 that she does not bring the last kind of booty home! She does good and not harm (31:12), possibly suggesting the supportive role, and applies herself to all aspects of weaving (31:13), emphasizing the independent wealth production. She obtains food wherever is best (31:14), whether on the estate in the local market, or from specialty shops.

TRANSLATION MATTERS

In 31:15, חק is more likely the fixed portion of food allotted to the servant-girls rather than "tasks."

She rises early (31:15), while it is still night, as is still true of many farmers today. Animals need to be tended to, and even if one has servants to do much of the work, the servants still need to be supervised, and, if חק means the fixed portion of food allotted to the servant-girls, then those female servants need to be fed; or if it means "tasks," as NRSV translates, then she has those tasks to set up. Verse 16 indicates that she is capable of entering into a real estate transaction, which one would not have thought possible in preexilic days. She develops a plan, then acquires the field. Next, through the fruit of her hands, possibly the earnings she has made from selling fabric she has spun beyond the needs of her family (31:24), she is able to hire the necessary labor to do the arduous work of planting the vineyard.

Verse 17 again describes her in military terms, girding her loins with strength and strengthening the arms. Her tasks are not military, but they do require the same physical vigor and tenacity as a warrior. Verse 18 involves two double meanings. She perceives/tastes that her merchandise/profit is good. Knowing that she is successful, she works late into the night. She is wealthy enough to have sufficient oil to keep her lamp burning, allowing her to do inside chores such as weaving and spinning (31:19). Verse 20 turns to the world outside her own household; she stretches out the same hands that spin to the poor and needy.

Proverbs 31:21-25 form the capstone to her spinning and weaving; she can dress the household in expensive crimson (31:21), normally worn by the upper class and royalty, reserving purple linen for herself (31:22). This connects her with Lydia in Acts 16:14-15, who was a seller of purple cloth. When the woman of strength's husband takes his place among the elders (31:23), he is treated with respect, either for his crimson garments or the reputation of his wife, or both. This is not to say that he spent all of his time there. He may well have been much involved in the agricultural activities of the estate. But the activities at the city gate we imagine were primarily a male preserve, and one that only those with reasonable wealth had the leisure to participate in. The story of Judith, however, does suggest that women could participate in community decision making. The woman of strength has a surplus to sell (31:24) and can be confident in the future (31:25).

Proverbs 31:26-31 are a concluding encomium. In addition to all the practical domestic matters, the woman of strength speaks with wisdom and either kindly teaches or teaches kindness (31:26); she manages the movements of her household diligently (31:27). Her husband and children praise her (31:28); she surpasses all women (31:29). Verse 29 says that many daughters have done valiantly, the same Hebrew word being used as the one that describes the woman of strength, חיל, strength, efficiency, wealth. Verse 30 is not saying that charm and beauty are evil but rather that they are transitory; they may fade over time. In contrast, a woman of strength who is the fear of YHWH[8] is to be praised. The Hebrew equates the woman with the fear of YHWH; she embodies this quality. She does more than fear God. She *is* fear of the deity. The fear of YHWH means awe and reverence for the deity. Since it is equated with the knowledge of YHWH and the beginning of Wisdom, this woman is the earthly counterpart of the divine personification of Wisdom in 8:22-36.

Verse 31 asks that a portion of the return on her labor be given to her, which assumes that her husband has the ultimate control over it. Finally, the second colon suggests that her works praise her in the gate. This might suggest that she cannot participate in the political activities there herself, even though she apparently can move about freely, doing business. The fact that Judith is involved politically in the story of which she is the protagonist, though, argues against this reading. Another interpretation is that her works are well known in the public sphere and give her, as well as her husband, a good reputation, not that she is forbidden to be there in any sphere of activity herself.

One of the perennial discussions about this passage is how to deal with a woman who seems to be superwoman. There are several things to be remembered. She is the manager of an estate with servants to help her. What does she actually do herself?

- She obtains food and the raw materials from which to weave clothing, we may assume with assistance in carrying the goods home from donkeys and servants (31:13).
  Modern equivalent: Visiting the farmer's market and grocery stores; getting raw materials for clothes generally not needed, though some people do still sew their own clothes and many knit and crochet, but the raw materials are generally obtained at local stores or mail order, not directly processed from the plants or animals.

- She provides food for her household (directing her servants; 31:14-15). Meal planning for an extended family with servants, especially with minimal technology, is a significant endeavor, but with enough helpers, the person in charge does not have an insurmountable task.

---

8. See discussion of this phrase at 1:7.

The diet was fairly simple: bread, grapes, olives, milk, honey, and a few fruits and vegetables to supplement the diet. Occasionally, there would be meat.

Modern equivalent: Planning a contemporary family's meals is much simpler today with the enormous variety of choices at modern markets and kitchen appliances. At a range of price points, someone with an hour a day can provide two reasonably healthy meals for a small family, though due to lack of time contemporary Americans are increasingly relying on fast food, contributing to the obesity epidemic. We typically do not have servants, but many middle-class and affluent families use services that provide house cleaning, gardening, and the like. It is the modern impersonal equivalent of servants.

- She spins to make the cloth for clothing from the wool and flax she has obtained (31:19). This was time-consuming work, but the resulting cloth lasted much longer than modern cloth.
  Modern equivalent: Mostly, people buy ready-made clothes in the West, relying on the labor of people in developing countries and the incredibly low wages they are paid. A few people spin because of the beauty and longevity of the homemade cloth. Some people knit and crochet, but mostly for special clothes.

- She sews garments from the cloth she has spun (31:22).
  Modern equivalent: Again, most people today buy relatively cheaply made ready-made clothes, with little awareness of the lives of those who make them. When I was a child, my mother, who did not work outside the home, made my clothes. I made some of my children's clothes, but since I worked outside the home, I bought most of their clothes. Today I wear hand-me-downs and -ups from my mother and my children, shop at second-hand stores, and sometimes buy new from catalogs. I sometimes sew for my grandchildren.

- She sells some of the garments she has made (31:24).
  Modern equivalent: Most women today work outside the home to earn a living. A few own small businesses and sell what they make or sell their services of various kinds.

- She buys a field to add to the estate and produce more food or add to pasture for the animals (31:16).
  Modern equivalent: Although some women are real estate investors, and a few invest in other sorts of commodities, most women receive most of their income from working at a job.

- She teaches (31:26). It is not clear whether the teaching was formal or informal.
  Modern equivalent: Most women are involved in informal teaching, whether of their children or in their community or at their place of work. Some women teach for a living, as I do, or teach in their church or homeschool their children.

- She stays busy before dawn until after sundown (31:15, 18). Because she was wealthy, she could afford to keep an oil lamp going at night. This was a luxury most people could not afford.
  Modern equivalent: Today in the West, we take electricity and lights at night for granted, so many women are up before dawn and work well into the evening hours, whether on their paid work or on tasks related to keeping house, home, and family going.

When I discuss the woman in 31:10-31 with my male and female students, many of them report to me that the portrait fits their mothers, not in every detail, of course, but in its spirit. Their mothers worked extraordinarily hard from before dawn until late at night, day in and day out, to provide for their families. They worked outside the home, sometimes as domestics, then came home and did the same sort of work at their own homes in addition to taking care of their children and everything else involved in managing a household. And some of them were single moms. I am in awe of them. My mother worked very hard too, but she was not juggling a job and managing our household on a very limited salary as was the case with some of my students' mothers.

The situation is just as difficult, if not more difficult, in developing countries where in many cases people do not even have access to clean running water or electricity and thus have to walk miles to lug buckets of water. What we consider minimal necessities are on their luxury list. So, from the point of view of modern Western women, the portrait in 31:10-31 may seem like an impossible superwoman. But she is a very real woman who exists throughout much of the world today and, without her, many of the world's children who make it to adulthood would not survive as long as they do. She is real and her value is indeed out of sight (paraphrase of 31:10).

Conclusion

The book of Proverbs seeks to entice the student of Wisdom along the path to a successful life, by engaging the learner in reflection in the full array of life's quandaries. Thoroughly embedded in its ancient milieu, it transcends its social location to call out to contemporary souls to heed its message to find the way to a truly fulfilling life. Though directed originally to young men, today it may profitably be read by women and men, young and old. With notable exceptions (especially corporal punishment), its teaching methods and advice are ageless. Although it can be mined for the sort of advice that the young wince at, through the "better than" proverbs, frequent criticisms of wealth for wealth's sake, injunctions encouraging protection of the poor or oppressed, and the constant reminder that the just poor are to be envied in contrast to the unjust rich, Proverbs can be seen as challenging the list of boring admonitions it is often thought to be.

From a gender-sensitive perspective, the way the final editors of Proverbs constructed the book indicates a concern to shift the perceptions of women by enveloping the body of Proverbs with a nine-chapter introduction (part 1) and the concluding twenty-one-verse acrostic Ode to the Strong Woman/Wife (Capable Wife; part 5). Part 1, advice mainly of fathers to sons about women, including the infamous strange woman, concluding with the banquets of Wisdom and Folly, where the feminine divine Wisdom clearly has the upper hand, is balanced by part 5, the Ode to the Strong Woman/Wife, divine Wisdom's human counterpart. Although the stereotypical strange woman is part of the outer envelope,

269

comprising about 15 percent of the outer shell in terms of the number of verses, the dominant feminine images are those of Wisdom and the Strong Woman, which comprise 22 percent of the verses.[1] Not only are they a larger part of the material, but both in chapters 1–9 and in the final poem, they are what concludes the sections. This leaves the reader with the image of Wisdom in the first section and her human counterpart, the Strong Woman, at the end of the collection as the final and climactic image of the section and, in the case of part 5, of the whole book of Proverbs. These outer layers set the tone for the rest of the book. Although the strange woman trope is not completely neutralized, at least she is overshadowed. The sages probably could not erase her from the tradition or the culture, but they did their best to limit her poison.

The middle section of Proverbs, parts 2, 3, 4a, and 4b, again contains advice, mainly of *fathers* to sons and, rarely, about strange/foreign women. These parts are balanced by part 4c, which is advice of a *mother* to her son, including counsel about intimate issues, though without reference to strange/foreign women. Even though parts 2–4b are much longer than 4c, the impact of a nine-verse speech of a mother to her son is considerable.

In this inner core of the book, there are only two references to strange/ foreign women, and really only one of these is obviously problematic from a gender-sensitive perspective, 23:27. The other reference, 27:13, which in the NRSV is translated as "foreigner" but in the Hebrew says "foreign woman" (נכריה), does not have clear sexual overtones. The texts that deal with the difficulties of living with quarrelsome wives (19:13; 21:9; 21:19; 25:24; 27:15) are also bothersome, but they are at least balanced by many more proverbs dealing with quarrelsome men. (See discussion and note at 21:9, 19.)

Another matter is worth reflection as we conclude this commentary, the attitude of the sages toward wealth and poverty, diligence and laziness. Material prosperity was important to the authors of Proverbs, as is exemplified in many of the proverbs, e.g., in 3:16 when it is proclaimed of Wisdom that "Long life is in her right hand; in her left hand are riches and honor" (see also 8:18). But there are many proverbs that make it clear that wealth is not the highest value, for wealth is ephemeral. Proverbs 11:4 says, "Riches do not profit in the day of wrath, but righteousness de-

---

1. The first nine chapters and 31:1-10 together have 287 verses. The verses that deal with the strange/foreign woman include 2:16-19; 5:3-6, 15-23; 6:24; and 7:5-27.

livers from death" (see also 11:28 and 18:11). Several proverbs condemn some of the immoral ways that people (try to) become wealthy. Proverbs 23:4 advises, "Do not wear yourself out to get rich; be wise enough to desist." In other words, wealth is a good thing, but one should not obsess over it and make it the only goal in life. The sages were especially concerned with ill-gotten wealth. They say, "Better to be poor and walk in integrity than to be crooked in one's ways even though rich" (28:6). They condemn both the miser (28:22) and the glutton (21:17) and seem therefore to urge a life of moderation as the route to wisdom, wealth, and happiness (see also 30:8).

The sages urge hard work in order to be successful in life, in particular to become wealthy. In five proverbs scattered throughout the collection they use the root חרוץ, meaning "sharp" or "diligent," to give this kind of advice, and it is no doubt true that in general diligence does tend to lead to success (10:4; 12:24, 27; 13:4; 21:5). They also bring up the opposite side of this coin, laziness, in fourteen proverbs, with the root עצל (6:6, 9; 10:26; 13:4; 15:19; 19:24; 20:4; 21:25; 22:13; 24:30; 26:15, 16). Proverbs 13:4 incorporates both of these roots: "The appetite of the lazy [עצל] craves, and gets nothing, while the appetite of the diligent [חרוץ] is richly supplied."

The sages also were aware of the problems the rich caused the poor. One proverb states, "Do not rob the poor because they are poor, or crush the afflicted at the gate; for the LORD pleads their cause and despoils the life of the one who despoils them" (22:22-23; see also 22:7, 16; 28:15; 30:14). Ultimately, the sages understood the common humanity of the oppressor and the poor, for they assert, "The poor and the oppressor have this in common: the LORD gives light to the eyes of both" (29:13). So, it is simplistic to suggest that the sages thought that the only cause of poverty was laziness. They were neither ignorant nor stupid. They understood that there were oppressors, who were part of the equation of wealth and poverty. Thus, a just person's duty was to help the poor, as Lemuel's mother advised her son in 31:9: "Speak out, judge righteously, defend the rights of the poor and needy." Similarly, the Strong Woman "opens her hand to the poor, and reaches out her hands to the needy" (31:20).

For the sages, the acquisition of and bonding with Wisdom, understood as deep knowledge, prudence, justice, and fear of YHWH, was the goal of education, and it took hard work, study, and discipline in order to achieve this goal. Their corporal methods of discipline we disagree with today (see discussion at 13:24). Nevertheless, we do understand the importance of discipline to learn any subject or skill, whether it be a sport, an instrument, a language, or a philosophical system. Since their audience was boys/young men and since wisdom was understood in their culture as feminine, they depicted her in personified feminine form. They urged the audience/readers to follow her rather than Folly, her personified opposite, and likewise to find a woman of strength, her human counterpart, for a wife rather than a foolish one, though this is mostly implied. What is explicit is that young men should avoid strange/ foreign women, though it is not entirely clear exactly what women the sages had in mind. Most of the encouragement is directed toward the young men to avoid being fools themselves. There are three types they should try not to be: inept dolts who are just unaware of what's going on; jerks or schmucks, i.e., really bad characters who cause a lot of trouble; and a third type only mentioned twice, who is churlish, like Nabal in the story of Abigail and Nabal, whose name is a nickname meaning fool. The corrupt are excoriated and contrasted with the just. The unethical are also condemned. The young men are told to avoid being scoffers and scorners, basically to pay attention in their lessons and take them seriously, because even though it may be hard for them to understand it now, it will pay off in the long run.

For readers today who are not young men seeking mates, we can still find value in this ancient book of aphorisms. Whenever we read a contemporary book whose protagonist is either a different gender, ethnicity, age, or nationality than our own, we temporarily take on that person's identity and learn something about another part of humanity without sacrificing our own. Rather, we are expanding our own boundaries. We can do the same when we read Proverbs. Alternately, if that does not feel comfortable, we can find modern parallels and rewrite proverbs as advice to young women. What kind of inept fools do we, as women, tend to become, and how do we act like jerks at times? We can advise young women to avoid behavior that will not lead to success even as we encourage them to be disciplined in their study, not only of academic and extracurricular subjects, but, even more important, of wisdom, in whatever tradition helps them to grow spiritually. Who are the strange/ foreign men (or just plain people) that they need to avoid? Many years ago when my daughters were young and I was struggling with this issue, I wrote a short version of Proverbs like this for them. It is a useful and creative exercise, perhaps especially for a youth group, and not just for women, but for young men as well, to update the advice in Proverbs to make it fit today's world. In the process of reflecting on the proverbs to contemporize them, a great deal can be learned.

I believe that Proverbs is not the conservative book of bromides that it is often thought to be. Perhaps the sages were wrestling with a new world in the postexilic landscape and crafted the book we now study out of older aphorisms, adding new material, and bringing the individual proverbs together into groups so that they would be read together and heard as poetic units to resonate with each other. Trying to see the connections between the proverbs in a group is in itself a fascinating process. The ancient Hebrews were poets, and one aspect of their poetry was the interplay between various elements within a colon or sentence, euphonically and substantively, as indicated in the introduction. Thus, I have tried to show that Proverbs should be seen not as a hodge-podge but as a carefully crafted, structured composition. I may or may not have gotten the structure right in my divisions, but I am convinced that a structure like this is what was intended so that the proverbs would not be read as individual entities but in groups so that they could help interpret each other. The result is an artistic tapestry a bit like a hologram, but on a multidimensional scale, that can change each time you look at it. It is beautiful, deep, and profound, as well as playful and joyful, but at the same time very vital. Read and heard this way, Proverbs invites the serious student of wisdom to engage some of the deepest and most important issues that confront humanity. Though the culture has changed dramatically since the book was brought into its present form, the core issue that we must wrestle with has not changed much. What is the most effective way to live a happy, successful life?

Works Cited

AAUW. "The Simple Truth about the Gender Pay Gap." https://www.aauw.org /research/the-simple-truth-about-the-gender-pay-gap/.

Alexander, Michelle. *The New Jim Crow: Mass Incarceration in the Age of Colorblindness*. New York: New Press, 2012.

Allen, Charles. "Cadenced Free Verse." *College English* 9 (January 1948): 195–99.

Archer, John. "Sex Differences in Aggression between Heterosexual Partners: A Meta-Analytic Review." *Psychological Bulletin* (2000). http://psycnet.apa.org /doiLanding?doi=10.1037%2F0033-2909.126.5.651.

Bailey, Randall C. "Beyond Identification: The Use of Africans in Old Testament Narrative and Poetry." In *Stony the Road We Trod: African American Biblical Interpretation*, edited by Cain Hope Felder, 165–69. Minneapolis: Fortress Press, 1991.

Bailey, Wilma. "Prepubescent Marriage: Baby Becky, Menarche and Prepubescent Marriage in Ancient Israel." *Journal of the Interdenominational Theological Center* 37 (2011): 113–37.

Baumann, Gerlinde. "A Figure with Many Facets: The Literary and Theological Functions of Personified Wisdom in Proverbs 1–9." In *Wisdom and Psalms*, edited by Athalya Brenner and Carole A. Fontaine, 44–78. FCB 2, 2nd ser. Sheffield: Sheffield Academic, 1998.

———. "Personified Wisdom: Contexts, Meanings, Theology." In *The Writings and Later Wisdom Books*, edited by Christl M. Maier and Nuria Calduch-Benages, 57–75. The Bible and Women: An Encyclopedia of Exegesis and Cultural History; Hebrew Bible/Old Testament. Vol. 1.3. Atlanta: SBL Press, 2014.

Bechtel, Lyn M. "Shame as a Sanction of Social Control in Biblical Israel: Judicial, Political, and Social Shaming." *JSOT* 49 (1991): 47–76.

Bellis, Alice Ogden. "The Gender and Motives of the Wisdom Teacher in Proverbs 7." *BBR* 6 (1996): 15–22.

————. *Helpmates, Harlots, and Heroes: Women's Stories in the Hebrew Bible*. 2nd ed. Louisville: Westminster John Knox, 2007.

————. "(The Queen of) Sheba: A Gender-Sensitive Reading." *JRT* 51 (1994–1995): 17–28.

Boyarin, Daniel. "The Gospel of the Memra: Jewish Binitarianism and the Prologue to John." *HTR* 94 (2001): 244–84.

Brenner, Athalya. "Proverbs 1–9: An F Voice?" In *On Gendering Texts: Female and Male Voices in the Hebrew Bible*, edited by Athalya Brenner and Fokkelien van Dijk-Hemmes, 113–30. BibInt 1. Leiden: Brill, 1993.

Bryce, Glendon E. "Another Wisdom 'Book' in Proverbs." *JBL* 91 (1972): 145–57.

Bureau of Justice Statistics, US Department of Justice. "Family Violence Statistics: Including Statistics on Strangers and Acquaintances." June 2005. https://www.bjs.gov/content/pub/pdf/fvs03.pdf, accessed 7/11/2017.

Burgo, Joseph. "Why We Should Humiliate Harassers." *The Washington Post*. November 19, 2017.

Camp, Claudia V. "The Female Sage in Ancient Israel and in the Biblical Wisdom Literature." In *The Sage in Ancient Israel and the Near East*, edited by John G. Gammie and Leo G. Perdue, 116–31. Winona Lake, IN: Eisenbrauns, 1990.

————. "What's So Strange about the Strange Woman?" In *The Bible and the Politics of Exegesis: Essays in Honor of Norman K. Gottwald on His Sixty-Fifth Birthday*, edited by D. Jobling et al., 17–31, 301–4. Cleveland, OH: Pilgrim Press, 1991.

————. *Wisdom and the Feminine in the Book of Proverbs*. BLS 11. Sheffield: Almond Press, 1985.

————. *Wise, Strange, and Holy: The Making of the Bible*. JSOTSup 320. Sheffield: Sheffield Academic, 2000.

Chapman, Cynthia R. *The House of the Mother: The Social Roles of Maternal Kin in Biblical Hebrew Narrative and Poetry*. New Haven: Yale University Press, 2016.

Collins, John. *Introduction to the Hebrew Bible*. 2nd ed. Minneapolis: Fortress Press, 2014.

Coogan, Michael D. "The Goddess Wisdom—Where Can She Be Found? Literary Reflexes of Popular Religion." In *Ki Baruch Hu: Ancient Near Eastern, Biblical, and Judaic Studies in Honor of Baruch A. Levine*, edited by Robert Chazan, William W. Hallo, and Lawrence H. Schiffman, 203–9. Winona Lake, IN: Eisenbrauns, 1999.

Copeland, Larry. "Life Expectancy in the USA Hits a Record High." *USA Today*. October 9, 2014. https://www.usatoday.com/story/news/nation/2014/10/08/us-life-expectancy-hits-record-high/16874039/.

Copeland, M. Shawn. " 'Wading through Many Sorrows': Toward a Theology of Suffering in Woman-ist Perspective." In *A Troubling in My Soul: Womanist Perspectives on Evil and Suffering*, edited by Emilie Townes, 157–71. Maryknoll, NY: Orbis Books, 1994.

Cozolino, Louis. *The Neuroscience of Human Relationships: Attachment and the Developing Social Brain*. 2nd ed. New York: W. W. Norton & Company, 2014.

Dradül Jampal, Trinley, the Kongma Sakyong II, *The Supreme Thought: Bodhichitta and the Enlightened Society Vow*. Halifax and Cologne: Dragon, 2013.

Ellis, Havelock. "Studies in the Psychology of Sex" (1927). Vol. 5. *Art and Popular Culture* (website). http://www.artandpopularculture.com/Studies_in_the_Psychology_of_Sex%2C_Volume_5.

Epp, Eldon Jay. "Wisdom, Torah, Word: The Johannine Prologue and the Purpose of the Fourth Gospel." In *Current Issues in Biblical and Patristic Interpretation: Studies in Honor of Merrill C. Tenney Presented by His Former Students*, edited by Gerald F. Hawthorne, 128–46. Grand Rapids, MI: Eerdmans, 1974.

Fiebert, Martin S. "References Examining Assaults by Women on Their Spouses or Male Partners: An Annotated Bibliography." *Sexuality and Culture* 18 (2014): 405–67. https://link.springer.com/article/10.1007%2Fs12119-013-9194-1.

Fischer, Kathleen. *Transforming Fire: Women Using Anger Creatively*. New York: Paulist, 1999.

Fox, Michael V. "Ideas of Wisdom in Proverbs 1–9." *JBL* 116 (Winter 1997): 613–33.

———. *Proverbs 1–9: A New Translation with Introduction and Commentary*. AB 18A. New York: Doubleday, 2000.

———. *Proverbs 10–31: A New Translation with Introduction and Commentary*. AB 18B. New Haven: Yale University Press, 2009.

Frick, Frank S. "Palestine, Climate of." In *ABD* 5:119–26.

Gelles, Richard J., and Murray A. Straus. *Intimate Violence: The Causes and Consequences of Abuse in the American Family*. New York: Simon & Schuster, 1988.

Giblin, Marie. "Dualism." In *Dictionary of Feminist Theologies*, edited by Letty M. Russell and J. Shannon Clarkson, 74. Louisville: Westminster John Knox Press, 1996.

Golshan, Tara. "Study Finds 75 Percent of Workplace Harassment Victims Experienced Retaliation When They Spoke Up: What We Know about Sexual Harassment in America." *Vox*. October 17, 2017. https://www.vox.com/identities/2017/10/15/16438750/weinstein-sexual-harassment-facts.

Goodfriend, Elaine Adler. "Adultery." *ABD* 1:82–86.

Hadley, Judith M. "Wisdom and the Goddess." In *Wisdom in Ancient Israel: Essays in Honour of J.A. Emerton*, edited by John Day et al., 234–43. Cambridge: Cambridge University Press, 1995.

Harrison, Beverly Wildung. "The Power of Anger in the Work of Love." *USQR* 36 (1981): 41–57.

Hart, David Bentley. *The New Testament: A Translation*. New Haven: Yale University Press, 2017.

Hatton, Peter T. H. *Contradiction in the Book of Proverbs: The Deep Waters of Counsel*. SOTSMS. Hampshire: Ashgate, 2008.

Hayes, Katherine M. *Proverbs*. Edited by Daniel Durken. New Collegeville Bible Commentary 18. Collegeville, MN: Liturgical Press, 2013.

Hayford, Jack. *New Spirit-Filled Life Bible*. Nashville: Thomas Nelson, 1982.

Heijerman, Meike. "Who Would Blame Her? The 'Strange' Woman of Proverbs 7." In *Reflections on Theology and Gender*, edited by Athalya Brenner and Fokkelein Van Dijk-Hemmes, 21–31. Kampen: Kok Pharos, 1994. Also in *A Feminist Companion to Wisdom Literature*, edited by Athalya Brenner, 100–109. FCB 9. Sheffield: Sheffield Academic, 1995.

Heim, Knut M. *Like Grapes of Gold Set in Silver: An Interpretation of Proverbial Clusters in Proverbs 10:1–22:16*. Berlin: de Gruyter, 2001.

hooks, bell. "Choosing the Margin as a Space of Radical Openness." In *The Feminist Standpoint Theory Reader: Intellectual and Political Controversies*, edited by Sandra Harding, 153–59. New York: Routledge, 2001.

"I Shall Not Be Moved." Wikipedia. https://en.wikipedia.org/wiki/I_Shall_Not _Be_Moved.

Kabat-Zinn, Jon. *Full Catastrophe Living: Using the Wisdom of Your Body and Mind to Face Stress, Pain, and Illness*. Rev. ed. New York: Bantam, 2013.

Kay, Katty, and Claire Shipman. *The Confidence Code: The Science and Art of Self-Assurance—What Women Should Know*. New York: HarperBusiness, 2014.

Kselman, John S. "Ambiguity and Wordplay in Proverbs xi." *VT* 52 (2002): 545–48.

Lang, Bernhard. "Lady Wisdom: A Polytheistic and Psychological Interpretation of a Biblical Goddess." In *Reading the Bible: Approaches, Methods and Strategies*, edited by Athalya Brenner and Carole Fontaine, 400–423. Sheffield: Sheffield Academic, 1997.

Lavik, Marta Høyland. "Are the Kushites Disparaged in Isaiah 18? Kush Applied as a Literary Motif in the Hebrew Bible." In *How Plausible Is a Kushite Role in Sennacherib's Retreat? A Conversation with Henry Aubin's* The Rescue of Jerusalem, edited by Alice Ogden Bellis. Piscataway Township, NJ: Gorgias Press, forthcoming.

Lee, Boyung. "Caring-Self and Women's Self-Esteem: A Feminist's Reflection on Pastoral Care and Religious Education of Korean-American Women." *Pastoral Psychology* 54 (2006): 337–53.

Lelwica, Michelle Mary. "Spreading the Religion of Thinness from California to Calcutta: A Critical Feminist Postcolonial Analysis." *JFSR* 25 (2009): 19–41.

Leonhardt-Balzer, Jutta. "צדק." In *New International Dictionary of Old Testament Exegesis and Theology*. Vol. 4, edited by Willem A. VanGemeren, 807–13. Grand Rapids, MI: Zondervan, 2012.

Lewis, C. S. *The Problem of Pain*. In *The Complete C. S. Lewis Signature Classics*. Rev. ed. New York: HarperOne, 2007; original, 1940.

Luc, A. "ערם." In *New International Dictionary of Old Testament Exegesis and Theology*. Vol. 1, edited by Willem A. VanGemeren, 539–40. Grand Rapids, MI: Zondervan, 1997.

Lypsyte, Robert. "Sexual Harassment: How We Men Can—and Must—Help Bring Down Sexual Predators." *The Guardian*. November 19, 2017. https://www.theguardian.com/world/2017/nov/19/sexual-harassment -assault-men-jock-culture.

Maier, Christl M. "Conflicting Attractions: Parental Wisdom and the 'Strange Woman' in Proverbs 1–9." In *Wisdom and Psalms*, edited by Athalya Brenner and Carole R. Fontaine, 92–108. FCB 2, 2nd ser. Sheffield: Sheffield Academic, 1998.

———. "Good and Evil Women in Proverbs and Job." In *The Writings and Later Wisdom Books*, edited by Christl M. Maier and Nuria Calduch-Benages, 77–92. The Bible and Women: An Encyclopedia of Exegesis and Cultural History: Hebrew Bible/Old Testament 1.3. Atlanta: SBL Press, 2014.

———. "Proverbs." In *Feminist Biblical Interpretation: A Compendium of Critical Commentary on the Books of the Bible and Related Literature*, edited by Luise Schottroff and Marie-Theres Wacker, 255–72. Grand Rapids, MI: Eerdmans, 2012.

Malchow, Bruce V. "A Manual for Future Monarchs." *CBQ* 47 (1985): 238–45.

Marcotte, Amanda. "Think Today's Couples Split Household Chores? Think Again." *LA Times*. May 11, 2015. http://beta.latimes.com/opinion/op-ed/la-oe-0512-marcotte-housework-men-20150512-story.html.

McKean, Erin, ed. *New Oxford American Dictionary*. 2nd ed. New York: Oxford University Press, 2005.

McKinlay, Judith E. *Gendering Wisdom the Host: Biblical Invitations to Eat and Drink*. Gender, Culture, Theory 4. JSOTSup 216. Sheffield: Sheffield Academic, 1996.

Meyers, Carol L. *Discovering Eve: Ancient Israelite Women in Context*. New York: Oxford University Press, 1988.

Miles, Rebekah. "Valerie Saiving Reconsidered." *JFSR* 28 (2012): 79.

Mitchell, Rebecca. "Gap or Trap? Confidence Backlash Is the Real Problem for Women." *The Conversation*. June 12, 2014. https://theconversation.com/gap-or-trap-confidence-backlash-is-the-real-problem-for-women-27718.

Mohler, Albert. "The Scandal of Biblical Illiteracy: It's Our Problem." January 20, 2016. https://albertmohler.com/2016/01/20/the-scandal-of-biblical-illiteracy-its-our-problem-4/m.

Moon, Josh. "Bus Boycott Took Planning, Smarts." *USA Today*. November 29, 2015. https://www.usatoday.com/story/news/local/blogs/moonblog/2015/11/29/bus-boycott-took-planning-smarts/76456904/.

National Women's Law Center. Fact Sheet. November 2016. Workplace Justice Sexual Harassment in the Workplace. https://nwlc.org/wp-content/uploads/2016/11/Sexual-Harassment-Fact-Sheet.pdf.

———. "National Snapshot: Poverty among Women & Families, 2015." https://nwlc.org/resources/national-snapshot-poverty-among-women-families-2015/.

Newsom, Carol A. "Woman and the Discourse of Patriarchal Wisdom: A Study of Proverbs 1–9." In *Gender and Difference*, edited by Peggy Lynne Day, 142–60. Minneapolis: Fortress Press, 1989. Also in *Reading Bibles, Writing Bodies: Identity and the Book (Biblical Limits)*, edited by Todd K. Beal and David M. Gunn, 116–31. London: Routledge Press, 1997.

O'Connor, Kathleen M. *The Wisdom Literature*. Wilmington, DE: Glazier, 1988.

O'Grady, Sarah. "Women Are MORE Dishonest Than Men: Females More Likely to Tell Every Day Fibs." *Express*. October 11, 2016. http://www.express .co.uk/life-style/life/719589/Women-more-dishonest-men-females-more -likely-tell-every-day-fibs.

Osiek, Carolyn. *Beyond Anger: On Being a Feminist in the Church*. New York: Paulist, 1986.

Patterson, Jim. "Women Face Dishonesty More Often Than Men during Negotiations." *Research News at Vanderbilt*. October 2, 2014. https://news.vanderbilt .edu/2014/10/02/women-face-dishonesty/.

Peck, Emily. "These 8 Men Have as Much Money as Half the World." *Huffington Post*. January 16, 2017. https://www.huffingtonpost.com/entry/income -inequality-oxfam_us_58792e6ee4b0b3c7a7b13616.

"The Pixel Project's '16 For 16' Campaign: 16 Organisations Working to Stop Child Marriage." December 6, 2013. http://16days.thepixelproject.net/16 -organisations-working-to-stop-child-marriage/, https://www.girlsnot brides.org/child-marriage-advocacy-successes-2014/, http://www.care.org /work/womens-empowerment/child-marriage.

Polinsky, Wioleta. "Dangerous Bodies: Women's Nakedness and Theology." *JFSR* 16 (2000): 45–62.

Pukui, Mary Kawena, and Samuel H. Elbert. *Hawaiian Dictionary*. Honolulu: University of Hawai'i, 1986.

Pukui, Mary Kawena, E. W. Haertig, and Catherine A. Lee. *Nānā I Ke Kumu: Look to the Source*. Queen Lili'uokalani Children's Center, 1971.

Relke, Joan. "The Archetypal Female in Mythology and Religion: The Anima and the Mother." *Europe's Journal of Psychology* 3 (2007), https://ejop.psychopen.eu /article/view/389/html.

Rice, Gene. "The Curse That Never Was (Genesis 9:18-27)." *JRT* 29 (1972): 5–27.

Richin, Leslie. "Watch Out Boy! Today in 1982 Hall & Oates Took on a 'Maneater.'" *Billboard.com*. December 17, 2014. https://www.billboard.com/articles /news/6406621/hall-and-oates-maneater-anniversary.

Rothman, Lily. "What to Know about the Real Case That Inspired the Movie Marshall." October 17, 2017. http://time.com/4972645/marshall-movie -true-story/.

Sadler, Rodney. *Can a Cushite Change His Skin? An Examination of Race, Ethnicity, and Othering in the Hebrew Bible*. New York: Bloomsbury, 2005.

Saiving, Valerie. "A Conversation with Valerie Saiving." *JFSR* 4 (1988): 99–115.

———. "The Human Situation: A Human View." In *Womanspirit Rising: A Feminist Reader in Religion*, edited by Carol P. Christ and Judith Plaskow, 25–42. San Francisco: Harper and Row, 1979.

Sakenfeld, Katharine Doob. *The Meaning of Ḥesed in the Hebrew Bible*. HSS 17. Missoula, MT: Scholars Press, 1978.

Schäfer, Peter. *Mirror of His Beauty: Feminine Images of God from the Bible to the Early Kabbalah*. Princeton, NJ: Princeton University Press, 2002.

Schroer, Silvia. *Wisdom Has Built Her House: Studies in the Figure of Sophia in the Bible*. Translated by Linda Maloney. Collegeville, MN: Liturgical Press, 2000.

Schüssler Fiorenza, Elisabeth. *Ephesians*. WCS 50. Collegeville, MN: Liturgical Press, 2017.

———. *Jesus: Miriam's Child, Sophia's Prophet; Critical Issues in Feminist Christology*. New York: Continuum, 1994.

Silverman, Rena. "Millions of Young Girls Forced Into Marriage." *National Geographic*. March 15, 2013. https://news.nationalgeographic.com/news/2013/13/130313-child-brides-marriage-women-sinclair-photography/.

Simmer-Brown, Judith. "Yeshe Tsogyal: Woman and Feminine Principle." *Shambhala Times*. August 19, 2009. http://shambhalatimes.org/2009/08/19/yeshe-tsogyal-woman-and-feminine-principle/.

Sinnott, Alice M. *The Personification of Wisdom*. SOTSMS. Aldershot: Ashgate, 2005.

Slow Italy (website). "Lactating Breast Italy." http://slowitaly.yourguidetoitaly.com/2012/11/lactating-fountains-of-italy/.

Snell, Daniel C. " 'Taking Souls' in Proverbs 11:30." *VT* 33 (1983): 362–65.

Stigers, Harold G. "1879." In *TWOT*, 752–55.

Suetonius. *Vita Divi Iuli*. Perseus Digital Library, 0121. http://www.perseus.tufts.edu/hopper/text?doc=Perseus%3Atext%3A1999.02.0061%3Alife%3Djul.%3Achapter%3D32%3Asection%3D1.

Tan, Nancy Nam Hoon. *The "Foreignness" of the Foreign Woman in Proverbs 1–9: A Study of the Origin and the Development of a Biblical Motif*. BZAW 381. Berlin: de Gruyter, 2008.

Tavris, Carol. *Anger: The Misunderstood Emotion*. Rev. ed. New York: Simon & Schuster, 1989.

Thirteenth. https://www.netflix.com/title/80091741.

Townes, Emilie M. *In a Blaze of Glory: Womanist Spirituality as Social Witness*. Nashville: Abingdon, 1995.

Toy, Crawford H. *The Book of Proverbs*. ICC. New York: Scribner's Sons, 1902.

"Transcript: Donald Trump's Taped Comments about Women." *New York Times*. October 8, 2016. https://www.nytimes.com/2016/10/08/us/donald-trump-tape-transcript.html.

Trible, Phyllis. *God and the Rhetoric of Sexuality*. OBT. Philadelphia: Fortress Press, 1978.

US Census Bureau. "Table FG10: Family Groups: 2016." https://singlemotherguide.com/single-mother-statistics.

Van der Toorn, Karel. "Female Prostitution in Payment of Vows in Ancient Israel." *JBL* 108 (1989): 193–205.

Van Dijk-Hemmes, Fokkelien. "Traces of Women's Texts in the Hebrew Bible." In *On Gendering Texts: Female and Male Voices in the Hebrew Bible*, edited by Athalya Brenner and Fokkelien Van Dijk-Hemmes, 57–62. BibInt 1. Leiden: Brill, 1993.

Van Leeuwen, Raymond C. "Proverbs." In *The New Interpreter's Bible: A Commentary in Twelve Volumes*, vol. 5, edited by Leander E. Keck et al, 17–264. Nashville: Abingdon, 1994.

Veary, Nana. *Change We Must: My Spiritual Journey.* Mililani, HI: Booklines Hawaii, 2001.

Walker, Alice. *In Search of Our Mothers' Gardens: Womanist Prose.* New York: Harvest/Harcourt Brace Jovanovich, 1983.

Washington, Harold C. "The Strange Woman אשה זרה/נכריה of Proverbs 1–9 and Post-Exilic Judean Society." In *Second Temple Studies: Temple and Community in the Persian Period 2*, edited by Tamara Eskenazi and Kent H. Richards, 217–42. JSOTSup 175. Sheffield: JSOT Press, 1994.

Webster, Jane S. "Sophia: Engendering Wisdom in Proverbs, Ben Sira and the Wisdom of Solomon." *JSOT* 78 (1998): 63–79.

Weems, Renita J. "Victim of Violence or Victim of Metaphor." In *Interpretation for Liberation*, edited by Katie Geneva Canon and Elisabeth Schüssler Fiorenza. *Semeia* 47 (1989): 87–104.

Wenham, Gordon. "Law and the Legal System in Ancient Israel: Part 2." https://www.the-highway.com/law2b_Wenham.html.

Williams, Delores. *Sisters in the Wilderness: The Challenge of God-Talk.* Maryknoll, NY: Orbis, 1993.

"The Woman at the Window." British Museum. http://www.britishmuseum.org/research/collection_online/collection_object_details.aspx?objectId=369006&partId=1.

"Womanish." *Urban Dictionary* (website). http://www.urbandictionary.com/define.php?term=womanish.

Worrall, Patrick. "Fact Check: How Many Women Face Sexual Harassment in the Workplace?" *4 News.* October 12, 2017. https://www.channel4.com/news/factcheck/factcheck-how-many-women-face-sexual-harassment-in-the-workplace.

Yalom, Marilyn, and Theresa Donovan Brown. *The Social Sex: A History of Female Friendship.* New York: HarperPerennial, 2015.

Yee, Gale A. " 'I Have Perfumed My Bed with Myrrh': The Foreign Woman (*'iššâ zārâ*) in Proverbs 1–9." *JSOT* (1989): 53–68. Also in *A Feminist Companion to Wisdom Literature*, edited by Athalya Brenner, 110–26. FCB 9. Sheffield: Sheffield Academic, 1995.

———. *Poor Banished Children of Eve: Woman as Evil in the Hebrew Bible.* Minneapolis: Fortress Press, 2003.

Yoder, Christine Roy. *Proverbs.* AOTC. Nashville: Abingdon, 2009.

———. *Wisdom as a Woman of Substance: A Socioeconomic Reading of Proverbs 1–9 and 31:10-31.* BZAW 304. Berlin: de Gruyter, 2001.

———. "The Woman of Substance (אשת־חיל): A Socioeconomic Reading of Proverbs 31:10-31." *JBL* 122 (2003): 427–47.

Yogendrarajah, Rathiranee. "The Impact of Micro Credit on Women Empowerment." *International Journal of Research in Commerce, Economics & Management* 2 (2012). https://papers.ssrn.com/sol3/papers.cfm?abstract_id=2431565.

Index of Scripture References
and Other Ancient Writings

12:16	12	15:9	41	17:3	225, 236
12:18	156	15:12	16	17:7	12
12:21	121	15:13-18	158–59	17:10-16	174–75
12:22	41	15:13	178, 181–82	17:10	16
12:23	129			17:14	179, 180, 202 n. 200
12:24	271	15:14	181		
12:27	271	15:16, 17	35	17:15	41
13:1-6	129–32	15:18	202 n. 200	17:16	16
13:4	184, 271	15:19-23	159–61	17:17-20	175–77
13:7-11	132–34	15:19	178, 271	17:19	202 n. 200
13:7	123	15:23	225	17:21-25	177–78
13:10	202 n. 200	15:24-27	161	17:21	12, 15
13:11	242	15:25	216	17:23	178
13:12-19	134–36	15:26	41	17:26-28	178–79
13:12	37	15:28-33	161–63	17:27-28	129
13:14	169, 271	15:28	129	17:28	12
13:19	41	15:33	9	18:1-9	179–81
13:20-25	136–39	16:1–22:16	lii, 164–212	18:2	16
13:24	198, 210, 218, 246			18:4	192
		16:1-9	164–65	18:6	202 n. 200
14:1-3	139–42	16:1-2	198	18:10-15	181–82
14:1	4	16:1	171, 189, 196, 198, 207	18:11	101, 271
14:3	12			18:13	182
14:4-9	142–44	16:2	12, 199, 201	18:15-19	183
14:5	191			18:16-19	182
14:6	16	16:5	41	18:19	202 n. 200
14:10-14	144–46	16:6	222	18:20-24	182–83
14:12	170	16:8, 16, 19, 32	35	19:1-10	183–86
14:15-18	146–49	16:9	189, 196, 207	19:1, 22	35
14:16	222, 231, 247	16:10-15	166	19:1	239
14:19-22	150–51	16:11	196	19:11–20:4	186–92
14:21	34, 90	16:12	41	19:11-14	186–88
14:23-27	151–53	16:16-33	166–71	19:11	192
14:27	169	16:18	254	19:12	192
14:28-35	153–55	16:20	34, 90	19:13	li, 95, 201, 235, 270
14:31	173	16:21	76		
14:34	190	16:28	202 n. 200	19:15-24	188–90
15:1-4	155–56	16:29	40	19:15	184, 192, 194
15:2	129	16:33	76	19:19	192
15:4	35	17:1-9	171–74	19:21	196
15:5-12	156–58	17:1, 12	35	19:23	222
15:6	97	17:1	202 n. 200	19:24	184, 192, 194, 271
15:8	41, 206				

Index of Subjects

strong drink, 191, 255; *see also* wine

student, xlix, 10, 18, 28, 33, 38–39, 44–47, 49, 53, 93, 135, 158, 169, 191, 260, 269, 273

suffering, xlvii, 146, 171–73, 221, 230

superwoman, 259–60, 266, 268

teachers, xlvi, 44–46, 48–49, 52–53, 92–93, 169

teaching, xlvi, 13, 28, 39, 44, 49, 65, 76, 78, 95, 134–36, 191, 214, 217, 268; *see also* knowledge

temple, 2, 68, 77, 150, 243

Terrell, Mary Church, 10

terror, 100–101, 203

Thomas, Clarence, 212

threshing, 197, 209

tongue, 37, 102, 105, 126, 155–56, 172–73, 177, 182–83, 185, 204–5, 228, 233

Torah, xlv, 53

torah, 13

Townes, Emilie, 172

treasure, 20, 101, 200, 204

tree, 117–19, 141, 145, 235, 243
  of knowledge of good and evil, 37
  of life, 37, 118, 134

trickster, 64, 110

trouble, 18, 31, 56–63, 112, 117, 124, 126–27, 136, 147, 153, 158, 161, 164, 167, 170, 174, 177–78, 185, 190, 203–4, 207, 221, 231, 272

Troy, Anne, 58–61

truth, 99, 125–26, 143, 194, 250

understanding, xliii, 7, 8, 16, 20, 24, 30, 34–35, 37–38, 49, 77, 82–83, 90, 92, 104, 155, 158, 160, 166–67, 172, 185, 207, 221, 241, 250

underworld, 94, 158

unethical people, 47, 65, 116, 124, 150, 221, 238–39, 272

unhappiness, 158–59

uprightness, 8, 25, 46, 131, 179

upstanding, 20, 22, 27, 38, 109, 112, 121, 144, 157, 160, 166, 206, 245

van Wijk-Bos, Johanna, 250

Vaughn, Dorothy, 188

vengeance, 133, 195

vigor, 52, 256

violence, 14, 57, 62–63, 98, 100, 118, 170, 190, 200, 230–31

violent, 40–41, 170, 190

virtue(s), 7, 24, 35, 76, 107, 114, 120, 140, 163, 168, 207, 259, 263

vowels, xliv–xlv, 18, 65, 149

vows, 75–76, 220

Walker, Alice, xlii

warning, xlvii, 13, 49–51, 54, 97, 101, 195

water, 53–55, 89, 94, 117, 130, 174, 181, 198, 228, 235, 255, 268; *see also* fountain

way. *See* path

wealth, L, 19, 35–36, 52, 82–84, 92, 97–98, 100–105, 108, 111–12, 117, 120, 122–23, 127–28, 132–34, 136–38, 145, 151–52, 156–59, 181, 183–85, 188, 207–11, 216, 236, 265–66, 269–70

weights, 106, 166, 193, 196

Wells-Barnett, Ida B., 10

wholeness, 22, 28, 109

wicked. *See* corrupt, guilty

widow(s), 34, 161

wife, wives, 2, 5, 52, 53–55, 65, 69, 118, 139, 175, 183, 187–88, 201, 255
  capable, li, 15, 94, 95, 106, 120, 254, 259–68, 269
  ideal, 4
  nagging, 198
  noble, 262–63
  quarrelsome, contentious, 201, 203
  strong, li, 3, 6–7, 15, 77, 94, 106, 120, 254, 259–68, 269

General Editor

Barbara E. Reid, OP, is a Dominican Sister of Grand Rapids, Michigan. She holds a PhD in biblical studies from The Catholic University of America and is professor of New Testament studies at Catholic Theological Union, Chicago. Her most recent publications are *Wisdom's Feast: An Invitation to Feminist Interpretation of the Scriptures* (2016) and *Abiding Word: Sunday Reflections on Year A, B, C* (3 vols.; 2011, 2012, 2013). She served as vice president and academic dean at CTU from 2009 to 2018 and as president of the Catholic Biblical Association in 2014–2015.

Volume Editor

Sarah J. Tanzer serves as professor of New Testament and Early Judaism at McCormick Theological Seminary in Chicago, Illinois. She has written several essays on feminist interpretation of ancient texts including "Wisdom of Solomon" in *Women's Bible Commentary* (3rd edition; 2012) and "Ephesians" in *Searching the Scriptures: A Feminist Commentary* (1994). Her other research interests have included the Dead Sea Scrolls, the Gospel of John, the historically Jewish Jesus, and most recently, how difference develops in biblical interpretation between Judaism and early Christianity.

Author

Alice Ogden Bellis is an ordained minister and professor of Hebrew Bible at Howard University School of Divinity in Washington, DC. Her books include *Helpmates, Harlots, and Heroes: Women's Stories in the Hebrew Bible* (Westminster/John Knox, 1994 and 2007); *Science, Scripture, and Homosexuality*, with Dr. Terry Hufford (Pilgrim Press, 2002; Wipf and Stock, 2011); and *Jews and Christians and the Theology of Hebrew Scriptures*, coedited with Joel Kaminsky (SBL Symposium Series; Atlanta: Society of Biblical Literature, November 2000).